Business Studies

Related titles in the series

Accounting
Advertising
Auditing
Book-keeping
Business and Commercial Law
Business Environment
Business and the European
  Community
Business French
Business German
Business Italian
Business Spanish
Commerce
Cost and Management
  Accounting

Economics
Elements of Banking
English for Business
Financial Management
Information Technology
Law
Management Theory and
  Practice
Marketing
Office Procedures
Organizations and Management
Personnel Management
Statistics for Business
Teeline Shorthand
Typing

Business Studies

Second edition

Geoffrey Whitehead, BSc (Econ)

MADE SIMPLE
BOOKS

Made Simple
An imprint of Butterworth-Heinemann Ltd
Linacre House, Jordan Hill, Oxford OX2 8DP

A member of the Reed Elsevier/plc group

OXFORD LONDON BOSTON
MUNICH NEW DELHI SINGAPORE SYDNEY
TOKYO TORONTO WELLINGTON

First published as *Business and Enterprise Studies* 1990
Second edition 1994

British Library Cataloguing in Publication Data
Whitehead, Geoffrey
  Business Studies. – 2Rev.ed
  I. Title
  658

ISBN 0 7506 1911 2

Printed in Great Britain by Clays, St Ives plc

Contents

Preface

This book provides a sound background for courses in Business Studies in schools and colleges. It follows closely the syllabus requirements of the various examining bodies in this subject, assuming no previous knowledge in the business field. At the same time it reaches a good level in each of the aspects covered, which are listed below. It cannot fail to develop a broad understanding of business and it shows clearly the need for enterprise in a modern industrial and commercial society.

The book brings out both the underlying purposes of business activity to create goods and services which satisfy the 'wants' of mankind, but also deals with the practical activities necessary for success in these endeavours. Production, marketing, distribution and exporting, personnel matters, accounting and many other related activities are introduced and described. The book embodies my own experiences in advising many people in the small-business field, and such aspects as cash flow, turnover, liquidity, the rewards to enterprise, etc. are fully discussed.

In writing this book I have received much help from many people, some of whom have provided artwork and given permission to refer to products and business systems. These are acknowledged elsewhere in the book, but I should like to express my appreciation of their efforts and those of the many other people who have assisted in its preparation. Despite this, I must emphasize that all the ideas expressed are my own, and should not be regarded as the views of any other person.

All the names used in this book for firms, companies, etc. are entirely imaginary and do not refer to real firms or institutions except where this is made clear. If I have inadvertently used the real name of any person or enterprise I apologize, but it is purely a coincidence.

I should particularly like to thank Jacquie Shanahan, the editor of the Made Simple series, and her colleagues for help and encouragement during the preparation of the book.

Geoffrey Whitehead

Acknowledgements

The assistance of the following individuals and firms is gratefully acknowledged:

Barclays Bank PLC
British Telecom
Cambridgeshire County Council
Comptroller General HMSO
Croner Publications Ltd
Formecon Services Ltd, Crewe (for permission to reproduce their export documentation and their classroom chart for double-entry book-keeping).
George Vyner Ltd of Huddersfield (for permission to reproduce their Simplex illustrations).
Kalamazoo PLC (for permission to reproduce illustrations of their Wages Systems).
The SITPRO Board (for permission to reproduce their Master Document).
Vacher's Parliamentary Companion

Part One
The External Environment of the Business

1
The nature of business activity

1.1 What is business activity?

Human life is an endless succession of 'wants'. From the day of our birth to the day of our death we 'want' things. The new-born baby wants to be washed, wrapped in clean garments, weighed, fed every few hours, soothed when he/she is fractious, kept warm and sheltered, etc. Everyone needs warmth, food, beverages, clothing, shelter and medical care. These are just the basic requirements to keep us alive and well. There are millions more things we all 'want' which, while they are not essential, are part of the way of life we have been born into. We need crockery, cooking pots, cutlery, personalized transport, toothbrushes, television sets, transistor radios, books, magazines, sports equipment, etc.

How do all these things that we want, both goods and services, become available? The answer is – by business activity. It is business that produces the food, clothing, shelter, furniture, soft furnishings, household utensils, etc., that we all need. It supplies us with all our means of transport, from the simple bicycle to the sophisticated airliner. It provides all our entertainment, from children's comics to the television programmes beamed to us from a satellite in space. Even the services we require, like the National Health Service, are dependent on business activity to a considerable extent. The doctor needs a stethoscope, drugs, surgical instruments, cylinders of anaesthetic gases, etc. The nurse needs sterilized bandages, hypodermic syringes, antibiotics and antiseptics of various sorts.

Business activity may be defined as any activity that creates goods or services to satisfy human 'wants'. The 'wants' may be easily satisfied, or may require involved and lengthy activities. For example, it is fairly easy to grow lettuces – we plant seeds, water them regularly, feed them with occasional supplies of appropriate fertilizer, cut them, wash them and market them at a fair price. It is not quite so simple to produce a television programme, or a sophisticated airliner. After one recent air disaster a spokesman for the Ministry of Transport said that part of the difficulty in deciding the cause of the catastrophe was that even the makers of the plane could not immediately identify what particular objects were, or where they were fitted on the aircraft, let alone identify particular scraps of metal. The most painstaking search through thousands of drawings and specifications was necessary to identify the recovered items and evaluate the part they might have played in the disaster.

Business activity is sometimes described as 'wealth-creating' activity. Many people misunderstand this, and think that business activity is something to do with millionaires. One does see the odd millionaire on television these days of course, and they are often in business, but wealth-creating is nothing to do with millionaires. The 'wealth' we are talking about is an abundance of goods and services. When cars roll off the production line every thirty seconds, or batches of bread come piping hot and golden brown from the ovens of some huge bakery – that is wealth. When we have an injection against some disease like tetanus, and throw the needle away to prevent anyone else using it because we have plenty more needles in the surgery, that is wealth. One traveller wrote home from the Cape Verde islands recently, saying 'There is very little food in the shops. The people mainly eat fish, and so do we.' He was missing the 'wealth' which he had formerly taken for granted – an abundance of goods at his local supermarket.

One difficulty about satisfying human wants is that people are spread around the world in a very haphazard way. For example, in Singapore some 3 million people live on an island which has a total area of only 600 square kilometres; about 5,000 people per square kilometre. By contrast, Canada has about 25 million inhabitants with almost 10 million square kilometres of land; about 2½ people per square kilometre. Some nations have within their huge territories almost every type of natural supply: timber, hydroelectric power, minerals, agricultural land, etc. Others have so few natural resources that they have to import everything they need: food, raw materials, oil, electric power, etc. All nations have to overcome problems of transport, distribution, warehousing and marketing to bring the goods that have been produced to the consumers who 'want' them. When we think of services it is often the other way round. We have to move the people to the services. We need ambulances to take them to hospital, air or road transport to get them to the dentist, or to college or university, etc.

Finally, note that business activity never ceases. We engage in business activity so that we can satisfy human 'wants'. When we do satisfy these 'wants' the very act of satisfaction consumes the useful good or service created and we must start again to supply a further batch. This is easy to see when we sit down to a good dinner and consume the various delicacies provided. It is not quite so obvious

Figure 1.1 The cycle of business activity

when, by wearing a garment, we gradually wear it out until it is only fit for the rag bag, or when we use a piece of office furniture or a machine until it is no longer of any further use. Economists say that 'consumption' destroys production, and we must go back to the beginning again and start another cycle of production. This cycle of business activity is illustrated in Figure 1.1. It goes from 'wants' through 'enterprise', 'production', 'distribution' and 'marketing' to 'consumption and satisfaction', and back to 'wants' again, as consumption destroys production. Figure 1.1 is self-explanatory. Study it carefully now.

Points to remember

- Business is a wealth-creating activity.
- Wealth does not mean money; it means an abundance of goods and services.

- Business activity creates goods and services to satisfy human 'wants'. We 'want' goods and services from the moment we are born until the day we die.
- 'Consumption' is the using and enjoying of goods and services.
- Consumption destroys production, and we have to start a new cycle of business activity.

1.2   Enterprise and the entrepreneur

We saw in Figure 1.1 that in order to create goods and services, enterprising individuals have to step out of the crowd and start getting things organized. We call these people entrepreneurs (a word which comes from the French, and means 'undertakers'). The English word 'undertaker' has a special meaning – a person who arranges funerals. The French word has a more general meaning – anyone who is prepared to see that a particular task is done efficiently. What does an entrepreneur do? He (or she) has many tasks, and we could answer the question by saying that an entrepreneur does whatever is necessary to bring the activity to a successful conclusion. Henry Ford built his first engine in his mother's kitchen, and very inconvenient she found it. He built his first car in the family's garden shed and when it was finished he had to knock the shed down to get it out. He spent his whole life trying to find better materials, better components, more skilled workers and more useful machines. Today Ford cars run over almost every road in the world. There are Ford factories in every major country, Ford dealers in every main town, Ford spare parts can be obtained everywhere. That is the sort of person an entrepreneur is. Ford died a wealthy man, worth 783 million dollars, yet one of the stories told about him is that he made his son spend two hours looking for a penny which he had flung into the bushes in a temper. It wasn't the money Ford was annoyed about – he had plenty of pennies. He just did not want his son to grow up wasting copper. Copper is a raw material that can satisfy human 'wants'. A skipping rhyme of the day used to say:

There was a young man called Henry Ford,
He took four wheels and a lump of board,
A couple of rivets and a petrol can,
He put 'em all together and the darned thing ran.

Figure 1.2   Henry Ford's 'Tin Lizzie' – the first mass-produced car

Exercise 1.1

Here are the names of ten famous entrepreneurs. Write the list down, and alongside them write what they are famous for undertaking, to satisfy human 'wants'.

1 Frank Whittle JET ENGINE
2 George Stephenson STEAMING
3 Florence Nightingale NURSING
4 F. W. Woolworth LOOLIES
5 Thomas Chippendale CIRCUS
6 Joseph Priestley AUTHOR
7 Eli Whitney AVIATION
8 Anton van Leeuwenhoek MICRO
9 John D. Rockefeller BANKING
10 Marie Curie RADIOACTIVITY

Answers at the end of the chapter.

1.3 Enterprise and the factors of production

What the entrepreneur does when a business is started up is to combine three things that make the production of useful goods and services possible. These three things are called the factors of production. They are land, labour and capital. Each of these words needs careful explanation.

Land

Land is anything that has been provided by nature as an endowment of resources which is available for use. The most obvious type of 'land' is geographical land. We use it for farming, forestry, factories and housing estates. We tunnel into it to extract metallic ores, chemicals of various sorts, oil, coal, water, sulphur, salt and countless other products. We domesticate wild plants and set up rubber plantations, sugar plantations, etc.

Another kind of 'land' is the waters of the sea and the fruits of the sea. We no longer go whaling, but we still fish; we collect lobsters and other crustaceans; we harvest seaweeds for fertilizers; we trap sea water in shallow lagoons to make salt; we are beginning to mine the oceans for metallic ores; we trap estuary tides to generate electricity and we are working to use wave power as an inexhaustible power supply.

Yet other kinds of 'land' are the gases of the atmosphere. We can obtain them all by refrigeration processes which separate them off, because they turn to liquids at different temperatures. Oxygen is useful, so are carbon dioxide, nitrogen and the inert gases, helium, neon, argon, etc.

All these resources known by the general term 'land' are gifts of nature. They are called **primary products** (first products) because they have been here from the very beginning of time. If an entrepreneur is a **primary producer** it means he/she harvests the bounties of nature. Thus fishing, drilling for oil and natural gas, farming, forestry, dairy farming, poultry keeping, rubber planting and similar activities are all primary production.

Labour

Labour is the human factor of production. It has been said that we need not worry when a new 'mouth' is born into the world, for it brings two hands to work for it. There are 5,000 million people in the world, most of them having some degree of skill and many of them so gifted that there is no work they cannot perform. We have bridged the mightiest rivers, made the waves and the air our servants for transport purposes, set satellites in space and sent probes to distant planets. We also make a lot of clothes, grow a lot of food, build a lot of houses, make innumerable furnishings, etc. We are cleaner than our ancestors, richer than our ancestors, healthier than our ancestors – yet even so there is a lot still to do. When the entrepreneur sets out to create goods and services he/she looks for help from other people. Just how the labour market works is one of the things we have to discover as we work through this book.

Capital

Capital is the third resource. It is a much misunderstood word. Many people think of capital as money, but it is nothing of the sort. Capital is the stock of tools and equipment that one period of production hands on to the next period, to enable production to take place. Tools and other capital assets like machines, computers, motor vehicles, etc., have to be made before we can use them, and while we are getting people to build them we have to keep them alive by paying them wages. Thus if 1000 people are building a bridge (a piece of transport capital equipment) we have to pay them wages so that they can go off to the shops at the end of the day and buy food. The entrepreneur who builds bridges needs money 'capital' to give to the bridgebuilders as a reward for their labour, working to create the real 'capital' asset, a bridge. The confusion between **money capital** and **capital assets** is understandable. We can distinguish them best if we learn two more words. In business, money is called **liquid capital**. It is liquid because it can flow anywhere. We can give it to a bridgebuilder to make a bridge, or a cement manufacturer to build a cement works, or to a local authority to set up a school. As they spend the liquid capital it turns into **fixed capital**, a bridge, a cement works or a school. Once you've fixed it you can't unfix it again for a hundred years or so when the bridge finally collapses, or the cement works is worn out, or the school is too old and inconvenient for further use.

Collecting capital is a very difficult process, as those who want to set up in business soon discover. The early capitalists got a very bad name for themselves because they had to accumulate capital the hard way – by saving up halfpennies. Dickens called them 'the iron gentlemen' because they had such hard hearts. They believed in thrift – saving money – so that it could be used to dig a mine, or build a railway, or a steamship. Today it is a little easier to get capital – there are plenty of banks willing to lend money to someone with a good idea. Unfortunately you do have to pay interest on it – and that creams off a lot of profit into the bank's pocket. If you want to keep all the profits of your business yourself you have to collect capital in the old-fashioned way, by saving.

To create wealth (an abundance of goods and services) entrepreneurs have to combine these three factors of production. Every farm, every factory, every mine, every hospital, surgery, clinic, school, library, office, etc., needs some land, some labour and some capital. You will find an enterprising person making decisions about all these items. They may call themselves various names – sole trader, partner, company director, office administrator, hospital almoner, head teacher, etc. They are showing enterprise.

1.4 What entrepreneurs do

Entrepreneurs combine the three factors of production in such a way as to develop an organization which can create goods and services. This needs the following sorts of decisions:

- Where shall we site the business (which particular piece of geographical land shall we buy or rent to set up our enterprise)?
- What sort of premises do we need? Are there some already built which are suitable or can be adapted? If not, who can we find to design a purpose-built property for us, and who will actually turn the plans into a plant, factory, office, laboratory (or whatever it is)? Premises are, of course, a capital asset.
- What machinery, furniture and fittings, storage tanks, ware-housing, small tools and equipment do we need? Who can supply them? Once again these are all capital assets.
- What raw materials (if any) shall we need, and from whom shall we obtain them? This means finding suppliers of all the various items we need, checking the quality, price and reliability of the goods they can supply and arranging terms of payment which suit both parties. These materials may be primary products (gifts of nature) or improved primary products. Improved primary products are called **secondary products**; manufactured goods. Thus iron is a primary product and a gift of nature, but steel nuts

and bolts, steel girders, sheet metal products, etc., are secondary manufactures; i.e. improved primary products.

- What staff do we need? What skills must they have? How shall we induct them so they know and understand our products, our customers, our systems of production and distribution etc?
- What finance do we need to do all this? Where shall we get this liquid capital, and when will we start to receive some income from our activities so that we can carry the business on? What cash flows in and out of the business can we forecast?

Points to remember

- Entrepreneurs are people who step out of the crowd and start to get production organized.
- They do so by combining the three factors of production – land, labour and capital.
- Land is any gift of nature – the land itself, the rocks and minerals, the animal and plant life of every sort, the produce of the seas and the gases of the atmosphere.
- Labour is the human resource – the skills, knowledge, ideas and wisdom of mankind.
- Capital is the stock of tools and equipment, premises, means of transport, roads and other infrastructure passed on by one generation to another.
- The role of the entrepreneur is that of decision maker – what shall we do and how shall we do it?

1.5   A project on business activities

There are five main types of businesses. They are:

1 Businesses in the primary field – where we take, or grow, the gifts nature has provided.
2 Manufacturing businesses – where we improve on the things nature has provided, in some sort of secondary production.
3 Trading businesses – where we buy and sell later at a profit.
4 Service businesses – which require materials, for example a landscape gardener who buys various types of materials and produces in the end an attractive garden.
5 Pure service businesses – such as accountancy, or a funeral director's business.

Obtain a copy of the *Yellow Pages* telephone directory. Choose any one of these types of business and by going through the index of headings, find all the businesses that come under the type you have chosen. For example, there are twenty-nine primary producers. The list starts with 'beekeepers' and ends with 'vegetable growers'. If different groups in a class choose different types, the whole range of *Yellow Pages* businesses will be covered. Think about each heading and ask yourself – Is that the type of business I am looking for to complete my list?

You should have discovered by the time you present your list to your teacher/lecturer that there are an awful lot of businesses about that you had never even heard of. This is what we mean by an advanced, sophisticated economy – with thousands of large and small firms offering an intricate pattern of goods and services; and all trying to earn a living.

1.6   Some first thoughts about showing enterprise

Those who are thinking about self-employment have to look at business from an entirely different viewpoint from the person who is thinking of taking employment with a firm or company. Some of the basic considerations may be listed as follows:

1   Which type of business am I going to enter?
2   What sort of knowledge or experience is required by this type of business?
3   Have I got the right type of knowledge or experience and if not how can I acquire it?
4   What sort of premises will be required, and where would they have to be located? Can I find such premises easily, or get any help with their construction if they have to be purpose built.
5   What are the likely costs of starting up in business? How much capital will I need, and how can I accumulate it – or at least some of it?
6   What accounting and other records must I keep? Which is the best system to use and have I the necessary skills?
7   What official requirements must I meet or barriers to progress may I need to overcome. These include planning permission, VAT regulations, tax records, building regulations, health and safety at work regulations and COSHH regulations (care of substances hazardous to health).

All these preliminary considerations and many more are dealt with in the various chapters of this book. Each chapter contains a checklist or suggestions list for various points of interest to those showing enterprise, and viewing the subject matter of business studies from the more vital and pragmatic viewpoint of the entrepreneur. A pragmatic person deals with problems as they emerge, finding solutions to practical problems and devising systems that will meet new requirements as they arise. All entrepreneurs are to some extent pragmatists.

1.7   Rapid revision

In this book you will find at the end of each chapter a rapid revision test, with answers on the left-hand side and questions on the right-hand side. Cover the page with a sheet of paper and slide it down to reveal the first question. Try to answer it in your own words. Then slide the paper down to reveal the correct answer, and the next question. When you know all the answers by heart you will be confident about this section of work. You can then go on to try some of the written questions.

Answers	*Questions*
–	**1 Why bother to study business**
1 Because business is the only activity that creates wealth, i.e. an abundance of goods and services. Without the creation of wealth we should all lead much less pleasant and satisfying lives, and possibly die of starvation.	**2 What is the universal condition of every baby born into the world?**
2 It is in a state of want. It has no clothes, no food, no shelter and is totally defenceless and helpless.	**3 What are the basic wants of mankind?**
3 Food, liquid refreshment, clothing, shelter, medical care and geographical territory – we must have somewhere to lay our heads at night.	**4 How are all these things provided?**
4 In a primitive society by communal work to provide food, clothing and shelter. In an advanced society business activity produces everything we need, and the social organization ensures reasonably fair shares for all (but not exactly equal shares).	**5 Why is business activity endless?**

Answers		Questions	
5	Because consumption of the wealth created destroys production and we must start a new cycle of production.	6	**What is the complete cycle of production?**
6	Wants – enterprise – production – distribution – marketing – consumption – satisfaction – wants – etc.	7	**Who organizes production in an advanced society?**
7	A self-selected group of enterprising individuals called 'entrepreneurs' – people prepared to undertake some facet of production.	8	**What do they actually do?**
8	They combine the factors of production – land, labour and capital – in an organization which creates goods or services which the general public wants.	9	**What is land?**
9	Any resource made available as a gift of nature, but especially geographical territory, the minerals of the earth, the gases of the atmosphere, the produce of the seas and the fruits of the earth, whether growing wild or cultivated and bred on our farms, forests, plantations, etc.	10	**What is labour?**
10	The human resource – muscle power, skills and ideas.	11	**What is capital?**
11	The wealth of assets (premises, plant and machinery, tools and equipment, motor vehicles and infrastructure) created in one time period for use in the next time period.	12	**Go over the test again until you are sure of all the answers. Then try the questions in Section 1.8 below.**

1.8   Questions on Chapter 1

1   Most of us at some time believe we could set up and run a business which would provide some good or service of use to our fellow men and women. Here is a list of questions posing ten of the problems you might face if you planned to go into business. Write down the letters (a) to (j) (leaving two lines for each answer) and against them give a brief answer to the questions, as if you were proposing to enter some field of business activity which appeals to you.

   1   Which type of business am I going to enter?
   2   Have I the necessary expertise and knowledge?
   3   How can I find out about the weak gaps in my knowledge, which are . . . and . . . ?
   4   Where shall I open the business?
   5   What kind of premises will I need?
   6   How much is it likely to cost to start up in business?
   7   What money do I have at present, and how much can I save in the next two years if I really try?
   8   Is there anyone I can get backing from with an injection of liquid capital?
   9   Can I drive a vehicle? If not, when can I start to learn and how can I finance the lessons?
  10   What system of book-keeping shall I use? How can I find out about it? (You could read a companion volume to the present one – *Book-keeping Made Simple*.)

2   Ivor Waywivem is knowledgeable about scooters and motor-cycles. He thinks he could set up a servicing and spare parts business in this field. What sort of land, labour and capital would be required for such an undertaking?

3   Mary is artistic, practical, full of ideas on fashion, materials, accessories, etc., and not very keen to stay on at school. Jane is academically inclined, intends to continue studying locally at the University and needs to earn money to support herself while she does so. How might these two pool their talents to set up in business?

4   'Business people are only interested in making profits' – young revolutionary idealist. 'On the contrary, I am only interested in making electronic keyboards' – wealthy entrepreneur. Discuss the merits of these two opinions about business activity.

5   What is wealth? How is it created? Who benefits from its creation? In your answer refer to *one* of the following: (a) a market gardener on the island of Guernsey; (b) a jeweller selling from a retail shop; (c) a compact disc manufacturer in the USA; (d) a UK fashion designer.

Answers to Exercise 1.1

1 Inventor of the jet engine;   2 Inventor of the first successful rail locomotive;   3 Showed us how to run an efficient hospital; 4 Started the 'variety store' which sold many different products in one shop;   5 Designed beautiful furniture;   6 Discovered oxygen; 7 Invented the cotton gin, which removed the greasy seeds from cotton;   8 Invented the microscope;   9 Started the Standard Oil Company (now broken down into a number of companies under the USA antitrust laws;   10 Discovered radium.

2
The environment in which businesses operate

2.1 The business environment

A business operates in an environment which has three sets of influences working on it. These are *local influences*, *national influences* and *international influences*. The term 'environment' means the whole climate of influences which are at work upon a business. For instance, a shortage of labour of a particular type may cause a firm to leave one area and set up in another. One car manufacturer whose sales in a particular country recently were cut to 10,000 cars decided to export only the largest and most expensive models – if it could sell only 10,000 cars it might as well sell 10,000 big ones. There are countless influences at work on businesses large and small, but the distinction between local influences, national influences and international influences is a good starting point. Before considering these influences in detail notice one important point – that the most important influence of all is the climate of laws which prevails.

2.2 Law

Law is a body of rules for the guidance of human conduct, which is imposed upon, and enforced among the citizens of a given state. It is well worthwhile learning that definition by heart, for it tells us much that we need to know if we decide to engage in business activity. The three vital parts of the definition are as follows:

1 '*imposed upon*' Laws are imposed upon the citizens of a state, by a sovereign body which has established itself in power. We have all heard of dictatorships, where a single individual has imposed his/her will upon a whole people. Sometimes it is not a single individual, but a group, like a particular political party. Many nations are democracies, a word which means 'rule by the people'. In the UK the sovereign body is 'The Queen in Parliament assembled'. This is a compromise between rule by a monarch, and

rule by the people. By convention Her Majesty is at the very pinnacle of the sovereign body but agrees not to carry out any activity which has not been authorized by Parliament on the people's behalf – except the personal affairs of the Royal Household. An Act of Parliament is imposed upon the people when the Queen puts the final seal upon it by giving it the 'Royal Assent'.

2 *'enforced among'*   It is not much good making laws if no one obeys them. We have a law against litter in the UK, but foreigners complain of the untidy state of our streets and public places. Laws must be enforced among the populace, and for that we need a police force, a prosecution service and a series of courts where trials can take place at various levels. The lowest courts are the magistrates courts, and the highest court in the land is the House of Lords, though the European Court in certain matters can impose its will even on the House of Lords.

3 *'the citizens of a given state'*   This part of the definition tells us that the 'national' law is more important than local law or international law. We live in a world which is divided up into about 200 nation states, each with its own set of laws. If we travel abroad we mean we leave our own country, with a set of laws we understand, and go into another nation state with its own set of laws. French law is very different from English law, the 50 United States of America have their own 'state's laws' but for the sake of easier movement across state boundaries a body of agreed 'Federal laws' applies in all the States of the Union. Russian laws are different again, and so is Japanese law, Chinese law or the laws of any other nation state. When a company sets up in business in the UK it has to obey the laws of the nation, but – as we shall see – it must also obey local laws (bye-laws); and many international laws also apply because the UK has ratified them by passing them through Parliament as British Acts of Parliament. Thus the Warsaw Rules which are about carriage of goods and passengers by air, were originally enacted into UK law in the Carriage by Air Act, 1932. The present Act is the Carriage by Air Act, 1961. Whenever an aircraft crashes, or makes a forced landing, or sends your cases to the wrong destination, or loses a cargo consigned from one country to another, the internationally-agreed Warsaw Rules apply.

Figure 2.1 illustrates this legal environment in diagrammatic form. Consider it now, and read the notes below the diagram.

Points to remember

● The environment in which a business operates is the total climate of influences at work upon it, and upon its proprietors.

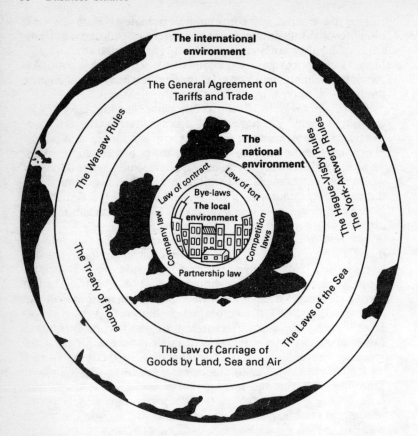

Figure 2.1   The local, national and international legal environment in which business operates

Notes:
1 The business operates in its own locality, from which it draws its staff, much of its raw materials or components or supplies, and from which it borrows most of its finance. It will be subject to local bye-laws, planning permission, etc.
2 That local environment is a small part of the national environment, which dictates the law and administrative framework within which the enterprise operates. In particular, contract law, criminal law, the law of tort (civil wrongs such as negligence and nuisance) and administrative law (taxation, value added taxation, health regulations, employment law, equal opportunities law, etc.) affect every business.
3 The national environment is in its turn only part of the international environment, which particularly affects exporters, importers, those who travel abroad and the business community's rights to freedom of the seas, freedom of the air, space communications, etc. There is no international body which can enforce international law, so international agreements are usually embodied into national law by a process called 'ratification'. The national laws thus enacted are binding on all businesses in the ratifying country.

- These influences may be local, national or international.
- The national influences are more important because they establish the legal system in which the business operates.
- Law is a body of rules for the guidance of human conduct which is imposed upon, and enforced among, the citizens of a given state.
- The sovereign body (the law-making body) in the UK is 'The Queen in Parliament'. It is a compromise system between monarchy and democracy.
- Local laws are often called 'bye-laws'.
- International laws usually have to be passed into national law by a process of 'ratification' before they can be binding on the citizens of a state.

2.3   The economic environment of business

Besides the legal environment in which businesses operate there is the very important **economic environment**. This is again affected by national considerations, because different nation states have different systems of production – different types of economy.

An economy is a system for organizing the production, distribution and exchange of goods and services. One celebrated economist defined economics (the study of economies) as 'The study of mankind in the everyday business of life.' The everyday business of life is to find food, clothing, shelter, geographical space (a home), liquid refreshment, health, etc. Without these things we die. We have already said that it is business that makes all these goods and services available; but it can only do so in a favourable environment. Some people think a 'free enterprise' system is the one most favourable to business activity. Others think the socialization of the means of production is a better method of providing goods and services. Still another group believes that a mixed economy is best, partly private enterprise and partly social enterprise. The terms for these three types of economies are **market economies** (the free-enterprise economies), **planned economies** (where social ownership of the means of production is important) and **mixed economies** (where free enterprise activities and social ownership each have a part to play). These are explained more fully in Chapter 4 (Section 4.3).

2.4   Scarcity and choice

Whatever the system of production decided upon there are certain principles which are inescapable and which we must all appreciate and understand. The first is that our 'wants' are enormous, and unending, but the means to satisfy our wants are limited. Resources are scarce, and must be used economically. *We have to choose the best uses for the resources available.*

Why are our 'wants' so enormous? There are many reasons, but two of the most important are:

1   *Appetite grows with feeding*   Consider a group of starving refugees, of the kind we see so regularly on our television screens; people for whom drought, war or political persecution have made ordinary lives impossible. They need food, clothing, shelter, etc. Suppose we are able to provide these, so that their present wants are satisfied. Does this put an end to their wants? No! People who are at last able to lift up their heads now see a wider horizon. They begin to think about a permanent home in the new territory, education for their children, a regular job, personal transport, tools and equipment. The more we have, the more we want; appetite grows with feeding. Even the very richest people can still think of things they want. Diamond necklaces, ocean-going yachts, private aeroplanes, holidays on Pacific islands, etc.

2   *Population growth*   One way of enjoying a more prosperous life is to have more children. The population of the world is measured today in billions. One billion is 1,000,000,000, one thousand million mouths to feed. It has been estimated that in 16,000 BC the world's population was 4 million. 16,000 years later in AD 1 it was 200 million. By the year AD 1800 it was 1 billion. Since then it has grown as shown in Table 2.1.

Table 2.1 shows that in the ten years between AD 1990 and AD 2000 the world's population will grow by as much as it increased in all the years of history up to AD 1800. One thousand million more mouths to feed in ten years, and most of the population increase will take place in the countries least able to afford to

Table 2.1   Growth in the world's population

Year	Number of people
AD 1800	1 billion
AD 1935	2 billion
AD 1960	3 billion
AD 1975	4 billion
AD 1990	5 billion
Estimates	
AD 2000	6 billion
AD 2050	12 billion

Source: United Nations

Name of natural resource	Scarce or abundant	Renewable or non-renewable?	Local or imported?
Iron ore	A	N	L (in the UK)
Diamonds	S	N	I
Wheat	etc.	etc.	etc.
Apples			
Ivory			
Teak			
Sodium nitrate			
Pine wood			
Beef			
Oil			

Note: Sodium nitrate is a chemical fertilizer found naturally in large deposits in Chile and Peru.

Figure 2.2

support these extra people. Even though the estimates given in Table 2.1 are based upon the assumption that birth rates in the years ahead will eventually fall to the point where zero growth occurs, by the middle of the next century there will be 12 billion people to feed and clothe. This will require a great deal of business activity.

An exercise about scarcity

Take a sheet of paper and head-up on it the columns shown in Figure 2.2. Copy the list of resources shown. Add ten more of your own to the list. Then answer the questions by filling in the columns; S for scarce or A for abundant; R for renewable or N for non-renewable; L for local (produced in your own country) or I for imported. The object of the exercise is to stimulate your interest in natural resources, so that all your life you avoid waste (remember Henry Ford and the lost copper coin). Sometimes you will find it difficult to answer – for example, we do have local supplies of iron ore in the UK but it is so impure that we actually import most of our iron ore from other countries which have plenty of good-quality ore.

Exercising choice in the use of resources

If resources are scarce, and need to be used carefully and in the most economical way, how shall we exercise choice? Do we need some powerful dictator to decide, and specify exactly how things should be used? There have been occasions in our history when this has been necessary – for example during the two World Wars. In those days everything was rationed – most car owners were allowed 2 gallons of petrol a month; we had one egg a week each, and one ounce of cheese, etc. At other times we have not particularly liked the 'great dictator' method of exercising choices. Dictators can get things wrong just as easily as ordinary people. Some countries around the world who do have this sort of central planning have found that it does not work too well. They finish up with too much of some things and too little of others.

In the free-enterprise market economies the market decides what things shall be produced. If a million housewives every day, pick up a tin of beans and say, 'This type of baked beans is the one I choose for my family!' the entrepreneur who produces the variety chosen will prosper. That business will expand, and take over other factories abandoned by less-skilled manufacturers, whose baked beans lacked the taste, flavour, etc., of the successful product. Take any industry you like and study the firms in it, and you will find some that are prosperous and some that are not so prosperous. The prosperous ones expand and the others decline. The prosperous ones capture a bigger share of the market, buy a larger proportion of the resources available, and make more of what the public want. The market decides – the purchasing power of the family acts swiftly and spells success or failure for every product.

As far as business is concerned, the consumer is sovereign. How resources are used (in Business Studies we say 'How resources are allocated') depends upon the consumer. If the housewife likes a product, more resources will be diverted to make that product. If the housewife rejects a product, that is a vote by the consumer against the use of resources to make that product. Even babies can allocate resources. If they shake their heads when mother says 'Do you like this?', mother leaves it on the counter and moves along to something the baby does like. The marketplace is where choices are made about the use of resources.

2.5   Cost and opportunity cost

Although the market is an excellent place to make decisions about the goods and services we select as consumers, there is another place where choice is exercised and that is at the point of production. An entrepreneur who steps out of the crowd and decides to get some particular type of production organized at once has to make choices. What natural resources shall be used and in what proportions? How much labour shall be taken on and of what types? What premises, tools and other capital equipment must be obtained if production is to go ahead? Some decisions of this sort are also made by governments, especially in mixed economies or planned economies where some sector of production is under official control. Thus, if industries like electricity, or gas, or railways, are nationalized the real power to decide how much should be spent on the various services they offer is under government influence (though the government does not necessarily exercise day-to-day control).

Whoever is deciding what to produce, the choices made involve costs of various sorts. There is the cost of the raw maerials to be used and the cost of the labour to be hired, and the cost of the assets to be acquired. However, from the viewpoint of society as a whole there is another kind of cost, which economists call the 'opportunity cost' or the 'alternative cost'. This is not a money cost, but a 'lost opportunity' cost. If we decide to use land, labour and capital to make one thing, we lose the opportunity to use those resources to make another. People who are busy making motor cars cannot at the same time be making household furniture, or growing wheat, or raising pigs.

This idea has been illustrated many times in history. Hitler offered the German people 'Guns or butter'. He actually forced them to choose guns, and for twenty years afterwards they had very little butter, but guns proved in the end to be a bad choice. The Soviet Union chose to develop heavy industry (steelworks, cement works, etc.) but finished up terribly short of the things light industry produces, such as television sets, clothing and consumer products of every sort.

In business we are constantly weighing up 'opportunity costs'. A publisher may have to decide between one author's book and another author's book. An engineering firm may have two inventions offered to it for development. Shall it pick the better mousetrap, or the improved kitchen utensil? It may not have the resources to develop both. If it chooses the mousetrap it must reject the opportunity to develop the kitchen utensil.

The 'opportunity cost' of anything is the next most favourable thing that we decide to reject by taking up the present opportunity. If I decide to buy a second-hand car I lose the opportunity to buy the music centre I had been hoping to purchase, for example. If the government decides to press ahead with building motorways it will lose the opportunity to rebuild the railway network. The cost of the motorway is the railway system we do *not* develop.

One final point about 'opportunity cost' is that when we choose one option we never know whether we would have done better if we had chosen the other option. If we decide to build an underground system in one of our cities we will never know if the alternative idea, an overhead transit system would have been a better choice. Once you decide on one thing, the alternative opportunity is lost forever.

Points to remember

- Besides a legal environment, businesses operate in an economic environment.
- An economy is a system for organizing the production, distribution and exchange of goods and services.
- There are three main types of economy – market economies, planned economies and mixed economies.
- Generally speaking, the 'wants' of mankind are endless, but the means of satisfying those wants are limited. We have to exercise choice if the scarce resources of the world are to be used in the best way.
- If we use resources for one purpose it means they cannot be used for another purpose. The 'opportunity cost' of choosing one particular good or service is the next most desirable alternative which we forfeited by our original choice.

2.6   A project on commodities

A project is an activity in which we study something that we find particularly interesting, to a considerable depth. It involves quite a bit of research, collecting facts, illustrations and information about the chosen subject. Since everyone has different interests no teacher or lecturer can really help you all that much, though they may give general advice. Parents may also give help, advice and encouragement. The minimum size of a minor project would be four sides of A4 exercise paper, nicely presented with information, illustrations, etc. A more normal presentation would be rather longer than this, say a booklet with eight sides of paper. A really exhaustive effort might be as much as twenty pages long.

Obviously you cannot do every project in this book in the course of a couple of years, and as you will have projects to do for other subjects one does have to keep a sense of proportion. All the same you should aim to have a try at a good many projects – and do some of them in a thoroughly satisfactory way.

This project is about natural resources, the gifts made available by nature which mankind can use. All you have to do is pick one commodity and find out everything you can about it, from libraries, reference books, organizations that deal with the product, firms that use it in their manufactures, etc. Here is a short list, but you are not limited to these items, you can pick any natural product you like. Try to deal with the following points:

1   What product is it?
2   Where does it come from?

3 What is it used for?
4 How much of it is produced?
5 What is the end product?
6 What processes does it pass through in manufacture?
7 What skills are needed to turn the natural product into a finished good?

Some suggested commodities are: gold; iron; softwood; cocoa; coffee; silver; leather; wheat; teak; oil; diamonds; barley; mahogany; wool; tea; bananas; rice; opals; coal; oranges.

2.7 The environment surrounding the new entrepreneur

If you are thinking of self-employment rather than employment in a local firm, company or other institution, the environment surrounding you becomes very immediate and local. The checklist which follows suggests all sorts of environmental factors and some of the ways of dealing with them.

Have I any legal matters which require attention?

Of course we all hope we shall not face such problems but it is wise to establish a relationship with a local solicitor, so that at any time you can say 'My solicitors are Wild, Hewitson and Shaw of . . . etc. A simple accident, or a complaint from a customer or a local householder nearly always requires a solicitor's help and advice. A solicitor's letter will usually collect a bad debt (it threatens the non-payer, because non-payment constitutes an act of bankruptcy in many situations). Write for an introductory interview and ask their permission to give their name in any situation. They will be delighted to help.

Have I any local government difficulties?

The most likely difficulty is some sort of planning permission for the use of premises in a particular way. At the very least you may have to register a change of use – the premises you take over may not have been used for the same type of business before. There may be matters of nuisance. A private nuisance upsets local people who sue you privately for redress of their grievances. A public nuisance is generally offensive (for example a bad smell, or interference with a public right of way). It may lead to criminal charges against you.

Are there any matters which the police or other bodies may view as needing attention?

For example, the police keep a register of keyholders for all business premises; people to whom they can turn for the keys in certain eventualities. Children often trespass on premises and get shut in, or have an accident and need to be rescued. Burglar alarms go off and ring and ring and ring until the whole neighbourhood is frantic. The Fire Department will want to inspect the premises to see if they meet the fire regulations, and the new COSHH regulations concerning substances hazardous to health must also be complied with. We have all heard of incidents where people have died due to toxic fumes from a burning factory, usually caused by poor storage of dangerous products.

Am I employing anyone?

If so, I shall have to keep proper records; pay wages or salaries in a proper manner; deduct tax and National Insurance contributions and pay them over to the Inland Revenue authorities; pay statutory sick pay (SSP) for the first forty days of an employee's illness in any one year (I can claim the money back from the Inland Revenue); and pay statutory maternity pay (SMP) to any woman who is absent from work while her baby is born and she cares for it during the first few months (I can reclaim this money too).

Are there any local firms or companies I should cooperate with?

Of course we are all busy running our own affairs, but we do need to be on reasonably friendly terms with everyone about us. We often need to give support to one another – keeping an eye on premises perhaps, answering telephones when someone is ill, running an accident case to the local Casualty Department etc. A burglary, or a bit of vandalism, or dangerous substances not properly stored, or motor vehicles inconsiderately parked are all things that call for support, or general protest, or apology by the offending party.

Do I need to help in local charitable works, or community projects?

One cannot leave one's own work to make too large a contribution to such events, but it is a common thing to give help in relieving distress. Business people who are successful tend to be charitable, for they know many people who lead hard lives through no fault of their own. At such times as Christmas or the midsummer fête, or other jollifications it is common to be asked to contribute both in time, goods and money.

These are only a few suggestions, but every environment is unique; it has features other environments do not have and they all enter into decisions about where to site businesses, how to market goods and services and how to cooperate cheerfully in making the local community a pleasant and agreeable place to work in.

2.8 Rapid revision

Answers	*Questions*
–	**1 What is meant by the 'business environment'?**
1 The total climate of influences which are at work on the business at any time.	**2 What are the three parts of this environment?**
2 The local environment, the national environment and the international environment.	**3 Which of these three is the most important?**
3 The national environment; because the world is made up of nation states which have their own climate of laws and administrative procedures.	**4 What is law?**
4 It is a body of rules for the guidance of human conduct which is imposed upon, and enforced among, the citizens of a given state.	**5 Who imposes law upon the citizens of the UK?**
5 The sovereign body – which means 'The Queen in Parliament assembled'.	**6 Who enforces law among the citizens of the UK?**
6 The police, the prosecution service and the system of courts.	**7 What do we call local laws?**
7 Bye-laws.	**8 How is international law enforced?**

Answers	Questions
8 It can only be enforced if it is passed into national law by a system of ratification of the international code, making it part of the national law.	9 **Why are the wants of mankind unlimited?**
9 Because (a) appetite grows with feeding and (b) we tend to have more children, as they are part of a higher standard of living. Population growth is the biggest factor in increasing demands by mankind.	10 **What are the twin problems of creating wealth?**
10 (a) We must face up to the fact of scarcity – the world's resources are limited; (b) we must therefore exercise choice, to decide how to use nature's resources.	11 **What is the opportunity cost of enjoying a good or service?**
11 The next most enjoyable opportunity we decided not to enjoy when we made our choice.	12 **Go over the test again until you are sure of all the answers. Then try the questions in Section 2.9 below.**

2.9   Questions on Chapter 2

1   Peter and Mary Giles are artistic, and are considering setting up in business. They will have a small workshop, in which they will produce works of art and artistic objects, and a shop in which they will sell not only their own products but artists' sundries of all sorts. What environmental influences might be encountered by Peter and Mary as they make their plans?

2   Isaac Olaleye is an accountant, working in an office over shop premises. The ownership of the shop changes, and the new owner who is continuing the business as a grocer, starts to make pickles and chutneys in the basement. The aroma is too strong for Isaac, and embarrasses his clients. What would you advise Isaac about this change in his working environment?

3   'Trading on the copper market yesterday involved 14,876 ingots of 50 kilograms weight.' (Market Trader)

'Copper is a scarce commodity; and we must be as economical as possible in its use.' (Professor of Economics)

How can a metal which is being bought and sold in such enormous quantities be 'scarce'? Why do we need to husband our resources like copper?

4   Rajiv and Abdul are both extremely fond of Maira, an art student. She wishes to see a film at the local cinema, but it is only showing at a time when Rajiv and Abdul should be attending a business studies seminar at the local technical college. Rajiv tells Maira he must attend the seminar, but Abdul cuts the seminar and takes her to the film. What is the opportunity cost of the lecture to Rajiv? What is the opportunity cost of the cinema visit to Abdul?

5   'As to the enforcement of this section (the company's address to appear on all correspondence) if a company fails to comply it is liable to a fine; if an officer of the company authorises the issue of a business letter that fails to comply he is liable to a fine and both the company and every officer are liable to a daily default fine for continued contravention.' (Companies Act, 1985, Section 351)

From the point of view of the environment in which a company operates, explain the importance of clauses like this in an Act of Parliament.

3
The objectives of business

ALEXANDER GRAHAM BELL

3.1 Profits and survival

There is a popular misconception that entrepreneurs are only interested in profit, and it is fashionable to denigrate the profit motive as
dishonourable. The truth is quite different, especially in the early
years of a business's activity. The fact is that people go into business
to provide some useful good or service, and hope to earn a living by
doing so. The profit earned is the reward to the entrepreneur for
showing enterprise, and in the early years of a business it is very
difficult to make enough profit to earn a really good living. Many
small business proprietors end up earning less than the people they
employ. Many hesitate to employ someone else, because they are not
sure they can earn enough to support two families. For such people
the objective is not profit – it is survival.

To survive as a small business the proprietor must earn the
following:

1 Enough to buy all the raw materials, new stock and consumable
   items like wrapping paper, packing materials, etc., required to
   carry on the business in the next trading period.
2 Enough to cover all the overheads: rent, rates (community
   charges), light and heat, carriage, postage, motor expenses,
   cleaning expenses, repairs and renewals, insurance, telephone
   expenses, etc., for the trading period.
3 Enough to pay any wages of employees, including the national
   insurance charges payable by an employer.
4 Enough to meet any capital expenses in the trading period, for
   example new tools and equipment, office equipment, etc.
5 Enough to pay any interest on money borrowed to purchase
   capital items in earlier periods, mortgages, loans, etc., and any
   repayments of capital due in the trading period.
6 A reasonable income for himself/herself. This is called 'drawings'
   and it is **money drawn out in expectation of profits made**. If no
   profits have in fact been made the sums drawn will be the

entrepreneur's original capital drawn out. The entrepreneur is said to be 'living on his/her capital' and will soon be appearing at the bankruptcy court.

We see, therefore, that for the small business, the most important thing is to survive from year to year, by earning enough receipts to cover expenditure, and leaving enough profit to permit reasonable 'drawings' for the proprietor.

To follow the expenditures involved in running a small business consider the illustrations in Figures 3.1 and 3.2. They show all the types of expenditure incurred by a small firm, in this case a landscape gardener. The expenditures are divided into two parts, the 'purchases' of the business (called 'Payments for Business Stock') and the overheads of the business (called 'Payments other than for Stock'). The word 'purchases' has a special meaning in business. It is used for the purchases of items which are bought to sell again at a later date, or (in the case of firms like landscape gardeners, builders and decorators, etc.) purchases which are embodied in the finished

Date or Chq. No.	To Whom Paid	Amount Paid			
		By Cash Col 7		By Cheque Col 8	
190146	CLAYHILL SANDPITS PLC			36	53
SEPT 6	LOWLANDS BULB Co LTD	28	42		
190148	IRISH TURF Co LTD			112	38
190149	CLAYHILL SANDPITS PLC			47	60
SEPT 7	MYHILLS GARDEN CENTRE	23	48		
SEPT 8	RUSTIC CHAIRS LTD	29	54		
	Totals	81	44	196	51

PAYMENTS FOR BUSINESS STOCK

Figure 3.1 Records of payments for business stock

Notes:
1 The entries are largely self-explanatory.
2 Where a payment has been made by cheque it is helpful to put the cheque number in. It can then be followed through on the bank statement when we receive it at the end of the month.
3 The total amounts spent have to be recovered by billing the customer for the materials used, a well as for the work done. If all these expenses were for the same job, what would be the total charged to the customer for materials used, if the proprietor always added 33⅓ per cent to cost prices for a profit margin? (Answer at end of Chapter.)

PAYMENTS OTHER THAN FOR STOCK				
Nature of Payment	Amount Paid			
	By Cash Col 9		By Cheque Col 10	
Rent	42	00		
Rates				
Light and Heat			27	56
Carriage				
Postages 19p, 19p, £1·26	1	64		
Paper				
Motor Expenses (PETROL)	13	54		
—do—				
Travelling				
Cleaning				
Printing & Stationery (LETTERHEAD)	11	25		
Repairs & Renewals				
Insurance (Business)				
Advertising				
Telephone				
Wages (Wife)				
Wages (Employees)	86	90		
Sundries 24p 36p		60		
Private Pension Contributions				
Inland Revenue (PAYE + NI)				
Drawings for Self (see Note. 10)			100	00
—do—				
—do—				
Capital Items (see note 7) (LAWN MOWER)			54	60
Totals	155	93	182	16

product supplied to the customer. Other things purchased (such as postage stamps, petrol for vehicles, stationery, etc., are not called 'purchases' but 'overheads' or overhead expenses.

3.2 Profits and expansion (growth)

When a firm or company has passed through the survival stage, it usually has a proven product (or preferably a group of proven products). These are distinct from other products on the market, and can command a ready sale. The firm begins to make more than enough profit to give the entrepreneur a decent living, and is therefore able to expand its activities. There is a great incentive to expand the business, because it makes the whole enterprise more secure. There are now perhaps many families dependent upon the success of the business, and everyone has an interest in keeping the prosperity going. Why is growth a good idea? The answer is that we can achieve the economies of large scale.

The economies of large scale

Scale means size. As we grow in size there are certain economies that can be achieved. A few simple examples would be as follows:

1 We only need one factory manager, whether the factory turns out 50 items, or 50,000 items or 50 million items.
2 A large building is nót much more expensive to build than a small one. For example, if we have a plot of land we can put up a one-storey building, or a two-storey building or a three-storey building on it without any increase in the size of the plot.
3 A machine to turn out a single item becomes more economical if it is used to make two, three, four or even 400 items. Henry Ford in his earliest car factories was turning out one new car every ten seconds, when some of his rivals were making only ten cars a year.

Figure 3.2 Recording overhead expenses

Notes:
1 Again, the entries are largely self-explanatory.
2 The entries in the top section are business expenses which can be deducted in the Final Accounts of the business (the ones where the profits are calculated). We call such expenses 'revenue expenses' and the tax authorities regard them as losses of the business, incurred in earning the profits.
3 Items in the lower section are not deductible for tax purposes, but are either drawings of the proprietor or long-term capital items which last many years, and therefore cannot be regarded as expenses of the present year only.

Accused of making huge profits, he replied, '*Manufacturing is not buying cheap and selling dear. It is the focusing upon a manufacturing project of the principles of power, accuracy, economy, system, continuity, speed and repetition.*'

We could go on giving such examples all day. In manufacturing the credit for more economical operations is often given to the three Ss, **simplification**, **standardization** and **specialization**.

1 *Simplification* means the use of simple materials, easily handled by mechanical means, without excessive craftsmanship. For example, elaborately-carved furniture depending upon the specialized skills of an artist or master craftsman, is too expensive except for the very richest home owners. The needs of millions of householders are more conveniently met by mass production methods, where a high degree of design skills can produce serviceable furniture, easily cleaned and polished, and yet aesthetically attractive.

2 *Standardization* is the breaking down of a complex unit into standard parts, easily assembled to give a variety of forms to meet a variety of needs. Thus the modern motor car largely consists of standard units which can be used on a variety of models, adapted to suit different tastes and fashions.

3 *Specialization* is the process of breaking a manufacturing process down into its individual processes and then making each process a separate activity which can be performed by a specialist operator. This process is called **the division of labour**, and it makes the largest single contribution to increased output. We have all seen, on television, assembly plants where complex electronic assemblies are put together by people who hardly seem to need to look at the work they are doing, so automatic has it become. Whether such work is enjoyable is debatable, and it may well be that it is not to everyone's taste, but there are people who are perfectly happy to do it.

It has been found that the division of labour in this way into processes and subprocesses is one of the chief causes of prosperity. The advantages of this type of specialization seem to be as follows:

1 People choose the work they like, and consequently work more enthusiastically and willingly.
2 They become much more skilled, with the repetition. Practice makes perfect.
3 They invent cunning short cuts and improved methods of working.
4 They can be supported by an array of power tools which speed up the processes and result in bigger and bigger output.
5 In some areas mechanization and computerization mean that

labour can be dispensed with altogether, and output can be achieved at very high levels by machines which are tireless.

The consequences of growth

There are many consequences of growth. Some of the more obvious ones are:

1 Output is increased enormously and the wants of mankind can be met more easily and a higher standard of living for all becomes possible.
2 The security of firms and companies is greatly increased because they are unlikely to meet financial problems and the provision of capital for new projects becomes a much more simple matter.
3 The security of employment offered to employees is greater, and strong ties of company loyalty develop. Good wages, good working conditions, health and pension provisions etc., can be afforded.
4 Sales and marketing move across national boundaries into world markets. A global approach to marketing and production means the growth of multinational companies, with plants and factories in every country, and a reduction in narrow nationalism. We become citizens of a world economy.

Of course, there are disadvantages, but to some extent the division of labour and specialization must be adopted if we are to produce the flood of products that are needed by people clamouring for an ever higher standard of living.

The diseconomies of large scale

The diseconomies of large scale are:

1 *Huge outputs require storage and distribution*   Huge outputs pour off production lines, and it is essential to remove them from the scene of production at once or the production lines will be blocked. There is, therefore, a big warehousing and distribution problem, which has to be solved by a network of depots around the country, and fleets of container lorries to carry the goods.
2 *Marketing problems*   Since income can only be generated by selling the product, marketing becomes an important feature. No longer can the village goldsmith make a ring for the wealthy farmer's wife and deliver it personally to her house. Millions of rings are being made every year, in great variety, and the customers are spread far and wide. We have to advertise them, find retailers to display and sell them, or set up mail order systems to supply customers by post. The Marketing Director, with support

from the Sales Department, the Advertising Department and the Public Relations Department, become a key figure in the company.

3   *The repetitive nature of work*   Some mass production work is boring, and repetitive, and although the operatives are highly-skilled it is over a very narrow field. One may be a highly-skilled car body welder and a member of the engineer's union but know practically nothing about engineering. Sometimes jobs are rotated to give employees a greater variety of work but the range is still rather limited.

Points to remember

- While business people are largely in business to make profit, in the early years the survival of the business is the more important consideration.
- To survive a business must be able to recover all its costs, including the replacement of stocks sold, the overhead expenses inseparable from business, the wages and salaries paid and the repayment of loans for capital items borrowed in earlier periods.
- Eventually growth begins to take place, in order to achieve the economies of large-scale operations.
- Production economies are usually achieved through the three Ss – simplification, standardization and specialization.
- Specialization means the division of labour into simpler tasks which can be performed at high speeds, often by mechanized or computerized methods.
- However, large scale does bring its diseconomies, particularly the problems of distribution, storage and marketing. The repetitive nature of work may also be a disadvantage.

3.3   Primary, secondary and tertiary production

We usually classify production activities (the chief objectives of business) into three divisions – primary, secondary and tertiary production. Primary, secondary and tertiary are simply words derived from the Latin for one, two and three.

Primary production

Primary production is the production of goods made available by nature, either in the distant past as part of the Earth's development or year by year, as the cycles of nature proceed. Thus, iron ore, tin, copper and other elements are natural resources which we cannot renew – we can discover them and use them, but as we do so we exhaust the supplies. They are non-renewable primary products. By contrast, timber, fish, wheat and barley are natural products which can be replaced by careful agricultural and animal husbandry programmes. They are renewable resources.

Secondary production

Secondary production is the production of goods which are an improvement upon natural products. Thus, a chair is more convenient to sit on than a tree trunk; a motor vehicle is an improvement upon the iron ore, bauxite, sand and other items from which its steel frame, aluminium components, glass windows, etc., are made. By years of scientific and practical study we have found how to change natural products into sophisticated secondary goods. In doing so we add value to the product. One Hollywood actress, complaining that the price of a diamond ring was excessive, considering that it was only a stone found in the ground was told by the irate cutter 'Madam, the diamond is free – look, I'll give you one.' And so he did. The work of the diamond cutter adds value to the natural stone; the work of the tailor or seamstress adds value to the cloth used, which was itself an improvement on the raw wool or raw cotton from which the cloth was made; and the work of the carpenter, joiner or cabinet maker adds value to the natural wood which is the raw material of these trades. Incidentally, perhaps it is worth mentioning that **Value Added Tax** is a tax imposed by the government on all value added to primary products as they move from their natural point of production to the final selling point. We shall learn more about VAT later.

Tertiary production

Tertiary production is the production of services, not goods. There are two kinds of services – **commercial services** and **personal services**. Commercial services are services connected with the distribution and exchange of goods. They include four branches of trade – wholesale trade, retail trade, import trade and export trade. The other four types of commercial services are called **ancillary services**, a word which means 'handmaiden' services, which go along with, and are essential to assist, trading activities. They are banking, insurance, transport and communications.

Personal services are services unconnected with goods. They include medical care, dentistry, hairdressing, education and similar activities which are provided directly to the individual concerned, and result in an improved standard of living for all those who can benefit by the services rendered.

In tabular form we could list some of the business people engaged in these activities as shown in Table 3.1.

Table 3.1   Types of production

Primary production	Secondary production	Tertiary production	
		Commercial services	Personal services
Farmer	Tailor	Wholesaler	Doctor
Beekeeper	Builder	Retailer	Dentist
Forestry worker	Car mechanic	Banker	Nurse
Coal miner	Carpenter	Insurance agent	Teacher
Oil driller	Potter	Importer	Policeman
Pearl diver	Baker	Exporter	Soldier
Fish farmer	Shipbuilder	Lorry driver	Undertaker
Herdsman	Electrical assembler	Telecommunications engineer	Psychiatrist

3.4   Private sector activity

Much of the business activity referred to above is provided by private firms and companies. They may be tiny businesses run by sole traders,who are in business on their own as butchers, bakers, grocers, carpenters, joiners, etc. They may be partnerships, with two or three partners cooperating together to run workshops, factories, garages, medical centres, dental practices, etc. They may be huge companies with hundreds or thousands of employees. Private enterprise is perhaps the natural way for business activity to start and develop, since everyone is different, and has his/her particular interests and talents. As explained earlier, we call the sort of person who shows enough enterprise to set up a business an **entrepreneur**. The private sector of business activity is sometimes called the **enterprise sector**.

We saw in Figure 1.1 that what happens when we start to show enterprise is that we step out of the crowd who are looking for employment and say: 'Here is something that I am particularly interested in, and which mankind needs.

It may be a good or a service.

- I think I could get this organized.
- I shall need some capital to get started so (a) I'll start saving and thus accumulate the capital I need, or (b) I'll find someone who can provide the money I need – either a partner, or someone who is prepared to join me in launching a company, or (c) I'll find an institutional investor (a bank or a finance company) that will lend me the money.
- I might need some help in the technical or business side of things, so my search for a partner may include finding someone who has

the skill I need. On the other hand an employee might be better than a partner, for an employee will do what I tell him/her to do, but a partner may have to be persuaded to do things my way.
● Finally I must find some premises.'

Everyone needs a geographical spot where a business can be started up. We have already seen that Henry Ford made his first engine on his mother's kitchen table, and his first car in a garden shed.

It is the combination of land, labour and capital that is the basis of any productive activity and it is the resulting output of goods and services which is the real wealth of the world, which its citizens can enjoy.

3.5 Public sector activity

There are certain things which we cannot leave to private enterprise. For example, we don't want people having private armies, or private police forces, nor do we want judges who are controlled by private lords and barons. Many people believe strongly in nationalization, particularly of industries which are natural monopolies, like the railways, the electricity industry, gas and water supply. It is true that in recent years some 'privatization' of public enterprises has taken place, but not all public sector activities are suitable for returning to private hands, and we are always likely to have some public sector institutions. Actually, about 60 per cent private sector and 40 per cent public sector institutions seems to be about right.

More will be said about private and public sector organizations later in this book. Here we need to understand how they are inter-related, and how the world of work is organized.

3.6 The interdependence of businesses

All business institutions are closely linked together in an intricate pattern or network of relationships which produces the goods and services which all the people require. At one side are the consumers, who want the goods and services. We are all consumers, so every person in the world has to be included in the picture. At the other side are the producers, who are producing the goods and services. We are all producers too (if we leave out the old and infirm, the very young and those people temporarily unemployed). Of course there are a few people who do not contribute to production – for example those who live by robbery, burglary, etc. – but they are usually dealt with by the law enforcement officers. In between the consumers and the producers is a series of links called 'the chain of production', which shows the various stages through which production passes before goods finally reach the consumer. Some links are quite short – as where a market gardener sells vegetables at his/her garden gate to passers by. Other chains of production have many links, for example, bananas grown in the West Indies may reach consumers in the UK only after a long sea journey, in a specially-designed vessel where the ripening of the bananas in transit can be carefully supervised. Unloaded at the ports they must then be warehoused while the ripening continues and eventually be distributed by the wholesalers to retailers who actually supply the families in every area.

As they move from producers to consumers all products change ownership, sometimes several times, with each buyer paying each seller at the moment of transfer. The economic term for these changes of ownership is 'exchange'. Exchange is the easy and convenient way to pass goods from one owner to another. The payment is called the 'price' and is frequently made in cash, though these days business people who are known to one another may agree to payment at a later date. To do this it is necessary to keep account of the payments due, and an actual book-keeping record is kept called 'an account'. The usual terms for account trading are monthly terms – that is to say that at the end of each month a statement is rendered to the debtor showing how much must be paid, and this is usually settled at some time within the next month. Meanwhile a new month's trading activities are already beginning. Readers who are studying Book-keeping (sometimes called Principles of Accounts) will be familiar with trading on 'open account' terms. A companion volume to the present one, *Book-keeping Made Simple*, explains the whole procedure in great detail.

These transactions are settled through the payment of money, and it is to the money system that we must next turn our attention (see Chapter 4). Before doing so we must make one further point about the interdependence of businesses.

As businesses become large-scale businesses there is a change in the relationships between them and other firms. Small firms become to some extent client firms of other companies, and may even be wholly-owned subsidiaries subject to direct control. Independent firms and companies may lose their freedom, and be entirely dependent upon orders from larger firms, who can consequently depress the prices paid to them and take most of the profits for themselves. Key workers may be attracted away by offers of higher wages and '*golden hellos*.' A 'golden hello' is a lump sum payment given to a key worker when he/she joins a big firm. It is an inducement to change jobs which many employees of small firms find difficult to resist. Many of the small businesses in your area (for example the shops) may in fact not be small businesses at all, but part of much bigger organizations which have taken over the small businesses and operate them instead as units of a much larger-scale organization.

Points to remember

- Production activities may be classified into primary, secondary and tertiary production.
- Primary production is the production of goods made available by nature.
- Secondary production is the production of goods which improve upon the natural product (as where wood is made into furniture, or iron ore is made into steel.
- Tertiary production is the production of services; either commercial services or personal services.
- Some of these production activities will be carried on by private sector firms, and other will be part of the public sector. In the UK this applies particularly to the personal services since such organizations as the National Health Service, the social security system and education are all public sector activities.

3.7 A project on chains of production

For this project it is necessary to study the chain of production as it affects a particular firm or company in your own home area. Since an entire class cannot descend upon a single firm or company it is necessary to select several companies in the area and choose a small team to study each. If possible it is best to have at least one member of the team who has a relative working in the firm who can furnish a good deal of routine information about the firm. Many firms are secretive about their affairs, fearing that rivals will use any information they divulge to increase their share of the firm's market. If you can choose a public limited company (PLC) things will be a little easier since all public limited companies must publish annual reports which the public may see, and this will give you a good deal of useful information. With other firms or companies it would be advisable to write officially asking if the management have any objection to your studying their chain of production, and asking for any information they can give you about their raw materials, products and market outlets.

The term 'chain of production' means the series of links which join producers to consumers. The following elements enter into the study:

1 What raw materials are used and where do they come from?
2 What final products are made, and to whom are they eventually sold?

3   What is the marketing structure? Is there a system of depots, or are deliveries made direct to wholesalers or large retail outlets?
4   What transport system is used to move goods from the point of production and where do they go?
5   Is there any servicing or similar after-sales link with the final consumer?
6   To what extent is the firm dependent upon other firms for its sources of supply, or its marketing, distribution and storage of the finished product?

Each member of the group should present a report giving an account of the firm's chain of production, as revealed by the inquiry conducted.

3.8   The objectives of a new enterprise

The young entrepreneur has a particular need to think carefully about, and record, the objectives of the business he envisages setting up. It has been said that 'writing maketh an exact man'. If we try to set down in writing the objectives of our new business we quickly find that we have to state our ideas very precisely if we are to feel satisfied that we have pinned them down exactly. The entrepreneur must have a business plan, but a plan is only a way to achieve objectives. The checklist below may help you.

1   What is the monetary objective of the new business?

We could answer this question by saying: 'I want to be a millionaire in five years.' Some people have stated such aims and actually achieved them. Others have failed. More modestly we might say that within two years we hope to have a net profit, as proprietor, of £300 per week. £20 per week is roughly £1,000 a year, so £300 per week is £15,000 per year. That is a fairly comfortable income for an ordinary person at the time of writing, but it would not be described as riches. State the objective as the figure you believe to be achievable, given hard work, and good luck.

2   What are the non-monetary objectives?

Monetary objectives are rarely enough, because if money is the only objective then any business would do – but most of us are heading into a business which appeals to us. We are doing it as much for the interest we have in the activity as the reward we hope to get out of it. Some typical non-monetary objectives might be:

(a) To establish a wide range of products in the light engineering field and market them to the building trades.

(b) To gain experience in interior decoration, particularly in the field of soft furnishings.

(c) To establish a wholesale vegetable round in the Richmond/ Twickenham area supplying retail outlets with top-quality fresh produce, organically grown.

Clearly there are many non-monetary objectives. The question is 'What are our non-monetary objectives?'

3 What constraints are operating to limit the achievements of these objectives

There are many constraints upon the new entrepreneur. Some of them are:

(a) *Personal constraints*   These include family ties; the need to earn a steady income whereas the early days of a business may be difficult in this respect; limited time available because of the needs of a growing family etc.

(b) *Skill constraints*   Few people have all the skills they need, and young entrepreneurs may be only too aware of their in- adequacies. The important thing is to extend the frontiers of your knowledge in every direction, but especially in these areas where the skills you need are the most immediate. Get books on the subjects you need to study and work through them. Any subject on earth can be mastered to a good level in twelve months, and to a really good level in two years. Much education in schools and colleges is very dilute – one has to wait for the slowest member of the class. Self-education is quicker. The Made Simple series, for example, has books on many aspects of business. Other skills can be acquired by short courses at evening institutes, colleges of further education, technical colleges etc. These places are the sweepers-up of lost skills. They can teach you anything and everything if you just hunt up the right college. Your local Regional Advisory Council (RAC) publishes a list of every subject, showing every college that teaches it. Your local library will have the booklet, or will get it for you.

(c) *Premises constraints*   Some premises cannot be used for certain forms of business activity. Be careful to select premises which have the necessary planning permission and always specify in any letters you write that any commitment you enter into shall be 'subject to planning permission being forthcoming'.

There may be many other constraints.

3.9   Rapid revision

Answers		Questions	
	–	1	Why do people go into business?
1	To provide some useful good or service that is wanted by mankind, and which they feel they can earn a living from supplying.	2	What form does the 'living' take?
2	It is the profit of the enterprise. Profit is defined as the reward to the proprietor of a business for showing enterprise.	3	In the early years what is the major problem faced by businesses?
3	Survival – the world is a competitive place and to meet the competition and survive it is essential usually to work long hours, and to take out from the business as little as possible.	4	What are the chief classes of costs that have to be covered?
4	(a) Payments for business stock (purchases to be resold at a later date, or embodied in the product); (b) overhead expenses – light, heat, etc.; (c) wages and salaries; and (d) capital items (tools, equipment, motor vehicles etc.).	5	What is the long-term objective of business?
5	To grow to the point where the economies of large scale can be achieved, and greater security for both the entrepreneur and the employees becomes possible.	6	What are the three Ss?
6	Simplification, standardization and specialization.	7	What was Henry Ford's definition of mass production?

Answers	Questions
7 'Manufacturing is not buying cheap and selling dear. It is the focusing upon a manufacturing project of the principles of power, accuracy, economy, system, continuity, speed and repetition.'	**8 What are the three types of production?**
8 (a) Primary production; (b) secondary production; (c) tertiary production (services).	**9 Explain these terms.**
9 (a) Primary production is the production of goods made available by nature, either as non-renewable basic raw materials, or agricultural products which can be produced every year; (b) secondary production is the production of improved natural goods, in some more usable form; (c) tertiary production is production of services, either commercial services or personal services.	**10 What are the chief diseconomies of large-scale output?**
10 You have a major distribution and marketing problem as a result of the vast outputs produced.	**11 What are private sector activities?**
11 Activities carried on by sole traders, partnerships and limited companies, motivated by the desire to make profits.	**12 What are public sector activities?**
12 Activities carried out by nationalized industries, or local or national government agencies, and financed out of taxation with official funds.	**13 Go over the test again until you are sure you know the answers. Then try the questions in Section 3.10 below.**

3.10   Questions on Chapter 3

1   List five primary occupations, five secondary occupations, five tertiary commercial services and five tertiary personal services.

2   Explain the part played in mass production by the three Ss (simplification, standardization and specialization).

3   Name four private enterprises in your own home town or district and four enterprises which are run as public sector organizations.

4   A. Grower is in business as a market gardener. His sales in a particular year total £33,500. His costs of production are: raw materials £825; wages £11,850; overhead expenses £5,284; and repairs to capital assets £1,345. What were his profits for the year?

5   Tina Ogilvie is a fashion designer who has just left college and is setting up in business with £5,000 borrowed from her father. The public limited company 'Fashions of Carnaby St PLC' has over fifty years' experience in the rag trade and a capital of £37 million pounds owned by 42,800 shareholders. What do you think would be the differences between Tina's objectives and the objectives of the public company?

6   Compare the chains of production of these three organizations:

   (a)   Bill and Joe Seafarer fish for crabs and lobsters off the Cornish coast and sell direct to hoteliers in their local towns.

   (b)   Peter and Mary Troutbeck run a fish farm and sell their output of fresh trout, in boxes of two fish ready for the customer, to a large retailer with a chain of shops all over the region.

   (c)   Farflung Fish Products PLC have a licence to fish off the Falkland Isles and market the produce from their factory ship as frozen cartons for sale in retail shops all over the UK.

7   Using a photocopy of the paper shown in Figure 3.3 record the following payments for business stock in the books of M. Phillips:

   7 July   Paid for supplies from R. Cork by cheque (No. 211730) £52.36. Also paid in cash to A. Farmer £19.36 for goods for resale.

   8 July   Paid to McKrill Biscuit Co. by cheque £195.60 (cheque No. 211731).

   9 July   Paid to R. Masterson by cheque (No. 211733) £27.25 and to The Mineral Water Co. Ltd, in cash £25.85.

   13 July   Paid to M. Laws by cheque (No. 211734) £179.56.

   After entering these items total the 'cash' and 'cheque' columns. (Answers at end of this set of exercises.)

PAYMENTS FOR BUSINESS STOCK			
Date or Chq. No.	To Whom Paid	Amount Paid	
		By Cash Col 7	By Cheque Col 8
	Totals		

Figure 3.3 This paper is for use with Questions 7 and 8 and may be photocopied for educational purposes

8 Using a photocopy of the paper shown in Figure 3.3 record the following payments for business stock in the books of R. Sheldrake:

14 August Paid to M. Rogerson by cheque (No 213223) £87.55 and to B. Laker in cash £43.50.

16 August Paid to A. Waterson by cheque (No. 213225) the sum of £225.80 for materials supplied.

18 August A delivery from R. Cook & Co., is valued at £48.50 but returns amounting to £7.25 are given by Sheldrake to the van driver. The net amount is paid in cash.

Total the 'cash' and 'cheque' columns.

9 Using a photocopy of the paper shown in Figure 3.4 record the following 'Payments other than for stock' in the books of T. Jones, who is in business as a greengrocer. He pays the following items in cash: rent £45; postage 27p, 32p, 46p and £1.40; petrol £8.75 and insurance £25.20. He also pays wages £87.50 in cash. He pays by cheque for a weighing machine £69.75 and for sundries £8.50. He also draws for his own use the sum of £80 by cheque. Enter the above items and total the two columns to find the total 'Cash' and 'Cheque' payments.

10 Using the type of paper shown in Figure 3.4 record the following payments in the books of Penny Whitehead who is in business as a fashion designer. She pays the following items in cash: postage

PAYMENTS OTHER THAN FOR STOCK				
Nature of Payment	Amount Paid			
	By Cash Col 9		By Cheque Col 10	
Rent				
Rates				
Light and Heat				
Carriage				
Postages				
Paper				
Motor Expenses				
—do—				
Travelling				
Cleaning				
Printing & Stationery				
Repairs & Renewals				
Insurance (Business)				
Advertising				
Telephone				
Wages (Wife)				
Wages (Employees)				
Sundries				
Private Pension Contributions				
Inland Revenue (PAYE + NI)				
Drawings for Self (see Note. 10)				
—do—				
—do—				
Capital Items (see note 7)				
Totals				

Figure 3.4 This paper is for use with Questions 9 and 10 and may be photocopied for educational purposes

£2.47 and £1.32; stationery £4.65 and travelling £12.50. She also pays wages £182.50 in cash. She pays by cheque for advertising £27.42 and a telephone bill for £281.74. She also draws for herself the sum of £100 in cash. Total the two columns to find the total 'Cash' and 'Cheque' payments.

Answers to Questions 7–10 above

7 Cash total £45.21, cheques £454.77;　8 Cash total £84.75, cheques £313.35;　9 Cash total £168.90, cheques £158.25;　10 Cash total £303.44, cheques £309.16.

Answer to question on Figure 3.1

Amount charged to customer = £370.60.

4
Money and business activity

4.1 The nature of money

'Money makes the world go around' says a popular song, repeating a proverb that is almost as old as money itself. Of course there was a time when there was no money. Prehistoric man, hunting in the woods of South-west Britain, and being hunted himself by the sabre-toothed tiger, had no money. The Phoenician traders had the use of money, but for many of their trades it was useless. They engaged in trade with primitive people by 'silent trade'. Anchoring off-shore they laid out a selection of trading items on the beach and retired to the main vessel. Overcoming their timidity the natives would inspect the goods and lay out alongside what they were prepared to offer in exchange. Retiring in their turn, the natives would watch as the traders examined the goods and if dissatisfied returned to their vessel. The natives would then increase the supply until the traders were satisfied and took the native supplies. They then took the 'foreign' goods and both parties were satisfied.

Silent trade is a form of **barter**. Barter is the exchange of goods for goods. It is widely used for trade even today, and when the value of money collapses in times of national unrest it again becomes the only way to trade. When the American colonies broke away from the UK and the British currency was unacceptable, barter returned as the chief method of trade. We shall see that barter has its problems, because, for example, a person may have something another person wants but be unable to obtain equal value in exchange. It may be necessary to carry a trade over to a later date. 'I owe Nathaniel Hawke one coil of rope' reads an old debt from the times of the American War of Independence. In primitive tribes some debts are often carried over from one generation to another. Fortunately interest does not enter into primitive trading, or such long-standing debts would become larger year by year.

The idea of 'money' is that it is something that is acceptable to everyone, so that the problems of barter can be overcome. It helps to understand the nature of money if we consider the problems of life without a money system where barter is the accepted method of exchange.

The problems of barter

The problems of barter are:

1 *The need to meet the other person's requirements* Economists call this the double coincidence of 'wants'. In barter, each person must want what the other has, and have what the other wants. If I have a fat goose and want a wedding ring, and the other person has a wedding ring and wants a fat goose we shall be able to satisfy one another's wants. If a goldsmith has no wedding rings but has only a silver bracelet we cannot trade.
2 *The values must be roughly equal* Even if we have a double coincidence of wants it still might not be possible to trade unless the values are deemed to be roughly equal. If the gold wedding ring is worth two fat geese the exchange cannot be made. Sometimes, by agreement, part of the trade could be carried over; one fat goose now and another fat goose at Christmas time. The jeweller, parting with the wedding ring, would know that, his/her customer being an honourable person, Christmas dinner was already provided. One American trading post in the early days 'before the West was won' had a notice which read:

> *Trading values with the Indians*
> 1 ordinary riding horse costs
> 1 gun and 100 loads of ammunition
> or 5 tipi poles   or 15 eagle feathers
> or 1 carrot of tobacco weighing 3 pounds

There were seventeen items on the list altogether.
3 *Some items are indivisible* Suppose a riding horse is worth two guns. What is one gun worth? Obviously half a horse; but it is impossible to cut a horse in half, without spoiling the horse.

With a money system you simply develop an article of some sort that is universally acceptable to everyone. Money does not have to take the form of round tokens of value made of copper, silver or gold. Many things have served as money – tools, nails, blocks of compressed tea, coloured beads. In Germany after the Second World War the currency collapsed and cigarettes became the acceptable currency, too valuable to smoke. British soldiers serving in the Army of Occupation were given fifty cigarettes a week free, and enjoyed a prosperity they had not previously known. In Tibet the trade with China before the Communist takeover was largely conducted in bricks of compressed tea. Ten million bricks a year changed hands on

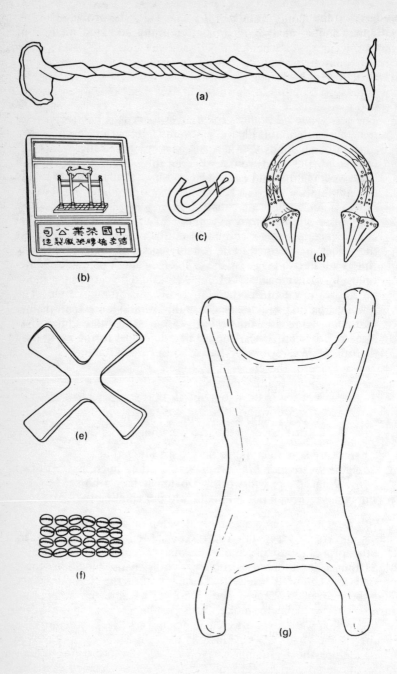

(a)

(b)

(c)

(d)

(e)

(f)

(g)

one trade route alone. They were compact, easy to carry, lasted a long time and a small part broken off made an enjoyable and nourishing cup of tea when enriched with yak butter.

Even today many nations engage in barter when they have insufficient foreign exchange. A nation that wants to buy UK goods may offer furs, or shoes, or furniture in exchange. This type of trade is called **countertrade**. Fortunately, some of the big banks help with countertrade. They keep on their databanks lists of traders prepared to handle various goods if the price is right. If they can find someone to buy the foreign goods at a fair price the exporter with a problem will arrange for the goods to be delivered to the 'barter and switch' merchant, and will be paid cash instead.

Later the minting of coins became the accepted way to produce money. Originally they were made from electrum, a naturally-occurring alloy of gold and silver. Subsequently they were made of the coinage metals, copper, silver and gold. The chief virtue of these metals for coinage is that they do not rust, though copper and silver do tarnish and look less beautiful as the years go by. It was usual to mark the coins with a distinctive sign. Wheat has always been used as money (the Greek word 'drachma' means 'handful' – of wheat). Wheat appeared on Greek coins and many coins had cattle on them. Another common idea was to show the head of a God, and the first Roman mint was set up in the Temple of the Goddess Moneta, whose head appeared on the coins. She gave us our word 'money'.

Later the face of the emperor was used, and today the Queen's head is the symbol of authority used on all UK coins.

What then is the true nature of money? A clear definition would be something like the following: *Money is a medium of exchange which is widely acceptable throughout a nation, so that goods and services may be purchased in exchange for an agreed amount of money. The*

Figure 4.1   Some early forms of money
(a)   Kissi pennies, from Sierra Leone; iron rods shaped like a man, with a head at one end and feet at the other.
(b)   Bricks of tea from Tibet.
(c)   Silver larins, from Lar, in the Persian/Arabic Gulf, made from silver wire in a fish-hook shape.
(d)   Silver manillas from West Africa, carried as bracelets. Also made of copper and brass.
(e)   Katanga crosses, from the Congo, made of copper.
(f)   Cowrie shells, used all over Africa, Asia and America, and even in prehistoric Britain.
(g)   The Mycenean talent, made in bronze to imitate an ox-hide. Cattle have always been used as money, and this money imitated the old, living currency. The Latin word for money, *pecunia*, comes from *pecus*, meaning cattle.

seller of goods and services is then free to use the money obtained to purchase further supplies, while any profit made enables him/her to purchase a balanced basket of goods and services to suit his/her particular needs.

4.2   The qualities of money

Money has to have a number of qualities if it is to play its part properly as a medium of exchange. These characteristics of money are listed as shown below. Money must be:

1   Generally acceptable
2   Stable in value
3   Durable, rustproof and difficult to imitate
4   Portable
5   Divisible into small units

1   *Generally acceptable*   Exchanges will not take place if money is not generally acceptable to all the citizens of the state. When coins were made of gold and silver they were generally acceptable – people will take gold and silver anywhere in the world. As coins came to be made of less valuable metals (token money) or of paper (which is practically worthless) it became difficult to make them generally acceptable. The solution was to have the sovereign declare the money '**legal tender**'. To tender is to offer payment. If I tender a £10 note to pay a bill it is a legal offer to pay, and every citizen of the state must accept it as a legal tender. If a shopkeeper or hotelkeeper refused to accept the note in payment I need not offer to pay again, for I have fulfilled my duty. The debt is not wiped out, but it is now up to the shopkeeper or hotelkeeper to ask me for the money, and when I offer the £10 note again he/she must accept it. There are limits to legal tender to prevent people being burdened with unfair amounts of coinage. For example, if I spend one penny out of £1 I do not want to receive ninety-nine pennies as change. The limits are:

- Notes, £2 and £1 coins are valid to any amount (although most of us pay large debts by cheque or some other form of paper or plastic payment).
- 50 pence, 25 pence and 20 pence pieces are valid tender up to £10.
- 10 pence pieces and 5 pence pieces are valid up to £5.
- Bronze coins are valid up to 20 pence per denomination.

There are many other methods of payment today, such as cheques, credit cards, Girobank payments, etc. These are not 'legal tender', and may be refused by traders who prefer not to be paid in these ways. We often see notices in shops 'Please do not offer to pay by cheque since a refusal may offend.' Such a shopkeeper is only prepared to sell goods in return for coins or notes which are legal tender. On the other hand many shops display notices reading 'Cheques accepted if backed by a cheque card.' Signs reading 'Visa, Access, Trustcard, American Express and Diners Club cards welcome' are to be seen everywhere.

2   *Stable in value*   Money should be stable in value. In the years from 1745–1914 the British currency was so stable in value that the rate of interest never varied. Today we suffer from a disease called 'inflation' which means that money falls in value gradually over the years. Sometimes we get 'runaway inflation' with money falling in value faster and faster. In some countries people go shopping early in the morning before the shopkeepers have time to put the prices up – since the value of money falls every day. One sad story tells of a Polish miser who saved all his life, denying himself many pleasures to do it. In the runaway inflation after the First World War he exchanged all his savings for one bread roll. His life savings had lost all their value.

3   *Durable, rustproof and difficult to imitate*   Making coins is an expensive business and they should have a long life. Most UK coins are expected to last fifty years. Printed notes rarely last more than about three months, and there is a great deal of work to do printing new ones on special security paper. Even worse is the security problem of destroying the old and dirty notes which are withdrawn from circulation. They are burned in special furnaces, under strict surveillance. All coins are made of metals which do not rust, since chemical reaction with the air would reduce the cleanliness of coins and their lifetime. Both coins and notes must be difficult to imitate. Hence the complex designs on banknotes, and the use of special paper to print them. Counterfeiting (making fraudulent imitations of money, either coins or banknotes) has always been an offence punishable by a long term of imprisonment. As we shall see, money is the way people are rewarded for producing goods and services. Anyone who makes his/her own money is fraudulently making a claim on the goods and services available, which destroys the very basis of the social system.

4   *Portability*   We all have to carry money around, and the weight of it can be a great disadvantage. Ideally coins should be as light as possible. One of the reasons why gold coins fell into disfavour was that gold is a very heavy metal. Notes are much more portable, and can be made of different denominations, £5, £10, £20 and £50. The Bank of England even makes £1 million notes, but they are only used for special occasions.

5   *Divisibility*   Notes and coins must provide a full range of values

so that even the smallest value items can be paid for. Traditionally the smallest coin in the UK was the farthing, a quarter of a penny in the days when there were 240 pence to £1. When we decimalized the coinage in 1971 the farthing was discontinued and more recently the halfpenny ceased to be issued. Inflation had done away with the smallest payments, and at present the smallest coin is the penny, which is one hundredth of £1.

Points to remember

- Money makes the world go round (see Section 4.4 for how it does it).
- Before the development of money, trade was largely carried on by barter, exchanging goods or services for goods (or services).
- The problems of barter are the need for a coincidence of wants; the difficulties in deciding equal values and the indivisibility of large items (like horses).
- The characteristics of money are general acceptability, stability of value, durability, portability, difficulty of imitation, rustproof qualities and divisibility into small units.
- General acceptability depends these days on the money being declared 'legal tender' by the sovereign power – which in the UK means 'the Queen in Parliament'.

4.3   Wants and economies

We create the wealth we need (an abundance of goods and services) by some system of production, distribution and exchange which is called the 'economy'. There are three chief types of economy: free-enterprise (or market) economies, centrally-planned economies and mixed economies.

The word 'economy' comes from the Greek word '*oikonomos*' which means a 'steward'. The two parts of the Greek word are *oikos*, a house, and *nomos*, a manager. So when we study economies we are really studying how we manage our house. Since the government is usually viewed as being in charge of the economy we might say it is in charge of the 'household' of the country. Is it behaving like a good steward, and running everything in a proper manner, so that we can all lead comfortable, secure lives? Sometimes we can confidently reply 'Yes – we've never had it so good.' At other times we may not be quite so sure.

First we must consider the three types of economy.

Market economies

These are free-enterprise economies, where the large majority of goods are made, and the large majority of services are provided, by the free enterprise of individuals, who step out of the crowd and start to organize production. In market economies people do not wait for the government to do things, they get on and do them themselves. Whatever they make, or grow or cut down (in the forests for example) they bring to market, so that those who want these items can come to the marketplace and buy them. A market is a place where buyers and sellers are in contact with one another to fix prices. Some of them are very ancient places. Some words in our language go back to the Stone Age. The word 'cheap' is the ancient word for 'barter' and many of our market towns, like Chipping Ongar and Chipping Campden still have this old word as part of the name.

The best example of a market economy is the USA, where as a matter of policy free enterprise is encouraged and the social provision of goods and services is kept to a bare minimum.

Planned economies

Planned economies are economies where the means of production, distribution and exchange are socially owned, and centrally planned. Free enterprise is severely restricted, and even punished. The typical example of a centrally-planned economy until about 1991 was the Soviet Union. Production could only take place if the central planning authorities approved. Unfortunately it is easy to make mistakes under this system and since punishment for mistakes was usually drastic, the planners lost confidence. The shortages that resulted from delays in the planning process became very frustrating to citizens. The essential point about central planning is that it was intended to be a way of ensuring that everyone got fair shares of the goods that were produced. The unfortunate effect has been that too few goods have been produced, because planners can rarely get things right – 'the best laid schemes o' mice an' men' said the poet Robert Burns 'gang aft agley', and so it is with planned economies. More important perhaps than the mistakes of the planners is the fact that the natural initiative and enterprise of the people is stifled. Since they have no way of influencing the remote, central authorities, they sink into a lethargy and indifference about the creation of wealth which is regrettable.

Mixed economies

Actually no economy can be completely free without any central authority, and no centralized economy can control every spark of free enterprise. There must be some things, like the armed forces and the forces of law and order which are centrally run. Equally, some production will be free enterprise if it is only people growing their own vegetables on a small allotment.

In fact, mixed economies may be regarded as a middle way. They have the vast majority of goods and services being provided by free enterprise, but a wide range of other goods and services are socially provided. Thus defence, law and order, education, health and social security services are provided by the state and a number of major industries, particularly transport, energy production, atomic power, water supply, etc., are nationalized and socially owned. These may be run in many ways. Some are controlled by boards and committees under the direct influence of central or local government departments – for example the health service, education, etc. Some are run by public corporations such as the Atomic Energy Commission or the Port of London Authority. Many smaller bodies are QUANGOS (quasi-autonomous non-governmental organizations). There are over 2500 such bodies in the UK.

Until a few years ago we could have said the UK was the typical mixed economy, but recently a number of activities have been privatized. Privatization is a system whereby socially-owned and operated assets are sold off to private operators, the funds raised being used to pursue other government programmes, or possibly to reduce the National Debt. Thinking of the UK as a mixed economy we find that about 60 per cent of total production is now privately run and 40 per cent of the nation's output is socially organized. Those who are familiar with the wide variety of goods in our shops and supermarkets will surely concede that the mixed economy has much to recommend it. Equally those who are found sleeping rough at night on the Thames Embankment may feel that however well it works, it hasn't proved to be a perfect system as far as they are concerned.

4.4 Money and economies

What part does money play in an economy? The answer is an enormous part. Money makes the world go round, particularly the free-enterprise world. It is no accident that in the USA people are said to worship the dollar (and it is often referred to as the 'almighty dollar'). Money represents control of goods and services. It is the medium of exchange, by which ownership of goods and the provision of services is obtained. We all need money if we are to buy a basket of goods and services for our daily needs. We must, therefore, continually obtain a supply of money. How do we get it? There are four chief ways. We get it as rent, interest, wages or profits.

1 *Rent (the reward to those who own land)* Some people are lucky and own land, which they can rent out to others, or use to grow food. Very few of us have land, because William the Conqueror seized it all many years ago and shared it out among his favourites. Land is one of those resources which are necessary if production is to take place. Those who were careful to choose among their ancestors friends of William the Conqueror, own land and can obtain money in the form of rent from those who require land for houses, factories, warehouses, etc. The term 'land' of course includes minerals, timber and other natural resources, the rents of which are often taken in the form of a royalty per ton of ore extracted.

2 *Interest (the reward paid to those who have capital (money savings) and can lend it out to those who need capital)* Nearly everyone has some savings although most of us have most of our savings tied up in pension schemes run by institutional investors. These investors take care of our savings, lending them out to borrowers at a rate of interest which gradually accumulates and eventually provides the money for the savers to live on in their old age. One of the institutions is the government itself which collects contributions from all working citizens under a National Insurance Scheme. These contributions eventually provide the old-age pensions to which all citizens are entitled.

3 *Wages and salaries (the rewards to labour)* Most of us have no land, and insufficient savings to earn enough interest to live on. What we do have is our health and strength and consequently the ability to work. We therefore seek employment of one sort or another and in return are paid wages or salaries. Karl Marx called those who have nothing to sell but their labour power the proletariat (after the Roman name for the lowest class in society). Some are proud to be members of the proletariat, and some use the term to denigrate those whose only real reward is the wages they can earn in employment. Whatever our attitude there are millions of us, the vast majority of the population.

4 *Profits (the reward to enterprise)* Who is it uses the land, the capital and the labour, and can afford to pay out the rent, interest and wages that the rest of us depend upon? It is the entrepreneurs – the enterprising people who set up firms and companies, or organize such official activities as the services provided by local authorities and central governments. They organize the provision of goods and services and if they are successful the profits made become their reward for the enterprise they have shown. Of course the profits earned by local and central authorities simply go into the general pool of funds to provide more goods and services as required. Anyone can become an entrepreneur. All you have to do is to step out of the crowd of people applying for jobs and

decide instead to be self-employed. There are a million rags-to-riches stories in any great nation. We have all heard of pop stars who became millionaires, of Marks, the East European refugee who began with a stall in Leeds with a sign that said 'Do not ask the price, it is one penny', and built Marks and Spencers. The man who founded the Ryder Cup in golf, for which American and European golfers compete, started by selling packets of seeds for one penny (when all his rivals charged two pence or three pence). The Ryder Cup is a solid gold cup, and it was purchased out of the profits on penny packets of seeds.

Other elements in the money cycle

Besides those who receive sums of money from rent, interest, wages or profits there are some who cannot obtain any rewards of a normal kind. There are those who are mentally ill, or physically handicapped; we have some who are too young to work and some who are too old. These older people may have provided pensions for themselves to support themselves in old age, while all are entitled at least to a small pension, the state pension. There are unemployed people temporarily out of work. All need support, and it is provided in the UK by the social security system. In 1992, the latest figures available at the time of writing, £37,000 million was made available in this way, to help those in difficult circumstances. This is a pile of £10 notes ten times as high as Mount Everest. It is clear there are a lot of people about who need help of one sort or another.

Besides these people who need help there are people who help themselves. Criminals of every sort steal from honest people every day. Burglars, smash and grab raiders, sneak thieves, embezzlers, counterfeiters and other dishonest people steal money and goods every second of every day. Naturally the honest people take a poor view of these activities and imprison anyone they can catch. The theft of money gives a person who has not helped create wealth the chance to share in the wealth created. It is unfair and punishable by the full rigours of the law.

We are now ready to see how money makes the world go round. Figure 4.2 shows how the mixed economy works. Look at it and study the notes below it.

Points to remember

- There are three types of economy – free-enterprise (market) economies, planned economies and mixed economies.
- The UK has a mixed economy with about 60 per cent of goods and services being produced privately and 40 per cent by state-run industries.

- There are three flows in an economy.
- The first flow is the flow of factors into production, for which the factor owners receive rewards of rent, wages and interest. Any residue left over is profit and is the reward of the entrepreneur. This is the income flow.
- The second flow is the flow of expenditure as the factor owners spend their incomes. Some of the spending is done for them by central and local government as they spend the taxes charged on social activities (social security, health, defence, etc.). Any savings are rerouted by the banks to those in need of capital.
- The third flow is the flow of exports out and imports in as foreigners buy our goods and in return we buy their goods. This flow has to be balanced somehow, to achieve a balance of payments.

4.5 A project on money

1 Most families today travel abroad occasionally and it is not uncommon to bring home notes and coins. Notes can be exchanged for sterling at most banks, but coins are not acceptable because banks are unwilling to return them to their country of origin. If your class or set cooperate it is possible to make an interesting collection of both notes and coins. For security reasons money has to be made difficult to imitate, and it is interesting to compare the designs used on notes to prevent forgery. It is also interesting to study the coins of different nations, and assess their portability, rustproof quality, durability, etc. Many charities collect foreign currency. It is worth the trouble for them to sort out all the foreign notes and coins and make arrangements to turn them into home currency. When your collection is finished you might like to send it to The Oxfam Stamp and Coin Unit, Murdoch Road, Bicester, Oxon.

2 There are over 200 countries in the world. Most of them have their own currency. Write down a list of thirty countries and write against each (a) the name of its currency; (b) the smallest unit into which the main unit of currency is divided and; (c) how many of the small units make one big unit. Example:

   UK: (a) the pound sterling; (b) the penny;
           (c) 100 pence in the £1.

If you have any difficulty, *Croner's Reference Book for Exporters* has a section for every country, which gives the details. You will find a copy in the Reference Section of any good library.

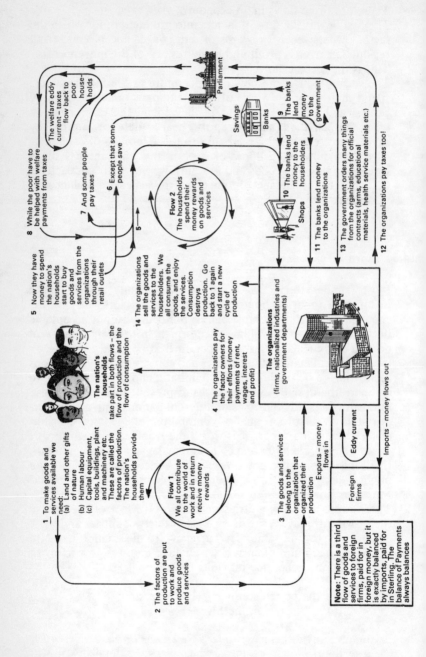

1 To make goods and services available we need:
(a) Land and other gifts of nature
(b) Human labour
(c) Capital equipment, tools, buildings, plant and machinery etc. These are called the factors of production. The nation's households provide them

2 The factors of production are put to work and produce goods and services

Flow 1
We all contribute to the world of work and in return receive money rewards

3 The goods and services belong to the organization that organized their production

The nation's households
take part in both flows – the flow of production and the flow of consumption

4 The organizations pay the factor owners for their efforts (money payments of rent, wages, interest and profit)

The organizations (firms, nationalized industries and government departments)

Exports – money flows in

Eddy current

Foreign firms

Imports – money flows out

Note: There is a third flow of goods and services to foreign firms, paid for in foreign money, but it is exactly balanced by imports, paid for in Sterling. The balance of Payments always balances

5 Now they have money to spend the nation's households start to buy goods and services from the organizations through their retail outlets

Flow 2
The households spend their money rewards on goods and services

6 Except that some people save

7 And some people pay taxes

8 While the poor have to be helped with welfare payments from taxes

The welfare eddy current – taxes flow back to poor households

Parliament

Savings

Banks

9 The banks lend money to the government

10 The banks lend money to the householders

Shops

11 The banks lend money to the organizations

12 The organizations pay taxes too!

13 The government orders many things from the organizations for official contracts (arms, educational materials, health service materials etc.)

14 The organizations sell the goods and services to the householders. We all consume the goods, and enjoy the services. Consumption destroys production. Go back to 1 again and start a new cycle of production

Figure 4.2 How the mixed economy works

Notes:

1 The nation's households are providing all the wealth created by the whole nation. They do it by contributing whatever factors they can supply. Some provide land, some provide capital, some provide labour and some provide enterprise and get the whole thing organized.

2 In return for supplying these factors they are paid their rewards in money. The landlords get rent; those who contributed capital get interest; those who contribute labour get wages; those who show enterprise get profit. However, some of this money is intercepted by the government as taxation of one sort or another – income tax, capital gains tax, corporation tax and value added tax, etc.

3 Now we all have money, we can spend it on a basket of goods and services to suit our particular needs. In this process we buy from the organizations the things we need – thus giving them back the money they have paid out, which they can then use to pay more factor owners in the next period.

4 If we don't spend all our money we save it; but we save it with banks, who promptly lend out the money to people who want more money than they have earned. Thus the banks may help us buy houses (by granting a mortgage) or furniture (by granting a personal loan).

5 The government is also spending a lot of money, (£220,000 million in 1992). Some of it is given to those on social security; some is spent on health, education, defence, etc.

6 If the economy is in balance all the money paid out by the organizations returns back to the organizations so they can use it again next month.

7 Notice that if the organizations sell to foreigners (export trade) they can earn foreign exchange to buy goods from foreigners (import trade). These two flows should equal one another – a balance of payments.

8 This is made possible by the use of money. Money makes the mixed economy and the free-enterprise economy go round. It does not work so well in the centrally-planned economy, because the value of money is artificially fixed by the central planners (and there often is not very much to buy). However, that is economics, not business studies.

4.6   Money and enterprise

Those who are in business deal with money in many different forms.
Once upon a time money meant coins of the realm or notes issued by
the Bank of England, though one or two other banks do issue notes as
well. Today coins and notes are only the small change of the business
world. No one dreams of paying for a new car, or a suite of furniture,
or a house in cash. We pay by cheque, or by credit card. It is too risky
to carry cash about, and it takes too long to count.

Answer the following questions, and then compare them with the
answers at the end of this chapter.

1   Tom Brown, a shopkeeper, cashes up the till at the end of the
    day. What coins might he have to handle?
2   Besides coins, he might have a large collection of bank notes.
    What are the likely values of the notes to be found in the till?
3   What other kinds of 'money' might be found in the till, and how
    would he deal with each of them?
4   A trader wishes to pay a supplier for goods supplied in bulk. What
    is the best way?
5   An employer wants to pay his staff their salaries. What is the best
    way?
6   A student member of the Chartered Institute of Bankers wishes to
    pay her annual subscription. What is the best way?
7   A bookseller wishes to buy books from a publisher in the USA
    with whom she has never dealt before. What is the best way?

Of course you may not be able to answer some of these questions
because the situation described is quite new to you. Look at the
answers now – see page 67.

4.7   Rapid revision

Answers	Questions
–	**1 What is money?**
1 Money is a medium of exchange. It has to be widely acceptable throughout a nation so that those who are in possession of goods will willingly exchange them for an agreed amount of money (the price) and those who are offering services will willingly perform them for an agreed amount of money (the charges, or the wage payable).	**2 What do those who receive the money then do with it?**

Answers		Questions	
2	(a) They may spend it on a balanced basket of goods and services for their own needs; (b) they may save some of it for use in the future, and if they do they usually invest it with a bank or other institutional investor, who lends it on, temporarily, to someone who needs cash.	3	**What are the coinage metals?**
3	Copper, silver and gold – but these days we also use aluminium and an alloy called cupro-nickel.	4	**Why were copper, silver and gold the best choice of metals for coinage?**
4	Because they have intrinsic value, that is they are worth having for their own sake, and this makes them generally acceptable.	5	**What do we call money that does not have intrinsic value?**
5	Token money. The commonest examples are paper notes and coins made of aluminium or cupro-nickel.	6	**Why do people take token money if it has no intrinsic value?**
6	Because it is declared by the sovereign power to be 'legal tender'. This means that anyone who offers it in payment of a debt is entitled to have it accepted as payment of the debt. If it is refused the debtor need not offer to pay again – it is for the creditor to ask for payment now – and to accept the money offered.	7	**What attributes must money display?**
7	It must be (a) generally acceptable; (b) stable in value; (c) durable; (d) rustproof; (e) difficult to imitate; (f) portable; and (g) divisible into small units.	8	**What is an economy?**

Answers	Questions
8 A system for producing goods and services, and distributing them throughout a nation.	**9 What are the three types of economies?**
9 (a) Free-enterprise (market) economies; (b) centrally-planned economies; (c) mixed economies, which have much of their economy free enterprise, but some parts of it are nationalized and run as state industries or state activities.	**10 Describe the UK economy.**
10 (a) It is a mixed economy; (b) 60 per cent of its goods and services are produced by private enterprise organizations – sole traders, partnerships, limited companies and public limited companies; (c) 40 per cent of its goods and services are produced by state-run enterprises, central and local government activities, nationalized industries run as public corporations and quangos (quasi-autonomous non-governmental organizations).	**11 How is money used in an advanced economy?**
11 (a) It is used to pay the owners of factors which have been used in the course of production; (b) the incomes that the factors earn are then taxed, to give the government its fair share of the wealth, to be used for social purposes; (c) the rest of the factor incomes can be spent to buy goods and services according to the choice of the citizens concerned; (d) if they do not spend it all the savings are deposited with institutional investors; (e) they lend the savings out to those who need capital; (f) foreigners buy goods and pay in foreign currency	

Answers	Questions
which is used to buy imports – but these always balance one another out; (g) some unjust claims are made by burglars, thieves, crooks and racketeers – but we do our best to stop this.	**12 What are the rewards to factors?**
12 (a) Land earns rent; (b) capital earns interest; (c) labour earns wages. Any profit left over goes to the entrepreneurs who organized production.	**13 Go over the test again until you are sure of all the answers. Then try the questions in Section 4.8 below.**

4.8 Questions on Chapter 4

1 (a) What is money? (b) How does money help in an advanced economy?

2 (a) What is barter? (b) What are the problems of barter? (c) Smith and Co, have a customer in Poland who would like to buy some of their machine tools. There is no foreign exchange available in Poland at the time and they are asked instead whether they would accept payment in either shoes or kitchen cabinets. What advice would you give Smith and Co?

3 Tom Smith is buying a secondhand car for £1,200. He offers to pay (a) in notes or (b) in 50 pence pieces. Is either of these methods of payment acceptable and why? If either method is not acceptable, why is this so? His friend suggests he pays by cheque, but the garage refuses to accept a cheque. Are they entitled to refuse?

4 What is a free-enterprise economy? Can everything in a country be run by free enterprise?

5 In theory, a planned economy should provide everything that the people of a country need. In practice planned economies rarely succeed in this aim. What are the defects in planned economies?

6 What is meant by 'wages is the reward to the factor labour'? Who gets the wages, and what do they do with them?

Answers to 'money and enterprise' questions

1 The most likely coins in the UK are the 1p, 2p, 5p, 10p, 20p, 50p

and £1 coins. More rarely there is a 25p coin and there is a £2 coin, but they are not in common use.

2   The most likely notes are the £5, £10, £20 and £50 notes. The Bank of England does produce higher value notes, even up to £1,000,000 notes, but they are not commonly in circulation.

3   The most likely other forms of 'money' are cheques from a multitude of banks and building societies. The wise trader will have demanded a banker's card as proof of ability to pay, and will have recorded the number of the card on the back of the cheque. The other likely form is credit card vouchers from one of the four main card-issuing companies – Barclaycard, Access, Trustcard and American Express. ˙

4   The best way is by crossed cheque, with 'A/c Payee only' entered between the crossing lines.

5   The best way is by bank giro, direct into the employees' bank accounts.

6   The best way of paying subscriptions, which tend to rise over the years, is by direct debit, with the Institute requesting the member's bank to debit the member's account with the correct amount.

7   The best way to buy goods from a foreign supplier who has no previous dealings with you is to ask your bank to notify a correspondent bank in the foreign country that an irrevocable letter of credit has been opened in the publisher's favour provided they provide evidence of shipment of the required books. The correspondent bank is asked to inform the publisher of the letter of credit, and the publisher will then be assured of payment. This procedure is described in more detail in the section on export trade.

5
The local environment of business

5.1 An intricate pattern of environments

When looking at our local environment we have to start by saying that every class or group of students will have a unique pattern of local institutions and enterprises to consider. The most that a general book of this kind can do is to set down the sorts of organizations and enterprises which are likely to be met in most areas and leave the student to consider the actual local pattern of his/her own area. We would expect to find some of the following types of institutions:

1 Free-enterprise units

Free-enterprise units are business organizations and voluntary organizations of every type. Their function is to provide goods and services to meet the needs of the general public, supplying them at such a price that all those who are engaged in the business process can receive their rewards of rent, wages, interest or profit. We shall certainly find sole traders, partnerships and limited companies running business enterprises of all sorts. There are five chief types of enterprises. They are:

(a) Farm, livestock or market-garden businesses, which have for their main aim the raising of produce for sale to the general public. They produce natural products, and are often spoken of as 'primary producers'.

(b) Manufacturing businesses, which have for their main activity the conversion of purchased raw materials into finished products, which are then sold at a profit. They are producing products which are an improvement on natural products. They are often spoken of as 'secondary producers'.

(c) Trading businesses which derive their main profit from the buying and selling of goods.

(d) Service businesses which require the purchase of materials as well as the use of skills. A typical example is the builder and

Table 5.1   Farm, livestock and market garden businesses

beekeeper	mushroom grower
budgerigar breeder	nurseryman
bulb grower	pig breeder/dealer
chicken raiser	potato grower
dairy farmer	poultry farmer
dog breeder	seedsman
farmer	smallholder
fisherman	soft-fruit grower
fruit grower	stud farm
hatchery	turf supplier
livestock breeder	turkey farmer
market gardener	vegetable grower

decorator who must purchase materials and work them into the customer's property or assets to produce a visible final effect.

(e)   Pure service businesses. Here expertise or skill in making arrangements is the vital part of the business, and little or no material is required to provide the service.

It helps to give some idea of the intricate pattern of businesses which might be met in any area by drawing up a list of the likely enterprises in each group. Using the local *Yellow Pages* telephone directory the author produced the list of examples of businesses in group (a) above shown in Table 5.1.

You may find examples of several of these in your own locality, and if you consult *Yellow Pages* you will certainly find some of each within a few miles of your school or college.

It would be equally possible to draw up a table for each of the other groups – a table of manufacturing businesses, or of trading businesses, or of service businesses which use materials and embody them into the service supplied, or of pure service businesses.

To start with you should take the list of twenty-five business activities given below and decide which of the five categories you would place them in. A more extensive project is given later in this chapter.

Exercise 5.1

Write down the following five headings, in abbreviated form: (a) farms, etc.; (b) manufacturers; (c) traders; (d) services using materials; (e) pure services.

Allocate the following twenty-five businesses to the respective groups. There are five of each: turkey hatchery; dairy farmer;

pharmaceutical company; DIY shop; goat breeder; fashion house; engineering company; aerial installer; seedsman; rubber stamp maker; caterer; grocer; market gardener; builder; garden centre; solicitor; sail maker; glazier; fencing contractor; confectioner; pottery; magician; disc jockey; driving school; accountant.

Some free-enterprise units are voluntary associations, not run for profit but to provide facilities for members of the association who have a common interest in a particular hobby or sport. They vary from local tennis clubs, football clubs, self-help groups for those with a problem (such as the care of elderly relatives or disabled members of their families) to local branches of national bodies such as the Automobile Association or the Royal Automobile Club. Such bodies have millions of members, thousands of employees and a budget of £50 million per annum would not be unusual.

2 Local government units

As this name implies all localities have a local authority of some sort or other which governs the community in the general interest of all the inhabitants. The general aim of local government is to achieve a good quality of life for the people living in the area. The authority is to some extent subject to the influence of the general population through the electoral system, since a dissatisfied electorate can vote it out of office the next time an election is held. At the same time some policies are laid down by central government, which uses the local authority as its agent in the implementation of national policies (and provides a great deal of money to ensure that the local authority is able to carry out the work). For example, many road maintenance activities are delegated by central government to local authorities and much of our educational system is supervised and financed in this way.

Local authorities provide many services for business people, such as fire and rescue services, waste disposal and sanitation services, pest control, animal welfare services, etc. They also exercise control over planning developments, conservation services, education and training, careers services, trading standards and similar items. They are active in two capacities, both as monitors of the behaviour of firms and the prevention of abuses, but also to promote and make easy the establishment of enterprises in their areas. Many authorities renovate derelict properties for use by small businesses or allocate land to build trading estates, warehouses and even whole factories. They will make funds available to build access roads, lay on power supplies, etc. One local authority attacted a major industrial firm into its area by agreeing to provide a reservoir so the industry had all the water it needed for the conceivable future. Every authority seeks to attract employment into its area by helping new enterprises to get established with rates 'holidays', grants of land, financial aid, etc.

3 Central government agencies

Many of the institutions we find in our local home areas are agencies of central government, carrying out a range of activities again aimed at enhancing the quality of life. They may take positive action to provide a service such as the Youth Employment Service, the Small Firms Service, the National Health Service, etc., or they may be exercising control to supervise undesirable practices; for example pollution of the atmosphere, river pollution, unsightly or hazardous industrial developments, unhygienic catering establishments, etc.

Almost every area has its Inland Revenue Department to maintain control of the tax system. The Customs and Excise Department controls not only the movement of imports and exports but the production of such products as cigarettes and tobacco, petroleum, and alcoholic drinks which have considerable taxes levied on them. Every trader whose turnover exceeds £45,000 per annum must register with HM Customs and levy $17\frac{1}{2}$ per cent value added tax (VAT) on every taxable item sold, paying this tax over to the VAT authorities after certain deductions. These agencies also help exporters, and will cover them at very cheap rates of insurance for such things as the failure of a foreign government to pay for goods and services supplied; default of the foreign buyer, etc. This department is called the Export Credit Guarantees Department (ECGD).

5.2 Studying the local business environment

Generally speaking, we cannot study too large an area in any detail, yet if we pick too small an area we may not have much business activity to describe. If an area is sparsely inhabited, with not too much business activity we must take a fairly wide area to draw any sensible conclusions about the economic scene. By contrast it would only be necessary to take a tiny section of most towns to find a good range of business activities and plenty of organizations to consider and discuss.

A list of the aspects we should consider when embarking upon the study of our chosen locality would include the following:

1   What is the name of the area, and how does it fit into the larger pattern of territory around it? What are the boundaries of the area chosen, and what lies beyond those boundaries in each direction?

2 Who lives in the area; what type of people are they and what skills and abilities do they have? How prosperous are they?

3 What business institutions can be identified in the area, and why are they located in this particular spot? What goods or services do they supply, and are they of national interest, international interest or do they only serve local needs? (For example the Royal Mint is in South Wales, but meets the needs of the whole country.)

4 What influences have been at work to locate these business units here? Have they been attracted in by positive inducements by local authorities or government departments, or have they come in of their own free will because it is a natural location to choose. Thus many firms and companies which trade with Europe have moved to the South-east corner of the UK where access to Europe is easy and convenient. In former times when UK trade was world orientated to meet the needs of a far-flung empire the western side of the UK was the natural location – and Bristol, Liverpool, Manchester and Glasgow were more prosperous than they are today. Sometimes imported raw materials are important, and industries locate near ports where these can be landed. Oil refineries are often on the coasts, and so are chemical works and flour mills. Cement works are often located on chalk hills or near limestone quarries, because imports play little part in cement production.

5 Is the area one where rapid development and growth is taking place, or is it a static environment with a more placid pattern of business activity? Is it a declining area, where old (smokestack) industries are falling into disuse and disrepair? Similarly, many inner cities are decaying, and require drastic improvements and redevelopment. The costs of such work can be enormous, and the new homes provided may be difficult to sell or rent at a price which is economic for any but the well-to-do. We often hear such areas described as 'yuppy-fied' – only the 'young and upwardly mobile' can afford to move in, and poorer families are dispossessed from areas where they had formerly been happy and contented.

6 What is the impact upon the area of the various business activities? Are they labour intensive, providing plenty of jobs for the local inhabitants, or are they capital intensive, with expensive machinery and equipment operated by only a few employees? Are there any adverse effects on the environment – fumes, smoke or noise pollution, traffic problems, noxious smells, parking difficulties, interruptions of rights of way and enclosures of land formerly enjoyed for recreational purposes?

5.3   A project on your local business environment

The stages for a detailed study of your local business environment are as shown below. Read through the suggested guidelines first to see the overall plan of the project, and then, over a reasonable period of time develop the project to be a really worthwhile, in-depth study of the chosen area.

1   Begin with some sort of map of the locality. Divide the area up into a number of convenient catchment areas, for which various groups can assume responsibility. Designate the boundaries for each area, and so far as possible let people study the area nearest their own homes. This ensures that their local knowledge will be used to the best advantage; goodwill of the general business community will be easier to achieve; some of the problems will be experienced at first hand and it will be easier to discover the true facts.

2   Each group should then draw up a general description of its chosen area. What sort of an area is it – industrial, residential, shopping centre, agricultural, recreational, etc?

3   Discover and pinpoint all the business enterprises in the area. This can be done purely by observation, without any formal questionnaire, simply by making notes of names and addresses culled from signs over the various shop, factory and office premises in the locality. Note whether they are sole traders, partnerships, limited companies or PLCs (public limited companies).

4   Discover and pinpoint other institutions, schools, colleges, hospitals, employment offices, clinics, council depots, fire stations, police stations, social services offices, trading standards offices, clubs and societies, etc.

5   Draw up a questionnaire which will give you a great deal of business information, if properly completed by the owners of businesses. Some of the questions suggested below may not be appropriate to your particular area of study. They should be replaced by more pertinent questions which occur to you. (For example a particular problem – a hazardous factory situated in the area perhaps – may merit a question to assess the views of local business people.) A suitable title might be 'Business Census for the . . . Area'. The second line of the questionnaire should read:

Special note: This questionnaire is only an educational exercise for use in preparing for an examination in business studies. It will not be used for any non-educational purpose, and your cooperation is greatly appreciated.

The questions we then might ask include the following:

(a)   What is the true name of the business? . . . .

(b)   Is it a sole trader business, a partnership, a limited company or a PLC? . . . .

(c)   Are you registered for VAT? . . . . If so, did you register voluntarily, or did you have to register because your turnover exceeded the required limit? . . . .

(d)   What is the nature of your business? . . . .

(e)   Do you purchase your supplies:
- (i)   Direct from manufacturers? . . . .
- (ii)   Direct from large-scale wholesalers? . . . .
- (iii) From a cash-and-carry outlet? . . . .
- (iv)   From a local wholesaler who calls as part of a 'round'?
. . . .
- (v)   From local producers (farmers, smallholders, etc.)?
. . . .

(f)   Are your customers mainly:
- (i)   Local householders . . . .
- (ii)   Other businesses . . . .
- (iii) Children and students . . . .
- (iv)   Mail order customers . . . .
- (v)   Large institutions . . . .

(g)   Would you describe the area as:
- (i)   Very prosperous . . . .
- (ii)   Reasonably prosperous . . . .
- (iii) Poor . . . .
- (iv)   Run-down and decaying . . . .

(h)   How many people do you employ?
- (i)   None . . . .
- (ii)   Casual workers only . . . .
- (iii) One only . . . .
- (iv)   2 to 5 persons . . . .
- (v)   6 to 99 persons . . . .
- (vi)   100 or more . . . .

(i)   Have you any criticism of the locality along any of the lines below? Mark it from 1–10, 1 being very bad in the matter under consideration and 10 being excellent:
- (i)   General police supervision . . . .
- (ii)   Extent of vandalism . . . .
- (iii) Cleanliness of the district, litter, etc. . . . .
- (iv)   Orderliness after dark . . . .
- (v)   Bus services to and from the area . . . .
- (vi)   Parking facilities . . . .
- (vii) Availability of health services, doctors, dentists, etc.
- (viii) Environmental standards, clean air, parks and open spaces, absence of graffiti, etc. . . . .

(ix)   Is there a Post Office conveniently situated ....
(x)   Please list any aspects of the locality which particularly please (or annoy) you ....
....

5.4   Checking up on a particular business

Part of your project on the locality might involve the study of particular premises to discover the business activity. Anyone purchasing a shop, for example, might carry out this sort of investigation, while in most big stores the actual customer activity across particular counters can be collected by codings punched into the till at the checkout. Since there are usually a number of shops in any area under study, each member of your group could pick a different shop and carry out this investigation. Figure 5.1 (reproduced from a book called *Self-employment not Unemployment*) shows the sort of method used. You should draw up a blank chart of the type shown (or photocopy the blank chart shown as Figure 5.2). Note the following points:

1   The address of the premises under investigation should be shown.
2   The date, and the day should be recorded (since some days might be busier than others).

Address of Premises: 24 River Drive, Oldtown			Date: 27:9:19--		Day: Wed.	
Times observed	8.00–8.15	10.30–11.45	12.30–12.45	2.30–2.45	4.30–4.45	Totals
Customers entering	ＬＨＴ ＩＩＩＩ 9	ＩＩＩＩ 4	ＬＨＴ ＩＩＩ 8	ＩＩＩ 3	ＬＨＴ ＬＨＴ ＬＨＴ ＩＩＩＩ 19	43
People passing by	ＬＨＴ ＬＨＴ ＬＨＴ ＩＩＩ 18	ＬＨＴ ＬＨＴ ＬＨＴ ＩＩ 17	ＬＨＴ ＬＨＴ ＩＩＩＩ 14	ＬＨＴ ＬＨＴ Ｉ 11	ＬＨＴ ＬＨＴ ＬＨＴ ＩＩＩ 18	78
Vehicles stopping Cars / Vans etc.	ＩＩＩ 3 / Ｉ 1	0 / 0	ＬＨＴ 5 / Ｉ 1	Ｉ 1 / 0	ＬＨＴ ＩＩ 7 / Ｉ 1	16 / 3
Vehicles passing Cars / Vans etc.	ＬＨＴ ＬＨＴ ＬＨＴ ＬＨＴ ＩＩＩＩ 9 Too many to count		ＬＨＴ ＬＨＴ ＬＨＴ ＬＨＴ ＬＨＴ ＩＩＩ 14 Too many to count		ＬＨＴ ＬＨＴ ＬＨＴ Too many to count	
Other details of interest	Lots of factory workers calling in	Police patrols seem to be quite frequent	Large lorry parked outside. Display completely hidden		Mostly school children – some rough behaviour	

Figure 5.1   Observing premises – the five-barred gate method

Address of Premises _ _ _ _ _ _ _ _ _ _ _ _ _	Date: _ _ _ _ _ _ _ _ _	Day: _ _ _ _ _ _				
Times observed						
Customers entering						
People passing by						
Vehicles stopping — Cars Vans Other						
Vehicles passing by — Cars Vans Other						
Other details of interest						

Figure 5.2 A blank form for observing customer activity (may be photo-copied for educational purposes)

3 Observers work best in short bursts – say 15 minutes or 30 minutes at a time. Suitable periods should be decided upon for the investigation.
4 The five-barred gate is the best method of counting – where a vertical line is recorded for the first four persons or vehicles observed, and the fifth one is represented by a crossed bar which gives an easy 'five-barred gate' for counting in fives.
5 The actual counts (called the raw scores) are written in each box at the end of the time interval. The totals could then be used to calculate the estimated number of callers for the day, and the week.

This exercise will teach you one thing at least. In studying business activity you cannot do much at your school or college desk, or from a textbook. You have to get out on the street, actually counting heads, classifying customers by the size of their actual purchases (so far as you can discover what was purchased), and looking at the total amounts rung up on the tills.

5.5 Presenting your report on the local business environment

A report of this type is best presented in the form of a booklet or file of material. If you are a typist or a personal computer enthusiast with a printer attachment you could present it in typewritten form. If not, present it in a clear, handwritten form.

Do not adopt too ostentatious or artistic a style of handwriting, and check spelling and punctuation carefully by re-reading your work at regular intervals as it develops.

A project is improved by including the following features:

1 A title page giving a clear title, and the name of the author (or authors if it is a piece of team work).
2 A preface, explaining what the project is about and how it came to be written.
3 A table of contents, detailing the various sections of the work.
4 An acknowledgement page to acknowledge help received and cooperation from fellow pupils, staff, local firms, etc.
5 The individual sections, as set out in the table of contents, where possible illustrated by data, charts, diagrams, illustrations and perhaps photographs.
6 A conclusion, in which the various threads of the project are drawn together and summarized. In some projects it might be helpful to make a short list of recommendations, for example ways in which the locality could be improved from the point of view of business people in the area.

Points to remember

- Every locality displays a unique set of institutions and business organizations.
- The five types of free enterprise businesses are: (a) farmers, market gardeners and other producers of natural products; (b) manufacturing businesses producing improved natural goods; (c) trading businesses; (d) services which also involve the use of materials, worked into the finished job; and (e) pure services.
- Other institutions include local government units and central government agencies.
- When studying the local environment we must select a unit of study which is extensive enough to show most of the features we associate with any community, but not so large an area that it is impossible to study it adequately in the time we have available.
- The chief aspects of interest are the nature of the locality, its people, their domestic arrangements, the pattern of businesses which serve them and the state of business in the area. Is it dynamic and growing, static or declining?

5.6 A *Yellow Pages* project

Choosing any one of the five groups of free enterprise units, and using the 'Index of Headings' as your guide, make a complete list, from A to Z of all the trades and occupations in your selected group. For example, if you selected 'pure services' the first 'pure service' you find is 'accident claims assessors' followed by 'accountants'. The last ones in the index of headings are 'Youth organizations' and 'Zoos'.

5.7 Rapid revision

Answers	Questions
–	**1 What are the features of a local environment?**
1 It is impossible to say unless you know the locality. Every locality is unique and presents an intricate pattern of business organizations serving the local community.	**2 What are the five types of free-enterprise businesses?**
2 (a) Farms, livestock and market garden businesses engaged in primary production; (b) manufacturing enterprises engaged in secondary production; (c) trading businesses; (d) services which incorporate materials and components into the finished job (e.g. electricians rewire old houses); (e) pure services.	**3 What is the ultimate purpose of business activity?**
3 To provide goods or services to the general public, supplying them at such prices that all the factors contributing to business activity can receive a fair reward for their efforts.	**4 What are the functions of local government institutions?**
4 (a) They provide a variety of services to the community, such as fire and rescue services, police, education, etc., either as a local government activity or as the agents of central government; (b) they exercise control over possible abuses, such as planning controls, health measures, monitoring hazardous situations, trading standards, etc.	**5 What features of local life are important to the business community?**

Answers	Questions
5 (a) The geographical layout, the access roads, railways, etc; (b) the local population, its composition, skills, level of prosperity, etc; (c) the other firms in the area and the extent to which they offer support, or competition; (d) what help or assistance is provided in the area by local or central government; (e) is the area expanding, contracting or static?; (f) are there any environmental advantages or disadvantages in the area?	6 **Go over the test again until you are sure of all the answers. Then try some of the questions in Section 5.8 below.**

5.8   Questions on Chapter 5

1   The following figures for annual turnover of a business are provided by the twelve firms in your own locality: £30,000; £76,000; £9,600; £98,500; £42,000; £19,000; £19,750; £84,700; £8,000; £59,000; £24,000; £2,800,000.

(a)   Find the average turnover of the firms in the locality, correct to the nearest £1.

(b)   Say whether you think the average turnover you have discovered is a good description of the turnover of firms in the area. If it is not very satisfactory explain why.

2   You are told that a building inspector employed by the local authority has placed a 'prohibition order' on your demolition site in the area. The order prohibits any further work on the site until a solid fence six feet high has been erected around the site at all exposed points. Why do you think the local authority is given such powers and what – as the site foreman – would you do about it.

3   It is learned that a foreign company which manufactures washing machines is prepared to re-develop a derelict area of your inner city provided certain proposals can be agreed to. These include:

(a)   A grant from local government of 40 per cent of the capital cost.

(b)   Access roads costing £1 million to be laid by local contractors and paid for by central government.

(c) A 'rates holiday', during which the foreign firm would pay no local taxes of any sort, is conceded by the local authority.

State a case for or against the acceptance of these ideas bringing out the advantages and disadvantages as you envisage them of such schemes.

4 Draw two pie diagrams to represent the following statistics of a town's business activities. The aim is to show (a) what part of the town's business units are small, medium, large and very large and (b) what part of the town's business activity is performed by each of these groups:

(a) *Size of firms*		(b) *Average turnover*	
Small (less than 5 employees)	25	Small	£40,000 per firm
Medium (5–24 employees)	20	Medium	£250,000 per firm
Large (25–99 employees)	4	Large	£1 million per firm
Very large (100 or more employees)	1	Very large	£10 million per firm
	50		

5 Why should central government set up offices in some large towns, acting independently of local government? Give examples of such organizations in your own local area.

Part Two
Business Structure and Organization

6
Business organizations

6.1 Types of business organization

Most businesses begin as small-scale enterprises and increase gradually (or perhaps rapidly) to large-scale organizations employing hundreds or thousands of people. The largest business organization ever formed in the UK was the British Transport Commission, set up in 1947. It had 900,000 employees. It ran all the railways, road transport services, buses and coaches and the canals. It proved to be so difficult to control that by 1953 it was broken up into separate units, and this process is still going on to some extent.

The smallest type of business organization is the 'sole trader' organization, which just has the proprietor in charge, with employees, if any. Frequently sole traders find difficulty in offering a full service to customers and therefore many of them take a partner and set up a **partnership**. The third type of business organization is the **limited company**.

The word 'limited' is short for limited-liability company – because the owners of such companies have limited liability. This is explained below. Finally, the very largest companies, which need so much capital that they have to ask the general public to buy shares in the company are called **public limited companies** or **PLCs**. We must study each of these types of business organization.

6.2 Sole trader organizations

As the name implies sole traders are in business on their own. They provide the capital that is required (or borrow it from a bank by a personal loan). They secure premises, or work from their own homes, and labour in the business with, or without, the help of employees. They have full legal responsibility for everything that is done, and take all the profits of the business.

PARTICULARS OF OWNERSHIP
OF
STYLISH HAIR*
as required by Section 4 of the Business Names Act, 1985

Full name(s) of proprietor(s)	*Address within Great Britain at which documents may be effectively served on the business*
Richard Thomas Smith	20 High St, Camford, Gloucestershire
Alicia Smith	20 High St, Camford, Gloucestershire

*Insert name of business

Figure 6.1   The statutory notice about the business name

Notes:
1   The purpose of this notice is to ensure that those dealing with the business know the identity of the owners, where to deliver goods and correspondence, and where to demand payment of money, should the proprietor fail to pay at any time.
2   From the legal point of view it is also the place where writs may be served. A writ is a legal document summoning a defendant to appear in court so that the claims a plaintiff makes against him/her may be heard, and justice may be done.
3   This information about the true name of the proprietor (or in this case the proprietors since it is a partnership) must also appear on all correspondence, orders for goods and services, invoices and other documents.
4   A leaflet is available about the correct method of display, from the Department of Trade, Guidance Notes Section, 55 City Road, London EC1Y 1BB.

The advantages of operating as a sole trader are as follows:

1   No formal procedures are required to set up in business, apart from the display of the firm's name. If this name is not the owner's true name but an invented name, the Business Names Act, 1985 requires a statutory notice to be displayed. This is illustrated in Figure 6.1.
2   Independence is a chief feature of sole-trader businesses. Having no one to consult, the sole trader can put his/her plans into effect quickly.
3   Personal supervision ensures effective operation at all times; customers are known to the proprietor who can cater for their tastes and avoid bad debts by a personal assessment of credit worthiness; employees are under personal supervision and waste is avoided.
4   He/she is accountable to nobody and (apart from the Inland Revenue authorities) need reveal the state of the business to no one.

There are certain disadvantages. These are:

1 Long working hours and little time off for vacations.
2 Sickness may mean the business gets into difficulties.
3 The proprietor has 'unlimited liability', which means that he/she is personally liable to the full extent of his/her private wealth for the debts of the business. Insolvency may mean the sale of the family house and furniture to pay the creditors.
4 Expansion is usually only possible by ploughing back the profits of the business as further capital. Of course money may be borrowed from a bank, or a partner, but this means a loss of independence. A sole trader can keep independent by taking a limited partner, but these are not easy to find in present conditions of fairly high taxation, and much safer investments widely available.
5 The business is part of the estate of the proprietor at death, and it may be necessary to sell the business to pay inheritance tax.
6 Like most small-scale enterprises it will be a high-cost enterprise because the degree of specialization will be small.

Sole traders do offer employment to staff of various sorts, but usually the number of jobs available is not large. There may be a need for office and clerical staff, but unlimited liability does not exactly encourage the employment of others, for the employer is always aware of the need to keep costs down, since any debts incurred are the personal debts of the proprietor, who has unlimited liability.

To overcome the disadvantages listed above sole traders frequently take a partner, and change to a partnership organization, or they may set up as a private limited company.

6.3 Partnerships

Partnerships are a popular form of business organization. Family groups, such as Sorrell and Son, Cook Brothers, etc., naturally form partnerships. In professional businesses – architects, accountants, solicitors, etc. – there are great benefits from partnership. These may be listed as follows:

1 Greater capital is available, so that expansion can take place.
2 The responsibility of control no longer rests with one person. This makes possible holidays and free weekends, and reduces the worry the sole trader experiences in times of ill health.
3 Wider experience is brought to the firm and some degree of specialization is possible; this is particularly true of professional partnerships. A physician and a surgeon may form a partnership; or lawyers with experience in different fields – divorce, criminal

law, commercial law – may combine to offer a more comprehensive service to the public.

4   Very often a young man teams up with an older man. The young man has his health and strength; his partner has the capital and the experience. Together they make a satisfactory team.

5   The affairs of the business are still private.

The great disadvantage of the partnership is that the partners are still liable to the full limit of their personal wealth for all the debts of the business. Thus if one partner has a spendthrift nature, and takes on financial responsibilities which the other partners would hesitate about, they are all liable for the debts he incurs. A good relationship between partners is essential and they must have mutual trust. Lawyers will tell you of partnerships which only last a few days – one of the partners suddenly discovering that the other, whom he believed he could trust and work with, was totally unreliable or otherwise unsuitable as a partner.

Problems also arise on the death of a partner. A well-established firm may suddenly find that a senior partner dies. Not only is his/her skill and expertise lost, but the heirs may not wish to continue in the business, and may wish to withdraw the capital. For this reason partners frequently take out life assurance on one another. When a partner dies the life assurance policy provides compensation to enable the partner's heirs to be paid without the firm being sold to raise the money.

There is a special type of partnership called a **limited partnership**. This permits a partner – often a retired partner – to leave money in the business and only risk that money. Such a partner is not liable for all the debts of the business – but is a limited partner, with limited liability. They are often called sleeping partners since they play no part in the running of the business. Limited partnerships are not all that common, because it is more satisfactory to set up a limited company.

6.4   Limited companies

First we must understand **limited liability**. Where a person contributes capital to a business but does not take any part in running the enterprise it seems unfair to expect that person to be liable for all the debts of the business to the limit of his/her personal wealth. It is fairer if he/she has 'limited liability', which means that their liability is limited to the amount of capital they have contributed. They can lose that amount of money, but no more. This makes people much more willing to put money into a business, because they know that they can lose only that amount of money. The provider of a share of the capital is called a **shareholder** and is issued with pieces of paper called **shares** (or share certificates). After a certain time shares can be consolidated into stock. These stocks and shares can be sold on the **Stock Exchange** in a way described in a companion volume *Commerce Made Simple*, should the shareholder wish to cease being a shareholder and to have the money back again.

There are two chief kinds of company – private limited companies and public limited companies. The latter type may advertise to sell shares to the public and are subject to strict regulations about this type of activity. Private limited companies are less rigidly controlled, but all companies are subject to two important Acts of Parliament, the Companies Acts, 1985 and 1989.

Floating a company

Under the rules of the 1985 Act the promoters of both public and private companies need to find only one other person prepared to join him/her as members in signing a Memorandum of Association. This document governs the relationship of the company with the external world. Its seven main clauses are as follows:

1 The name of the company, ending in the word 'limited' for private companies, and the phrase 'public limited company' for public companies. This use of the word 'limited' is a warning to all people who do business with the company that the shareholders have limited liability. Those who supply companies with goods without payment cannot look to the shareholders to pay them if the company gets into difficulties. The shareholders' liability is limited to the money they contributed when buying the shares.
2 The address of its registered office.
3 The objects of the company. This states what the company will do when it is established, and forms the legal basis for its activities. It will have to keep its activities within the fields specified, or the Courts may rule them *ultra vires* (beyond the powers). This is a protection to the shareholders. Suppose that I invested £500 in a company that was to develop a revolutionary type of aero engine, which I believed had a great future. I suddenly discover that the directors are using my money to buy sugar which happens to be rising on world markets. I would naturally feel that this was not the purpose for which I had subscribed my capital, and would be able to obtain an injunction restraining them from using my money in an *ultra vires* way.
4 A statement that the liability of the members is limited.
5 The amount of share capital to be issued and the types of share. For a public company, the minimum capital (s.118 of the Companies Act, 1985) is £50,000.

6   An undertaking by the signatories that they do desire to be formed into a company registered under the Acts, and to undertake to purchase the number of shares against their names.

7   By Schedule 1 of the 1985 Act a seventh rule requires that the names etc., of the first director (or directors) and the first company secretary shall be stated, in a prescribed form.

Having drawn up and signed the Memorandum of Association, it is necessary to draw up detailed Articles of Association, which control the internal affairs of the company. Such matters as the procedure to be followed at meetings, the powers of the managing director, the borrowing powers that may be exercised, etc., are considered and agreed. A set of model articles, called Table A, is printed in the Acts and becomes the Articles for any public company which fails to register any Articles. A simpler set may be adopted by private companies.

Registration of the company

The promoters of the company may now proceed to register the company under the Acts. They present to the Registrar of Companies the Memorandum of Association; the Articles of Association; a statement of the nominal capital, on which a tax of £1.00 per cent is payable; and a statutory declaration that the Companies Act has been complied with.

If all is in order, the Registrar will issued a **Certificate of Incorporation** which bestows upon the company a separate legal personality. The company can now do all the legal things that an ordinary person can do; it can own land and property, employ people, sue and be sued in the Courts, etc. Before it can begin trading, however, it must secure the capital it needs. With a private company this will largely be contributed by the founders anyway, and it may commence trading. With a public company the capital must be obtained from the public, either directly or indirectly through the **institutional investors**. Institutional investors are organizations such as insurance companies, pension funds and investment trusts who collect money from the general public for use in an emergency at some future time. For example, one famous insurance company, the Prudential, collects £35 million every week from the general public in the UK. It is, therefore, always on the look-out for safe investments in reliable companies, and if a new company is 'going public' and becoming a public limited company it will be quite willing to take some shares. Later, when an emergency arises or a customer reaches retirement age and needs to draw the pension promised, the institutional investor will sell the shares to provide the money required.

A public company must produce evidence to the Registrar before it commences trading that it has obtained the minimum capital re-

required. The Registrar will then issue a **Certificate of Trading**, and the company may commence trading.

Buying an 'off-the-shelf' company

The easy way to set up a company and become a company director is to buy an 'off-the-shelf' company registered by a company registration agent. Look up in your local *Yellow Pages* telephone directory under 'Company registration agents' and you will find a list of local firms who register various companies, usually with a capital of £2. They usually charge about £120, which covers the various expenses they have incurred and leaves them a profit on the transaction. You can now either use the name they suggested or pass a resolution of the company to change its name, change the directors and company secretary to your own names, and raise the capital if you wish to do so to a higher figure. Once the changes have been registered you can go ahead and organize your business, print stationery, rent premises if necessary and start up your business. As your business grows you may, once you reach a suitable size, apply to become a public limited company, with your shares being quoted on the Stock Exchange. Figure 6.2 illustrates this procedure.

A comparison of sole traders, partnerships, limited partnerships, private limited companies and public limited companies is given in Table 6.1 (see pages 92–3).

Stationery for limited companies

The Companies Act, 1985, Section 351 requires certain items to appear on the official stationery of limited companies.

1 The place of registration of the Company and its registered number, as shown on the certificate of incorporation.
2 The address of the company's registered office.
3 In the case of an investment company the fact that it is an investment company must be clearly stated.
4 The expression 'limited liability' if the company is one that is excused from putting the word 'limited' or PLC at the end of its name.
5 If there is any reference to the amount of capital of the company it must be the paid-up capital, and not the authorized capital (because authorized capital may not actually be available if it has not yet been called for).

Points to remember

• The chief types of profit-making enterprises are sole-trader businesses, partnerships, private limited companies and public limited companies.

Table 6.1   Comparison of private enterprise units

	Aspect	Sole trader	Partnership	Limited partnership
1	**Name of firm**	Any name provided it is either the proprietor's true name, or their names, or names and addresses of the proprietors are displayed at business premises.		
2	**How formed**	By commencing business without formality except (1) above	By agreement, which may be oral or written; limited partnerships must be registered with the registrar of companies	
3	**Control of the firm**	Proprietor has full control	Every partner is entitled to manage	Only the general partner(s) can manage the business
4	**Liability for debts**	Liable to the limits of personal wealth	Partners are jointly and severally liable for debts and torts to the limit of their personal wealth	General partners fully liable; limited partners not liable beyond the capital contributed
5	**Relationship between owner and business**	The business is the owner, or owners, and has no separate legal existence		The business is the same as the general partners; the limited partner is not the business
6	**Membership of firm**	One	Two or more	Two or more
7	**General powers**	At will	At will, subject to agreement; if no agreement, Partnership Act 1890 applies	
8	**Transfer of ownership**	By sale of 'goodwill'	Only with unanimous consent	
9	**Controlling Acts**	None	Partnership Act, 1890	Limited Partnership Act, 1907
10	**Disbanding of firm**	At will or by bankruptcy	Firm may go bankrupt or be dissolved by notice or mutual consent	
11	**Advantages**	Independence. Personal control of staff and granting of credit. Decisions acted upon at once	Increased capital. Days off and holidays possible. Wider experience of partners. Privacy of affairs	Limited liability for some partners. Larger capital
12	**Disadvantages**	Long hours, no holidays. Illness affects conduct of business. Unlimited liability. Small capital.	Unlimited liability. Death or retirement ends firm. Profits must be shared	Unlimited liability for the general partners. Also as for partnerships

Table 6.1   (continued)

	Limited companies	
	Private	*Public*
1	The registered name, registered under the Companies Acts, 1985–89.	
	Names for private companies end in the word 'Limited'	Names for public companies end in the words 'Public Limited Company'
2	By registration under the Companies Acts, with due legal formality	
3	Directors control the company. Members have no control at all, but may elect a new board at the Annual General Meeting if they wish to do so	
4	Limited liability for all members – only liable to the limit of capital contributed	
5	The business is a separate legal personality from the members	
6	Minimum two, no maximum limit under Acts	
7	As laid down in Memorandum of Association and Articles of Association	
8	Shares may only be transferred with consent of fellow shareholders	Shares are freely transferable
9	Companies Acts, 1985–89	
10	Company may go into voluntary or compulsory liquidation	
11	Limited liability. Death of shareholders does not affect the firm. Capital can be collected from any number of members. Privacy to some extent on affairs	Limited liability. Death of shareholders does not affect the firm. Very large sums of capital can be collected from any number of members
12	Publication is required, but turnover need not be revealed, unless it exceeds £8 million and profits of small companies (with less than £2 million turnover) need not be revealed	Full public knowledge of affairs. Minimum capital for a public company, by s. 118 of the 1985 Act, is £50 000

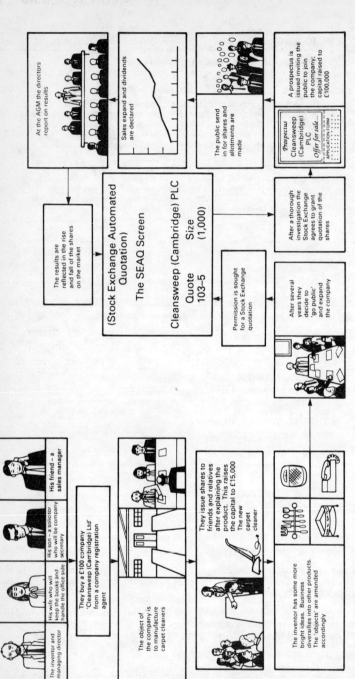

Figure 6.2 How a company is formed and financed

- Sole traders and partners have unlimited liability which means they are liable for the debts of the business to the full limit of their personal wealth.
- Limited companies have to be given the status of incorporation, i.e. they are bodies created by law which can do all the things ordinary human beings can do except the personal things like getting married and having children.
- You can buy an 'off-the-shelf' company that has already been registered for about £120.
- The shareholders of companies have limited liability. They are not responsible for the debts of the business and can only lose the money they have actually invested in the shares. Their personal possessions cannot be taken to pay the debts of a business which gets into difficulties.

6.5   Other types of organization

All the types of organization discussed above are profit-making organizations. They satisfy the 'wants' of mankind by producing goods and services that are required and making their charges high enough to earn a profit, which is the reward of their enterprise. In many ways it is a very satisfactory system, for the organizer of the business has an incentive to work hard and keep providing the goods and services we all want. Unfortunately there are limits beyond which we cannot press the profit system. If a firm starts to profiteer – make more than a fair reward for its services by preventing competition, or taking advantage of a monopoly position – it must be controlled. Also there are some 'wants' that cannot be satisfied by the profit system. We cannot make profits out of mentally handicapped people, for example, for they are usually too poor to afford the services they require. Many people could not afford to pay for education, and it must be provided 'socially' by local or central governments.

Other services are provided by a self-help type of organization. Most of these are non-profit-making clubs and societies. The members join the association and pay an annual subscription, which entitles them to enjoy the services provided by the club. Famous examples are the Automobile Association (AA), the Royal Automobile Club (RAC) and there are numerous retailer and producer 'Cooperative Societies'. Some producer cooperatives are profit-making; most retailer cooperatives are not considered as profit-making – although they do make surpluses which are shared out among the members. The 'profits' made are simply regarded as overcontributions by the members, and are returned to them in some way, either as a 'dividend' or as improved services to members.

These other organizations therefore may be listed as follows:

1 Government departments (the Civil Service).
2 Local government departments.
3 QUANGOS – quasi-autonomous non-governmental organizations – these are set up by the government but are not part of the
   Civil Service – though some civil servants may serve on them. An
   example would be the British Overseas Trade Board which helps
   exporters solve the problems of exporting. The word 'quasi'
   means almost – they are almost autonomous organizations but
   Parliament has a controlling influence.
4 Nationalized industries.
5 Producer cooperatives.
6 Retailer cooperatives.
7 Clubs and societies.

The public sector institutions are described more fully in Chapter
7.

6.6 Employment in these various organizations

All these organizations offer employment in a wide variety of fields.
Some have more opportunities than others. For example, a small firm
with only a few employees may offer a wide variety of tasks in the
working day and a greater degree of responsibility. On the other
hand, supervision by the employer is close and continuous and
suggestions for better methods of working may be unwelcome or be
rejected outright. In larger firms there are more job opportunities,
specialized equipment may be more easily available, wide experience
can be gained by moving round the firm and recreational and other
facilities may be better than in the small firm.

More points to remember

- Not all activities are appropriate to profit-making enterprises.
  Some must be carried out for social reasons by official bodies,
  such as the National Health Service.
- Some are best carried on as non-profit-making clubs and
  societies, such as the Automobile Association, or the cooperative
  societies.
- Some official bodies, set up by the authority of Parliament are
  quangos; quasi-autonomous non-governmental organizations.

6.7 Projects and activities on business organizations

1 A survey about business names

Take the High Street of your own home town, or the nearest local town and carry out a survey of at least part of it to discover the names of every business in it. A good method is to select a substantial section of the High Street, between any two side roads. Write down all the street numbers in your section and the names of each business. In a column alongside the name write the type of business it appears to be. Watch out for:

(a) Sole traders
(b) Partnerships
(c) Businesses trading under a made-up name which is not the true name of the owner or owners. Are they displaying the notice required by the Companies Act, 1985?
(d) Private limited companies
(e) Public limited companies
(f) Cooperatives
(g) Friendly societies

Collect bills or invoices from as many businesses as possible – for example by making a small purchase or asking for a bill for this project. Such a document should reveal the true owners of the business.

What percentage of businesses in your survey comes under the heading of each type (a)–(g) above?

2 A class collection of stationery

Make a collection of stationery from limited companies. Include letters, invoices, credit notes, compliment slips, etc. Check that the details required by the Companies Act, 1985 actually do appear.

6.8 New enterprises and a choice of business units

Those who are thinking of starting up in business have about five choices open to them, but one of these is unlikely to be available. This is to set up as a public limited company, for which the minimum capital required is £50,000 and therefore out of reach of most budding entrepreneurs.

The following checklist develops the thought pattern which most traders might follow:

1 How important is limited liability to me in this business? Sole traders and partners are liable to the limit of their personal wealth

for the debts and the torts of the business. The word 'torts' means 'civil wrongs' – such as negligence, nuisance and defamation. Company directors are not liable in this way, but if they borrow money they may be asked for some sort of security.

2   If limited liability is important, buy an off-the-shelf company or register one yourself, either personally or by the use of a company registration agent (see *Yellow Pages*).

3   What is my capital situation? Have I saved enough to be able to start up without outside financial help? Can I get normal trade credit from suppliers despite my lack of a proven track record?

4   If the capital situation is weak how do I intend to get the capital I require:
    (a)   By borrowing.
    (b)   By taking a partner.
    (c)   By floating a private limited company and finding outside investors who can help.
    (d)   By looking for grants and/or equity investors from official bodies (for example tourism projects can get some help in this way).
    (e)   By joining a cooperative – but cooperatives have special rules which need investigating. See your local CDA (Cooperative Development Agency).

5   In the light of (4) above what is my chosen form of business unit to be?

6   What name shall I trade under – and if it is a name other than my own true name I must make out the notice required to display under the Business Names Act, 1985. Make every effort to avoid a name that might be used by someone else – the best way is to include your own home town in the name like 'Landscaped Gardens of Brighton'. It is easy to check whether such a name is used in your local area.

7   Do not print letterheads, business cards, etc. or paint noticeboards, shopfronts, etc. until you are quite sure the Registrar of Companies has accepted your company name, and you have all the details required by law, and by sound business practice.

8   One outlet open to many new enterprises is as a franchised operation. A **franchise** is a permit to start up a new enterprise using the skills, expertise and organization of a well-established business. The franchisor permits the use of these skills to the franchisee in return for a lump sum payment and possibly an annual fee. A directory of franchise opportunities is available from Franchise Development Services Ltd, Castle House, Castle Meadow, Norwich NR2 1PJ (Tel: 0603 667024).

6.9 Rapid revision

Answers	Questions
–	**1 What are the main types of business organization?**
1 (a) Sole traders; (b) partnerships; (c) limited partnerships; (d) private limited companies; (e) public limited companies.	**2 What are the advantages of being a sole trader?**
2 (a) Independence; (b) no formal procedures for setting up in business; (c) personal supervision of every aspect by the proprietor.	**3 What are the disadvantages?**
3 (a) Unlimited liability; (b) long hours and no holidays; (c) problems when sickness occurs; (d) limited amount of capital; (e) at death, inheritance tax applies.	**4 What are the advantages of partnerships?**
4 (a) Shared responsibility means time off, holiday and sickness can be covered; (b) more capital is available; (c) a better service can usually be offered because wider experience is available; (d) the affairs of the business are still private.	**5 What is a limited partnership?**
5 One in which one (or more) of the partners has limited liability, but the other (or others) are general partners, liable to the limit of their personal wealth.	**6 What is a limited company?**
6 A form of organization where the members of the company have limited liability. This means that they can lose their shareholdings invested in the company, but no more – so their homes cannot be taken and sold to recover the debts of the company.	**7 What is a public limited company?**

Answers	Questions
7 A larger type of company (the minimum capital is £50,000) which is allowed to offer its shares to members of the general public. Other companies are called private limited companies and may not sell shares to the general public – only to friends and relatives.	8 **What other types of organization are there?**
8 (a) Government departments; (b) local government departments; (c) nationalized industries; (d) QUANGOS; (e) producer cooperatives; (f) retailer cooperatives; (g) clubs and associations.	9 **Go over the test until you are sure of all the answers. Then try the questions in Section 6.10 below.**

6.10   Questions on Chapter 6

1   Peter Thompson is a sole trader who regularly works seven days a week, twelve hours a day. He is considering taking a partner. Advise him of the advantages and disadvantages of partnerships as a form of business organization.

2   Why should an industry like the gas industry be nationalized in so many countries, when road haulage is frequently run by private enterprise firms?

3   A is thinking of setting up a limited company with his friend B. How would they set about it, and what would be the advantages of this form of organization?

   (a)   The word 'limited', is a warning to all who do business with limited companies. What are they being warned about?

   (b)   Farrant, a small shopkeeper can obtain paper bags very cheaply from a friend in the paper industry. He is approached by a limited company with a chain of baker's shops with an order for 1 million paper bags. Farrant is enthusiastic about the huge order, but his wife is more cautious. Why is she hesitating, do you think?

5   Design a letterhead for the firm of Clearsky Ltd, who are in the airfreight business. They are authorized IATA cargo agents. Their address is 20 Airport Way, Heathrow, Middlesex TW6 3JD. Their telephone number is 081 089 42951. Their telex number is 7387954. They are registered in England, No.

00092951. Their registered office is at the address given above. The directors are Michael Clear, Peter Clear and Andrew Clear. The Secretary is Kenneth Purkiss, ICSA. The letterhead carries the following notices: All contractual engagements subject to published conditions of air carriage, available on request. Insurance risks are covered only on receipt of written instructions, specifying risks to be covered and full value of cover required.

6 Design a letterhead for Gallerie Espanol, an art gallery situated at 17958 King's Road, Chelsea, London SW3 8UP. The proprietors are Thomas and Mary Greco. Their telephone number is 081 399 7642. The letterhead bears a statement: Specialists in Spanish and Latin American works of art. At the foot of the page is a notice reading: Special note: We reserve the right to charge both buyers and sellers a commission when acting as agents.

7 What is the distinction between a private limited company and a public limited company? How does a private company become a public company?

8 A school leaver is offered two jobs:
   (a) A post in a small office where three people only are employed.
   (b) A post in a large government department where the intake of school leavers alone is more than thirty. Discuss the relative merits of employment in such organizations and (assuming the posts are in the subject areas which interest you) say which you would accept.

9 What are the disadvantages of a one-man business? Why do so many of them continue to exist?

10 Explain the term 'limited liability'. Mrs Jones, who is a widow with £10,000 to invest is considering putting this money at the disposal of a friend who is manufacturing bedroom furniture under the name of Sleepwell Knightly, Ltd. Advise her about the wisdom of this investment.

11 List reasons why a sole trader would consider turning his business into a limited liability company.

12 If someone tells you they have shares in a limited company, what do they mean? What financial benefit are they to that person?

7
Public enterprises

7.1 The need for public enterprises

From 1945 to 1979 the UK was the best example in the world of a mixed economy, with a large number of private enterprises offering a wide range of goods and services, but with a good many enterprises run in the national interest. These were in four main forms – central government organizations, local government organizations, nationalized industries run as public corporations and quangos, or quasi-autonomous non-governmental organizations. Just why those institutions came to be run in the way they were is a long story and a little of it will be told in this chapter, but first we need to talk about the balance of a mixed economy.

What we are trying to do in a mixed economy is strike a balance between *free enterprise* (in which people are allowed to do whatever they like, and are free to use their natural talents to enrich themselves – so long as they do not adversely affect others) and a fair share of health, wealth and happiness as far as that can be achieved. The British have always been strong supporters of such ideas, and some of our earliest roots as an advanced nation were nurtured on the practical philosophy of Jeremy Bentham, who taught that every action of men, institutions and government should be measured against the yardstick of human happiness, and whether it achieved 'the greatest good for the greatest number of people'. In striking such a balance we want to achieve as high a standard of living as possible, with reasonable fair shares for all, but there is a dilemma. Many of the things social organizations do are of necessity not self-supporting. If we run North Sea Oil, or British Coal, or British Telecom as a nationalized undertaking we should be able to make a profit, or at least break even, but we cannot hope to do so out of caring for the mentally handicapped, or the National Health Service (a *free* service) or even education. Such organizations must be paid for by taxation and the only source of taxation is the 'free-enterprise' sector, because the social sector is by definition not self-supporting. It follows that if we expand the social sector too much, the private sector – the wealth-creating sector – will become too small to support it.

What happened by 1979 was that the social sector was very buoyant, and even expanding, while private enterprise was sinking under the burden of excessive taxation, which creamed off the fruits of enterprise to such an extent that enterprising people hesitated to come forward and organize production. The result has been a decade of government policies designed to restore the balance in the free-enterprise sector's favour. A number of nationalized bodies have been privatized, and more are to follow. The social side of the economy has been curtailed, but largely by promoting greater efficiency rather than by lowering the quality of services. The aim is to get the private enterprise sector back to about 60 per cent of the economy – it had fallen to less than half – and that 60 per cent to be highly productive using new technologies. The old 'smokestack' industries were to be finally phased out. Many readers will question the wisdom of such policies, holding that they mean hardship for some people, but it is very difficult to deny the underlying economic sense of the policies. If the wealth-creators do not get enough incentive to keep the farms, factories and other wealth-creating firms going the 'social sector' will be starved of resources anyway. The figures are clear. The 1992 figures were:

Total national output (wealth created)	£456,387 million
Amount of this wealth taken by the public sector	£210,026 million
Balance left for private sector	£246,361 million

The public sector, despite considerable privatization, was still taking 46 per cent of the wealth. Why do we need all these public enterprises?

Central government services

We need central government services for the following reasons:

1 There are some things only central government can do – defence, law and order, the Court system, etc.
2 There are some things that are best provided nationally, so as to get even standards across the nation – health, education, social security, etc.
3 There are some things that are of national importance – energy, agriculture, mineral resources, forestry, exports, nuclear power, overseas trade, etc.

The various government departments assume responsibility for these matters, and if necessary set up establishments around the country to encourage, supervise and control them.

Local government services

There are some things that are best carried out at a local level, because they vary from place to place and it is important to know the local needs. Some of the things the central government takes responsibility for have to be handled by local agents and often the best agent is the local government organization. For example, education is a matter of national importance but must actually be implemented in the localities.

The chief services provided by local government are:

1 Civil defence
2 Public order and safety
3 Education
4 Social services
5 Housing and community amenities
6 Recreational and cultural services
7 Transport and communications
8 Drainage and coastal protection

Public corporations

For a variety of reasons there are certain major industries which are run as national corporations. For example, atomic energy is inherently dangerous and not many people are in favour of it being privately run – although some attempt is being made to privatize it at the time of writing. Coal was nationalized at the end of the Second World War after a century of bad treatment of the miners by the mine owners. Against many protests mines are now being offered for sale, but there are few applicants. Gas, electricity and water were nationalized after 1945 as services of national importance where great gains could be achieved by a central administration. All have recently been privatized, and all have shed staff in the process and become leaner, more competitive industries.

Quangos

Quangos stands for quasi-autonomous non-governmental organizations. Quasi means 'almost', so they are almost autonomous (self-governing) but actually there is usually some minister or official somewhere to whom they do in fact report. Some people translate the term as quasi-autonomous national government organizations, but this is not really correct – the essential point is that they are set up in most cases to give independent advice to ministers and to that extent it is important for them to be autonomous bodies. They are made up of experts in a particular field – some of them paid appointments and others voluntary positions (but with all expenses paid). Altogether there are about 2500 such bodies, with about 10,000 paid personnel and 25,000 unpaid appointments. With such a huge list of organizations it is impossible to mention many but, for example, the Medical Research Council has eleven paid members and the National Environment Research Council has about twenty-five members (but 2400 staff scattered around the country). There is hardly any aspect of our lives which is not reviewed by a quango, and commented upon in reports to ministers of one sort or another.

7.2 Central government departments

The central government is run by the Prime Minister from the Cabinet Office. The Cabinet consists of the Prime Minister's team of ministers, each of whom has charge of a department. The full list is shown in Table 7.1. An up-to-date list of the actual ministers can be found in the current edition of *Vacher's Parliamentary Companion* which is available in most libraries, and many Business Studies Departments do subscribe to it for its quarterly up-date on Parliamentary personalities.

It is impossible to do more here than illustrate briefly the organization of a department and the work it does. The example chosen is the Department of the Environment.

7.3 The work of the Department of the Environment (DOE)

The Department of the Environment consists of the Secretary of State for the Environment, the Minister for Local Government and Planning, the Minister for Housing, Inner Cities and Construction, the Minister for the Environment and Countryside, two Parliamentary Under-Secretaries of State and some 5000 members of staff.

The Secretary of State for the Environment, supported by the Department, has responsibility for eight major areas of activity. These are:

1 *Local government* Responsibility lies for the constitution, organization, powers, functions and finance of local authorities in England. These matters in Wales, Scotland and Northern Ireland are in the hands of other Departments. Local government is an area where all sorts of abuses of power could easily arise if there was not some sort of central control to ensure even standards over the whole country, with clear rights of the authorities and clear duties to people living in their areas.

2 *Housing* Housing policy is an area which affects all sections of the community, but especially the less-well-off section, who cannot afford private housing and must look to the public sector – council

Table 7.1   Her Majesty's Chief Officers of State

The Cabinet	
Prime Minister, First Lord of the Treasury and Minister for the Civil Service	Secretary of State for the Environment
Lord Chancellor	Secretary of State for National Heritage
Secretary of State for Foreign and Commonwealth Affairs	Secretary of State for Employment
	Secretary of State for Social Security
Chancellor of the Exchequer	Chancellor of the Duchy of Lancaster and Minister of Public Services and Science
Secretary of State for the Home Department	Secretary of State for Scotland
President of the Board of Trade	Secretary of State for Northern Ireland
Secretary of State for Transport	Secretary of State for Education
Secretary of State for Defence	Secretary of State for Health
Lord Privy Seal and Leader of the House of Lords	Minister of Agriculture, Fisheries and Food
	Chief Secretary to the Treasury
Lord President of the Council and Leader of the House of Commons	Secretary of State for Wales

Law Officers	
Attorney General	Solicitor-General
Lord Advocate	Solicitor-General for Scotland

Ministers not in the Cabinet (M/S denotes Minister of State)

Parliamentary Secretary, Treasury and Chief Whip	M/S for Defence Procurement (Minister of Defence)
M/S Foreign and Commonwealth Office and Minister for Overseas Development	M/S for the Armed Forces (Minister of Defence)
M/S Foreign and Commonwealth Office	M/S for the Department of the Environment (Minister for Housing, Inner Cities and Construction)
M/S Foreign and Commonwealth Office	
M/S Home Office	M/S for the Department of the Environment (Minister for Local Government and Planning)
M/S Home Office	
M/S Home Office	
Financial Secretary, Treasury	M/S for the Department of the Environment (Minister for the Environment and Countryside)
The Paymaster General	
M/S Dept of Trade and Industry (Minister for Energy)	M/S Department of Employment
	M/S Department of Social Security (Minister for Social Security and the Disabled)
M/S Dept of Trade and Industry (Minister for Industry)	
M/S Dept of Trade and Industry (Minister for Trade)	M/S Scottish Office (Minister for Health and Home Affairs)
M/S Dept of Transport (Minister for Public Transport)	M/S Northern Ireland Office
	M/S Northern Ireland Office
M/S Dept of Transport (Minister for Aviation and Shipping)	M/S Department of Education
	M/S Department of Health (Minister for Health)
	M/S for Agriculture, Fisheries and Food
There are also 46 Junior Ministers	M/S Welsh Office

Source: Vachers' Parliamentary Companion August 1993

housing, etc. The Department's policies cover owner occupation, the private rented sector, new towns, council housing, housing associations and the general oversight of housing conditions, repair and refurbishing of run-down properties etc. It has powers to allocate resources and financial subsidies for housing associations and local authority housing.

3 *Construction industry sponsorship* The construction industry is one where sound controls are necessary if building standards are to be maintained. The Department controls the building regulations, coordinates research work, administers the Building Research Establishment and the Fire Research Station and represents the UK in negotiations with the European Community on construction industry matters. In particular, the Department seeks to encourage the competitiveness of the construction industry by promoting a wider understanding of the opportunities presented to the industry in the Single European Market and worldwide.

4 *Environmental protection* The Department supervises policy on waste disposal, air pollution, radioactive wastes and all other aspects of environmental protection. It represents the UK on international environmental bodies, and runs Her Majesty's Pollution Inspectorate.

5 *Land use* The Department gives guidance on planning policy, regional development and has a Planning Inspectorate to maintain and improve the planning system.

6 *Inner cities* The decay of inner cities in the last forty years has led to DOE programmes for urban regeneration, development grants, grants for restoring derelict land and has led to the establishment of urban development corporations to restore the inner cities.

7 *Water policy* The Department sponsors the provision of water services, supervises water quality, and has recently played a major part in the privatization of the water industry. The Department has a major role to play in forcing the industry to meet European Community standards, through its Drinking Water Inspectorate.

8 *Wildlife and countryside conservation* The Department sponsors policy on rural development, the conservation of the countryside and the protection of wildlife. It sponsors a number of quangos, such as the Countryside Commission, and the Nature Conservancy Council which carry out a wide range of activities in this field.

Until recently the Department supervised the Property Services Agency which looked after and managed the government's Civil Estates and Defence Estates. Much of these have now been privatized. It also supervises a number of quangos, although they are, in effect, autonomous bodies charged with various duties in the environmental field.

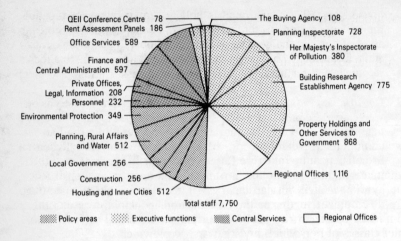

Figure 7.1   What the staff of the Department of Environment work on

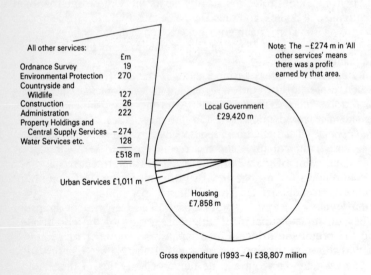

Figure 7.2   Where the money goes

What the staff do and where the money goes are illustrated in Figures 7.1 and 7.2. The figures give some idea of the expenditure involved in such an important ministry and their division among the various fields of activity which call for the attention of ministers.

7.4 The Civil Service

Ever since 1854, when the Northcote–Trevelyan Report recommended that recruitment to the Civil Service should be by competitive examination, and promotion by merit rather than seniority, the quality of the Civil Service has been high. Today the State is the largest employer in the country, with about 750,000 civil servants administering the work of some twenty departments. There are four chief classes of personnel, and one or two minor classes. They are:

1 The administrative class
2 The specialist class
3 The executive class
4 The clerical class
5 Other classes (clerical assistant class, typing class, personal secretary class and the messenger class)

The administrative class forms the top 1 per cent of the service, with major responsibilities on policy formulation for the various government departments, advice to the ministers concerned and supervision of the major areas of work in each department.

The specialist class includes the very wide range of professional, scientific and technical expertise which is required in such wide-ranging activities as defence, health, education, land planning, economic planning etc. About one-quarter of all personnel fall into this category of specialist advisers, inspectors, surveyors, technicians etc. at various levels.

The executive class supervises the general activities of the department in the regions and localities, prepares budgets, forecasts and reports and conducts the department's activity within the framework of agreed policy.

The clerical class is the lowest level of staff, at which most young recruits enter, and from which they may work their way up into the executive class.

In an organization as extensive as the Civil Service, with such a large labour force employed in such a wide range of activities, it is essential to ensure that communications are maintained efficiently. The other classes are designed to ensure that the organization is never starved of secretarial and typing personnel, and is adequately supported by routine services of every sort.

7.5   Quasi-autonomous non-governmental organizations

Quangos have been referred to earlier, as organizations which are 'almost' governmental. When we say that activities are almost governmental we mean that there is an element of governmental control in them, but for some reason the government thinks it more appropriate to delegate the responsibility to some other body, which will perform the activity along the guidelines laid down, but outside the direct control of a politically-motivated government. This might be desirable in many situations – for example, to avoid allegations of bias from organizations affected by a particular procedure or to ensure a perfectly fair investigation of an accident or incident. Sometimes it may be helpful just to clear a whole section of work from a busy department into the care of a specialist group appointed for the particular problems concerned.

For example, the Department of the Environment has the following non-departmental bodies associated with it.

1   The Housing Corporation
2   The Commission for New Towns
3   The New Towns Development Corporations
4   The British Board of Agrément
5   The Historic Buildings and Monuments Commission
6   Royal Commission on Historic Monuments
7   Board of Trustees of the Royal Armouries
8   The National Heritage Memorial Fund
9   The Sports Council
10 The Urban Development Corporations

Points to remember

- In a mixed economy we try to get a reasonable balance between free-enterprise activities and public-sector activities.
- There are certain things that only central governments should do – for example defence, law and order, the Court system, etc.
- There are certain other things that only central government can do if standards are to be uniform across the nation. Examples are education, health and social security.
- Each government department has broad areas of activity which it controls and influences and a minister (or several ministers) to be responsible to Parliament for its affairs. The senior ministers form the Cabinet, led by the Prime Minister.
- The sovereign body in the UK is 'The Queen in Parliament'.
- The Civil Service is a body of paid officials, divided into a number of classes of seniority, which act for the government in implementing and enforcing its policies.

7.6 Local government

A major reorganization of local government in the UK took place in 1974. The map of Great Britain (Figure 7.3) shows the new counties established at that time. (There was, in addition, a major reorganization in Northern Ireland which reduced the number of local authorities to twenty-six district authorities.) However, the full system introduced then included a tier of authorities at Metropolitan County Level, the seven designated Metropolitan areas being Greater London, Greater Manchester, Tyne & Wear, Merseyside, West Midlands, South Yorkshire and West Yorkshire. These areas all proved to be excessively bureaucratic (and highly politicized), spending very heavily on a huge range of 'social' policies at a time when widespread restrictions were being called for by central government. This led to the abolition of this tier of local authorities, power returning instead to the District (or Borough) Councils. To deal with sections of the necessary services which were more logically handled by a larger authority (police, fire, local transport, waste disposal, etc.) **joint authorities**, made up of delegates from the local councils, were set up.

The present arrangements are illustrated in Figure 7.4.

Organizations are vitally affected by the work of local authorities, for controls are inevitable on any type of human activity in heavily-populated advanced economies. Central government cannot possibly do more than exercise general controls over planning, environmental quality, industrial development, health education, the transport infrastructure, etc. The detailed work must be delegated to local authorities who can actually deal with manageable areas of land, reasonable numbers of people and even individual cases. Effective power must be accessible to the firms and organizations it is seeking to control, and must therefore be local, without being parochial.

The general pattern of councils set up in 1974 was a two-tier system, and this still applies in the non-Metropolital areas. If we consider these as the typical local government authorities today we may outline their activities as follows:

First-tier authorities

The 'first-tier' authorities are the County Councils in England (39) and Wales (8) and the nine Regional Councils in Scotland. In addition, the three Island Councils of Shetland, Orkney and the Western Isles are all-purpose councils so that they do perform the 'first-tier' activities. The major duties of 'first-tier' authorities are not completely uniform throughout the country, and some flexibility does exist between the 'first-tier' and 'second-tier' councils.

Figure 7.3   Local authorities in Great Britain (Crown Copyright)

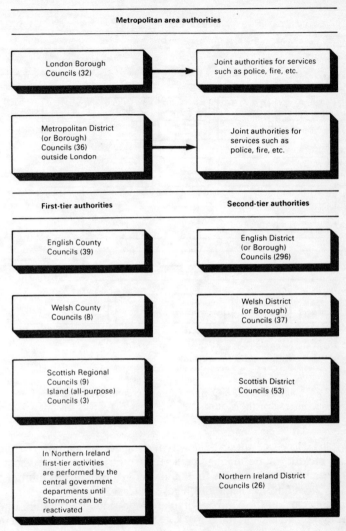

Metropolitan area authorities

London Borough Councils (32) → Joint authorities for services such as police, fire, etc.

Metropolitan District (or Borough) Councils (36) outside London → Joint authorities for services such as police, fire, etc.

First-tier authorities

Second-tier authorities

English County Councils (39)

English District (or Borough) Councils (296)

Welsh County Councils (8)

Welsh District (or Borough) Councils (37)

Scottish Regional Councils (9) Island (all-purpose) Councils (3)

Scottish District Councils (53)

In Northern Ireland first-tier activities are performed by the central government departments until Stormont can be reactivated

Northern Ireland District Councils (26)

Figure 7.4 The pattern of local authorities in the UK

In Figure 7.5 the committee structure for one medium-size County Council – Cambridgeshire – shows the major activities in diagrammatic form. The Council is responsible for administering most of the local services which are best organized on a county-wide basis. These include education, social services, roads, police, fire and rescue services, transport planning, strategic planning, consumer protection, library services, waste disposal and some environmental services. In

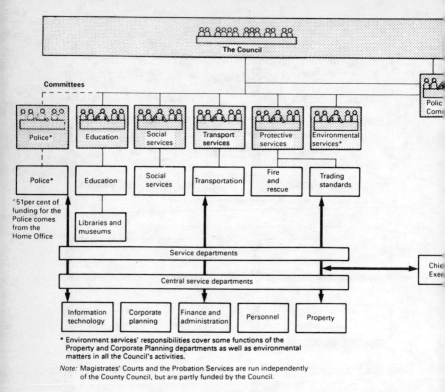

Figure 7.5   Cambridgeshire County Council committee structure (Reproduced by courtesy of the Council)

order to carry out these field activities it needs 'support' services. These include estate management (the County owns 50,000 acres of land) architectural services to its hundreds of properties, administrative services and financial and legal services.

In London and the Metropolitan areas outside London the London Borough Councils and the thirty-six District (or Borough) Councils in other Metropolitan areas provide all the services required, both first tier and second tier, but where a service does require a larger catchment area for effective operation the 'joint authorities' referred to earlier operate the service.

In Northern Ireland first tier duties were formerly exercised by the Northern Ireland Parliament at Stormont, but the dissension of recent years led to these duties being operated by the Civil Service under the control of central government in London, until such time as more reasonable arrangements can be arrived at.

Second-tier authorities

These authorities are not subordinate to the first-tier authorities; they have their own functions and rights. Naturally a good deal of cooperation is essential between the two tiers, and goodwill is necessary if problems which arise are to be resolved amicably. For example, in any particular county some areas will be growing faster than others, and may take an unfair proportion of capital development perhaps contributed to by other areas which are not benefiting to the same extent. Such situations may cause difficulties.

The general name for second-tier authorities is District Councils, but a special procedure permits application to be made for Borough status (in Scotland 'Community' status) which does not change the powers of the authority but may be of ceremonial or historical importance.

The District Councils control passenger transport, local planning, housing and related activities, building regulations, local amenities, cemeteries, etc. In the Metropolitan areas they are now the main councils and perform as all purpose councils carrying out both first-tier and second-tier activities as explained above.

Lower authorities

District Councils must establish parish councils (in Wales community councils) to cater for local needs and give local populations a voice in their affairs. In very small communities a parish meeting serves the same purpose.

As far as private enterprise business is concerned, what the local authorities do is of very great importance. Such activities as planning permission, inspection of building work, putting out council contracts to tender, etc. are very important for businesses. The 'business rate' system is now managed from a central organization, since the Council Tax levied on property owners in any locality only applies to non-business properties. This can have a bad effect on councils, since too heavy a business rate drives business away to other areas where rates are lower, and most business representatives will argue that the rate should be kept to a reasonable and fair level. This is now done centrally, with Central Government setting a **Uniform Business Rate**, but it is at a high level. Some protests are being made at the time of writing.

By contrast, councils have it in their power to encourage businesses by assistance with premises, infrastructure developments (roads, railway sidings, water supplies etc.), housing and educational and training requirements. This is particularly the case in inner city rehabilitation areas, development areas etc.

7.7   A project on the public enterprise sector

Using your local telephone directory make a list of the public enterprise activities in your area. The project begins when you look for central government bodies in your local directory. The most likely names to look for are as follows: Trade, Department of; Health & Social Security, Department of; Employment, Department of; Export Credits Guarantee Department; Home Office; Industry, Department of; Defence, Ministry of; Agriculture Fisheries and Food, Department of; Environment, Department of; The Welsh Office, the Scottish Office and the Northern Ireland office may be important in your area; Transport, Department of; Energy, Department of; Education and Science, Department of; Your Local Council; Inland Revenue; Courts.

Make a note of the names and addresses of all the premises occupied by these bodies. Then choose any one of them and write a short report on its activities. You can do this if you visit them and ask for a leaflet about this activity. If different members of the class choose different bodies you will avoid swamping the system or abusing the generosity of staff in assisting you with your project. Reporting back to the class is a useful way of developing self-confidence in speaking to groups.

7.8   Rapid revision

Answers		Questions	
–		1	What is a mixed economy?
1	An economy where a balance is struck between private enterprise and public enterprise. Ideally a 60 per cent free enterprise economy is about the best, with 40 per cent of the economy going to socially-essential activities.	2	What are the traditional and essential central government activities?
2	Defence, law and order and the Courts system.	3	What other activities are best performed by central government?

Answers	*Questions*
3 Education, health, social security, atomic energy etc.	**4 What other role can central government play?**
4 It has a duty to ensure prosperity for its people, and therefore all major aspects of production, distribution, and trade are subject to general supervision (while being largely the result of free enterprise business activity).	**5 What does the British legislature consist of?**
5 (a) The House of Commons; (b) the House of Lords; (c) the Queen, whose Royal Assent makes a Parliamentary Bill an Act of Parliament	**6 Where does effective power lie?**
6 With the Cabinet.	**7 What is meant by 'the collective responsibility' of ministers?**
7 All ministers are held to be responsible for the agreed policies which result from Cabinet discussion. Even if he/she opposes a policy in the Cabinet discussion a minister must support the policy outside the Cabinet, since it has been agreed to by the Cabinet as a group.	**8 What is the minister's responsibility for his/her department?**
8 He/she is fully responsible for all its acts and shortcomings, and must answer to Parliament for them.	**9 What is the Civil Service?**
9 A large body of paid employees which carries out the detailed work of departments, implementing policy and enforcing regulations.	**10 What are quangos?**

Answers	Questions
10 Quasi-autonomous non-governmental organizations set up by Act of Parliament to administer particular fields of interest. Their independent status ensures impartial treatment of all affected by the regulations concerned.	11 **What local authorities run the London Metropolitan Area, and the six metropolitan areas outside London?**
11 The thirty-two London Borough Councils and the thirty-six Metropolitan District (or Borough) Councils.	12 **What is special about the police, fire service, etc. in these metropolitan areas?**
12 Since they need to serve a larger area than just a single borough or district they are run by 'joint authorities' made up of delegates from the councils concerned.	13 **What are the first-tier authorities in other areas?**
13 (a) Thirty-nine English County Councils; (b) eight Welsh County Councils; (c) nine Scottish Regional Councils; (d) three Island (all-purpose) Councils; (e) in Northern Ireland the first-tier activities are run by the government departments in London.	14 **What are the second-tier authorities?**
14 They are the 296 District (or Borough) councils in England, thirty-seven in Wales, fifty-three in Scotland and twenty-six in Northern Ireland. There are no second-tier authorities in the metropolitan areas.	15 **Go over the test again until you are sure of all the answers. Then try the questions in Section 7.8 below.**

7.9   Questions on Chapter 7

1   What is private enterprise? What is the public sector? Why do we need both? In your answer refer to a number of activities which are best left to the public sector, and justify the exclusion of private enterprise from these activities.

2 Why is local government an essential part of the management of the country? How can it keep business people in its locality?
3 What is a quango? A minister proposes to set up a National Ports Council to advise him/her on matters pertaining to the efficiency, management and well-being of ports. What sort of things do you think might be enquired into and reported upon by such a body?
4 'There is no need to worry about noisy Question Times in the House of Commons. At Question Times I find out about things going on in various Departments which might otherwise escape my attention.' (The Prime Minister) What qualities make a good 'Question Time' member of the House of Commons.
5 What is a first-tier local authority? What is a second-tier local authority? What sort of responsibilities do they have and how are they financed.

8
The internal organization of businesses

8.1 The management of businesses

Every business has to be managed. There is a lot to worry about even for a sole trader, who has no need to consult anyone, and is free to do whatever he/she likes. There is the product, or the range of products, or the services being offered to worry about. We have to find suppliers for everything we need, not only raw materials and components but all the capital items (premises, machines, motor vehicles, furniture and equipment) and consumable items (stationery, fuel, packing materials, etc.). There is the marketing of the product, advertising, appointing agents to handle various types of goods, keeping track of sales and of payments by debtors. There is staffing, transport and distribution, research and development, accounting records, finance, and so on. For the sole trader it is an endless round of work. With a partner there is some help, and some respite because a worry shared is a worry halved, but now there is the need to consult with the partner, and get agreement on many points before the actual solution can be tried out.

The vast majority of businesses today are limited companies. We have already seen that this is because the owners of a company have limited liability, and are not liable for the debts of the business to the limit of their personal wealth. There are about 700,000 limited companies in the UK and the 1000 really large companies do about 90 per cent of all the business in the UK. The other 699,000 companies are relatively insignificant, though they all play a 'niche' part in the economy or they would go out of business. A niche is a little place in a wall where a statue or some interesting ornament or decorative pot of flowers can stand to play its useful part in beautifying the whole edifice. A business that has found a niche for itself has found a position where it can play a useful part supplying either a new product, or a useful service to the world at large, but generally speaking to bigger businesses around it. It is these bigger businesses on which the whole nation depends. For this reason when we look at the management of businesses it is most sensible if we look at the organization of limited companies, because they give the truest and fairest picture of how our society is run. Even the public sector organizations, like the nationalized industries and the government departments follow largely the same pattern of organization.

8.2   The Board of Directors

The Board of Directors is responsible for the management of a company. It is distinct from the owners of the company, who are called the shareholders, except that the Articles of Association of a company may require directors to have a qualifying holding of shares which they must purchase within two months of appointment. The composition of the Board is very important, because all decisions taken by the Board have legal implications and it is essential to have a good balance between the crucial employees of the company who are actually going to put the Board's plans into effect (the executive directors) and outside advisers who are knowledgeable about various aspects of the company's business. These are usually only part-time directors, who are available for consultation by telephone at any time but otherwise just attend monthly Board Meetings for an annual fee (say £2,000–£3,000 per annum in a normal-sized company). Figure 8.1 shows a typical Board of Directors with the Chairman taking charge of the meetings and all the major departments of the business represented by executive directors, while a team of part-time directors advises the Board about various aspects. Study the diagram now, before reading the detailed descriptions of the functions of the various members.

The Chairman

The Chairman is the senior member of the Board, with the power to call meetings and arrange the agenda after consultation with the other directors (who may suggest items for discussion). The Chairman, whether male or female, is in an influential position and all remarks are addressed to the Chair. This ensures that only one person can speak at a time, for the Chair can only give attention to one person. It is forbidden to make private remarks from one member to another while a third party is addressing the Chair – for accurate minutes of what is said have to be kept, and the minuting secretary cannot take notes if several people are talking at once. If a meeting becomes rowdy the phrase 'Through the Chair please' will remind everyone of the proper way to speak at meetings.

The Chairman has a special agenda called the Chairman's Agenda, which contains rather more detail than the ordinary agenda sent to

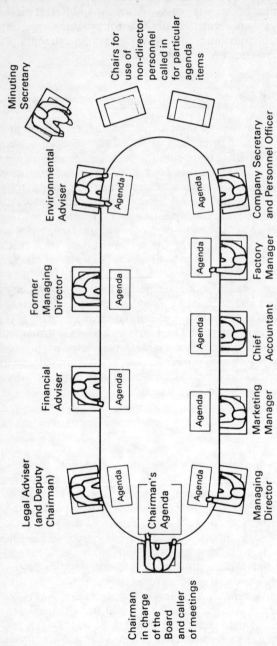

Part-time directors

Minuting
Secretary

Chairs for
use of non-director
personnel called in
for particular agenda
items

Legal Adviser
(and Deputy
Chairman)

Financial
Adviser

Former
Managing
Director

Environmental
Adviser

Chairman's
Agenda

Agenda

Agenda

Agenda

Agenda

Chairman in charge
of the Board
and caller
of meetings

Managing
Director

Marketing
Manager

Chief
Accountant

Factory
Manager

Company Secretary
and Personnel Officer

Executive directors (full-time employees)

Figure 8.1 A Board of Directors

the other directors when the meeting is called. It may, for example, contain the Chairman's notes about particular items, the names of any people to be called in to report to the Board at some stage, and a place to record any resolutions, amendments, etc., to be voted on at the meeting.

The Chairman has a casting vote in the event of a tie between the 'Yes' and 'No' votes on any resolution before the meeting, and it will often be exercised in such a way that an extreme measure is not proceeded with, rather than the reverse.

The Deputy Chairman

The Deputy Chairman takes the place of the Chairman when he/she is absent or ill. There is no firm rule for deciding whom to appoint as Deputy Chairman, it is up to the Board, but clearly it needs to be a knowledgeable and respected Member of the Board, rather than an inexperienced person.

The part-time directors

These people usually have some reason for being invited to join the Board. They may be former executive directors who have now retired but whose knowledge and experience will be helpful. They may have special experience that may be helpful to the Board, particularly legal experience or financial experience, or technical expertise. Thus we might expect to find a medical practitioner on the Board of a pharmaceutical company, or a professor of electronic engineering on the Board of a computer manufacturer. They may have been appointed as a result of some arrangement made earlier. For example, a merchant bank which has made large loans to a company might insist on a representative of the bank being accepted as a part-time director, so the bank is fully aware of the company's financial situation.

The executive directors

Executive directors are full-time employees of the company, occupying senior positions within the company. The chief executive director is the **Managing Director** who occupies a key position. He/she has a dual capacity – to put into practice the policies laid down by the Board, but also to be able to present the results to the Board, bringing back to the Board any views expressed or experiences of the departments in trying to implement the Board's ideas.

The other executive directors are leading personalities in the various departments of the business, Production Department, Marketing, Accounting, etc. These departments are often called 'functions' since they have a particular function to perform within the company, and require specialist knowledge and experience. The **Company Secretary** is a name which is liable to mislead students. It is the name given to the Head of Department of the office responsible for keeping the register of shareholders, and registering changes of ownership when shares are bought and sold (for example on the Stock Exchange). The post is usually held by a person with legal qualifications, since compliance with the complex rules of the Companies Acts, 1985–89 is part of the secretary's responsibilities, and in any takeover or merger the company secretary will have an important part to play. The post therefore has nothing to do with secretarial duties of the shorthand/typing variety.

The work of the various functional departments is described in the next section.

8.3   The orientation of companies

There are two main types of orientation – **production-orientated companies** and **market-orientated companies**. Production-orientated companies are chiefly concerned with the complexities and technicalities of the goods they are making, and do not worry too much about the market. If they get their products right, and constantly update them to take account of the latest state-of-the-art developments, the customers will usually come forward and order the product. Thus the aircraft industry has a complex and evolving technological basis, which is constantly being improved. Although they do have to find customers, and attend air shows around the world to meet them, their main emphasis is the production of a range of aircraft which meet public needs.

Market-orientated firms are firms which have a proven product, often of a non-technical nature – such as a face cream, or a window cleaning fluid, a soap powder or a toothpaste. Such firms are interested in achieving nationwide or worldwide use of their products – ever bigger markets for what is really a relatively simple product but meeting a need which is very widespread. They are almost always in the position of selling a branded good – one to which a particular trade name (or brand name) has been applied. The implication is that the product is unique, whereas it is not – except that any brand may have secret ingredients which do give it a special flavour or property. Thus a product like Bold washing powder may be slightly different from Persil or Daz or a number of other powders, but at a pinch – if the customer is in a hurry – any one of them will do. Such firms are market orientated – the product is simple and unchanging – the need is to get it into the hands of a very wide range of customers.

The orientation of companies affects their organization, giving a different emphasis and importance to various departments. In general the membership of the Board will be affected by the emphasis given – for example the factory manager of a market-orientated firm might not be accorded Board status, whereas the production-orientated firm would certainly have the factory manager on the Board.

8.4   Relationships within an organization

There are three main types of relationship within an organization which represent the three chief types of organization – line organizations, functional organizations and line and staff organizations.

Line organization

Line organization is a direct relationship between members of staff running vertically down from the most important to the most subordinate position through a chain of command. At the top is the Board of Directors, with the Managing Director as the Chief Executive Director. Below the Managing Director is an executive director in charge of a particular aspect – for example the Factory Manager. Below that are various layers of middle management and supervisory staff, and below that lower-level staff, such as craftsmen and apprentices. Each person knows the person immediately above and below him/her. Orders pass down the line from above, and reports (and possibly protests) pass up the line from below. It is a structured, disciplined type of organization, almost in military style. It is an efficient system, especially in emergencies, but it can be irksome to those at lower levels – who may develop a 'nobody ever tells us anything' attitude, and a tendency to grumble about 'them upstairs'. There are two ideas that spring from line organization. They are the concepts of 'chain of command' and 'hierarchy'.

1   *Chain of command*   As illustrated in Figure 8.2, a line organization is essentially a command organization with a chain of command moving from the very highest level to the lowest level. This is an effective way of getting the decisions made at Boardroom level carried into effect by passing instructions down from the Board, through the Managing Director to the executive directors (who may – or may not – have been present when the decisions were actually made). They then relay the orders to the various heads of sections within their departments, who give instructions to the personnel in their sections and actually get the necessary work under way. Problems that arise are relayed up the chain of

command in a procedure known as 'feedback'. How high the problem goes depends upon the nature of the information fed back – but everyone at management level has discretion within the policy laid down. Thus a section head with whom a problem is raised might be able to say: 'Oh yes – that is easy enough – do it this way' and the instructions will go down the line again. On the other hand, the section head might say: 'I don't know – but I'll find out and get back to you on the point.' He/she then raises the matter with the person above, and either gets a clear ruling or the matter goes higher still – right back to the Board if necessary.

2   *Hierarchy*   The word hierarchy refers to the chain of command in certain religious orders (the word actually means 'high priest') but it is widely used for any organization which is organized in successive grades – as with 'line organization'. The essential feature is that information and instructions pass up and down the hierarchy and those who short-circuit the hierarchy by (for example) going straight to top management instead of through their superiors are likely to be severely frowned upon by those who are ignored. There is some justification for this – since top management should not be bothered with trivialities. If the matter is one where discretion would have been exercised lower down if the proper procedure had been followed then the offending person is clearly at fault. Difficulty does arise when an employee feels that he/she is being unfairly treated, and possibly victimized or harassed by the supervisor concerned. There has to be an appeals procedure of some sort. The chain of command breaks down if an individual can block genuine protests in an arbitrary manner and a genuine protest to a third party – such as the Personnel Officer – will usually be sympathetically received.

Line and staff organizations

There are certain sections of the organization of any big institution which do not operate in a 'line' formation with generals at the top and new recruits at the bottom, but instead exercise a fairly high-level influence on certain aspects of the company's affairs. Generally speaking these are not large departments, but specialist departments (sometimes just a single officer) – more often a small group of high level staff with secretarial and clerical assistance. Such groups are called 'staff' groups, almost always based at Head Office, and examples would be the Legal Department, Personnel Department, Public Relations Department and very often Research and Development (R&D) Department.

Functional organizations

Line organization actually occurs in all other types of organization, so each 'function' within a company will have a line organization within its own particular section. Some functions do spread across the whole field of a company's activity – for example the Costing Department will be collecting cost figures from every department and the Accounts Department will be paying wages for every person on the payroll. There is, therefore, a set of relationships established across the pattern of vertical line organizations to give horizontal links between departments. For example, the subject of Health and Safety at Work, which is usually the responsibility of the General Administration Officer, will affect every department and a cooperative and friendly relationship between the General Administrative Officer and all Heads of Departments will be essential.

The major functions in any organization are purchasing, manufacturing, marketing, transport and distribution, finance and accounting and general administration. Most of these will have executive directors in charge of them, each supervising a group of middle managers who in turn will have subsections which are their main areas of responsibility.

A general pattern of such an organization is shown in Figure 8.2, but the reader must expect to find an infinite variety of patterns in the organizations encountered in real life.

Points to remember

- Every business has to be managed, and the vast majority of them are run as limited companies, where the capital is provided by individuals called shareholders, but the management of the company is in the hands of a Board of Directors.
- The Board is composed of the Chairman, a number of full-time executive directors and a number of part-time non-executive directors. A Deputy Chairman will be appointed by the directors.
- The function of the part-time directors is to bring special expertise and general experience to the company. They may also be appointed by an outside body, with a watching brief, where a company has borrowed heavily from a financial institution, or a large body of shares is owned by a particular institutional investor.
- Executive directors have a main part to play in the day-to-day activities of the company; they are often departmental heads. The chief one among them is the Managing Director.
- The Managing Director has a dual function – to put into practice the policies laid down by the Board, and to report back to the

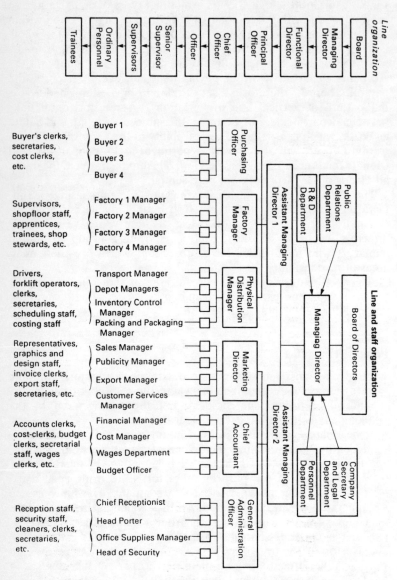

Figure 8.2 Patterns of organization

Board any problem areas in the proposals which have been found impractical for some reason.
- Some companies are product-orientated, with products that need constant revision and improvement. Some are market-orientated, with a routine product, with a long life span, and their chief aim is to sell it in wider and wider markets.
- The three main elements in business organization are line organization, line and staff organization and departmental organization by function.

8.5 The principles of organization

We live in an intricate world where there are many problems, and many different solutions to them. The size of an organization affects its conduct and the principles on which it can be operated, but given a firm of reasonable size with a good subdivision of activities and responsibilities the following principles will be found to have some place in the organization.

Clear objectives

An organization cannot be set up unless we know what it is intended to do. It is for top management to lay down the objectives of the company or firm, and publish them to all concerned. By this we mean that departmental heads must be appointed, informed of the objectives and told to convey to low-level staff the general plans of the organization. All departments must work cooperatively to achieve these objectives (sometimes this is called the **unity of objectives**). This idea can be carried further in some departments than in others – for example sales staff can be set personal objectives for achievement and manufacturing operatives can be set output targets. This detailed planning of tasks is sometimes called **management by objectives**.

Span of control

Although extraordinary managers do occasionally appear, most managers find it difficult to control more than three or four subordinates. This is called **span of control**. Where the span of control is too wide some aspects of the organization will be too loosely supervised. This may mean that some section heads become lax or overconfident, and they may begin to follow policies which are at variance with the true objectives of the organization. It is, therefore, better to put in an extra tier of staff to keep the span of control reasonable. Thus in Figure 8.2 the Managing Director would find it difficult to supervise six departmental heads and the insertion of an Assistant Managing

Director tier, with two assistant MDs reporting to the MD, and each controlling three departments reduces the span of control to manageable proportions. Notice that the 'staff' departments, although technically reporting to the managing director are not supervised in the same close way as, for example, production departments, and an occasional reporting back session might be all the control needed. Such reporting back would often be problem-orientated; for example a particular legal difficulty, or personal problem, or consumer relations difficulty.

Delegation

A single objective specified by the Board may have widespread implications for staff all the way down to grass-roots level. The actual implementation of parts of the objective may be delegated down the line, and ideally should go down as low as possible to a level of management where the actual activities are carried on and can be directly supervised. Delegation gives authority to the delegate, and makes him/her responsible for the execution of the tasks delegated Responsibility requires not only the execution and supervision of the task, but a duty to feed back information on any difficulties, and to report back at intervals, and on final completion. Discretion may have to be exercised within the policy laid down, and the extent of the discretion should be made clear. To take a very simple example – suppose car park charges are 50 pence per hour. A person who arrives at the pay booth 1 hour and 1 minute after entry may complain bitterly if charged £1, claiming that queuing at the pay booth had taken ten minutes. An exercise of discretion, so that anyone presenting a ticket less than five minutes over the hour would not be charged extra might be agreed. That is discretion within a policy.

Unity of command

This principle holds that all staff should know who is in charge of them, and there should be only one supervisor for each person, wherever they are in the hierarchy. This prevents trouble, for example orders from two supervisors might conflict and the junior person might be uncertain what to do. Even worse, he/she might play the two supervisors off against one another. It is true that this rule can break down in confused situations, especially, for example, in law and order situations or military situations. In such circumstances it may be understood that all lower ranks will behave correctly if they '*obey the last order given*' by someone who has authority. This places the onus on the officer concerned not to countermand existing orders unless the circumstances clearly merit it.

Advancement

We shall see later (see Chapter 16) that staff are more contented when they see prospects of advancement, and can achieve in their working situation personal self-esteem and the respect of their peer groups (i.e. equals). If it is a principle of the organization that every office boy or girl has the prospect of eventual promotion to the Boardroom, labour turnover will be reduced and a spirit of enthusiasm and cooperation will prevail, rather than the bored disinterest which is commonly shown by those who know they are in dead-end jobs. Such a policy needs to be supported by a good training programme and the positive encouragement of those who seek self-advancement by acquiring professional status in the various functional areas – accountancy, finance, purchasing and supply, marketing, physical distribution management, freight forwarding, personnel etc. Boards of directors who encourage a grow-your-own policy will never be short of management material and staff trained in this way who move away to obtain promotion form a network of useful contacts in the wider industrial field. One judge defined goodwill as 'The probability that the old customer will return to the old outlet, in the old place, at some time in the future.' In personnel terms a policy of encouraging advancement increases goodwill and yields future dividends to the organization even from those who no longer work for the company but took their qualifications and experience elsewhere – often into related industries rather than to direct competitors.

8.6 The departmental system

A fuller discussion of the work of various departments is given in Part Three of this book, but it is worthwhile mentioning their main activities at this point. The need for departments arises from the wide variety of skills that are needed in any major business. For example, a manufacturing activity may require knowledge and skills in all sorts of technical procedures – metalworking, woodworking, glasscutting, painting and polishing. These are all very different from one another, but they can be grouped into a single department, the **Production Department** or **Factory**. Yet all this effort will have been fruitless if we cannot find any customers. The problems of marketing our product are totally different from the problems of making it, and we may need people skilled in advertising, selling, packaging etc. This group of activities is best performed by a separate Marketing Department.

The problem of the Managing Director, and ultimately the Board of Directors is to coordinate these activities so that they all go together

in the desired direction. A brief description of the various departments is as follows:

Purchasing Department or Buying Department

When we buy anything we want to get value for money. We need to
be able to specify the quality of the raw materials and components we
need; we have to negotiate a fair price so that we are not overcharged
and if we buy in bulk we can expect to get a more competitive price.
Consequently we don't let *anyone* buy for our company. We have a
team of specialist buyers·who alone may spend the company's money
on goods and services of every type. Every member of the staff who
needs anything from a tonne of steel to a pencil puts in a requisition
for it to the Buying Department and eventually the item will reach
the requisitioning party – but it will have been purchased by a
properly-run Buying Department. Usually the head of this department is a member of the Institute of Purchasing and Supply, a
professional body which sets high standards of education and training
for its members.

Production Department or the Factory

The Production Department sees to the manufacture of all the
products of a company. It starts with raw materials, whatever they
may be, and finishes up with a variety of saleable products and – quite
probably – a certain amount of waste. It tries to be as efficient as
possible and find uses for the waste material, or returns it for
recycling – for example scrap metal. One of the problems of production is the disposal of waste material – particularly waste material
which is harmful to the environment.

Marketing Department

Every company has a marketing problem. There are very few companies with a monopoly of the market (so that everyone who wants
the product must come to the company to buy it). Nearly everyone
has to search for customers, persuade them they need the product,
help them install it and give support during the initial period where
staff get used to it, and so on. Only a good product gets repeat orders,
so the Marketing Department will feed back to Head Office all the
snags customers meet, and the complaints customers make. The
Marketing Department plans advertising campaigns, keeps in touch
with wholesalers and retailers, sponsors public events where the
company's products can be displayed, etc.

Transport and Distribution Department

Physical distribution management is an important activity. It involves clearing the production lines which otherwise would get flooded with goods pouring off the ends of the lines, and getting the output away either into the warehouse, or into depots conveniently situated around the country, or direct to the customer – either the wholesaler, the retailer or the final consumer. All sorts of ways have been devised for clearing the production lines, and most of them involve the use of unitization procedures. Unitization is the making of one single load out of a great many smaller loads, by the use of pallets and containers which can be shifted in one movement by a forklift truck or a straddle-carrier. The Transport and Distribution Department is concerned with the making up of unit loads and their actual movement by road, rail, sea and air.

The Accounts Department

This department is concerned with all the financial aspects of business. It raises the original capital required; looks after all receipts and payments; ensures that wages are paid correctly and without any fraud or deception; keeps VAT records and other Customs and Excise accounts; maintains cost records so all sales items can be properly priced; works out the profits of the business; recommends to the Board the dividend that should be distributed (if any) and what reserves should be kept to meet future eventualities including growth of the business. It has a watching brief over all departmental expenditure – based on budgets for each department. Thus if the factory has budgeted a certain expenditure on wages for the year and by May it appears that the department instead of spending five-twelfths of the budget, has spent six-twelfths (i.e. half) the accountant will want to know why. Have wages been increased, or have staff numbers increased, or was the department's budget badly forecast? The department cannot go on as it is, or there will be no wages to pay anyone in November and December.

The General Administration Department

This department looks after all the routine affairs of the business – reception, porter services, cleaning, toilet facilities, canteen facilities, etc. The General Administration Officer is the first person we turn to with any problem concerning buildings, access to buildings, car parking, use of premises for functions, conferences, etc. and all domestic arrangements (i.e. arrangements within the firm or company). The officer needs to be an experienced, unflappable person, able to meet visitors at the highest level and to deal with all members of the staff and the public.

The Personnel Department

The Personnel Department is charged with the duty of obtaining for the firm such staff as it requires, with the necessary skills and abilities, experience and knowledge. It is not, as is popularly supposed, simply a welfare organization to look after staff. Naturally a Personnel Officer will try to keep staff, and help staff with any problems both within the firm and outside, but his/her function is to find labour of all sorts and grades as required. If the pattern of work changes he/she may be just as anxious to dispose of unwanted staff as to find new staff, and redundancy arrangements are just as much part of personnel work as recruitment.

8.7   A project on business organization

Draw up a business organization chart for the firm or company which employs you. If you are in full-time education draw up an organization chart for the school or college you are attending. In your chart you should be sure to designate:

(a)   The person in overall charge of the organization.
(b)   His/her immediate inferiors, i.e. the Board of Directors or the Senior Management Committee of the institution concerned.
(c)   People who might generally be described as 'middle management'. If the organization is so large that you could not possibly do this for the whole company at least do it for the department of which you are a member.
(d)   Then fill in the variety of low level positions in your own department.

Write a short explanation of the organization of the company or institution to complete the project, and bring out where any line of authority lies, whether there are any 'staff' features and what the departmental structure is.

8.8   Business organization and the new enterprise

The type of organization a new enterprise requires will vary with the type of business unit proposed. Dealing with the viewpoint of a sole trader we may say that few sole traders can manage entirely on their own, but will have some sort of support, whether unpaid family support, paid family support or paid employees. Certain principles should be decided upon, and written down for future reference, for example:

1   All orders to be signed by the sole trader – on properly drawn up forms which state clearly: 'No order is valid unless signed by the trader personally.'
2   All deliveries to be opened in the trader's presence and checked against the advice note and the original order.
3   All cheques to be signed by the trader personally.
4   Till receipts to be given to all customers and all tills to be openly displayed and not concealed in any way.
5   Written warning to be given to any employee found to be guilty of any malpractice, either with regard to goods or money.
6   Receipts to be given for all cash taken if a till is not used (otherwise Inland Revenue will suspect that records are less than complete).
7   If the sole trader is responsible for the book-keeping records state the day and time when this will be done (if not kept up to date earlier). For example, after closing hours on the last working day of each week is the best time. Most simple systems roll over into the next week at this time and the regular completion of the week's records at that time keeps such things as VAT records and receipts and payments records up to date and ready for inspection should this be required. If actual book-keeping is largely done as events occur we still need a regular review at a given time to ensure all is well.
8   A cash flow forecast should be prepared monthly and rolled forward as the year progresses, to give time to prepare for shortages by seeking an overdraft or loan, and to tuck away surpluses in a Deposit Account where they will be safe and not be a temptation to spend.
9   Interim final accounts should be prepared each quarter as quarterly figures for takings, purchases and overhead expenses are totted up. This lets us know how we are doing. It also involves a stocktaking check, which detects stock losses due to theft by staff, shoplifting, breakages, deterioration, etc.
10 All work done to be paid for on completion unless a credit period has been agreed with a customer. If so, bills to be made out promptly and delivered to the customer stating the date payment is due.

There may well be many other aspects to be considered.

8.9   Rapid revision

Answers	Questions
–	**1 Why are the vast majority of important private enterprise outlets limited companies?**
1 Because the shareholders have limited liability and are consequently more willing to invest in companies, as they only stand to lose the money they invest, not their entire worldly wealth.	**2 Who actually runs a company?**
2 The Board of Directors.	**3 What is the composition of a typical Board of Directors?**
3 A Chairman; a Deputy Chairman; a number of executive directors, including the Managing Director and the heads of all the major departments; a number of part-time non-executive directors.	**4 What is the point of having non-executive directors?**
4 They can bring useful experience or specialist knowledge to a company at quite small expense. They are also sometimes appointed at the insistence of outside companies who have either loaned considerable sums to the company or have taken quite a large share of the equity (ordinary shares) and feel entitled to have a representative on the Board.	**5 What are the twin functions of the Managing Director?**
5 (a) To implement the policies approved by the Board; (b) to report back to the Board on general progress and any	

Answers	Questions
difficulties arising from the attempt to put the policies into effect e.g. industrial relations problems, technical problems, marketing problems etc.	**6 What is meant by the orientation of a company?**
6 It means the main direction of its activities. The two main groups are product orientation and market orientation.	**7 What are the main features of a product-orientated company?**
7 (a) It has a product which is constantly in need of up-dating and variation, for reasons of overall efficiency, safety etc. – good example are automobiles and aviation; (b) the main emphasis is on the product, and the customers tend to seek out the suppliers.	**8 What are the main features of a market orientated company?**
8 (a) The product is in a finished form, and any changes in it are largely cosmetic only, of the type 'My powder gets clothes whiter'; (b) the aim is to sell to a very wide market, and maintain market share; (c) the product is usually branded e.g. Bold, Daz, Persil, Omo, etc.	**9 What is line organization?**
9 A military type of organization, where orders travel from the top level down the line to the least important members of staff, and reports travel back up the line.	**10 What is a 'staff' organization?**
10 It is one where certain specialist officers with a high-level, well-qualified staff are set up to deal with problems, usually at Head Office. Examples are legal departments, public relations departments, and personnel departments.	**11 What is a departmental organization?**

Answers	Questions
11 It is one where the main functions of a firm or company are organized as departments, with a line organization below the Head of Department but an obligation on the Heads of Departments to cooperate to achieve the objectives of the company.	**12 Go over the test again until you are sure of all the answers. Then try some of the questions in Section 8.10 below.**

8.10   Questions on Chapter 8

1   What is meant by the term 'organization chart'? Grove Nurseries (Ashbourne) Ltd has a Board of Directors of whom the Managing Director is the Chief Executive Director. Three other directors are the Chief Accountant, the Marketing Director and the Head of Purchasing. Each of these has three middle management staff, each of whom has four lower level staff. Draw a chart showing the organization of the business.

2   Explain the duties of the Chairman of the Board of a public limited company, and the part a non-executive director might play in a company's affairs.

3   'The solicitor described Mr Smith as the Chief Executive of an important public limited company, and a part-time director of forty-three other companies. The offences under consideration had been reported by a member of the middle-management team in the Accounts Department.' What are the meanings attached to the terms 'public limited company', 'part-time director' and 'middle management' in the paragraph above?

4   (a)   What is meant by delegation?

    (b)   The Board of a public company has approved in principle the holding of a conference in which fellow members of the industry will be invited to discuss environmental problems associated with their industry. A subcommittee of three senior staff is to be formed to see the project through. Which officials would you consider should be appointed to this subcommittee and what points would you list as being essential agenda items for their first meeting?

5   Why are objectives so important in the affairs of a firm or company? What is management by objectives?

9
The location of businesses

9.1 The need for premises

Every business requires premises, though many of them do start up in the entrepreneur's home. Remember Henry Ford, building his first engine on his mother's kitchen table. However, because many businesses make a noise, or produce fumes or smoke which may be unhealthy or irritating to ordinary citizens there are quite extensive planning requirements these days and not everyone can set up just where he/she chooses.

Some of the rules affecting planning permission are as follows:

- The character of the area and the local amenities should not be affected, for instance by noise, fumes, smells, parking problems or badly increased traffic.
- Is the land envisaged in the long term as being needed for socially-desirable developments, schools, roads, water resources, public parks, etc.? If so, conflicting proposed developments will be rejected.
- Are local services like water, gas, electricity and sewerage services available?
- Is the site itself undesirable (for example do old mine workings exist in the area)?

At the very least it will be necessary to make a 'change of use' planning application in which the Planning Authority for the area is informed of the intention to set up a new business at a given address. The local Planning Officer will look at the circumstances to see if any infringement of the local bye-laws or plans is likely to occur and if not the application will be recommended and passed at the monthly planning meeting. Even if no objections are raised this usually takes at least two months.

It is more likely that the location of a business is going to have some sort of impact upon the local community and a longer period of time must be allowed so that objectors to the proposal can have an opportunity to prepare and present a case for refusing the application. Before considering this possibility we will review the choice of a location from the point of view of the entrepreneur seeking to establish a new business.

9.2   Considerations when acquiring premises

The chief considerations may be as follows:

1   The working area available, including possible office space, storage space and parking space for vehicles. Room for future expansion may be important.
2   The availability of services, particularly electricity, water and gas (which is not available in many areas) and sewerage.
3   Whether the actual buildings are available already, or need to be built. If existing premises are available will they need adapting or redesigning (for example they may need to have a loading bay built on)?
4   What is the likely rateable value, and what is the rate per pound payable? UK business rates are now set centrally and are less under the influence of local councils.
5   Is the area convenient for (a) a Post Office; (b) banking services; (c) access for visitors and parking; (d) bus, train and possibly air services?
6   Are there plenty of work people in the area (if the business is going to need employees)?
7   Are business-to-business services and supplies good in the area? Many businesses save money by buying in services from other businesses if they only need the service occasionally. For example many people do not have a photocopier but pop round to the local copy shop. Many firms do not have a company car – but use a local 'Hiravan' or (as one local hire firm call themselves) 'Hire-a-banger'. For the odd delivery job a 'banger' may be good enough. Business-to-business services make setting up a much easier problem.
8   Are there any special requirements for this particular business which need to be met when the location of the business is being decided?

9.3   Setting up a business in a domestic property

In order to assist the employment situation the government has introduced an Enterprise Allowance Scheme which allows an unemployed person who wants to try self-employment to draw £40 per week for one year to help him/her to get started. A married couple, if both are genuinely unemployed, can obtain £40 per week each. Many such businesses start up in the domestic premises of the parties concerned and the question of whether a business of that type may start up in that location at once arises.

The general rules are:

1 Will the home still be mainly a home, used substantially as a private residence?
2 Will any part of it manifestly no longer be a home – for instance will it be a workshop, or a laundry, or changed to some clearly business use.
3 Will there be a marked increase in visitors to the premises, and will they present traffic problems, noise and obstruction to other residents?
4 Will the business disturb the neighbours, by noise, fumes, unpleasant odours or traffic movements at unsocial hours?

9.4 What happens when objections are raised?

If a development is likely to cause local objections the developer will be required to display public notices in prominent places for a short period before the matter comes up before the Planning Committee of the local council. Anyone who wishes to do so may raise objections, and in the initial stages these views will be considered by the Planning Committee. There is a rule that there is always a *'presumption in favour of development'*. This is a legal term which states a fundamental freedom of UK citizens. If a person wishes to develop an enterprise, and if it does nobody any harm, or if the balance of good it does is in favour of proceeding with the development, the planning authorities have no right to prevent it. Everyone is free to enrich himself/herself, and it is hoped that in doing so benefits will also accrue to the general public as well. We are all interested in prosperity.

On the other hand, if the balance is not in favour of the developer, permission will be refused. The developer may then appeal, and if necessary a public enquiry will be held. If permission is granted, the objectors who feel their views have been overruled may bring an action to compel a more careful consideration of their points of view, but the legal expense is an important consideration, since if a case is lost the objectors may have to pay the costs of the developer as well as their own costs. Another rule of law is that the law takes no account of trivialities, so that minor objections are rarely worth going to law about.

9.5 Restrictive covenants in leases and deeds

One point that many householders are not familiar with is that there are often restrictive covenants in leases and deeds which prevent property being developed in a particular way. A covenant is a promise, and when land is developed to build an estate of houses it is often the case that the person selling the land extracts certain promises from the developer which are passed on in the deeds to the new house owners. These may prevent the householder from using the premises for business purposes, even if planning permission is given by the local authority. It is always wise to have a lawyer check deeds for this kind of restrictive clause.

Points to remember

- Every area has its own local development plan which envisages possible future uses for the land. Any proposed development which does not conflict with this regional plan will be approved because there is a 'presumption in favour of development'.
- However, if the development is likely to have adverse effects on local residents – smoke, fumes, noise, traffic problems, parking problems, etc., permission may be refused.
- Anyone proposing to locate in a new area, whether by setting up in business or by moving in an existing business will consider its individual needs carefully. These are premises, services (gas, water, electricity, sewage disposal and telephonic communications), labour, room for future expansion and support from other businesses, such as banks, postal services, lawyers, printing, plumbing, building, decorating and cleaning services.

9.6 A project on starting a business in your own home

In this project you are asked to imagine that you are setting up a business in the career you hope eventually to follow, or if you have not yet decided upon that, in your favourite hobby. You are then asked to assess your own home as a suitable place for starting the business. If your own home could be used, what changes, alterations, etc., might be necessary. What would be its favourable aspects and its limitations. Think through all the processes and procedures that would be necessary and write a report about the whole idea.

If your home would definitely not be of any use in such a project say why not. Outline the type of premises that would be needed, the location that you would have to look for, and write a full report setting out the detailed requirements.

9.7   Other reasons for location

When studying any locality it is always worthwhile asking yourself
'Why was this particular plant, factory or other business establishment set up in this particular spot?' The answers can tell you much
about both the needs of business and the responses business makes to
inducements offered by central and local government. The following
reasons for location might be identified in your own home area. Each
of them is discussed in a separate paragraph below. When you have
studied these in detail decide if any of them are relevant to your own
home town.

1   Closeness to a source of raw materials.
2   Closeness to a source of power.
3   Closeness to a means of transport.
4   Closeness to a financial centre.
5   Closeness to a supply of labour.
6   Closeness to the market.
7   Suitability of climate.
8   Stability of political atmosphere.
9   A natural geographical catchment area.

Closeness to a source of raw materials

Historically, closeness to a source of raw materials was always an
important consideration when locating any business. It is less influential today because our transport systems are so much more
efficient that bulk raw materials can be moved relatively easily,
especially in ships like ULCCs (ultra-large crude carriers), tankers
and ore carriers. The best example today of location near a source of
raw materials are the cement works, which are dotted around the
chalk hills and limestone hills of the UK. The chief ingredients of
cement manufacture are chalk, clay and flint, all fairly heavy commodities. Cement itself is fairly easy to transport, either in bulk
vehicles with pressure discharge facilities which force the product out
at the destination, or in sacks which are easily handled by forklift
trucks on pallets. It is, therefore, sensible to locate near the raw
material, and move the finished product.

Closeness to a source of power

Traditionally, closeness to a source of power was an important
consideration. In the Industrial Revolution the iron industry moved
from Kent and other forest areas to the North of England where
water power was available from streams running off the Pennines.
Later, when steam power became available industry relocated to the

coal fields. Today in the UK we can get power at the touch of a switch in every corner of the country, so location near a source of power is less important. In other parts of the world, where long distance means loss of power due to the heating up of cables, location close to a source of power is important, and industry grows up around features like the Aswan Dam in Egypt, or the Dneiper Dam in Russia. Some aluminium smelters, which use huge quantities of power, are located at very isolated power dams where the electricity can be used more economically on site than by distributing it over huge distances. The best example is Kitimat in British Columbia.

Closeness to a means of transport

Transport is essential to every business, but if roads are good as they are in the UK almost everywhere can have reasonable transport. However, there are economies to be achieved by locating in the following areas:

(a)   *Close to ports*   Especially if imports are an important element in the industry concerned. Thus oil refineries are almost always located on estuaries such as the Thames Estuary, Southampton Water, the Clyde, etc. The South Coast and East Anglian ports which are accessible to Europe have grown in importance as trade within the European Community has increased.

(b)   *Close to motorways*   Practically every motorway junction is today a potential site for industry and housing because access to the motorway network gives a cost advantage in transport. Despite some horrific crashes, motorways are the safest roads in the country, delivery speeds are high despite the occasional traffic jam, motorway service areas are excellent rest points and changeover points for lorry drivers of bulk haulage vehicles. A firm doing long haul deliveries between factories and depots can select a service area half way on the journey and arrange for drivers starting at each end of the journey to meet there. A vehicle leaving Newcastle and driving south to say the Peterborough area can meet a vehicle driving up from the West Country. The drivers change vehicles and return home with goods which have travelled 300–400 miles in a single day.

(c)   *Within a freeport area*   If an area is designated a freeport, whether it is an actual seaport or an airport, it means that imported raw materials and components can be landed, re-packaged, manufactured or assembled within the freeport area without paying customs duty. The resulting product can then be re-exported without any levy of customs duties or if it is to be sold in the home market the customs duty is paid as it crosses the boundary of the freeport area and enters the general hinterland of the home country. This is often an administrative convenience for industries which pay heavy import duties – for example tobacco, wine and spirits. The customs duty is not paid until much closer to the selling date of the finished product, or in the case of re-exports need not be paid at all.

Closeness to a financial centre

Finance plays a large part in the successful conduct of many enterprises and those who wish to join and participate in the various markets tend to locate near, or actually in, major financial centres. This might not seem as essential as in former times, since telephonic and computerized communication now makes it as easy to deal in New York, Tokyo or Sydney as in London. On the other hand, one still needs staff who are knowledgeable in the various fields of finance, banking, insurance, foreign exchange, countertrade, forfaiting and similar activities. Countertrade (sometimes called compensation trade) is trading with countries who are short of foreign exchange, and who want to pay partly in goods. Forfaiting is a way of obtaining payment from foreign importers by getting a guarantee facility from a bank in the importer's country. The people who know how to do these things are in short supply, and tend to be found already working in the major financial centres. It is wise to locate in these areas if you are proposing to set up these kinds of financial sector businesses.

Closeness to a supply of labour

The importance of labour which is knowledgeable and skilled has been referred to above. There have been some important examples of location near a labour force, for example the Ford works at Dagenham was located where it is partly because it was on the River Thames with good shipping facilities but mainly because the whole area was a developing London-overspill area at the time (in the 1920s) and there was an abundant, easily-trained labour force available. Many firms locate in new towns because of the labour that is available as people move to the new town from overcrowded inner-city areas. Milton Keynes, the first new city, is a particular example of a labour force being made available in what was previously a fairly sparsely inhabited rural area.

Closeness to the market

Certain products do not travel well in their finished form, either because they are perishable or easily damaged. A good example is quality furniture, which is often bulky; has doors, drawers and fittings which are easily strained in transit and is often highly polished and easily blemished. Such products are best produced in factories as close to big markets as possible. You therefore find that furniture factories are often located on the outskirts of major cities, so that the majority of the output has only a short distance to travel before it reaches the market.

These problems can be reduced by proper packaging, and the modern materials for packaging, such as polystyrene, have certainly reduced the need to be close to the market. Similarly, cheaper furniture which can be sold in kit form and put together by the householder when the package arrives, do travel more easily and more economically. Quality furniture, however, will always be best produced as close to the market as possible.

Suitability of climate

Climate is less important today than in former times because we can control the climate in factories today with such devices as central heating, humidifiers, air conditioning, etc. The best example of climatic influence over location was the setting up of the cotton industry in Lancashire during the nineteenth century – the generally damp conditions being better for cotton spinning, since the threads break if they are too dry. In dry weather the floors were hosed down with water, which led to the cotton workers wearing wooden clogs. Today's climate is less of a problem.

Stability of political atmosphere

Political stability is very important to business. Not only must we be able to get our raw materials without difficulty but we must be free of any worries about the expropriation of assets, or the seizure of finished products. At one time the oil companies built their refineries near the source of the raw material in such countries as Iraq and Iran. When these assets were expropriated by the various types of governments which assumed control the oil companies realized that it was better to bring the crude oil in in tankers to be refined in the UK and other European countries where stable governments meant that business activities could be pursued more safely. The student might usefully observe from afar the effects on business of unstable governments around the Third World, for example in South America, Africa and South-east Asia.

The effects of a natural geographical catchment area

Some parts of a country form a natural geographical catchment area where businesses can only locate logically in one particular spot. For example, the rivers and roads may be forced by the topography in a particular direction and as a result a particular location acts as a bottleneck where all the business activities naturally occur. Both central and local government, and all major firms, depots and offices will gravitate towards the logical point and the whole area will be run from this natural centre of activity. Students should consider their own areas and ask whether such a natural site exists in the area, and what institutions, industries and markets have been established.

9.8   Location and industrial inertia

Industrial inertia is the tendency of an industry to stay in the same place once it has established itself, even though the original reasons for its location have long ceased to exist. The best example is Sheffield, which was originally established as the steel centre for the UK because it was near the essential raw materials – iron ore, limestone and coal. The iron ore was long ago exhausted and has to be brought in from Spain and Sweden, but the steel industry still survives, though in a more modest form, producing many special steels.

You may be able to find local examples of industrial inertia in your own home area – for example warehouses still operating in premises or from land near rivers and canals even though there is no inland waterway traffic calling at them, and all goods are handled by road.

9.9   A project on the location of industry

In any locality it should be possible to work out (or perhaps find out) why a particular business enterprise is located where it is. You should study a number of different businesses, some old and well-established businesses and new ones being established right at this moment. We might, for example, find that some businesses were simply set up in this present situation because local authorities built a business park and made sure all the necessary facilities were available. We might find that access to a motorway, or to a port were important considerations. Your project brochure should consist of a number of pages based on the location report shown in Figure 9.1.

Location report

Name of firm ....
Address ....
....
.... Post code ....
Nature of business ....
....
Estimated number
of employees ....

Do any of the following factors
seem to be important in the
location of this firm? Write Y for
Yes, N for No, P for Possibly

Closeness to its source of
  raw materials   ...
Closeness to main road
  network   ...
Closeness to a port   ...
Closeness to a railway
  station   ...
Closeness to an airport   ...
Do you think the land was
  cheap, at least when the
  firm started?   ...
Do you think the climate
  made any difference to
  the location of this firm? ...
Is the firm environmentally
  undesirable, and did this
  influence the location?
Did it locate where it is
  because there is a
  reasonable market for its
  goods or services?   ...
Do you think being near a
  housing estate or some
  supply of labour was
  important for this firm? ...
Would you say the firm is
  situated in a natural
  geographical area to
  which business would
  naturally flow?   ...

Information discovered
Give a brief account of any points.
Put N/A if 'not applicable'.
What raw materials are used? ....
....
How are they brought into the
  firm? ....
....
What finished products are made?
....
....
How do they leave the firm? .....
....
Does the firm use road vehicles? ..
Does it use inland waterway
  barges? ....
Does it use shipping? ....
Does it have private rail sidings? ..
Does it use air freighting services?
....
What sort of skills do the
  employees seem to have ....
....
....
Does the firm serve local people?
....
Does it serve other businesses? ...
What sort of power does the firm
  use? Tick: Water power ....
  Gas .... Electricity ....
  Steam ....
Are these facilities handy nearby.
  Tick if they are: Post Office ....
  Bank .... Police ....
  Solicitors .... Garage ....
  Station .... Taxi ....
Does the firm get any special
  support from the local
  government?
....
Does any central government body
  seem to assist it? ....

Report: So far as I can discover the main reasons for this firm being
located where it is are ....
....
....
....

Figure 9.1 A form for checking up on the reasons for the location of
firms and companies

9.10 Rapid revision

Answers	Questions
–	**1 What is the essential rule about the use of premises for business purposes?**
1 They are subject to planning permission which must be obtained in advance.	**2 What is the presumption in any planning application?**
2 There is a presumption in favour of development.	**3 What is the idea behind this presumption?**
3 (a) The idea is that everyone is interested in prosperity, and we should not interfere with any activity that might bring prosperity unless there is a good reason; (b) everyone is free to use his/her talents to enrich himself/herself, and we should not interfere with this freedom without good reason.	**4 What are the basic considerations in any planning decision?**
4 (a) Will the local amenities be affected by smoke, fumes, noise or smells? (b) Will the development increase traffic or present road safety problems? (c) Is the land earmarked for some other social use, schools, recreation grounds, water resources, road developments, etc? (d) Is the site undesirable (old mines, flooding, etc.)? (e) Will there be problems laying on services, gas, water, electricity, telephone lines, etc?	**5 What considerations enter into the choice of business premises?**

Answers	Questions
5 Is the space available adequate, including office space, warehousing, access to premises, car parking, etc? (b) Is there room for future development? (c) Are the premises suitable or do they need expensive alterations and refitting? (d) What is the rateable value, and business rate payable? (e) Are all domestic services available – gas, water, electricity, sewerage, telecommunications, etc? (f) Are all ancillary services available – post offices, banks, solicitors, buses, trains and possibly airport services? (g) Is labour available in the area, of the right quality and potential? (h) Are local 'business-to-business' services good – copy-shop, stationery, printing, vehicle-hire etc. as required?	6 **What is a restrictive covenant in a lease or contract?**
6 It is a clause which restricts the person moving in from using the premises in a way deemed undesirable by the original developer. It may refer to the buildings themselves (e.g. any alterations to use yellow bricks only) or to the purpose for which the premises are to be used (e.g. not to be used as a fast food restaurant).	7 **List the likely reasons for locating a business in a particular place.**
7 (a) Closeness to raw materials; (b) closeness to a source of power; (c) closeness to a means of transport – a motorway, port or airport; (d) closeness to a financial centre; (e) closeness to a supply of labour; (f) closeness to the market; (g) suitability of climate; (h) stability of political environment; (i) a natural geographical catchment area.	8 **Go over the test again until you are sure of all the answers. Then try questions in Section 9.11 below.**

9.11   Questions on Chapter 9

1   Tom Smith is setting up a small manufacturing business, but the only premises he can find (although reasonably priced) are rather larger than he really needs. What arguments would you advance in favour of taking the premises?

2   Penelope and Catherine tell you they have decided to open a home workshop to wash, dry and iron clothes for local house-wives. They have made no sort of plans at all, except to order two washing machines, two tumbler driers and some ironing equipment. What would you advise?

3   Explain the viewpoint of a local authority Planning Department when asked to approve the development of an existing market garden into a pig farm, for open-air rearing of fifty sows with litters.

4   *To whom it may concern:*   Take notice that I, John Henry Williamson, of 2859 Hopview Lane, Murview, Dorset, have applied for planning permission to use the field behind this property for a breaker's yard and used car lot. Objections may be made to Murview Rural District Council by 31 March 19.... What objections might be raised to such a proposal?

5   Consider the capital city of your own country.
   (a)   Why was it originally established where it is.
   (b)   What caused industry and commerce to develop it to its present size.
   (c)   If it is still growing, what factors continue to make it attractive as a location.
   (d)   If it is declining, why is it no longer attractive as a location.

6   Why are motorway junctions causing property values and land values to rise in the immediate surrounding area.

7   In your own country select two examples of location near each of the following: (a) a source of raw material; (b) a river; (c) the seashore (if available); (d) a railway; (e) a main road; (f) a source of power; (g) a centre of government.

10
The size of businesses: growth, merger and takeover

10.1 The small business

Nearly all businesses start small and may take a considerable time to grow. On the other hand, newspapers are full of rags-to-riches stories about young people who break out of their small businesses within a few years to reach a flotation on the Stock Exchange and overnight millionaire status, so it seems some firms do grow much faster than average. A good idea, a useful invention, good fortune in being in the right place at the right time and many other reasons might be advanced for this better-than-average performance, but perseverance, hard work and a nice calculation of risks have usually much to do with it.

Most entrepreneurs start out as sole traders, and the advantages of being a sole trader have already been listed (see Chapter 6). However, from the point of view of the size of a business the sole trader organization is at a disadvantage. Unless the niche occupied by the trader is naturally small (a village will rarely need more than one watch repairer) it is difficult for a small business to achieve the 'best' size for a business. The 'best' size in economics is referred to as the **optimum size**. It is often decided by the machinery or equipment that is used in the industry. For example, a plain paper copying machine may be able to run off 20,000 copies a month. A trader who is only likely to need 100 pieces of copying a month will find it is not worth buying a copier, while a firm that needs 500,000 copies a month, produced on long print runs will find that a plain paper copier is no use, and it must look at high-speed offset copiers. The sole trader will probably find this beyond his/her pocket, and most look around for financial backing. The solution may be a partnership with a like-minded person, but it may be necessary to become a limited company and seek the cooperation of someone with spare capital. This is often referred to as **venture capital**. The organization or individual with surplus funds is prepared to take shares in the business and a part-time directorship, providing funds and expert advice, for the mutual benefit of the trader seeking to grow and the investor seeking a safe return on the investment. More of this later. First, consider the factors affecting the size of the business, which may generally be divided into two classes – technical factors and market factors.

10.2 Factors affecting the size of a business

1 *Technical factors*   Often the technology in use decides the size of the business. Frequently a technical process will only operate if it is at a critical size, or it may only be economic if it is operated at a certain minimum level. A sewing machine can sew up one garment at a time, but a sophisticated lay of material where garments are cut out through fifty layers of cloth and with the patterns cut out by laser beam is going to keep a great many machinists busy. Such methods are only possible for the large mass-production firm, and they will undercut any individual seamstress, or bespoke tailor who is using more individual methods.

2 *The division of labour*   We know that specialization is the key to high productivity and therefore to wealth creation. The small business is unable to take full advantage of the division of labour into specialist activities and processes, because this requires a large number of employees each with his/her own specialist skills. The various activities are arranged sequentially, with work flowing through the factory or around the site, or even around the office with each individual performing his/her particular activity.

3 *The least-common-multiple principle*   In many manufacturing situations this principle influences optimum size. For example, if a component is made on a machine which can process five items per hour and then goes to a second process on another machine which can only process three items per hour, the ideal arrangement will be an output of some common multiple of five and three – the lowest of which is fifteen. Thus an output of fifteen items per hour will keep three machines of the first type and five machines of the second type busy. If output is to be greater than fifteen per hour we should raise output in steps of fifteen – to thirty, forty-five, sixty units per hour, etc. In this way we can purchase further machines in economic groups of three and five, and they will all be kept busy. Of course, the least common multiple principle does not apply to all processes – for example where an item can be made very quickly (say 15,000 items per hour) we would not envisage continuous production but would use **batch production**. We make a batch of 15,000 volume control knobs, or whatever the item is, and take them into store to be issued as required. When the batch is getting near the end we requisition a further supply from the Production Department.

4   *Market size*   The size of the market is very influential in deciding optimum size. Many items are in limited demand, and a small firm, using small-scale methods of production, can meet the demand. This is particularly true of craft items, where the individual skill of a craftsman is being used to make individual items. Musical instruments, golf clubs, false teeth and countless other items are made in this way. Where some sort of standardization is possible, and the demand is large enough, some degree of mass production can be introduced. Thus although spectacles are needed in every case to suit the personal needs of an individual, the defects in the human eye which need correction by spectacles follow such similar patterns that almost every type of corrective lens can be produced by mass production methods and be available as standard items. In other cases, cars for example, mass production methods can be used and designs only need to include minor adaptations to suit individual peculiarities such as an adjustable driver's seat or adjustable mirrors. The production of goods for the general market, rather than the 'bespoke' market, is invariably large-scale production.

5   *Bespoke mass production*   A more modern development is the linking of mass production with bespoke engineering in what has been called 'flexible manufacturing'. The idea is that mass production still takes place, but not necessarily by big organizations, but by relatively small firms who find out, or are shown, how to make small parts, miniature components. Having mastered the intricacies of their little bit, they then make them by the million for everyone who needs them, the goods being available *ex catalogue* at very economical prices and yet of the very highest quality. The design engineer wanting three widgets, a wotsit and a pair of thingammies browses through the catalogues and orders the bits. Almost any piece of electronic apparatus can be made in this way. It makes it easy for someone with a bright idea, a knowledge of what the public wants (or can be made to want) and a small amount of capital to break into production using components that are already invented and available. Just where these ideas, which are in their infancy, will lead remains to be seen, but it brings a new approach to research and development. How can we use bits we, and other people, have made for some original purpose in different ways to create new products and new applications?

10.3   The economies of large-scale operations

It is usual to divide the economies of large-scale operation into two parts – the internal economies which can be achieved within the firm and the external economies which are achieved outside the firm. They are often listed as follows:

1   Technical economies

These are economies where the use of some piece of technical equipment raises output and productivity. For example, a large firm can buy the most technically-advanced machines, high-powered and fast. It can install complex layouts for flow production, feeding components in at the best point. It can use robot devices for routine processes. Its network of physical distribution can be highly mechanized, with unit loads weighing up to 44 tonnes being moved by container cranes, straddle carriers and heavy duty forklift trucks.

2   Marketing economies

There are many ways in which the marketing of products can lead to cost-cutting and more economic working. For example, a large firm usually distributes its products to regional depots, serving a natural, and manageable catchment area. There are huge economies to be had in the 'in-plant' printing field. For example, Debenhams need 30 million tickets for labelling displays in their shops every year, and have found that by setting up a specialist department they can streamline the creation of attractive notices, price-tickets, etc., and at the same time achieve a useful uniformity throughout the group. Such uniformity also achieves good control of displays from the legal point of view, for example to ensure compliance with rules about consumer credit, pricing of items in sales, etc.

Packaging can often achieve economies, for example the package in which children's toys are marketed can, if properly designed, be part of the display material, drawing attention to the product, its price, etc. The mere display of the package is effective store promotion, without any need for specialist display notices or window dressing.

3   Administrative and other economies

A large firm can afford specialist teams in all sorts of administrative areas – for example a Personnel Department can find staff more efficiently and cheaply if it has routine procedures for finding labour of the types and numbers required, inducting them carefully so they settle in well and listening to complaints if they threaten to leave. A specialist Accounts Department will similarly exercise control over costs and a collection of payments from debtors. It will obtain discounts from suppliers, supervise wages, prevent abuses such as misuse of the telephone systems, etc. These are the financial economies of large scale. Other economies can be achieved in research, and in welfare, safety, etc.

Points to remember

- The best size for any business is said to be the optimum size.
- This optimum size may be decided by the market, or by the capital equipment necessary, or by some other limiting factor which controls the best size for that particular business at that particular moment in time.
- Generally speaking large scale brings certain economies of scale, particularly technical economies, marketing economies and administrative economies.
- The division of labour into specialist activities generally encourages more economic operations, because the operatives become very skilled over a more limited range of activities and thus produce more output of improved quality.

10.4   How firms and companies grow

There are many aspects to growth. First, all growth costs money, because growth requires us to extend our premises, buy more plant and machinery, office equipment, motor vehicles etc. We may need to extend into new areas, setting up branches, depots, area offices, etc. The most satisfactory way to finance growth is to do it out of the profits of the existing business, a process known as **self-financing**. If the business is a sole trader or partnership business, the profits must be large enough to permit the proprietor or partners to have reasonable amounts of drawings for their private needs and still leave some funds to use for expansion. If this is not the case the business can grow by borrowing money from banks, finance houses and similar institutions, but these institutions will charge interest – usually at least 14 per cent and often rather more. This means that the cream of the profits made as a result of the expansion will be skimmed off by the interest payable.

This is also true of companies, but remember that the profits made by a company, although they belong to the shareholders can only be paid out to them if the directors recommend a dividend. If the directors do not recommend a dividend the shareholders will naturally be annoyed, but the directors may pass the dividend on the grounds that expansion of the business is more important, and in the better interest of the company as a whole. Usually a compromise will be arrived at, the directors recommending only a small dividend and keeping back most of the profits for use in expanding the business.

Business finance is a major study in its own right and we cannot deal with it too fully in a book of this sort – but there is more about it in Part Three of this book (see Chapter 11).

Vertical integration

The word integration means 'to complete an important thing by adding parts to it'. We can add parts to a firm in three ways – **vertically, horizontally** and **laterally**. Thinking of vertical integration first, we could allow our company to grow by adding parts above and below the existing parts. For example, suppose a car manufacturing company finds that it is always having difficulties with its suppliers of raw materials and components, such as steel, tyres, glass for wind-screens etc. It may, as the opportunity arises and profits become available for extending the business, extend downwards to become its own raw material and components supplier. It might acquire a steel works, and produce only the grades, qualities and thicknesses of steel it needs, controlling the quality to meet its requirements. It might acquire a rubber factory and makes its own tyres. It might go even further down and buy a rubber plantation in Malaya to provide the raw material for the rubber factory. Equally it could extend vertically upwards, buying car-transporter firms which will move its products to the garage sales outlets, and garages that will actually sell its cars. In that way it becomes a completely integrated company from raw materials producer, through manufacturing and distribution to the final retailer.

In rather a similar way the cooperative societies own tea gardens in the Far East, with factories which ferment and chop the leaves, blending houses which mix the teas to give a variety of blends and retail outlets where the tea is sold to the final consumer. This is vertical integration.

Horizontal integration

Horizontal integration takes place at the same level as the existing firm. We see this happening all around us in the UK these days as more and more branches of major retailers open up in every town throughout the length and breadth of the country. Thus there is a Marks and Spencer in almost every town, and a Boots, and a branch of W. H. Smith etc. These outlets are served by local wholesale depots which deliver daily on a 'just in time' (JIT) basis. 'Just in time' is a concept which tries to supply retail branches just in time before they run out of a particular item. Most of these stores have EFTPOS sales tills. EFTPOS stands for 'electronic funds transfer at the point of sale'. All the items in the shop are marked with bar codes read by electronic devices which not only show the item purchased on the till screen but also search the computer's memory for the price, record

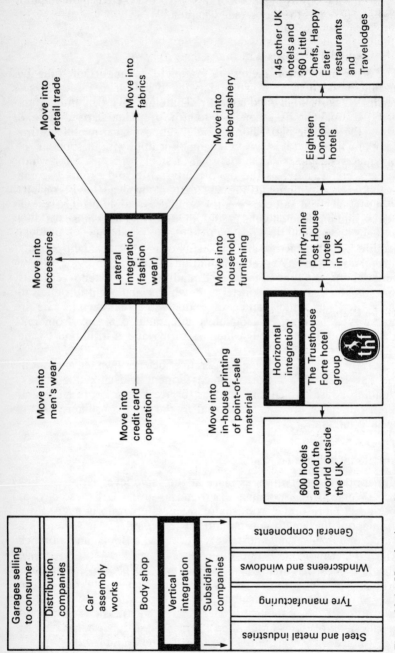

Figure 10.1 How businesses grow

Lateral integration (fashion wear)
- Move into retail trade
- Move into fabrics
- Move into haberdashery
- Move into household furnishing
- Move into in-house printing of point-of-sale material
- Move into credit card operation
- Move into men's wear
- Move into accessories

Horizontal integration
The Trusthouse Forte hotel group — thf

- 600 hotels around the world outside the UK
- Thirty-nine Post House Hotels in UK
- Eighteen London hotels
- 145 other UK hotels and 360 Little Chefs, Happy Eater restaurants and Travelodges

Vertical integration

Garages selling to consumer	Distribution companies	Car assembly works	Body shop	Subsidiary companies

Subsidiary companies:
- Steel and metal industries
- Tyre manufacturing
- Windscreens and windows
- General components

the stock movement as the goods are sold and if the customer pays by credit card seek authorization for the transaction and charge the money to the customer's account. The stock records, fed through to the depot, alert the depot that stocks of the item are getting low and the computer arranges a further supply JIT.

With horizontal integration a company that has established itself in one area and developed a good system in its business affairs grows by doing the same thing in the next town and the next town, and so on. It is repeating the same processes in every branch, using the skills and the expertise it has developed and broadening its share of the market.

Lateral integration

Lateral integration is a process of growth by a side-step into a related industry. Thus a firm manufacturing toothbrushes and 'Doing very nicely thank you', might move into toothpaste manufacture, and then into cosmetics, and then into hair shampoos etc. It adds on products as it has the funds to finance the expansion, hiring extra staff with the necessary 'know-how' and gradually establishing itself in a wider and wider range of goods and services.

10.5   Planning for growth

The small business grows in slow stages as the initial projects become success stories and make it possible to go further with new projects which, hopefully, in their turn will be successful. As growth occurs we reach a point where we need to start planning ahead in a formal way. We can no longer rely on a vague feeling that we must look for new products and new projects. We have to have a more organized approach to growth. The stages are:

1   Understanding where we are now – our present position.
2   Deciding where we want to get to.
3   Developing a business strategy.
4   Putting the plan into action.

Understanding where we are now

This involves looking carefully at our present position and studying all the figures that are available about our business. Some of these are:

1   *The turnover*   Turnover is best expressed as the sales made (less any returns). It is sometimes, therefore, called the 'net turnover'. For a company selling products of various sorts we have these figures collected into a Sales Account (*less* Sales Return Account)

which records all the goods invoiced to customers. If we don't sell goods, but give a service the turnover is simply the fees we have invoiced to customers for our services rendered. Increasing our turnover is the main requirement for the growth of any business.

2   *The number of employees*   This is an easy figure to arrive at. Most managers know exactly how many people they employ – but in a big firm the Personnel Officer will know the figures. However, it isn't just the numbers that matter, it's the quality of their labour; the skills they have, and the training that they need if we move into an expansionary phase. Growth requires us to invest in people, as well as in machines, and we have to retrain as required. Another aspect of the present labour position is the labour turnover. What percentage of workers leave in any year. To find this we use the percentage calculation:

$$\frac{\text{Number of leavers in year}}{\text{Number of employees}} \times 100$$

For example, if 275 people leave in the year out of 986 employees, we have:

$$\text{Labour turnover} = \frac{275}{986} \times 100 = 27.9 \text{ per cent}$$

This is more than one-quarter of our staff leaving each year.

3   *The life cycle of every product*   Every product has a life cycle. There will be some that still have a long life ahead of them and we can expect them to earn profits for years to some. Others will be selling less well than they did. Perhaps our plan can give them a new lease of life – new packaging, new variations – but still basically the same product. Others will be getting to the end of their life cycle. Have we got new products coming along which will replace these obsolete lines?

4   *The plant and machinery and other assets*   Not only do all machines wear out, but methods of manufacture change. A quarter of all the goods made in the UK today are made of materials not even invented twenty-five years ago. New materials usually mean new plant and machinery. We must look carefully at all such items – will our factory be totally out of date in ten years?

Deciding where we want to get to

Planning is usually short-term planning for the small company. The aim is to see where we want to go in the next two years and we can then ask ourselves what staff we need to achieve the plans envisaged, what premises, equipment, etc. will be required, what it is all going to cost and how we are going to finance it etc. This amounts to saying that we need to develop a business strategy for the next two years. We need to quantify (express in numerical and financial terms) what it is we hope to do and we need to designate someone to oversee each particular programme. If there is an area which cannot be handled by existing staff we need to appoint a suitable person, with the right qualities and skills.

In deciding where we want to get to we have to look at the business world in which we operate and our particular industry. We know what our present situation is, because we have just reviewed it. The question is 'Where do we want to go now?' This may be a matter of market share – we want to grow to a certain point which we believe is possible and to develop a strategy to get this growth. It may be that we plan to fill a particular niche in the industry and have to overcome certain opposition to get there. It may be that we have to change direction, because certain lines are reaching the end of their life cycle, and the new products mean a shift into new materials, new ranges, new suppliers etc. Whatever it is we need to:

1 Define the vision we have of the future.
2 Set specific, attainable, objectives for the two-year period ahead.

The specific objectives can be graded by time into short-term objectives (the things we have to do first), longer-term objectives and final objectives as we approach the end of our two-year allowance of time. Of course, by the time we get to the end of that two years we shall have rolled the objective forward again, but we should, all the time, be passing milestones laid down earlier in the planning programme.

Developing a business strategy

The stages in creating an effective business strategy are as follows:

1 Define the vision of the future and specify the objectives we must attain to achieve the vision.
2 Consider the various ways we could achieve each objective (the options open to us) and discuss which is the best option. If you cannot be sure then set a date in the near future, after preliminary enquiries have been made, when a firm decision will be made.
3 Appoint one individual to act as project leader for each objective and to be responsible for progressing it so far as is possible. A deadline for reporting back on each objective should be set.
4 Help the individual by examining the present organization in the light of the objective. In particular, try to identify any obstacles to success in the present organization and the possible remedies for them. Which features of the present system shall we retain and which shall we need to change?

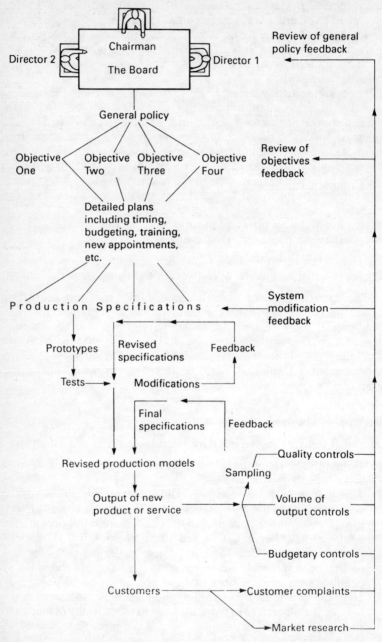

Figure 10.2   Planning for growth

5 Budget for the changes. A budget is a forecast of the expenses involved. It is usual to appoint someone as **budget officer** who will call for a budget from each project leader. The **budget period** is the time interval for which the budget is required. Often it is one year, but it may be less, and it may be rolled forward every half year. We may have a **sales budget**, a **production budget**, an **administration budget**, a **'special event' budget**, a **capital expenditure budget** and so on. Each budget will be broken down into its basic parts, materials, labour, office overheads, capital expenditure, fuel, transport etc. – it depends upon the budget. Once the budget is complete it will be reviewed by the management (in a very big company there might be a special Budget Committee) and once it is agreed the project leader can start to spend. The actual costs incurred will be compared with the budget, and any **variance** will be investigated. A variance can arise from outside the business (inflation etc.) or inside the business (wage increases, spoilt work, excessive overtime etc.). They could just result from poor budgeting – the person who drew up the budget having taken insufficient care to enquire about prices, time required for a job etc. The aim of the plan is to achieve the objective, on time, and inside the budget. Budgets are an essential activity for growing businesses.

Putting the plan into action

To put such a plan into action it is necessary to give the project leaders a clear signal that they may start work on their projects and clear accounts of any restraints on timing, cost, etc., within which they must work. They will then start to get their teams moving, reporting back on such snags as arise, about which management should be informed. Costs will be recorded as they occur and compared with the budgeted figure; warnings being sent of any adverse variance that arises so investigations into the causes can be made. A succession of feedback activities will ensure that modifications to the plan are implemented quickly (see Figure 10.2) and once the new product or service is launched the results will be monitored to see whether the growth envisaged is actually being realized and the objectives achieved.

10.6 Growth and company status

Some companies start by being set up on Day 1 of the business as an 'off-the-shelf' company purchased for £120 from a company formation agent. Others start as sole traders, develop into partnerships and eventually register as private limited companies as part of the growth process. All such companies must have names that end in the word Limited (which is usually abbreviated to Ltd) or the Welsh equivalent. The requirement to have the word 'limited' in the title is to warn those dealing with the company that the directors have limited liability and cannot be held personally liable for the debts of the business, unless they give a personal guarantee. There are thousands and thousands of such small companies which have capital of less than £1,000, and as the only security a creditor who deals with such companies has is the original capital, there is not much money available to pay all the creditors should such a company get into difficulties. Be wary, therefore, of dealing with limited companies. You can do a company search on any company at the Companies Registration Office which has premises in Cardiff and in London. Of course, many private limited companies have been in existence for many years and have accumulated considerable capital and are absolutely reliable. One advantage of the limited company format is that the company never dies (except by a legal process called winding-up). Whereas sole traders and partners are mortal, limited companies do not die, and the death of the Chairman, Managing Director or any other official make no difference to the company.

Private limited companies may not offer their shares on the Stock Exchange. They can only collect capital from the friends and acquaintances of the officials, which can include the staff, but they must not advertise to the general public offering their shares for sale. A full listing on the Stock Exchange involves an application for a quotation to the Stock Exchange – a process known as 'going public'. Public limited companies must be approved by the Stock Exchange Council, and offered a 'listing' on the Stock Exchange list of companies. They must have a capital of at least £50,000 and a name that ends in the words 'Public Limited Company' (usually abbreviated to PLC) or the Welsh equivalent. The shares of such a company may be bought and sold on the Stock Exchange, and the companies are subject to public scrutiny to a considerable extent – for example they must publish a set of accounts each year which are available to any members of the public who are interested, and are also on file at Companies House where they may be inspected on payment of a small fee.

Today there are two other markets – the USM (Unlisted Securities Market) and the Third Market. These are markets where the shares of larger private companies who are considering going public in the fairly near future may be bought and sold. There are investors who are particularly interested in such companies, which are important growth points in the economy of the country, and although they are not public companies such investors often make approaches to the company after buying a few shares.

10.7 Mergers and takeovers

Merger, or *amalgamation*, is where two firms or companies agree to join together because it will be advantageous to both. Most of the big companies today were formed in this way. For example the 'Big Four' banks, Barclays, Lloyds, National Westminster and Midland started off in the eighteenth century doing a little banking as a sideline business. The original Lloyd was a Birmingham ironmaster, for example. Other famous names in banking were Smiths of Nottingham, who were drapers, and Backhouse of Darlington who were merchants. When small banks got into financial difficulties (bankruptcies) many poor people who had put their life savings in the banks were ruined, and it became clear that only big banks, which were widely spread around the country could survive the slumps in business that were all too common. They began to merge into groups, often with a London bank joining up with several country banks in various parts of the country. In 1896 nineteen banks came together to form Barclays Bank, for example. In the next section we have extracts from an account of the Trusthouse Forte hotel group, which includes a reference to the fact that Trusthouse Forte was set up in 1970 as a result of a merger between Trust Houses Group Ltd and Forte Holdings Ltd. Generally speaking, mergers result in the new company achieving the economies of large scale, sharing facilities and assets and operating more efficiently. The criticism of them is that competition may be reduced, to the disadvantage of the consumer. To overcome this it is possible for the Director General of Fair Trading to advise the Minister concerned that a proposed merger should be referred to the Monopolies and Mergers Commission to decide whether the merger is in the public interest. A monopoly is defined in law as a situation where a firm has at least 25 per cent of the UK market.

Takeovers

Takeovers are the result of one company purchasing another company's shares until it has a controlling interest. This point is actually reached when it has 50 per cent of the shares and one more share. Since voting in a company is based upon one vote for each voting share (there may be other shares which are non-voting) the person with 50 per cent + 1 share must win any vote, and can therefore take over the company. Actually, takeovers occur in many cases because a small company gets into financial difficulties and needs help. The directors of the company which is in difficulties may look around for help and come to a voluntary agreement to be taken over, on the best terms they can. Such takeovers are not of great public interest, but others are more spectacular.

A public company is one where the shares can be bought and sold on the Stock Exchange, and consequently it is possible to achieve a takeover by buying 50 per cent + 1 (usually for convenience we say 51 per cent) of the voting shares. Actually in many cases this is not possible, because when a share is allowed to be quoted the Stock Exchange does not insist upon all the shares being put on the market, so long as there are enough to make a market – which is usually regarded as 30 per cent of the shares. The directors of the private limited company which is going public may retain a controlling interest by keeping back 70 per cent of the shares in their private hands. The view taken is that sooner or later all the shares will in fact come on the market, because:

1   Families are notorious for failing to work together, and if some shares are in the hands of each member of the family sooner or later someone will decide to opt out of the business and sell the shares on the open market.
2   Death strikes everyone sooner or later and when it does inheritance tax will fall upon that person's estate at death, and this will usually mean some, at least, of the shares will have to be realized to pay the tax.

If we take it for granted that eventually all the shares of a public company will be marketed then it becomes possible to buy 51 per cent of the voting shares, and take over the company. The person wishing to take the company over usually offers a price a little above current market price, and hopes that shareholders who are not too happy about the company for any reason will sell to them. Thus if the company has been niggardly in its dividend policy many shareholders will sell and get out while the price is high, and the bidder will be able to buy these shares. In one recent takeover a major bid was launched with an offer of £2,400 million. The extraordinary thing was that the bidder was only a £2 company. The directors who had purchased it 'off-the-shelf' especially to make the bid were going to borrow the whole of the £2,400 million from merchant banks and other institutions and felt sure that by proper management once they had taken over the company they would be able to repay the sum borrowed. Almost always the aim of such a takeover is to break up the company (often a large, unwieldy group of companies) selling them off as separate businesses at a price which will enable the borrowed money to be repaid and leave a profit for the bidder. Whether this is a good thing for the economy is debatable. It is certainly a bad thing for the existing directors who previously were comfortably employed in a safe business. It may be a bad thing for the workforce, since some parts of the group which have been badly run in the past – with considerable overmanning – may now be run more efficiently with a smaller labour force. It may be a good thing for the nation if a high-cost, low-productivity company becomes a low-cost, highly-productive series of new companies. What is quite certain is that the new directors of the company will probably make an excellent profit somewhere out of the deal – although of course they ran the risk of making a loss.

Asset stripping and takeovers

The least desirable feature of takeovers is **asset stripping**. Where a company keeps its dividends low, and its shareholders are discouraged by the poor return on their investment they will be disgruntled and easily persuaded to sell their shares. At the same time the company itself will be flush with funds, because it is paying out so little in dividends. This means it may have plenty of cash, or plenty of investments, or plenty of other assets, such as plant, machinery, stocks, etc. An alert bidder may realize that if he/she buys up enough shares (at the present cheap price) and gets control of the company it will be possible to distribute the accumulated funds to the new shareholders (himself/herself). This is called asset stripping. The accumulated wealth, which really belongs to the old shareholders, is available for the takeover bidder, now that the shares have been purchased in a perfectly legal way. A board of directors which is niggardly in its dividend policy, invites such a takeover from an astute investor with enough funds to buy a controlling interest.

10.8   A project on growth

Most public companies give details in their published accounts of the growth of the company over recent years. Also companies which are going public, and offering their shares to the public for the first time, are required to publish a prospectus giving the very fullest details about the company, its progress over the years, etc. Such prospectuses are usually published in the popular press, in the more serious types of newspaper, particularly the UK *Financial Times*. It is possible to build up a small collection of prospectuses and published final accounts by writing in for them when you see them being reviewed in the business pages of your daily paper. This costs a few pence for stamps, but gives you a real opportunity to study a range of companies.

Your project is to obtain the growth details of one company from either its final accounts or its published prospectus and make a short report about its increase in size over the years. We are particularly interested in:

1   The turnover of the business (as far as you can discover it) over the years.
2   Its capital – how has that grown over the years.
3   Its profits – how have they grown over the years.
4   Its number of employees.
5   Any details of its share of the market today would be interesting.

The following extracts from a press release by Trusthouse Forte give some idea of the company's growth.

Trusthouse Forte – Britain's Biggest and Best

Trusthouse Forte is a British company serving the daily needs of millions of customers across the world with an annual sales turnover of £2,044 million. As the largest British-based hotel and catering group, with its roots in the historic coaching inns of the past, and proudly bearing the traditional White Hart as its logo, it is today a progressive, modern organization operating over 800 hotels worldwide with 75,000 rooms, some 3500 different catering outlets and providing in-flight meals for passengers on 150 international airlines.

It is the most profitable hotel company in the world. In recent years, it has received many major awards as the best hotel group in Britain and Grosvenor House, the Group's flagship, was in 1984 voted by *Caterer & Hotelkeeper* magazine 'Hotel of the Year' and in 1988 was named the RAC five star hotel of the year. In 1986, the Group's Albany hotel in Glasgow received the award.

Trusthouse Forte was formed as a result of a merger in 1970 between Trust Houses Group Limited and Forte Holdings Limited.

Lord Forte of Ripley, Chairman of Trusthouse Forte PLC, founded Forte Holdings Limited in 1935. The major expansion of the company began in the post-war period and soon Forte activities spanned the whole range of catering, duty-free shops, motorway service areas, and from 1958, hotels in Britain and overseas. By 1970 the company had forty-one hotels.

Trusthouse Forte operates in over thirty countries including the Bahamas, Bahrain, Barbados, Belgium, Bermuda, Canada, France, Italy, Jamaica, Majorca, Malta, Monaco, Netherlands, Portugal, Sardinia, Spain, Switzerland, United Arab Emirates, West Germany and USA.

The group has 250 hotels in Great Britain ranging from traditional country inns to modern city centre properties with full facilities, for both the tourist and business traveller. Twenty-one hotels have health and leisure club facilities with fifteen more planned. There are fifteen hotels in central London, including such famous names as the Cumberland, Strand Palace, Russell and Waldorf and four at London Heathrow Airport.

The company provides a complete range of services to the modern traveller at twenty-three service areas on motorways and major roads, serving 30 million customers a year. There are over 300 Little Chef and eighty-five Happy Eater roadside restaurants throughout the country offering meals to 25 million people a year.

A chain of budget-priced accommodation units introduced in 1985 adjacent to Little Chef restaurants proved so popular that they are now marketed under the brand name of Travelodge.

The flight catering needs of 125 international airlines are provided for by THF Airport Catering Services. Every year over 15 million meals are served to passengers in flight, ranging from high-class cuisine to snacks on short sector flights from twenty airports in Europe.

Trusthouse Forte has a worldwide staff of over 70,000 and provides new career openings each year for up to 2000 young people. The company has two management training colleges and spends £15 million in direct training costs.

Trusthouse Forte is proud of its contribution towards the £5,000 million a year earned in foreign currency by the tourist industry – Britain's largest invisible export. The company received the Queen's Award for Export Achievement in 1980 and again in April 1985 in recognition of the £450 million it generated in overseas earnings.

10.9 Rapid revision

Answers		Questions	
	–	1	**What is the best size for any business?**
1	We call it the optimum size, but it varies from time to time and from stage to stage. It depends on the techniques being used, the extent of the division of labour, etc.	2	**What are technical factors in deciding optimum size?**
2	Some technologies only work if the scale is large. For example, steelworks, mines, cement manufacture, oil refining etc. cannot be carried on in small-scale works. There are many things to do and lots of division of labour.	3	**What is the least common multiple principle?**

Answers	Questions
3 A principle which says that if different machines work at different rates we need to operate at a scale which enables us to work with enough machines to keep them all busy at once. So if one machine makes three items an hour and another only makes two items an hour having two of one and three of the other will make six items of each in an hour. Six items is the least common multiple of two and three.	4 **Why does market size influence scale?**
4 If the market is tiny there is no point in a large-scale undertaking.	5 **What is bespoke mass production?**
5 It is a system where mass production techniques are used to produce very long runs of components, thus getting the economies of scale. These bits are then available in catalogues for ordering up by technicians making a 'bespoke' (tailormade) piece of equipment for a customer. There is no need to keep designing new bits – the bits are all available. All we need is a system for putting the necessary bits together into a finished product.	6 **What are the economies of large scale?**
6 (a) Technical economies; (b) marketing economies; (c) administrative economies; (d) research economies; (e) financial economies; (f) welfare economies.	7 **In what ways can businesses grow?**
7 (a) Vertically – from top to bottom – so raw materials, production, distribution and market outlets are all under control; (b) horizontally – so more and more branches are	

Answers	Questions
spread wider and wider around the country, and the world; (c) laterally – into related activities –so that more and more products form a dense pattern of lines, all supporting one another.	**8 What are the stages in any expansion programme?**
8 (a) Decide where we are now; (b) decide where we want to be in (i) the short term and (ii) more long-term; (c) develop a business strategy for achieving the aims envisaged; (d) draw up detailed plans; (e) put the plans into effect, with good management control and feedback.	**9 What are mergers?**
9 Voluntary amalgamations between firms for their mutual benefit to achieve more economic working. Mergers used to be frowned upon as reducing competition, but in fact many mergers are logical and inevitable if the industry concerned is to operate efficiently and meet foreign competition.	**10 What is a takeover?**
10 A situation where one company purchases 51 per cent of the voting shares of another company and can therefore dictate policy. The company taken over becomes a subsidiary of the other company, and the successful bidder becomes a holding company.	**11 Go over the test again until you are sure of all the answers. Then try the questions in Section 10.10 below.**

10.10   Questions on Chapter 10

1   Supersox Ltd believe that their business is now worth £1 million and they suggest that this might be the time to go public and offer shares on the Stock Exchange. What would they have to do, and is there any advice you would give them?

2   Peter Dore's business is now well established but it seems to be stuck at its present size and unable to make any growth worth speaking of. How would you suggest that he improves the situation with a view to larger scale operations?

3   'My business meets all the local requirements, and I see no need at all to grow at the present. I have a comfortable income from the business anyway.' Comment on this proprietor's attitude to business, mentioning any adverse aspects that occur to you.

4   Almost all large businesses are limited companies. Why is this form of business organization the most appropriate for large scale businesses.

5   Explain vertical integration as a business method of growing larger.

6   Explain horizontal integration as a business method for expansion.

7   What is a takeover? What is asset stripping?

Part Three
Business Behaviour

11
Financing a business

11.1 Sources of finance

The chief sources of finance for a business are as follows:

1 Self-financing.
2 Hire purchase and leasing finance from finance companies and merchant bank subsidiaries of the major banks.
3 Bank loans and overdrafts.
4 Debenture finance.
5 Equity finance.
6 Official grants and loans.

We must consider each of these in turn.

Self-financing

Almost all businesses start off by a certain amount of self-financing. There is a great deal to be said for an entrepreneur having a major stake in his/her business and few of those who lend money, such as the banks and finance houses will put much money into a business where the person running it has no personal financial stake in it. The average person works harder, and is more careful about the money spent, if it is his/her own money, or he/she has a great deal to lose if the business fails.

Self-financing starts with saving. Many a millionaire started out by washing other people's motor cars, or serving in a subordinate position to earn a bit of cash to get started. One founder of a world famous airline disappeared as a young man and was actually reported missing to the police. He eventually turned up carrying people's cases to the aeroplanes, in the days when baggage handling was not mechanized and it was all done by hand. When he did eventually get started he was influential in making sure that it was easy to get the luggage on board. He had combined self-financing with useful research to kill two birds with one stone.

Self-financing is not used just at the start of the business, but right the way through. As a business grows it is the ploughing back of profits into the business to obtain better machines, methods of work, storage facilities etc., which is the real key to progress. The early capitalists were known, not for their lavish lifestyles, but for their miserly behaviour. They were interested in profits, not for the high life it could bring them, but for the growth they could achieve as they reinvested the profits into the business. The reason why self-financing was, and always will be, so important is that you do not have to pay interest on the money you are investing. It is yours, earned by earlier profitable activities and any profits the expanding business makes will be similarly available. By contrast, borrowed money creams off much of the profit into the pockets of the banks and finance companies. If a manufacturer is paying 14 per cent or 20 per cent or even 29.8 per cent (the current credit card rate) for borrowing money this rate of profit will be creamed off the top of any profits made. Highest rate of interest of all used to be the money-lender's rate, which was fixed at 4 per cent per month. At compound interest this is 60 per cent per year.

Hire purchase and leasing finance

Hire purchase is the purchase of assets by the payment of a small deposit (often one-third or one-quarter of the purchase price) followed by a succession of instalments until the full purchase price is paid. Since this system is mainly used by ordinary householders to purchase what are called 'consumer durables' like cookers, furniture, television sets, etc. it is closely controlled by the Consumer Credit Act, 1974 and an official, the Director General of Fair Trading ensures that such arrangements are properly conducted. Many small businesses purchase assets in this way. The trader who is supplying the machine does not finance the purchase personally, but relies on a finance house to provide the rest of the purchase price. The trader thus gets paid the normal price for the item supplied, in two parts – the deposit and the balance from the finance company. The finance house draws up a hire purchase agreement in which the original price, the deposit paid, the balance outstanding, the interest added, and the instalment due, must all be shown. A typical calculation might be:

		£
To supplying one BD 3110 Toshiba photocopying machine – cash price without tax		828.50
Add VAT at $17\frac{1}{2}$%	=	144.99
Normal price if purchased in cash	=	973.49
Less deposit at 20%	=	194.70
Amount borrowed from finance house	=	778.79
Add interest at 11% for 2 years = 22%	=	171.33
		950.12

Repayable in twenty-three monthly instalments of £39.58 and one final instalment of £39.78.

Leasing finance is a rather similar system of finance, usually provided by finance houses, in which the trader asks the finance house to buy exactly the machine required, and to lease it to him/her for a monthly rental. The machine never becomes the property of the business that is using it. It is owned and maintained by the finance house, but is placed at the service of the trader who requires it.

The advantage of leasing equipment in this way is that the trader does not have to find the capital to buy machines, vehicles etc. The finance house looks after the provision of the capital, owns the asset when it is purchased and maintains and cares for it all its working life. The trader simply pays a regular daily, weekly or monthly charge for it. This is particularly useful in contract work, where, for example, a crane will only be wanted for a few days or weeks. For some cranes the charge is as much as £1,000 a day, but it is better to pay a few days' hire charge and then return the crane than spend £250,000 to buy the crane outright.

About one-third of all finance house money is spent on buying equipment for leasing. In one recent year the figure was £5,000 million. There are about ten major finance houses, which together form the Finance Houses Association. A number of them have been taken over as specialist subsidiaries of one of the big four banks; each finance house serving its particular bank where this kind of business is required and borrowing most of the money it needs from its own Head Office (though it would be free to borrow on the money markets if funds were available there at a cheap rate).

Bank loans and overdrafts

The logical place to borrow money is the bank. The UK has the best banking system in the whole world. It combines great size (for financial security) with ready availability (through a branch-banking network in every corner of the land). Local bank managers have a duty to get to know new entrants to the business community in their areas. They will arrange an interview for all those in need of business funds, and will consider their plans, advise about difficulties which the applicant may not have foreseen, and encourage and help in every way possible. It is in the bank's interest to ensure that every new business succeeds. The branch banking system depends upon a steady number of active accounts. Business people retire every year and a local manager must find new accounts to replace accounts lost in this way. An application to a bank for finance is dealt with in detail later in this chapter.

Bank finance is made available in two main ways – by loans and overdrafts. An overdraft is a way of making finance available to meet

PLEASE COMPLETE AND RETURN THIS FORM TO YOUR BRANCH.
IF YOU ARE NOT A BARCLAYS CUSTOMER, PLEASE RETURN IT TO YOUR MOST CONVENIENT BRANCH.

BARCLAYS BUSINESSLOAN APPLICATION FORM

Please complete in BLOCK CAPITALS. ALL questions to be answered.

1. Full name of business   Limited company/sole trader/partnership*
                                                                            Delete as applicable

2. Business address

                                                            Telephone no.

3. Nature of business

4. Proprietor(s) (directors/partners etc) *Please refer to question 10

i. Surname (Mr/Mrs/Miss/Ms)*   Forename(s)
   Delete as applicable
Home address

Telephone no.   Date of birth

ii. Surname (Mr/Mrs/Miss/Ms)*   Forename(s)
    Delete as applicable
Home address

Telephone no.   Date of birth

iii. Surname (Mr/Mrs/Miss/Ms)*   Forename(s)
     Delete as applicable
Home address

Telephone no.   Date of birth

(Please list others separately, if necessary)

5. Present bankers

Branch

6. Purpose of loan

Is it to start up a new business? YES/NO Delete as applicable

7. Total amount of proposed expenditure £

8. Amount of loan required £   Period of loan   years

(If you're using the loan to purchase an asset, the term of the loan must be less than the expected life of the asset.)

9. Date loan required (if known)

Figure 11.1   A business loan proposal form

████████

† 10. Life, accident and sickness cover will be arranged automatically for the first named person in section 4 overleaf, UNLESS we are advised to the contrary. Monthly loan repayments with single person insurance can be found in the repayment table enclosed.

Please mark box 'X' if cover is not required. ☐

If more than one person is to be insured, or someone not listed in 4 overleaf, please list below details of ALL persons to be insured (maximum 3 persons). A quotation will be provided on request.

i. Surname (Mr/Mrs/Miss/Ms)* _____ Forename(s) _____
Delete as applicable
Position _____ Date of birth' _____

_____

_____

ii. Surname (Mr/Mrs/Miss/Ms)* _____ Forename(s) _____
Delete as applicable
Position _____ Date of birth' _____

_____

_____

iii. Surname (Mr/Mrs/Miss/Ms)* _____ Forename(s) _____
Delete as applicable
Position _____ Date of birth' _____

_____

_____

*Insurance cover cannot be arranged for over individuals aged 65 or over at the outset of the loan.

AUTHORITY to Barclays Bank PLC.
I authorise you to make any enquiries you deem necessary for credit assessment.

Applicant's signature _____ Date _____

Published by Barclays Bank PLC.
Corporate Marketing Department. Reg. No. 1026167. Reg. Office: 54 Lombard Street, London EC3P 3AH.
January 1989. 9970003. ED. BB261029. D09402. Member of IMRO.

short-term difficulties, which will correct themselves in a few weeks. For example, a trader who is stocking up for Christmas may get very short of funds in September and October when wholesalers deliver all the goods that will be required. In November and December, when the pre-Christmas rush is on, the trader will be paying in plenty of cash.

If a bank lends a trader money on overdraft in September and October (and charges interest on the money borrowed) it will be corrected in November and December as goods are sold, and the customer's account will be restored to a satisfactory position.

Loans are rather more formal than overdrafts. An application form has to be completed, stating the purpose for which the loan is required, the amount envisaged, the period over which repayment would be made and so on. A typical business loan form is shown in Figure 11.1. If the loan is substantial it would be usual to put up a fully developed proposal to the bank, showing the financial state of the business, but for smaller loans the application form is sufficient and a quick decision would be made.

Debenture finance

When companies wish to obtain capital they may of course approach a bank or finance house just like any other person. Remember, a company is an incorporation, that is, it is a body created by law which can do most of the things that an ordinary human being can do. It can buy and sell, borrow money, employ staff, etc. However, Parliament does impose certain rules upon companies, and the way in which they raise their funds is fairly closely controlled. They must issue shares to the people who wish to become members of the company, and once the company is registered and officially incorporated they may also issue debentures if the Articles of Association (which are the rules of a company and govern its activities) permit. A debenture is a loan to a company, secured on the assets of the company. It earns a stated rate of interest, usually about 8 per cent per annum which is payable every six months, whether the company makes a profit or not. A debenture is a safe investment because it gets its interest paid whatever happens to the company, and if the interest is not paid the **debenture trustee** (usually a firm of accountants) who holds the debenture deed, can step in and seize the assets of the company. These can be sold to repay the debenture holders. Debentures are often issued by fairly large companies. They are sometimes called loan capital, because like the share capital they are retained in the business for many years, but strictly speaking they are not 'capital', but only loans to a company. In any dissolution of a company the debenture holders have a prior claim on the money obtained by selling the assets of the company. If anyone is going to lose their money it will not be the debenture holders.

Equity finance

Most of the finance of a company should ideally come from the sale of shares to ordinary shareholders, who then become the part-owners of the business, and entitled to an equal share in the profits of the business. For this reason ordinary shares are often called 'equity shares' or 'equity finance'. If a person is really interested in a company, and believes it has a great future ahead of it, he/she should be prepared to back this belief by buying shares in the company. When shares are first issued they are sold at par, which means 'at their face value'. Thus a £1 share will be sold for £1, and a 50 pence share will be sold for 50 pence. However, once a company has been set up for some years and has grown by ploughing back the profits of the business a share will rise above par, because the share is entitled not only to get back the money that was originally invested but also its share of the undistributed profits of earlier years which have been ploughed back. That is why we hear of £1 shares being valued at £4.95, or something like that. Equity shares are entitled to an equal share of all the profits earned.

Less happily, equity shares also stand to suffer any losses that occur. If a company makes losses, so that some of the original capital is lost, the shareholders cannot hope to get all their money back. The shares will fall in value and become worth less than par.

One further thought is this. If you buy a share in a major bank and pay – say – £9.55 for a £1 share, when you come to sell the share you hope you will get at least £9.55 for it. If it sells for £10.20 you have made a capital gain of 65 pence per share, but if it sells for £8.20 you have made a capital loss of £1.35 per share. That is why, when there is a panic on the stock market, everybody gets so agitated. If you had shares worth £1,000 and by the end of the day they had fallen to half their value you would have suffered a loss of £500. That is why some people never buy shares. There is an element of risk involved.

Preference shares are not equity shares. They do not share equally in the profits. Instead they get a fixed rate of dividend, say 8 per cent, and no more. They get preference on their dividend, so that in a bad year when the ordinary shareholders get no dividend they may get their 8 per cent, but they do not get more than 8 per cent in a good year, when the ordinary shareholders might get 20 per cent, or 30 per cent, or even more.

The great advantage of raising money by share issues is that vast sums of money can be raised; far more than any individual could raise. These days £1,000 million may be raised in a single issue of shares. Another advantage is that the shares only obtain a dividend if this is recommended by management at the Annual General Meeting. They cannot, like banks or debenture holders, force the company into liquidation if they do not get their dividend.

Official grants and loans

Some finance can be obtained from official grants and loans. Most of the current schemes are described later (see Chapter 21). As a general principle funds of this sort are designed to meet the particular needs of areas which for one reason or another have fallen on hard times. For example, if major factories close, or ports cease to be in operation, or mining conditions cause pit closures, schemes to relieve distress in the area concerned may mean that funds are made available to encourage entrepreneurs to move there and develop factories, depots or tourist attractions. The sums can be considerable, but the aim is not to enrich individuals, it is intended that the money provided should be spent in the area of development, paying wages and creating jobs which will benefit the whole area.

Points to remember

- Self-financing is the way most small businesses start, though small loans are usually available from banks and finance houses.
- Self-financing by ploughing back profits is also the best way for a business to grow in its early years, but a judicious amount of borrowing is permissible provided the profit earned will cover the interest and still leave the entrepreneurs a reasonable income.
- Hire purchase is a useful and inexpensive way of obtaining assets. As the procedure is controlled by rules laid down by the Director General of Fair Trading your legal position with regard to ownership of the goods, repossession by the supplier, early termination of the contract etc. is all made clear in the hire purchase agreement. Read the small print – by law it has to be large enough for you to read it easily.
- Leasing is a method of financing the purchase of capital assets by allowing a finance house to purchase them and lease them to us for a monthly rental. This rental is fully deductible as a business expenditure for tax purposes and the asset remains the property of the finance house.
- The logical place to borrow money is from a bank, either by way of overdraft or loan. The bank will be interested in discussing the amount, the period of the loan and the security that can be offered, but the procedure – especially to an established account

holder – is quite simple and in many cases can be arranged over the telephone.

- 'Equity finance' is financing a business by issuing ordinary shares. It is the ideal way of financing a company since any capital obtained is long-term capital, without interest – its right is to share in the profits of the company. It is similar to self-financing in that the new shareholders become members of the company.
- Debentures are loans to a company. They do earn interest, which is usually payable half yearly, and they are secure in that a debenture trustee looks after the debenture holder's interests and may seize the assets of the company for sale to repay the debenture holders if the company gets into financial difficulties.

11.2   Applying for finance

Fortunately we live in a world where there is no shortage of capital. In the early days of capitalist society the problem was to find the capital to start even the smallest enterprise. Today not only is the world running with capital, it can be moved from one end of the earth to the other in less than a second. The shortage today is of viable projects which are worth developing. There are many people with worthwhile ideas, who do not know how to present a proposal in a form which bankers and others will appreciate. The presentation of a business plan calls for a careful, detailed explanation of what is proposed; the starting point from which it is to be launched (i.e. the present state of the company or firm); the finance required, costed as accurately as possible using present-day prices; the security that can be offered to the bank or other investors; the proposed method of repayment (including the timescale) and the likely profit from the venture.

To give some idea of the kind of detail required the format for such a proposal has been set out in Figure 11.2. Alongside it have been written some notes of further points which may be of interest.

This may sound a daunting set of information for obtaining a loan, but it is not only of use to the bank. It helps the person showing enterprise to go through this sort of rigorous exercise and makes it much more likely that the project, whatever it is, will be successful. Those who are setting up in business can get help with the preparation of such a proposal from a number of organizations. For example, the local TEC (Training and Enterprise Council) offers help in this area. See your local telephone directory. A valuable source of information and help in your local area is provided free of charge from the Enterprise Initiative on 0800 500 200.

Loan request to Development Bank of Europeana PLC
2956 High Street
Lowborough
Lowland

for Ivor Waywivem, 2129 Shore Drive, Leystone on Sea

1 Nature of business
  (a) Give an exact description of the business proposed, the product to be manufactured or handled, or the service to be offered.
  (b) State the proposed area for developing the project, the catchment area for customers, the type of organization required, etc. Refer to the more detailed specifications to be found later in the proposal (see 3 below)

2 The proprietor(s) and other staff
Businesses only happen because entepreneurs make them happen. You need to give:
  (a) Your own qualifications, age, experience, training for this particular business, experience in industry generally and this industry in particular. In particular your knowledge of business, ability to keep books of account, computer skills (if appropriate) etc.
  (b) Similar details of anyone in your family who will help with the business, and detail in what capacity this will be.
  (c) If other staff are important – for example key, skilled personnel in any field, give the fullest details about them. It may be necessary to get them to write their own section or to state that they approve of the ideas expressed and do intend to participate wholeheartedly in the project.
  (d) If the organization is to be a company the full details must be declared, names of directors, secretary, principal shareholders, stated objects in the objects clause of the company, a statement of any personal guarantees to be given by any such people (if any) should be included.

Further points that may be needed

1 An existing business should give exact details of its present position, the expansion envisaged and why it is justified in asking for financial assistance.

2 An existing business should send a full account of personnel; their track records, and a full account of the company's present state of affairs.

Figure 11.2　Application for a loan (*continues on pages 185–7*)

3 The detailed proposal
This should include:
(a) The proposed trading name.
(b) The proposed premises (if selected). If to be built, the proposed cost, situation re planning permission, architect's name, details, etc. of any official help available, etc. Send diagrams, plans, site photographs, builders' estimates, suppliers' estimates, timetable envisaged.

3 An existing business should include:
(a) Details of current situation and why expansion is necessary.
(b) If application is for an emergency an explanation of the nature of the crisis and why you didn't anticipate it.
(c) An explanation of current organization, profitability, accounting system and financial position.

4 Analysis of the market
(a) A detailed description of the market area, the location, total spending power available, share of market you hope to achieve.
(b) Details of market research carried out, support from local bodies such as Chamber of Commerce or Trade Association.
(c) State of competition – demonstrate that you know of all the competitors. Why you feel you can still succeed. Weaknesses they display and how you hope to avoid them. Can you beat them for quality, design, price, market appeal, etc.

4 An existing business should review its present market position, give reasons for expansion, and analyse the likely impact of the new proposal on the existing proposal.

5 The financial requirements
(a) The proposal should now produce detailed figures of the amount of money required, carefully costed to show what it will be spent on and the timing of the project – because not all the money is required at once. The bank should be asked for blanket approval for the whole project but only a gradual provision of the actual money. To release all the money at once inclines those putting the early stages in hand to overspend, leaving the later stages – often the marketing aspects – starved of funds.
(b) Be careful to think the project through to the very end, so that all aspects of costs – such as warehousing, transport and advertising costs are fully anticipated. A later application

5 An existing firm will already have established a track record with the institution to which it is applying for funds. This should mean that the proposal is more favourably viewed – and the applicant merely has to acquaint the bank with the proposed new programme.

Figure 11.2 (*continued*)

5 The financial requirements (cont.)
for a secondary budget will only
reveal the applicant's poor
preparation of the original
application. To think a project through
to the very end you have to budget for
raw material purchase, manufacture,
packaging, distribution, warehousing,
marketing, distribution to final sales
point and after-sales servicing, if
necessary. All costs have to be
budgeted for, including general
overheads, interest on loans,
accounting costs for hire purchase
customers, etc.

(c) Make it clear how much of the finance
required can be obtained by self-
financing and cash generation as the
project gets under way. Thus if some
partial product is readily saleable and
can bring in income as the product
develops it should be costed as a
favourable cash flow to reduce the
finance required.

6 The profit envisaged and the method of repayment
When stating the case for a loan the bank
is interested in knowing how you
envisage being able to meet the loan
repayments, which includes both the
interest and the capital sum granted. The
proceeds expected have to be enough to
support all the expenses that are likely to
be incurred, and still leave enough to give
the proprietor some reward and cover the
loan repayments. Preferably the rewards
should be able to cover all this with ease,
rather than depending upon good luck, or
a favourable set of circumstances, to
produce the desired result. The method of
repayment may be specified by the bank,
but where the nature of the project
requires a 'repayment holiday' until the
project is under way the bank will always
listen to sensible proposals. Thus a
business cannot start manufacturing until
the factory is built and can start up
production, so the bank cannot look for
repayments to begin until that time. Put a
sensible suggestion forward.

6 An existing business should
relate the new situation to
the past record of the firm/
company, and reference to
earlier loans successfully
completed may be
appropriate.

Figure 11.2   (continued)

7 Security for the loan
Most banks will hope to take security for any large loan they make. This will ideally take the form of a mortgage, or second mortgage, on premises, or a debenture (if the directors are authorized to issue debentures). Some people cannot offer such security – for example if the only premises they have are rented premises. Instead the directors of a company may be asked for a personal guarantee, and other traders (who will be liable anyway to the full limit of their personal wealth) may be asked if they have a friend or relative who can offer a guarantee. Life assurance is helpful – since at least if the applicant dies the bank will get its money from the assurance company – while an existing life policy may have a surrender value if the applicant proves unable to pay.

7 Once again, the present position of an existing business may enable the bank to arrange security of the existing assets.

11.3 Fixed and working capital

The word 'capital' can be used in many ways. We usually think of capital as being money, but that is only because money represents anything we can buy with it. If we have money we can go out and buy anything we need, such as premises, machinery, equipment, motor vehicles, furniture and fittings and stock for resale. We can ask people to work for us and promise them money (wages or salaries) in return. So money is capital in a very adaptable form – we can change it into anything we like. In fact money is called **liquid capital**. We use the word *liquid* because money can flow anywhere – it only takes a second to send it to Australia. Cash flows, in and out of a business, are very important, but this is explained elsewhere (see Chapter 14 and Figure 11.3). What do we do with money capital?

The first thing is, we spend a lot of it on assets of the business. These are said to be fixed capital, because they cannot flow anywhere. We purchase premises to work in, machines and tools to work with, motor vehicles for transportation, computer systems for design, accounting, stock records etc. All these things are fixed assets. They are purchased to use in the business. The capital we spend on them is called 'fixed capital' and the assets are called 'fixed assets'.

Once we have all the fixed assets we are ready to begin production of the goods we intend to make, or to offer the services we intend to offer. Before we can do so we need further capital – not for fixed assets, but for current assets. Current assets are assets which are not

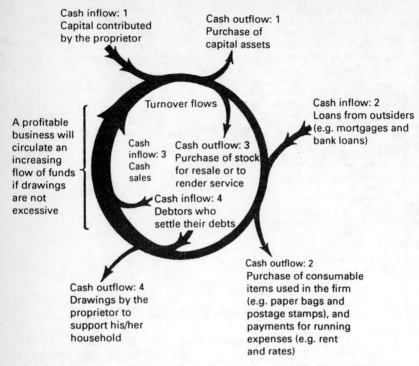

Figure 11.3 Cash flows as liquid capital is turned into fixed capital and working capital

fixed but current (from the French word *courrant* – meaning running). What current assets do is turn over in the business, as they run round in an endless cycle of activity. We buy raw materials, and make them into stock, which we then bring to market and sell to people who become our debtors and eventually pay us in cash. Then we take this cash and buy more materials to start a further cycle of activity. The chief current assets are raw materials, work-in-progress, finished stock, debtors, money in the bank and cash in hand. These current assets are used to work the business. They are often called 'working capital'. However, as there are always some current liabilities due to be paid up in the short term out of current assets, we usually define the working capital of a business as 'current assets *less* current liabilities'.

If we want to take a look at the capital of any firm or company – for example if we are thinking of buying it, we ask to see its Balance Sheet. A Balance Sheet may be taken out at any moment in time, but the most usual time to draw up a Balance Sheet is at the end of the

R. Marshall & Co (Saltplace) Ltd   Balance Sheet as at 31 December 19xx

Fixed assets	At cost	Less depreciation to date	Value today		Authorized	Issued
	£	£	£	Ordinary shareholders' interest in the company	£	£
				Ordinary shares of £1 fully paid	200,000	100,000
Intangible assets						
Goodwill	3,000	1,500	1,500	Capital reserves		
				Premium on Shares A/c		25,000
Tangible assets						
Premises	60,000	–	60,000	Revenue reserves		
Plant and machinery	45,000	9,000	36,000	Plant replacement reserve	20,000	
Fixtures and fittings	15,500	3,150	12,350	General reserve	50,000	
Motor vehicles	19,760	8,250	11,510	Balance on Appropriation A/c	27,265	
Total fixed assets (fixed capital)	143,260	21,900	121,360			97,265
						222,265
Trade investments (market value £41,650)			36,000		Authorized	
				8% Preference shareholders' interest in the company	50,000	
Current assets				8% Preference shares of £1		50,000
Stock	46,250					
Work-in-progress	31,775			8% Debentures		40,000
Debtors	12,965					
Cash at bank	117,340			Reserve for corporation tax		42,000
Cash in hand	1,370					
		209,700				
Less Current liabilities						
Creditors		12,795				
Net current assets (net working capital)			196,905			
			£354,265			£354,265

Notes: 1 This is the Balance Sheet of a Company, in the style required by the Companies Act. 1985. 2 You can see the fixed assets on the left-hand side – showing how much capital has been tied up in fixed assets. 3 Below the fixed assets are the current assets, but the current liabilities have been brought over from the right-hand side and deducted to show the net working capital. 4 Trade investments are shares in subsidiary companies. They aren't quite fixed (we could sell the shares on the Stock Exchange) but if we do we lose control of the subsidiary company. (They are sometimes called 'assets which are neither fixed nor current'.) 5 On the liabilities side we see who provided the capital to provide all these assets. Most of it comes from the ordinary shareholders, either from their original capital or from profits left in the business as 'reserves'. The preference shareholders contributed £50,000 and the debenture holders loaned the company £40,000. The reserve for corporation tax is more profits waiting to be paid to Inland Revenue – the Government's share of the profits.

Figure 11.4 A Balance Sheet showing fixed and working capital

financial year when we work out the profits of the business. Such a Balance Sheet is shown in Figure 11.4. Look at it now and the notes below it.

11.4   The risks of business enterprise

All enterprise is risky. We are offering goods or services to the general public which we believe they will wish to purchase at a price which will enable us to earn a profit. It is the profits of the business that reward the entrepreneurs and if the business proves to be unprofitable the entrepreneurs will get into financial difficulties and may possibly go bankrupt. A careful look at what we mean by risks is helpful in Business Studies, because we need to understand risks if we are to survive in business.

We generally divide risks into two kinds of risks, **insurable risks** and **non-insurable risks**.

An insurable risk is one the probability of which can be calculated mathematically, based on statistics collected over a great many years from a great many people. For example, we can calculate the risk of burglary by collecting statistics about burglary over the whole country, and keeping the figures up-dated over the years as more and more burglaries are committed. The people who collect this kind of statistics are called **actuaries**, and they use them to predict the chances of a burglary occurring in any particular area. For example, burglaries are commoner in big cities than in rural areas. Not only are there more criminals about in big cities but people do not know their neighbours so well. Everyone in rural areas knows everyone else and a strange car or lorry would be noticed and people would wonder what it was doing in that area. Even if the driver commits a burglary there is more chance he will be caught. In city areas the same vehicle would be lost in the traffic in seconds.

Actuaries work for insurance companies, predicting risks. They enable the insurance company to fix premiums which will cover losses by burglary, fire, storm damage and various other hazards. Anyone who wishes to insure may ask for cover to be arranged, and on paying the agreed premium they will be held covered. This does not take long to arrange; in fact you can do it over the telephone in five minutes sufficiently well to be 'held covered' while the insurance company sends you a proposal form and you have time to fill it in and pay the premium.

Insurable risks

The common insurable risks are as follows:

Fire insurance
Fires are a serious problem. They do terrible damage, very quickly and a business may not only lose its stocks, its premises, its business records etc. but also any chance of earning profits until everything can be rebuilt. We call such things as loss of profits 'consequential losses'. You can cover all such risks, for a fairly reasonable premium. A premium is a sum of money paid into an insurance pool. The pool of money thus collected will be used to compensate the people who do suffer the loss insured against. We have all heard of a football pool – where the lucky few win all the money in the pool. An insurance pool is rather similar but it is the *unlucky* people who are helped from the pool – so it is really a more sensible idea than a football pool which is just a gamble.

Vehicle insurance
By law every vehicle must be insured, or rather the driver of every vehicle must be insured. Driving while uninsured is a punishable offence. Of course you may drive and not have an accident, but if you do have an accident and damage property, or injure or kill anyone – who is to cover the damages if you are uninsured. Often as much as £1 million damages are awarded. The injured person looks to the responsible driver's insurance company for compensation. The actuaries can predict the likelihood of any driver having an accident. They take the type of car, the area lived in, the driver's past record, etc. into account when they fix the premium.

Accident insurance
Beethoven's Fifth Symphony begins with four loud notes. When asked what those notes meant he is reputed to have replied: 'That is how fate knocks on your door?' Fate knocks on someone's door every second of the day. In fifteen seconds the San Francisco earthquake killed a whole freeway-full of motorists, as well as many other people. Accident insurance covers all such risks, and insurance companies sent millions of dollars to California to meet claims.

Marine insurance
Marine insurance is insurance of goods and passengers travelling by sea. It is a very important branch of insurance, and Lloyds of London is the greatest marine insurance organization. It knows where every major ship in the world is, on every day of the year.

Life assurance

The word 'assurance' is used about covering the life of people, because, unlike all other risks, we can be quite sure we shall die. We may never have a fire, or a burglary, or an accident, but if we insure our lives one day we will die, and the insurance company will have to pay up. They are assured of having to pay the people named in the policy as beneficiaries. Life assurance is a very important form of cover, not only for the business person but also for all key staff. If we lose our best designer, or our skilled mechanic, or our export manager we may suffer serious losses. All such people can be covered by life assurance.

Non-insurable risks

There are some risks about which we cannot predict the probabilities. No one will offer us insurance on these risks, for they cannot decide on a fair premium to cover the risk. The only person who can cover this risk is the entrepreneur himself. The business person who is showing enterprise must take these risks into his/her calculations. We often hear people say 'It is a calculated risk?' They mean they know there is some chance that they will lose their money but they have a good idea that they won't lose on the project, but on the contrary will be all right and make a profit in the end. There is a break-even point, where every business activity recovers all the money spent on it and starts to make a profit. This is explained later. First of, all, consider the following risks.

1   The risk that the product I am thinking of making may not be as popular as I hoped it would be.
2   The risk that I may misjudge the price people will be willing to pay and as a result will be unable to sell it to most of the people I designed it for.
3   The risk that I may prove to be a fool in business, unable to make sound decisions on many of the things that are vital to success in business.

These are the sort of things which no one can insure against. We have to bear a certain amount of risk ourselves, and if we see that things are not going to work out have some sort of contingency plan to get out of our difficulties. The most usual precaution we take is only to start a new project in a small way. We try out a limited production run, with the minimum output to start with. We do a test mailing to a small area, and see what the response is. If the response is good we make a slightly larger batch the next time, and so on.

11.5   The services of banks to the business community

Reference has already been made to the ability of banks to provide overdrafts or loans to businesses. Banks offer a wide range of other services, and in recent years they have developed these to such an extent that there are few aspects of business activity that banks are not concerned with. Many of the things banks do for ordinary customers have important implications for businesses, as the following sections will show. Each service referred to has been described from the business point of view.

Current Account services

A Current Account is a facility which places at the service of every account holder all the other facilities of the banks. These include the safeguarding of funds; their transfer from one person to another without leaving the bank; and the use of a cheque card to guarantee to every shopkeeper, hotelkeeper, etc. that any cheque signed by the account holder at the time the card is presented will be honoured up to a known limit (which is usually £50 at the present time). The word 'current' means that the account is a running account, which may be added to – by a further deposit of funds – or subtracted from – by writing cheques to make payments as and when required. The customer who opens an account by depositing funds gives up ownership of that quantity of funds, in return for an absolute assurance that he/she may demand funds to the same value (plus interest if the account is an interest-bearing Current Account) at any time. Not all Current Accounts are interest-bearing, but some carry a small rate of interest today.

The cheque system is described below, and is the most useful service offered to customers by any bank, but there are many other facilities, night safe services etc.

Cheques
A cheque is an order to a banker to pay money to someone at once. Technically it may be written on any piece of paper or indeed on anything. One wag wrote a cheque out on his cricket bat. A group of London fishmongers wrote one out on a shark, and took it round to the bank to be cashed. The manager duly obliged, stamped the cheque 'Paid' and returned it to the customer who had presented it. These days bankers prefer cheques to be of a certain size because they are dealt with by machines, so they issue books of cheques to their customers. Odd bits of paper do not fit the machines. This is also true of cricket bats and sharks. There are many advantages of paying money by cheque:

1   It is just as easy to pay £1,000 as it is to pay £5. You do not need 200 pieces of paper as you do with £5 notes.
2   A cheque can be safeguarded by crossing it so that even if it is stolen it is useless to the thief.
3   The money never leaves the bank so it is perfectly safe.
4   In some countries, for instance in the UK (by the Cheques Act, 1957), the cheque is a receipt. It is proof, once it has been paid, that you did pay the money.

Figure 11.5 shows four ways in which a cheque may be safe-guarded. An explanation of each cheque is given below.

(a)   This is an open cheque; it can be cashed at the bank by anyone who presents it and says he is T. Jones. He will have to endorse it. This means he must sign his name on the back when he cashes the cheque. Although this is not much of a safeguard it does have a deterrent effect on thieves, because signing the name T. Jones on the cheque when you are not Mr Jones means you have committed the crime of forgery, which is more severely punished than mere theft. There is an even more unsafe cheque, called a 'bearer' cheque, which is made out 'pay bearer'. This is very unsafe indeed and does not require endorsement, because the name of the bearer is not important. Anyone who presents it is entitled to payment on it. Generally speaking it is safer to cross a cheque, and banks issue books of cheques that are already crossed for those who prefer to play safe.

(b)   This is a general crossing – two lines with or without '& Co'. It will not be cashed across the counter of the bank but must be cleared into a bank account. It is therefore much safer than (a), but it can be cleared by anyone so long as R. T. McGuiness (Camside) Ltd have endorsed it (written their name on the back). Notice that it is possible to pay this cheque into *any* account. It does not have to go into the account of the person named on the cheque, McGuiness. This is possible because it is an Order Cheque. At the end of the line it says 'Pay R. T. McGuiness (Camside) Ltd .... or order'. This means that if McGuiness Ltd endorse it 'Pay R. Brown' and sign their name, the bank concerned will obey the order and pay R. Brown not McGuiness Ltd. The simpler rules about endorsement are as follows:

  (i)   No endorsement is necessary if the payee pays an order cheque into his own account.
  (ii)   If the payee orders the bank to pay someone else he/she must endorse the cheque. The new payee will also endorse it when it is paid into his/her account.

(a)

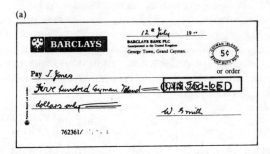

(b)

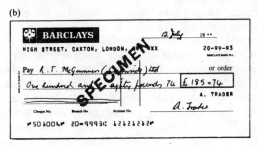

(c)

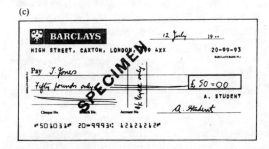

(d)

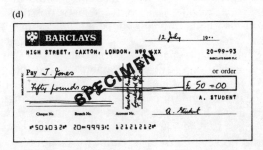

Figure 11.5 Safeguarding a cheque

(c)   A recent Act of Parliament, the *Cheques Act 1992*, has changed the law about cheques which are crossed 'a/c Payee' and has led to most banks issuing all cheques to customers in books where every cheque is crossed in this way. The effect of this crossing under the Act is that the cheque is not an 'order' cheque; in other words, it cannot be endorsed and passed on to someone else to be paid into his/her account. It can only be cleared into the account of the named payee.

(d)   This is a special crossing, since the bank into which it is to be paid is clearly stated. It must be paid into that account and no other.

Deposit Account services

Besides Current Account services, which are linked to the use of cheques and all other means of money transmission, and to loans and overdrafts, the customer will usually open one or more Deposit Accounts, where money may be left to earn interest completely separate from the Current Account facility. The general purpose of Deposit Accounts is as savings for the individual concerned, and this may be true for many small businesses run by sole traders and partnerships. Businesses, however, have other uses for deposit accounts. First of all there are two main uses which are concerned with the need to put money by safely until it is required. These are VAT payments and income tax payments.

VAT money is money collected under the Value Added Tax regulations, which all traders over a certain size (turnover exceeding £45,000 a year) must charge to customers, and then pay over to the Customs and Excise authorities. Payment has to be made every three months. Since most shopkeepers have a turnover of about £3,000 a week at least, and many traders have much more, the tax collected on such a figure is £450, which over thirteen weeks comes to £5,850. This is a lot of money to find every three months and the only safe way is to put it away in a Deposit Account, where it is available when required, and also earns interest which is a bit more profit for the trader.

Similarly, business people pay their income tax in two parts, half on 1 January, and half on 1 July, while companies pay corporation tax in a single payment on 1 January. There is no PAYE (Pay As You Earn) income tax scheme for business people. The tax payable is best saved up from week to week so that when the time for payment comes the money is available in the Deposit Account and can simply be transferred into the Current Account for payment by cheque.

Another use for Deposit Accounts is to build up a sinking fund. Consider a business that has machinery worth £40,000. All machinery suffers from wear and tear – a process called depreciation – and it is

usual to depreciate the asset by a percentage each year. A common
method is the straight-line method of depreciation. Here you say, for
example:

Machinery value   £40,000
Lifetime   10 years
Value after ten years as
second-hand item, or as scrap   £4,000

$$\text{Therefore depreciation per year} = \frac{£40,000 - £4,000}{10}$$

$$= \frac{£36,000}{10}$$

$$= \underline{£3,600 \text{ per annum}}$$

This depreciation means that each year the machinery falls in value
by an estimated £3,600, and this is a loss of the business.

If we write down the value of the asset in this way we record the
loss against the profits of the business, and say that the owner of the
business cannot have all the profits made, because £3,600 of it must
be put away to buy new machinery in a few years' time. The £3,600 is
put in a special deposit account. It earns interest every year, and a
new £3,600 is added each year, until, in ten years' time, all the money
is used to buy the new machinery that is required. This fund is called
a sinking fund, because that is the name used in the olden days when
funds were set aside to meet the obligations of a country under some
agreement or treaty, so that on the day the payment was due they
could sink (i.e. wipe out) the debt without any difficulty. We can set
up a sinking fund for any purpose, but the replacement of machinery,
motor vehicles and computers (these days) are some of the more
important.

The bank giro service

A bank giro service is one where payments move round from one
bank to another (these days usually electronically) without having to
leave the bank. They are always credit movements, and are often
called credit transfers. The commonest uses are:

1 *Paying wages direct to employees' bank accounts*   This is the easy
   way to pay wages. The Wages Department does all the calculations for wages (or at least the computer does) and prints out a
   detailed wages slip to give to the employee, but no actual money
   is included in the pay envelope. Instead the company sends a list
   of employees to the bank, with a credit transfer bank giro slip

saying how much money is to be credited to the employee's account. The company pays the whole payroll with one cheque, and the individual amounts are credited to the employees' accounts. No chance of a wages snatch; no notes to be counted or coins to be handled, and the wages are made available on the correct date with no interruption to the ordinary work while employees collect and sign for their pay.

2 *Counter payments by home agents* Many mail-order firms have home agents who sell household items to their friends and relatives and collect payments weekly from them. This money is paid over the counter of any bank, with a bank giro slip, for the credit of the mail-order house – wherever it may be. The money is taken into the bank's funds and the credit slip moves through the clearing system, so the home agent has no problems. In a rather similar way rates, community charges, gas, electricity and telephone bills can be paid over the counter in Post Offices, building societies and banks.

Standing orders

A standing order is a method of making regular monthly payments to such organizations as building societies for mortgages, or to finance houses for hire purchase payments. The customer gives the bank instructions in writing, and the computer is instructed to debit the customer's account (removing the money) and credit the account of the payee who is due to receive the money. Every month the computer sends the instruction through, waiting just long enough for the branch to check whether the customer has enough money to pay the instalment due. If the branch approves the payment the money moves, and the customer can never overlook the payment.

Direct debit movements

Sometimes money has to be paid by a customer but the customer does not know how much it is, or it is likely to vary. In this situation it is more sensible for the organization which wants the money to ask for the money. For example, professional organizations like the Chartered Institute of Transport, the Chartered Accountants and similar bodies may vary their subscriptions from year to year. If the member has made out a standing order the payment – when it arrives – may be for the wrong amount. It is much better if the member signs a **direct debit mandate**. This is an authority to the bank to pay any amount requested by the professional body on request. The system is also used by organizations such as the AA and the RAC, which have members all over the country, some of whom may not get to hear of any change in the subscription for a particular year.

Night safe services

Leaving money on premises overnight is always unwise. It is usual to empty all tills and leave the tills open. A burglar who finds a till which is locked may think there is money in it and smash it open – to no useful purpose and at great inconvenience to traders. Banks offer a night safe service which enables firms to pay in money after closing hours, in locked leather bags. The bag falls into a special vault where it may be collected next day by the trader for paying into the bank. Banks will only open the bags themselves if asked to do so, and on the understanding that any discrepancy between the money available and the figure on the paying-in slip enclosed in the bag is for the firm to explain. Some firms use the service every day. Others only use it when they need to – for example youth centres and evening institutes only collect fees once a term, and on such occasions may use the night safe service by special arrangement.

Banker's drafts

Suppose a trader wishes to obtain goods worth £1,000 from a supplier with whom he/she has not traded before. It would be inconvenient to pay in cash, but a cheque in the trader's own name would not be acceptable as the trader is not known to the supplier. Any bank will supply its customers (for a small charge) with a banker's draft, made out to the supplier, for the sum required and crossed 'A/c payee' so that it is not available to anyone else. Suppliers are always prepared to take such drafts in payment, because they are issued by major banks, which are absolutely reliable.

Peformance bonds and guarantees

There are many situations where an absolutely reliable promise to pay (a bond) or a guarantee are needed. For example, the customs authorities of many countries allows goods to pass through their territories without paying any duty, if they are destined for some other country. However, suppose a dishonest driver breaks open the load and sells the goods in the country, when the duty has not been paid. In such situations the customs authority would look to the driver's employers to pay the duty which had been avoided. Many banks will offer a guarantee that payment will be available and this is acceptable to the customs authority. The trader who needs the guarantee pays a fee for the service, but of course if the bank ever did have to pay up they would come back to the trader for reimbursement of the duty paid, leaving the firm to find the driver and recover the money paid (or charge the driver with an offence). Most such events can be covered by insurance, but the insurance company will only cover the loss if the driver is charged and brought before the Courts.

A performance bond is a little different. If a trader puts in a tender for a big contract, the organization offering the contract (which is usually for a large sum, possibly millions of pounds) does not want to be bothered by people who, if awarded the contract, would not be able to perform it. They therefore demand that when you put in the tender you also give a performance bond from a major bank (or insurance company) saying that you have got the necessary funds to perform the contract. The applicant sees his/her bank, ensures that a bond will be provided and knows that if the contract is awarded the bank will lend enough money to complete the contract.

Credit cards

There are many types of credit cards, but in all of them the principle is that the bank is virtually saying to all who deal with the card-holding person: 'We believe that the person named on the card is reliable up to a certain figure.' This is usually £50, but if the card is a credit card the person being asked to supply goods may phone and ask if a greater amount is covered. One boatyard in the South of England sold a yacht to an Arab customer for £80,000. He produced a credit card in payment. The trader rang the company concerned and was told: 'Oh yes, that gentleman can certainly have the yacht and pay on his card.' Later the boatyard rang to say: 'Well, we're delivering the yacht to him, but as we have to pay you 3 per cent on all card sales do you realize we shall have to pay you £2,400 commission on that sale.' To this the credit card company replied: 'Well, you must just weigh that against the thought that if you had not sold the yacht you would have lost a very considerable profit on the vessel.'

There are many people today who think that credit cards are issued too easily and that they encourage poor people to get into debt. There are of course some people who do get into difficulties but generally speaking the proportion is very tiny. What has happened is that a specialist organization, the bank, has stepped in between the buyer of goods and the seller of goods to take over the lending of money. In general this is done fairly, and more efficiently than before. The trader benefits because if there are any bad debts the bank suffers, not the trader. The customer is able to pay without the supplier needing to ask embarrassing questions about the customer's ability to pay. The amount the customer is in debt is a secret between the customer and the bank, and the system works very well for all parties.

These are only a few of the services banks offer to customers. Others are dealt with elsewhere in this book. The essential point is that the bank will always be the first person business people turn to when they want to safeguard funds in their possession, or to borrow money for business purposes. There are few problems banks cannot solve, but they will advise if they feel any course of action is unwise. A sound relationship with a banker, and respect for the activities of bankers, is in the best interests of every trader.

11.6 A project on self-financing

Mark Twain said that every millionaire he had ever met claimed to have hit the town where he made his fortune with only 5 cents in his pocket. Mark Twain said he had tried it many times but never found it worked for him. Think up ten (respectable) ways you could try to raise money to launch yourself into business. What job could you, personally, take to earn money? What relatives could you approach? What friends might be encouraged to take a few shares in a company if you decided to promote one? What assets do you have that you could sell? Look upon £1,000 as the amount that you should really try to raise. Give yourself an imaginary two years in which to raise it. (Thought: – You might like to spend the two years pondering which business to start up in. You will find a daily study of the *Yellow Pages* telephone directory a great help in triggering off ideas.)

Your project should consist of a selection of the best ways you can think of to raise money – each one developed in about 10–15 lines of writing explaining the advantages of the method and the possible snags in trying to follow that method. (Further thought – open a suitable bank account to put the money in. Many banks will actually start you off with a small sum – about £10. Insist on having both a Current Account and a Deposit Account. If they won't agree to that at least ask for a Current Account that earns interest. Don't open up an account with every bank you see. The essential point about developing a good relationship with a bank manager is to put your business his/her way and in return he/she will always be prepared to assist you when you really do need help.)

11.7 Rapid revision

Answers		Questions	
	–	1	**What is self-financing?**
1	It is the provision of the initial capital of a business by the proprietor, and the ploughing back of profits in subsequent years to avoid borrowing at a high rate of interest.	2	**How does borrowed capital affect a business?**

Answers	*Questions*
2 It creams off much of the profit into the pockets of those who supplied the capital. This is all right so long as the yield from the business is big enough to allow the entrepreneur some reward for his/her services.	3 **Why is hire purchase finance chiefly used by small businesses?**
3 (a) Because it is simple; (b) because it is controlled by the Director General of Fair Trading and is reasonably trouble free; (c) because the security lies in the assets purchased, and all the trader can lose is the use of the asset if he/she gets into financial difficulties.	4 **What are the advantages of leasing?**
4 (a) The asset is purchased by, and belongs to the lessor; (b) the lessee (who is actually using the asset) only pays a monthly fee for its use; (c) this fee is tax deductible as a business expense, whereas if the small trader purchased the asset he/she could only claim depreciation on it against tax.	5 **What is the natural institution to turn to for a loan?**
5 The bank. Banks exist to lend capital to those who require it.	6 **What information does a bank need before sanctioning a loan?**
6 (a) General information: (i) business background, (ii) key personnel, (iii) a well-developed plan if the business is new, including the target market, the products or services to be offered, any references available; (b) current financial information: (i) recent financial accounts –	

Answers		Questions	
	audited if it is a company, (ii) past bank statements, (iii) amount required; the uses the loan will be put to; cash flow forecasts and details of any security available.	7	**What is equity finance?**
7	Finance raised by issuing ordinary shares.	8	**Why is equity finance advisable?**
8	Because equity finance only gets a share of the profits if the directors declare a dividend, and cannot threaten a company (as bank borrowing or debenture funds can do if the business fails to pay the interest due).	9	**What is a debenture trustee?**
9	A person or institution (like a bank) authorized to hold the deeds associated with an issue of debentures and keep a watching brief over the affairs of the company so that when signs of instability appear it is possible to step in and seize the assets secured to protect the debenture holders.	10	**What is fixed capital?**
10	Capital tied up in fixed assets.	11	**What is working capital?**
11	Capital left over to work the business after the fixed assets have been purchased.	12	**What is the formula for working capital?**
12	Working capital = current assets − current liabilities.	13	**Go over the test again until you are sure of all the answers. Then try some of the questions in Section 11.8 below.**

11.8   Questions on Chapter 11

1   Explain why self-financing is the best way for a new business to find its capital. Explain why self-financing is still a good way to finance a business even when it is well-established.

2   Naomi Clarke is proposing to purchase a computer to assist in designing her fashion garments. The purchase price is £2,685 + VAT of $17\frac{1}{2}$ per cent. She is paying a deposit of £250. The balance, including the cost of an insurance policy to cover the loan £88.15, will be charged interest at a flat rate over three years of $8\frac{1}{2}$ per cent per annum. Draw up these figures as they would appear on a hire purchase agreement, showing the monthly repayment over thirty-six months.

3   Peter Russell is preparing to purchase a van for use in his business. The price is £4,240 plus VAT at $17\frac{1}{2}$ per cent. He will trade in an old vehicle for £850 which will act as a deposit. The balance, including a premium of £108.45 for an insurance policy on the loan, will bear interest at 9.5 per cent over two years. Draw up these figures as they would appear in the hire purchase document and show the monthly repayment over the two-year period.

4   (a)   Why should a business person have both a Current Account and a Deposit Account?
   (b)   In which account would you put:
     (i)   A cheque received from a customer for the completion of a job.
     (ii)   VAT money for safe keeping until required.
     (iii)   Cash takings from tills.
     (iv)   Profits to be set aside for the replacement of depreciating assets.

5   Explain the following crossings on cheques:
   (a)   A general crossing.
   (b)   A crossing 'A/c payee only'.
   (c)   A special crossing.

6   (a)   I expect the yield on this new product to be a clear $12\frac{1}{2}$ per cent profit but I need to borrow £5,000 to purchase new equipment.
   (b)   I expect the yield on this new product to be a clear 60 per cent but I need to borrow £25,000 to purchase new machinery.
   Which of these two projects seems the more worthy one to lend money to, and why? Loans are currently being made available at 12 per cent per annum. What criticism can be made of the question?

7   Suggest four ways in which money may be paid, using the services of a bank. Which method would be most appropriate for paying:

(a) A trade supplier.
(b) A hire purchase account.
(c) A subscription to the AA (which may vary from year to year).
(d) A new supplier who states that cheques can only be accepted from established customers.

8 What is fixed capital? What is working capital? From the Balance Sheet of Clear Vision shown below work out its fixed capital and its working capital.

Balance Sheet of Clear Vision
(as at 1 January 19xx)

Fixed assets	£	£	Capital	£
Machinery	4,280		At start of year	13,496
Furniture and fittings	2,580			
Office equipment	1,120			
Loose tools	2,360			
		10,340		
Current assets			Long-term liabilities	
Stock in hand	3,000		Loan from Helpful	
Debtors	2,156		Bank PLC	5,000
Cash at bank	4,450		Current liabilities	
Cash in hand	50		Trade creditors	1,500
		9,656		
		£19,996		£19,996

12
Production

12.1 The objectives of business

Fundamentally a business aims to create goods or services which satisfy human wants in some way, and enable the proprietors of the business to achieve a variety of satisfactions, among which the achievement of profits may be central, but not always so.

Many activities are either non-profit-making, or not totally motivated by profit. Others are purely profit-inspired, but even so they may bring great advantages to the users of the good or service irrespective of whether the business concerned is also very profitable to its owners.

To achieve profits, or whatever other satisfactions are aimed at, the enterprise must achieve its objectives in production, distribution and marketing of the good or service. It must maintain sound control, particularly financial and cost control. It must solve all the technical problems that arise, develop systems of work which meet all the restraints imposed on business by central and local government and it must keep within the law, both the public law (which includes constitutional law, criminal law and administrative law) and private law (which includes contract law, tort and property law). In the long run its objectives must include future planning, research and development, so that new products or services are developed as old ones reach the end of their life cycle. All this is rather daunting, risks have to be taken, plans have to be made, judgement exercised and staff motivated. We cannot study it all at once, so we will begin with production.

12.2 Production: innovation and development

An American proverb says: 'If you invent a better mousetrap the world will beat a path to your door.' Practically all firms are trying to invent a better mousetrap, whether it is a good or a service. There are a number of sources of better mousetraps. They include:

The clever idea suggested by the outsider

An outsider may write or phone with an idea and ask if the firm is interested. Generally speaking it is wise to keep an open mind on such suggestions. The person may have a totally unworkable idea or scheme. On the other hand they may have a genuinely useful and marketable idea or scheme. Some general rules are:

1   Alert staff to the fact that management is always interested in practical ideas and schemes, and that any such enquiries should be passed to a named individual who has a proper procedure for dealing with outsiders.
2   This named individual should have written – preferably pre-printed – information, telling the outsider that the firm is not interested in vague ideas but is interested in well-thought-out proposals, which include drawings (or even prototype products) where necessary; some estimate of the market envisaged, particulars of any patent registered, etc.
3   Since outsiders are always fearful of having their brainwaves stolen and even great and powerful companies have been found doing this (and have had millions of pounds (or dollars) damages awarded against them), any preprinted advice should make it clear that inventors can rely on the honesty and integrity of the firm in a fair evaluation of the idea, and a proper reward or royalty if the idea is proceeded with.

The suggestion box

Many firms run a suggestion box in which suggestions can be made to a special team of top managers, without going through the usual channels. The 'usual channels' means that one passes on ideas to superiors, who pass them on to their superiors. By this route the originator of the idea may not get either the recognition or the reward to which he/she is entitled. Superiors often condemn ideas from junior staff out of petty spite, or even jealousy. They may put the idea up as if it originated with them, and not give credit where it is due.

The 'suggestion box' idea works better perhaps in improving an established system of work, or an existing product, rather than in producing a completely new idea. This is natural, for the low-level people concerned are actually working the existing system, and know what the weaknesses are. Thus a process which results in spillages of expensive, or even dangerous, liquids is very apparent to the person who has to keep cleaning up each time a spillage occurs. A suggestion to get around the problem will save both the liquid, and the time wasted cleaning up, let alone any adverse effects on the working environment. One cleaner who suggested a solution to such a problem earned £1,000. This had been calculated as 50 per cent of the savings to the firm in the first year the new idea was used. Generally speaking suggestion box ideas are rewarded on the basis of a share in the benefits achieved.

The Research and Development Department

Most firms have someone in charge of innovations, and large firms have a special department called R & D (Research and Development). Where people are employed to discover new ideas, or new solutions to old problems, the fruits of their labour belong to the employer, not to the individual, because they take the position with the intention of producing such results. In recent years some recognition, in the form of merit awards, royalties, etc. tends to be given, or the employee may accept a lower remuneration in return for some share in the proceeds of the work done.

The chief activities include:

1   Innovative work along lines proposed by the Board of Directors and given to the R & D Department as a directive or instruction.
2   Problem solving in response to failures in the system of work or some aspect of an existing product.
3   Problem solving in response to complaints from customers using the final product, fed through to R & D by the selling force.
4   Problem solving in response to public disquiet conveyed to the R & D Department by the Public Relations Department. Such matters may be about environmental effects, hazards not previously reported, etc.

The essential result of all these aspects of research and development work is an improved product or service, a better system of work, and recommendations to top management about new products, new methods of using waste, new packaging and wrapping materials etc.

Market research

Market research is a programme of work where we investigate all aspects of a market to discover:

- Whether there is a broad body of people interested in a good or service we are proposing to market.
- Whether they would, if mutually approached, pay a price for the good or service which would not only cover our costs in producing the product or service but leave a reasonable margin of profit over afterwards as well.

- Whether the market is likely to be a recurring market, or a one-off market. The most profitable sales are nearly always the repeat sales – the first sales usually are made before we have reached a break-even point and moved into profitability.
- Whether there are any special features of the proposed product which might affect sales – for example some colours or sizes might have more appeal than others, or might appeal to particular age groups or ethnic groups. We might avoid approaching people who are not likely to be interested, and target our advertising better at those who are, if our research reveals facts we had not thought of before.

Before starting any market research programme it is always best to think the whole thing through carefully first. Can we discover what we wish to know by **desk research**. This involves working through any published material in such places as local libraries, the libraries of professional bodies such as the trade association to which we belong or the local Chamber of Commerce. Consider the following points:

- How many people are there who might be interested in our product?
- How affluent are they?
- What is the total market – the total amount of money likely to be spent by these people on our type of product.
- What share of the total can we hope to achieve: 1 per cent or 10 per cent or 50 per cent.
- Who are our main competitors and how can we compete with them in the best way? Will it be on price, or on quality, or on after-sales service, or something else.

In-house research

We may already have helpful information in-house. **In-house research** means looking at information available within our own firm – the results of earlier surveys, letters from customers, files of magazine cuttings which some firms take the trouble to cut out and keep to give an information base on topics of interest to the company, etc. Another source of in-house market intelligence is the reports coming in from representatives, agents, wholesalers and retailers who handle our products. If they are properly alert to our needs they will relay on to us the views of customers not only about defects in our products but about products they wish we produced. Any suggestions of this sort might quickly be turned into new and worthwhile products with wide public interest. Such people may also report on the affluence of customers, telling us which sectors of the population find prices too high and which snap up our products because they believe them to be cheap at their present prices.

Field research

Field research is the investigation of the market by means of questionnaires and interviews conducted as part of a new programme for approaching consumers and other users actually in the field i.e. the shopping precinct, or the housing estate or a particular trade or industry where we market our product.

Census

A census is an investigation in which we ask every single member of the population. The word 'population' does not mean every citizen of the country (except in the case of the National Census, held in the UK in the first year of every decade – i.e. in 1981, 1991, 2001 etc.). Thus the 'population' in a piece of field research about student textbooks would be all the students in the nation, whereas if it was an enquiry about the sale of law textbooks the 'population' would only be the law students in the nation – a much smaller figure. In fact, because of the cost involved, we can rarely conduct a census, especially if the numbers in the population are large. Instead we try to ask a sample only of the population.

Sampling

Sampling is where we conduct an enquiry by using a **representative sample** of the total population. There can be many kinds of sample. Ideally sampling should be **random sampling** which may be defined as a system of sampling where each member of the population has as good a chance of being selected for interview as any other member of the population. Unfortunately purely random sampling results in a very scattered enquiry. Thus if we selected 5000 UK citizens (out of a total of 55 million) they would be so widely spread around the country it would be very expensive to send interviewers to see them. Among the various methods of sampling we may list:

1   *Systematic sampling*   This is where we select, for example, every tenth member of the population. If we choose the starting point by random methods, for example by drawing one of the numbers 1–10 out of a hat and then systematically selecting every tenth item we have **systematic random sampling**. Suppose three came out of the hat. Then we ask the third, thirteenth, twenty-third, thirty-third etc. person in the list which contains the whole population.

2   *Stratified sampling*   Sometimes a systematic sample will not give a true and fair view of the views of the population, because some particular group is missed out entirely. If there is an enquiry about the economy and none of the unemployed are asked to express their view we shall not get a fair view of the economy. If 10 per cent of the population are unemployed we shall need one in ten of

those questioned to be unemployed if we are to get a true and fair view. In that case we may need to stratify the population into layers with different interests and include representatives of each strata – a stratified sample.

3 *Multistage sampling (also called AREA sampling)* This is a cheap way of sampling a very broad population. Suppose we take all the counties of the UK and select five of them at random. Suppose those five authorities have electoral wards, and we select eight of them. Suppose those eight wards have 50,000 households and we select 2 per cent of them, which is 1000 householders. We now have 1000 people to interview but they are all in eight wards, scattered around the country. If we send eight interviewers, one to each area, with a list of the householders they are to interview we shall have a fairly inexpensive inquiry which is nevertheless representative of the whole population.

4 *Quota sampling* With quota sampling we make the cost of the enquiry less by allowing the interviewer to select any one they meet until the quota allotted to them has been filled, when they must not use any more people in that category. For example, an enquiry about the likelihood of a motor vehicle accessory (say a car cushion) being adopted might be addressed to quotas as follows:

(a)	Those who buy a new car costing £20,000 plus	2
(b)	Those buying new cars costing £10,000–£19,999	8
(c)	Those buying new cars in the £5,000–£9,999 range	35
(d)	Those who buy good second-hand cars	45
(e)	Those who only buy 'old bangers'	10
	Total	100

The interviewer will ask whoever he/she likes to give an opinion, but once he/she has filled the quota of people in that group any further people encountered in that category will be regretfully refused.

Questionnaires
Market research is often carried out by getting people to complete a questionnaire. Some bodies like the Consumer Association, which publishes the magazine *Which*, use questionnaires very extensively to find out what the public thinks of products which are in use on the market, or services which they have used (such as tourist services, hotel services etc.). The questionnaire method is relatively cheap, since we only have to produce the form itself and post it to the persons invited to respond to it. It does have drawbacks. We may list:

Advantages
1 The questionnaire, if well devised, covers the whole topic we wish to investigate and if completed responsibly will give the research bureau a great deal of helpful information.

```
         **********              ..*........
         **********              ..*........
         **********              ..*........
```

(a) A census – all members of the population are interviewed or invited to complete the questionnaire.

(b) Systematic random sampling. The third item was selected at random. We interview the third, thirteenth, twenty-third, etc.

(c)

Income ranges	Number to interview
£30,000+	50
£20,000–£29,999	150
£15,000–£19,999	180
£10,000–£14,999	220
£5,000–£9,999	320
Under £5,000	80
Stratified sampling	1000

The proportions to be interviewed reflect the % nationally of people in the strata concerned.

(d) Multi-stage sampling

Of 166 institutions of higher education we choose a random 10 per cent = seventeen. The seventeen institutions have a total of eighty-four departments. We choose a random 10 per cent = eight. The eight departments total 3500 students. We choose a random 10 per cent = 350.

350 students interviewed.

(e) Quota sampling by ages and sexes.

		Sex
Age	Male	Female
Under 16	0	0
16–19	16	16
20–35	28	28
36–60	38	38
Over 60	18	18
	100	100

Figure 12.1 Choosing interviewees for market research

2 It is relatively inexpensive, even if a stamped addressed envelope (sae) or reply paid envelope is sent out with the form.
3 The answers do not all come in at once, so that the response is staggered and if we process the forms which do arrive every day we can keep on top of the work and not be overwhelmed by it.

Disadvantages
1 As there is no interviewer, the person responding may misunderstand the questions altogether. One enquiry about burglaries was misread by one respondent as 'budgerigars' and the answer to the

questions were consequently confusing. Asked whether they were put to flight the reply was 'They kept up near the ceiling for over two hours.'

2 Bias may enter into the answers, especially if the respondent has a particular interest in the industry or service concerned.
3 The odd 'joke' response can be expected, and has to be disregarded.
4 The rate of response is often less than it would be if the interview method had been adopted instead.

Design   The design of the questionnaire is important. Points about the design are:

1 The form cannot be too long, or people will not respond to it – getting tired before they get to the end of it.
2 So far as possible several answers should be provided from which the respondent can select the one that seems most appropriate.
3 A system should be prepared beforehand to record the responses as they come in, perhaps on the five-barred gate system (see Figure 5.1).

Interviewing
Where it is decided to use interviewers for a market research programme we must be prepared for a more expensive survey than one carried out by a questionnaire. The questionnaire itself will still be necessary but now the interviewer will take the respondent through the questionnaire asking the questions and recording the answers as they are given. There is less chance of the respondent not understanding the questions, since the interviewer can explain any difficult parts. The joke response is also much less likely when the interviewer conducts the completion of the form. There may still be some difficulty in getting responses from the selected interviewees, because they may be out when called upon or unwilling to cooperate. The interviewing method is certainly most useful in situations where completion of the questionnaire is compulsory and the threat of a fine, or imprisonment, ensures cooperation. However, this is rarely possible on a market research programme.

Interviewers must be trained, especially in avoidance of bias. Ideally they should be as keen as the organizer of the enquiry to find out the true facts about the situation under investigation, and should be told that the recording of false answers, or, even worse, a more favourable answer than is really being given, is totally undesirable. As is often said about computers 'garbage in, garbage out'. If your raw data from the enquiry is false, any conclusions you draw from the enquiry will be false too.

Questionnaire: Window Cleaning

Our company is bringing out shortly a new window cleaning product which is for the do-it-yourself window cleaner. We are interested in your opinions on this subject and would be grateful if you would complete and return this questionnaire. Please tick the box which is nearest to your choice of answer.

1   How are the windows in your house cleaned?
By a professional window cleaner ☐
By the man/woman of the house ☐

3   Is a branded-name window cleaner used on them?
Yes ☐   No ☐   If yes, what brand is it? ....

4   What do you estimate it costs you to get your windows clean?
(a)   By a window cleaner ....
(b)   In cleaning materials if you do it yourself ....

5   How many windows are involved?
(a)   On the ground floor ....
(b)   On the first floor ....
(c)   Higher than the first floor ....

6   We are offering a free bottle (plastic) of our new product to people who complete this questionnaire. Would you like one?
Yes ☐   No ☐   If yes, please insert name and address here.
....
....
....
.... Post code ....

7   Should you find the product satisfactory and wish to purchase a further supply which retail outlet would you be most likely to go to for the product?
Name of retail outlet ....
Address (if known) ....
....
If address not known please give the district ....

Thank you for completing our questionnaire. Please post it in the reply paid envelope supplied. If this has been mislaid please post to
Cleaner Windows (Tibshelf) Ltd
Freepost 12
xxxxxxxx
Derbyshire DE12 9QR

Figure 12.2   A questionnaire

Points to remember

- The objectives of a business can only be achieved if the whole procedure of production, distribution and marketing is successfully pursued.
- Research and development to produce new products and improved versions of existing products or services is also essential.
- Some of the chief sources of new ideas are: (a) external sources – bright ideas from inventors etc.; (b) suggestion box ideas; (c) commissioned research from the Board, and research to solve problems drawn to our attention by the public, customers etc.
- Market research involves a detailed study of the market using desk research, in-house research and field research based on questionnaire and interviews.
- Censuses are investigations of the entire population; more usually we have to be content with sampling and drawing conclusions about the whole population from the sample. Samples should be random, but to get an economic programme of work it is usual to use either a systematic random sample, a stratified sample, an area (multistage) sample or a quota sample.

12.3 The process of production

There are countless systems of production and it is impossible to do more than give a general outline. Students should try to visit factories and workshops in their home areas and study the system of production in use. The basic idea is that we take raw materials, which are usually a gift of nature, and turn them into a more convenient and useful product than nature provided, by working on them in some way. We may turn iron ore into motor cars, bauxite into aeroplanes, crude oil into petrol, oak trees into furniture, sand into windows and scientific glassware etc. In doing these things we add value to the natural product and make a profit for the enterprise after covering costs. Henry Ford explained what manufacturing is. 'Manufacturing is not buying cheap and selling dear. It is the focusing upon a project of the principles of power, accuracy, economy, system, continuity, speed and repetition.'

The elements of the process of production are raw materials, labour and a system of technology for bringing the labour to bear upon the raw materials in such a way as to change them into a more serviceable form. In order to have such a system we need tools and equipment of every sort, adequately deployed in premises designed to make them effective, management to plan and control the processes and a general administration to ensure the wellbeing of the plant, the employees and the product at all stages of its manufacture.

Such a system involves heavy expenditures, both in the form of prime costs (the actual materials and labour) and overhead costs (the costs of the general enterprise). A detailed study of these costs is helpful in seeing how value is added at every stage of production.

12.4   Types of cost

We all know what is meant by the cost of anything in everyday life – it is the price we pay for it to the retailer who supplies it to us. This final 'cost' however is made up of many other costs added in at various levels, and to the producer of goods or services who is cost conscious it is these elements of costs which are the chief concern. Before discussing these various types of cost it is interesting to see how the final retail price is built up. This is shown in Figure 12.3.

The types of cost to be considered are as follows:

Direct costs or prime costs

Direct costs are costs which become directly incorporated into the product. The commonest direct costs are the raw materials used, the wages paid to employees involved directly in production, and any design costs. Direct costs can be related directly to a particular product. Thus if a port authority calls for a particular piece of lifting apparatus to be manufactured the raw materials, labour and design costs will be charged to the contract (under a system known as Contract Accounts) and will have to be borne by the port authority. Since these are the first batch of costs associated with any product they are often called **prime costs** (primary means 'first').

Indirect costs or factory overheads

These are costs which cannot be attributed to any particular product, but are spread out over all the products made. For example, factory rent, factory rates, the foreman's wages, telephone expenses, maintenance costs of machinery and many similar items. Some materials cannot be allocated directly, for example shuttering may be used in concrete work several times. Such costs will have to be allocated to the various **cost centres** within the factory and are said to be **absorbed** by the cost centres. The system is sometimes spoken of as **absorption costing**. Of course it is possible for debate to arise as to what method is fair for absorbing costs in this way. Thus if overheads were allocated on the basis of a percentage of prime costs, or on a basis of a percentage of the number of units produced we might get very different amounts to be charged to a particular product. It is for the Cost Accountants and the Production Manager to agree a fair basis.

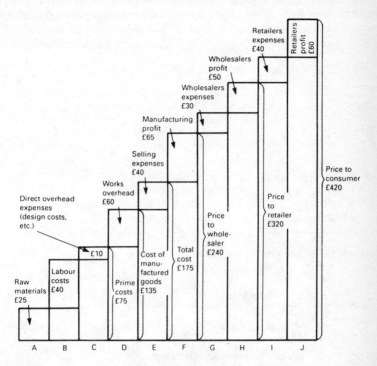

Figure 12.3   How the final retail price is built up

Notes:
1 There are three prime costs entering into the cost structure – raw materials, labour and direct overheads. Then there are the general works overheads which cannot be directly related to any product, but have to be averaged out over all outputs.
2 We also have selling expenses, wholesalers' expenses and retailers' expenses entering into the cost structure.
3 There are three elements of profit entering into the final cost, the manufacturer's profit (column F), the wholesaler's profit (column H) and the retailer's profit (column J).
4 We sometimes buy direct from the manufacturer or direct from the wholesaler, and when we do we expect to obtain the goods more cheaply.
5 However, this may be an illusion, because we will ourselves be doing some of the work previously done by the wholesaler or retailer. For example, we may be going to collect the goods (transport) or running the risk they will be damaged in transit (insurance) or arranging a loan from the bank (finance).
6 The economic argument in favour of the full pattern of distribution shown in the diagram (and justifying the full costs) is that since at every stage the work is being carried out by specialists the whole process will be more efficiently carried out than if amateurs (you and me as consumers) try to do part of the work to save expense. In fact accidents, waste of time, fuel etc. will make the overall process more expensive.

Suppose all units of output are fairly similar even though there are five different products. The factory overhead charge might be allocated as follows:

$$\frac{\text{Total overhead}}{\text{Total number of units produced}} = \frac{£50,000}{10,000 \text{ units}} = £5 \text{ per unit}$$

Every item produced, therefore, would have £5 added to it for factory overhead costs and would have to earn that extra £5 in its final selling price. Factory cost would therefore be made up as shown in Figure 12.4.

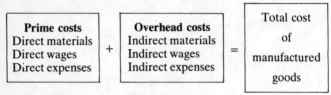

Figure 12.4   The cost of manufactured goods

12.5   Types of production

There are a number of ways in which production can be classified, and each has its associated method of costing. The two broad areas are **specific order costing** and **operation costing**.

Specific order costing

Under specific order costing we have:

1 *Job costing*   Here the 'job' is a particular piece of work which has been ordered by a customer, or possibly by one of the departments of our own company to save buying in an item. For example, in the construction industry it might be the building of an oil platform, or in the printing trade it might be the printing of a book. The schedules of work required to process the various parts of the job will be drawn up and as materials and labour are allocated to the work the various costs will be recorded and charged to the job.

2 *Batch costing*   This is rather similar, but the order usually comes from a department of our own firm. The item required is usually a component of a larger product – for example in the motor car manufacturing industry it might be brake blocks or switches or rear light housing. Relatively simple items can probably be produced quite quickly and continuous production would not be needed. A batch – say 10,000 items – would be made and taken

into stock by the department concerned. An agreed minimum stock level – say 1000 items – will be locked away separately, or 'bagged up'. No one is allowed to break into the minimum stock without first requisitioning a further batch of 10,000. By the time the last 1000 items have been used up the Production Department will have produced the new batch. With computerization the computer can be programmed to print out a requisition as the minimum stock level is detected by the computer.

3 *Contract costing* This is used for long-term contracts, such as motorway building, bridge building etc. The costs incurred will be allocated to the contract, and from time to time quantity surveyors will measure up the work done and arrange a part-payment for the completed work.

Operation costing

This is the costing of continuous operations. There are two kinds – process costing and service costing.

1 *Process costing* This is used where production is continuous, as in the oil industry, cement making, breweries and many food processes. The costs of the raw materials and labour etc. are averaged out over the whole output to find the cost per gallon, or per sack, or whatever the unit of production is.

2 *Service costing* With services we cannot allocate costs directly. For example, transport costs when a vehicle is loaded with an assortment of crates and packages, for delivery at various points along the vehicle's route. The costs are added together and an average price is worked out using some sort of appropriate unit. For transport we often use the tonne-mile. Thus a crate weighing ½ tonne and travelling 20 miles is charged with 10 tonne-miles at 40 pence per tonne-mile. This sounds a little complicated but becomes very easy once we are used to it and it is repeated every day as deliveries take place.

12.6 Cost sheets

Whenever goods are supplied, or services are performed, there is a pricing problem to be overcome. The trader who buys goods to sell again has only to add on his mark-up. The manufacturer has a more difficult task, for the materials he manufactures are built into the finished product either to meet the needs of the particular job – job costing – or as part of a process – process costing. A person who provides services, like a building contractor, freight forwarder or a repairer will usually use job costing or work to an agreed contract and use contract costing.

Cost sheet serial number:

Customer's name and address:

Telephone number:

Job number:

Job description:

Materials used	F	£	p	Components used	F	£	p	Foundry charges	F	£	p	Machine shop charges	F	£	p	Cost summary	£	p
																Materials		
																Components		
																Foundry		
																Machine shop		
																Drawing Office		
																Packing Dept.		
																Transport Dept.		
Total				Total				Total				Total				Other charges		
Add oncost at 50%				Add oncost at 50%				Add oncost at 200%				Add oncost at 150%				Total costs		
Total to summary				Total to summary				Total to summary				Total to summary				Add profit		
																Invoice total		

Drawing office	F	£	p	Packing dept.	F	£	p	Transport dept.	F	£	p	Other charges	F	£	p
Total				Total				Total				Total			
Add oncost at 100%				Add oncost at 75%				Add oncost at 100%				Add oncost at 200%			
Total to summary				Total to summary				Total to summary				Total to summary			

Final Report: Note here any problems connected with this order.

Figure 12.5 A simple cost sheet (Note: this illustration may be photocopied for class use)

Simple costing usually involves the use of some type of cost sheet on which the details of costs incurred can be noted. From the cost sheet the actual price to be charged for the job can be calculated. A simple cost sheet is ruled to provide adequate space to record the various types of costs which are incurred on any particular job. There will usually be space for materials used and for components 'bought-in' to be used as required. Thus a commercial vehicle-body builder might use materials like timber, sheet alloy, etc., but might buy in components like lighting fittings or refrigeration machinery for use in the vehicles under construction. Other departments – machine shops, foundries, etc., may perform parts of the work, and service departments like the transport department may need to charge their costs to the contract or job in hand. When the job is complete, and time has been allowed for all the cost centres concerned to send in their charges, the cost clerk will proceed to draw up a summary of costs which will give the grand total of costs to be recovered. Overheads will usually have been calculated to give an average figure to be added to all the costs incurred. This is shown on the cost sheet as an 'oncost', and will vary for each department according to the size of the overheads in that part of the organization. A typical cost sheet is shown in Figure 12.5.

12.7   Break-even points

One of the important aspects of any production plan is to know at what point we shall break even on any particular project, or product. We can always work out a break-even point, but it is best to consider the problem by drawing up a break-even chart. Briefly we may say:

1   We break even when we have covered our total costs, and from that point on we can begin to make profits.
2   Total costs are made up of 'fixed costs' and 'variable costs'. To explain variable costs first, they are the costs incurred in making our product, and they are called 'variable' because they vary with output. So if I make pizzas with pizza pastry costing 10 pence and other items costing 10 pence, and if the labour cost is 5 pence the variable costs of my pizzas are 25 pence. So long as I sell them for more than 25 pence I shall make a profit on any particular pizza. Let us say I sell them for 50 pence. Then I have covered my variable costs, and have 25 pence left over. This 25 pence is called the 'contribution'.
3   To what does it contribute? The answer is it is a contribution towards covering my fixed costs (often called overheads), and once they are covered, and I have broken even, they are profits of the business. Fixed costs must now be explained. They are the

costs that have to be borne whatever the output of the business. Thus I need a factory whether I make 1000 pizzas or 100,000 pizzas. I need a managing director, a lorry for distribution purposes etc. These are all part of the 'fixed costs', which do not vary directly with output – though I might need a bigger lorry if output grows. Suppose my total fixed costs are £2,000 and I sell one pizza. I have a contribution of 25 pence towards my fixed costs and no profit. I shall need to sell 8000 pizzas to cover my fixed

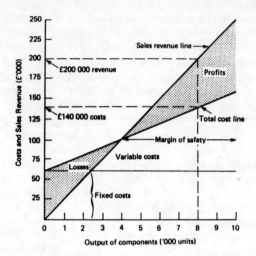

Figure 12.6   A break-even chart

Notes:

1   The fixed costs are £60,000, whatever the output and are shown as a horizontal line parallel to the x axis.

2   The variable costs are £10 per unit and are shown by the sloping line starting at £60,000 and rising to £160,000 at an output of 10,000 components.

3   The receipts of the business are £25 for each item sold, and these begin at the zero point on the graph and rise to £250,000 at an output of 10,000 units.

4   The point where the total cost line is cut by the sales revenue line is the break-even point. It occurs at an output of 4000 components. Here the 4000 × £25 received (£100,000) exactly equals the total costs of £60,000 + (4000 × £10) (the variable costs).

5   From that point on every extra unit sold provides £10 to cover its own variable costs and a £15 contribution to profits.

6   At 8000 units output the takings are £200,000 covering £60,000 fixed costs, £80,000 variable costs and £60,000 profits.

7   The margin of safety is the amount by which sales exceed the break-even point. If the margin is wide the business has every prospect of continuing. Suppose costs rose, either fixed or variable costs. The break-even point would move to the right (it taking more sales to reach the new break-even point now that costs have risen). Suppose we now pass the increased cost on to the consumer by raising our prices. The higher prices mean a higher contribution (see above) and the break-even point moves back towards the left. Our margin of safety is restored.

costs, so 8000 pizzas is my break-even point. After that I shall begin to make a profit.

4   If I sell less than 8000 pizzas I shall make a loss. If I sell exactly 8000 pizzas I shall break even. If I sell more than 8000 pizzas I shall begin to make a profit. Suppose I sell 10,000 pizzas. The first 8000 will contribute enough to cover all the fixed costs as well as the actual cost of materials etc. The remaining 2000 will earn £1,000, of which £500 is the variable costs of the extra pizzas and the other £500 is profit. So I begin to move into profit once the break-even point is passed. Figure 12.6 shows the break-even chart of a component manufacturer in the car industry who makes a component for sale at £25. The fixed costs are £60,000 and the variable costs of each unit sold are £10. Study the diagram now and the notes below it.

12.8   Job satisfaction and production

We all want to enjoy the fruits of production and expect to have available in our shops an enormous variety of goods of every sort. Regrettably, we are not quite so enthusiastic about actually producing the goods that everyone wants, and too many people think that working in a factory is beneath them; something that should be done by lesser mortals. Similarly much of the work of transport and distribution is done in fairly dreary places, which are not easily turned into a source of job satisfaction. This attitude to production is really mistaken, and for those who have the vision to see that production activities are absolutely essential, and the chief source of any nation's prosperity, the factory can be a stimulating place. For many people, however, the repetitive nature of the work, and the small requirement it makes on the intellectual capacities of the worker make factory work unattractive except for the paypacket it produces. The workplace ceases to be a place where the artistic and aesthetic capacities of the worker can be exercised, and the truly fulfilling part of life has to be sought elsewhere in family life, hobbies and similar pursuits.

This situation could be improved if managements, and society generally, were prepared to concede status to the factory worker, recognizing the vital part production plays in everyone's success. Proper levels of wages in particular must be negotiated to reflect the contribution made by the shopfloor, and representation of shopfloor workers on all committees is essential. Being so much nearer to the point of production, and knowing the practical problems, means that shopfloor workers have much to contribute to planning and design – and can save money with their suggestions. These may well anticipate and prevent bottlenecks in the production process, and even accidents such as explosions, tainting of one product with another, elimination of dangerous manoeuvres, etc.

We often hear calls for trade union representation on the boards of companies, a practice which is much more common in some countries (such as West Germany) than it is in the UK. While this is undoubtedly desirable, there is just as strong a case for having representation, not just from a union point of view, but from the point of view of the production process involved, on all committees in a firm. For example, if a firm has an Export Department it might be well worthwhile bringing a representative of the shopfloor onto any Export Panel. The delegate would not only voice the shopfloor's view of export problems to the Export Panel, but would take their views of the urgency of meeting quality and delivery deadlines back to the shopfloor.

12.9   Telecommunications and production

The 1980s and 1990s have seen new methods of manufacturing with robot machines, computerized design systems and electronic databases which have changed many of the ways we work. Increased international competition has meant that more use is made of standardized components, and outside designers who may be based anywhere in the world. This requires production managers to be in touch with suppliers, customers and sources of new data around the world.

The methods used are described more fully in Chapter 19, but production managers are vitally concerned with these new developments. For example, the development of JIT (just in time) programmes means that orders are placed so that only the correct quantity of materials and components comes into the factory every day. This means that the Production Department cannot requisition supplies from the Purchasing Department and wait while they place an order with a supplier. They need to place orders every day – send 17 units for Wednesday – send 35 units for Thursday etc. The use of facsimile copiers (FAX) to place orders moves the ordering responsibility into the Production Department. There are many similar savings. A useful booklet *Turning Ideas into Reality* is available free of charge from British Telecom International, Holborn Centre, 120 Holborn, London EC1N 2TE.

12.10   A project on production

Draw up a cost sheet for any field of activity with which you are familiar. It could be based on your experience in your present employment, or in an earlier post, or in a part-time job if you have such experience. Figure 12.6 may help to give you some ideas on the style and layout of such a document.

12.11 Rapid revision

Answers	Questions
–	**1 What are the aims of businesses?**
1 To create goods or services to satisfy wants, and make a profit in the process.	**2 'If you invent a better mousetrap . . . (*continue the sentence*)**
2 . . . the world will beat a path to your door?'	**3 What are the chief sources of 'better mousetraps'?**
3 (a) Bright ideas from outsiders; (b) suggestion box ideas from the shopfloor; (c) new products generated in-house by the R & D Department; (d) improved versions of old products to meet problems or criticisms directed to the firm's Public Relations Department; (e) market research findings.	**4 What are the chief approaches to market research?**
4 (a) Desk research; (b) in-house research; (c) field research.	**5 What is a census?**
5 Investigation of the whole population (or at least the whole 'population' likely to be interested in the product under consideration).	**6 What is a sample?**
6 A smaller number than the whole population chosen to be as representative of the population as possible.	**7 What is a random sample?**

Answers	Questions
7 A sample is random when every member of the whole population has as good a chance as any other member of the population of being selected for the sample.	8 **List the chief types of sample**
8 (a) Systematic samples; (b) stratified samples; (c) multistage (or area) samples; and (d) quota samples.	9 **What are the chief methods of production?**
9 (a) Job production (to manufacture a particular item for a customer); (b) batch production (to make a batch of components); (c) contract production (to comply with the terms of a particular contract); (d) process (or flow) production of a continuous nature; (e) service production, in which a service is supplied to meet a contract for services.	10 **Why is job satisfaction important in factory work?**
10 Because a person who cannot experience job satisfaction will lose interest in the employment concerned, and may become a frequent absentee, or move from job to job (placing a great strain on such departments as the Personnel Department and the Training Departments, endlessly trying to recruit and train new staff).	11 **Go over the test again until you are sure of all the answers. Then try the questions in Section 12.12 below.**

12.12   Questions on Chapter 12

1   Explain how the final price charged to a consumer for an appliance such as an electric iron or a television set has been built up?

2   What is job costing? What is process costing? Compare the calculations necessary to cost a job like building a footbridge over a main road, with those necessary to work out the cost of a gallon of petrol at an oil refinery.

For the next two questions make two copies of the cost sheet in Figure 12.6 and use them to record the costs for the following jobs performed by Prefabricators PLC for the customers named. What was the total charge to the customer in each case?

3 Serial number: 0001. Job number: 284. Light Engineering PLC, 24 Somers Way, London E5 2TS. Telephone 01 008 3124. Job description: spiral staircases. Materials: steel rod, £38.50; brass rod, £72.85; bolts etc., £8.54. Foundry charges: spiral assemblies 84 at £5.80 each. Drawing office: plans, £45.80. Transport charges: £39.50. Other charges: quality control, £23.50; painting shop, £38.50. Profit to be based on 40 per cent of total costs.

4 Serial number: 0002. Job number: 285. Rail Enthusiasts Club, Glen Railway Station, Aberdovey. Telephone 0436 012. Job description: admission turnstiles. Materials used; steel bars, £38.50; steel sheet, £42.50; sand and cement, £15.80. Foundry charges, £31.64. Machine shop charges: drilling, £12.85; shaping, £7.56; turning, £14.25. Drawing office: plans, £35.80. Transport Department: delivery £28.50. Other charges: paint shop, £28.50 inspection and testing, £18.50. Profit to be based on 45 per cent of total costs.

5 What is a suggestion box? Describe the suggestion box method for collecting new ideas from existing staff.

6 Explain the sampling method known as 'quota sampling'. Suggest how it might be used in assessing the demand for a new type of car vacuum cleaner.

13
Marketing

13.1 An introduction to marketing

All business organizations have some interest in marketing, but for many firms and companies it is absolutely vital. These are the sort of organizations which are 'market orientated' rather than production orientated. Production-orientated firms are more interested in their product and the difficulties of making it and keeping it efficient than they are about the marketing of it. The customers who want their products will seek them out, rather than the supplier having to look for a customer. With the market-orientated firm the problem is to find the customer and having found him/her to keep him/her for as long as possible – years and years if that can be managed.

Such firms have a number of problems. They have a product, a good product that has been tested and found to do a particular job well. It is wanted by almost everyone in the world. The problems are:

1 To bring the product to the attention of everyone, so that they start to demand it in their shops or by mail order.
2 To package it attractively so that it is noticed, and is tried by the customer, and once it has established itself is instantly recognized and picked out by the customer.
3 To bridge the gaps between the producer and the consumer. There are two gaps, the geographical gap and the time gap. The geographical gap has to be bridged by transport, and the time gap has to be bridged by merchandising skills. Merchandising skills vary with every product. Butter needs refrigerating, prepared foods need to be kept chilled, diamonds have to be locked away in vaults, bananas have to be ripened gradually, etc.
4 To arrange the actual sale of products – what economists call the exchange of products, where one person ceases to be the owner of the goods and another person becomes the owner. These exchanges are arranged by a system of wholesaling and retailing.

A definition of marketing

We can, therefore, define marketing as a procedure by which goods or services which are available to satisfy wants are offered to the general public, and if necessary moved across the geographical and time barriers which separate producers from consumers, so that services can be used, and goods can be exchanged, passing into the hands of the final consumer for a money payment called the price. This price reimburses the producer and any intermediaries for all the costs incurred, and also leaves a profit over as a reward for their efforts.

13.2   The personnel in the Marketing Department

If we consider the work of the Marketing Department, and the people in it, and the things they do we shall understand what an important part marketing plays in every firm, but especially in market-orientated firms. The department is often a 'super-department', the Marketing Manager having a general supervisory role over a number of departments such as Sales Department, Advertising Department, Packaging Department, various warehouses, Despatch Department, Export Department, etc. The justification for this 'super-department' approach is that there is a need for coordination of the work of marketing through the various stages, so that no opportunity is missed, in a competitive world, to market the product ranges on offer. There are excellent employment opportunities in all these areas, and many marketing staff gain experience while studying in their spare time to achieve full professional status and membership of the various prestigious bodies such as the Chartered Institute of Marketing, the Institute of Export, the Institute of Freight Forwarders, etc. We can see this idea of the super-department most easily in Figure 13.1. Look at this diagram now before considering the explanations given in the sections which follow.

13.3   The functions of the Marketing Director

The chief responsibility in marketing lies with the Marketing Director who is almost always a director with full Board status. He/she will draw up plans for a marketing policy which will be presented to the Board, and after due discussion and perhaps some modification will be formally approved by the Board and minuted as a Boardroom decision. From that point on it is for the Marketing Director to achieve the plans with the help of the various departments under his/her control. It is here that many marketing strategies fail, because

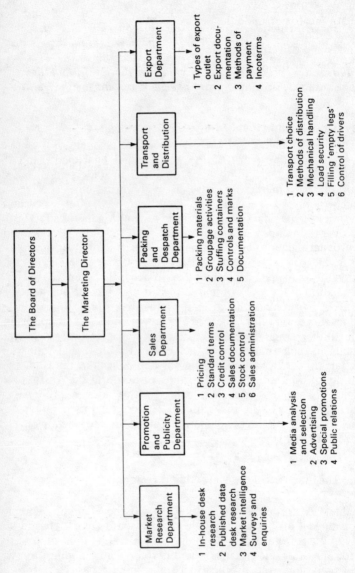

Figure 13.1 The Marketing Department of a major company

there is all the difference in the world between drawing up a plan and actually achieving it. The strategy has to be achieved by the enthusiasm and energy of many members of staff, right down the scale to the very lowest levels, and the latest appointee. The Marketing Director has to persuade the key people in each department that the plans are sound, the objectives are achievable and that any changes in attitudes and drive that are necessary must be made.

The main elements of marketing are:

1 The product, or range of products if there are several.
2 The price.
3 The promotion.
4 The distribution.
5 The final exchange with the customer, and payment of the price.

In order to achieve each of these the Marketing Director has to ensure the widest understanding of the new marketing policy. Thus, to win the hearts and minds of all staff the fullest explanations of points 1–5 above are required, as follows:

The product range

All staff must know about each product. They must have actually seen it, and if possible also have used it. They must understand what it is made of; what it has cost; what it is used for; what sort of rival products are on the market; what special features should be stressed when comparing the product with its rivals; what servicing is likely to be required, etc. Nothing sounds worse to a customer on the telephone than a member of staff who says 'I don't think we make one of those.' Similarly a member of staff who clearly does not know the name of a product, or its use or suitability for a particular task, or its price range, etc. creates a poor impression to outside ears. The Marketing Director must convey the facts to staff, and develop in staff the attitudes and types of behaviour needed to sell the product range well to all sorts of customers wherever they are.

The price

Pricing is always difficult. If we price too highly we may not sell the product, but we should always price as high as the market can bear. Only a good margin of profit will carry the overheads of the business and leave something extra to reward the shareholders or other entrepreneurs. Since all new products bring in competitors sooner or later, profit margins are always eaten into in the long term by competition. Therefore, a reasonably high margin of profit is desirable on all new products so that a fair return on capital invested can be achieved before competition moves in. The Marketing Director must not only get staff to know the prices of all products, but must train them to resist any price-cutting suggestions from customers. If such 'reductions' are going to be conceded they must be built into the prices offered so that after the 'reduction' we are left with the price we really wanted anyway. Many price lists bear a clear statement that staff are not authorized to allow departures from the advertised prices, and any such changes will not be binding on the Sales Department. Most representatives (who are usually paid by commission) are so anxious to make a sale they will agree to discounts which were not envisaged in the Board's marketing strategy.

The promotion

Every product has its own market, which must be approached through the appropriate medium. A whole new field of media studies has opened up in recent years and those with a good background in Business Studies might well consider moving into 'Media Studies' as a logical development. The Marketing Director must identify the main market for each product. There may well be specialist groups who are interested in a particular product, and who should be approached through the specialist magazines and free periodicals which are called by the general name of 'the business press'. Even a product destined for the final consumer may be of interest to business people, and may generate bigger orders from the trade if advertised in the specialist business press rather than to the public as a whole. Thus a new type of fishing rod is of interest to anglers, but is most likely to be ordered by wholesalers and retailers who have the ability to display it at the best points for attracting customers who are anglers. The retail price has to be conceived as being high enough to give manufacturer, wholesaler and retailer a profit since this is the way most products are sold in a sophisticated economy.

An organization called the British Business Press, at 15–19 Kingsway, London WC2B 6UN, is an association of leading publishers of business and professional magazines. It specializes in researching business-to-business advertising and analysing the efforts of the business press not only in reaching out to markets for a host of products of interest to business people, but also for being a major source of news about new products, new markets, etc.

One recent survey revealed that in 1988 UK manufacturers spent £1,000 million on 'business-to-business' advertising of which the specialist business press took £345 million and television only £12 million.

Promotions may take other forms than advertising, such as attendance at exhibitions in such centres as the National Exhibitions Centre at Birmingham, or Olympia in London. Most organizations have at least one exhibition a year – we have all heard of the Motor Show, or the Ideal Home Exhibition, etc. Smaller local exhibitions are mounted all over the country, and travelling exhibitions such as 'Road Shows' and 'Promotion Trains' are mounted by many manufacturers and major companies such as utilities (gas, water and electricity companies).

The Marketing Director not only has to supervise all these programmes and events but even more has to generate enthusiasm in staff. He/she must work on, and persuade key staff to give the promotion their very best efforts. Students might ponder the following thoughts:

1   It is easy to take an attitude of indifference to all that is going on, and to soft pedal on any project – appearing to support it without actually really doing anything worthwhile.
2   It is easy to take the attitude that there is very little to be gained personally by putting your shoulder to the wheel – someone higher up will probably take the credit anyway.
3   This does not alter the fact that by getting really involved you will get to know everything about the promotion; what is being marketed; who it is mainly directed towards; who gives good service and who gives poor service; where the real effort has to be put in, etc. This kind of knowledge can be invaluable later on; it gradually brings recognition and status; and no one can take it away from you once you've acquired it. The Marketing Manager who finds that you have quietly looked after one bit of work and not only organized it but seen it through to fulfilment is going to be pleased, relieved and appreciative. The really valuable member of staff is the one who assumes responsibility (however low the level) and does so as a matter of principle – not looking for or needing any reward; but assuming that experience is its own reward.

The distribution

We live in a mass-production world, and distribution is essential to clear the production lines as an endless stream of product pours off the end of the line. The last stage of production is packaging and whatever the type of package used the product has to be ready for removal not only to a warehouse next door, but to depots hundreds and even thousands of miles away. The usual method is to load the packages on to pallets, wooden (or perhaps even compressed cardboard) platforms with room beneath them for the forks of a forklift truck. As the pallet is filled (which depends upon the strength of the packaging since packages with reasonable strength can be piled three or four high) the forklift truck lifts the pallet and takes it straight to a container for transport to a depot somewhere well away from the factory. The pallets are designed to fit into the container exactly. The standard size of a container is 8 ft × 8 ft square, so that a 2 ft square pallet will go four times into the width of the container and will eventually fill it completely. Thus a 40 ft container will hold 80 pallets in a single layer. Piled 4 foot high to each pallet it will hold a second layer, 160 pallets in all. If every pallet holds 32 packets it means 5120 packets can travel in a single container. The container will then be taken either to the distant depot by road haulage, or to the freight-liner terminal to be lifted onto a railway waggon, or to a port to be lifted into the cellular-holds of a container ship.

The Marketing Director has to plan the distribution system and select the most appropriate means of transport for the products concerned. Many products are in powdered form – cement, sugar, flour, meal for cattle feed, etc. Others are packaged in cartons, and depend upon the contents for their strength (cartons of tinned products for example). Others need to be crated in wooden crates, because the contents are relatively fragile and the crate must provide the strength required. Polystyrene packaging material may be used to ensure safe transit.

Security is important for all cargoes – they are all valuable. Pilfering is common; hijacking of vehicles is a common occurrence; insurance must be arranged for every consignment.

Documentation is very important, not only for the actual destination of the cargoes, but the documentation that helps move goods – allocating them to vehicles, ferries and deep-sea container ships. Some cargoes travelling by rail go to Japan via the European rail networks, the Trans-Siberian Railway and then by sea to the destination in Japan. If holdups at frontiers are to be avoided the documentation must be foolproof, meeting international requirements and moving according to international agreements; in the case of rail the COTIF convention. COTIF stands for the French words for the Convention of the Intergovernmental Transport Organization for International Movements by Rail (Chemin-de-fer – hence the F).

All such export movements are of course carried out by the Export Department which must know about and understand all the various regulations for moving goods overseas by road, rail, sea and air.

Exchange

Exchange occurs at any point where goods change ownership, payment being made by the new owner to the old owner. In the ordinary marketing sequence the manufacturer supplies the wholesaler who becomes liable to pay at the moment the supply is made, but in practice pays rather later, according to some agreed period of credit. The wholesaler supplies the retailer in turn, and may give the retailer a period of credit too. The retailer supplies the final consumer, usually for cash, or payment by cheque or credit card, but possibly under a hire purchase agreement. All such sales are governed by the Sales of Goods Act, 1979, which lays down quite complex rules about both the time of payment and the time of delivery. It is a most instructive Act of Parliament and well worth studying. The Marketing Director will lay down procedures for the handling of all goods being supplied to customers, whatever their status. The general principle is that goods will only be supplied against payment except to accredited customers with whom an agreed arrangement for credit has been laid down. This is explained more fully in Chapter 14.

Points to remember

- Marketing is an activity where goods and services are brought to the attention of consumers so that they may be aware of their availability, price, uses, etc.
- Market-orientated firms are particularly concerned with the market, and the need to obtain a good share of the market, over as lengthy a time as possible. They have a proven product – the difficulty is to get every one to buy it at a 'fair' price which yields at least a reasonable profit.
- The post of Marketing Director is an important post, usually of boardroom status, and normally the Marketing Director will be a member of the Chartered Institute of Marketing.
- The elements of marketing are an understanding of the product, its price, its promotion, its distribution, the method of exchange, with the final consumer or end-user and the method by which payment will be secured.
- It is essential to know all about the product, its name, construction, colour, price, technical details, availability, etc. Every detail may be important when discussing the product with a customer.

13.4   The Sales Department

The Sales Department is concerned with finding the customers for the company's products. It may have a team of representatives each allocated a territory which is to some extent a natural catchment area. It may rely on direct mail or advertisements in the trade press to bring in the initial enquiries or alternatively representatives may gradually extend their business within the territory by a certain amount of 'cold calling' (calling without an appointment) or after an appointment has been secured by a preliminary letter. Salesmanship is an art. One cannot be too timid if one wants to make a sale, but aggressive salesmanship can set up opposition for the future, and repeat orders are essential if businesses are to prosper. However anxious one is to secure an order it is unwise to agree to terms which are less than the specified normal prices, and some purchasing officers are just as aggressive as the salesman they deal with in striking a hard bargain. Do not concede reductions unless you absolutely have to, and be sure the Marketing Director has approved the order before accepting it. Some elements in the sales procedure are as follows:

Voluntary offers

A business relationship has to start somewhere and it often begins with a voluntary offer. This is an invitation to a customer to do business with you. It often takes the form of a circular letter accompanying a catalogue, or a number of brochures or a press release. Contract law is important here. A contract is made when a valid offer to supply has been accepted by the offeree (the one to whom the offer was made) and a clear arrangement about price (the valuable consideration) has been agreed. A voluntary offer is not an actual offer, it is only an invitation to treat (in other words an invitation to people to make offers to buy). This means that the circular letter, catalogue, etc. is not an offer, only an invitation to customers to offer to buy – when we will be happy to accept their offers if they agree to pay the price we are charging. The result of a voluntary offer is an enquiry from the potential customer.

Enquiries

Of course the enquiry may be an actual order – particularly if the circular or other advertising material contained an order form – or it may be an enquiry asking for more details, prices, etc. It is important to reply at once. Following up orders before the customer's interest cools off is vital – but at the same time it must be guarded. One member of a sales team offered to supply goods, at the quoted price delivered to destination, but was alarmed to find that this 'offer' was immediately accepted at the agreed price, and the place of delivery specified was Tokyo. It costs a fortune to send goods to Tokyo – the representative had been thinking of delivery in the UK. We have to be very precise and the best way is to have a set of Terms and Conditions of Supply, printed on a special form, which is sent out with every response. The response refers directly to: 'Our Standard Terms and Conditions which form the basis of any contract made.'

Orders

An order is a formal offer to buy, which may be accepted by us to make a binding contract, but the usual thing is to acknowledge the order only, and say it is receiving attention. This gives us time to check the details of the order. Is the price right? Have we got the goods to fulfil the order, or can they be made quickly enough to meet any deadline? Are there any difficulties envisaged? Only when we are sure we can fulfil the order should an acceptance of the order be notified, and from that moment it becomes a binding contract. A binding contract is one that will be upheld in the Courts if either party fails to do what it promised to do. Thus the purchaser can sue the seller for non-delivery, and the seller can sue the purchaser for non-payment.

Repeat orders

Every attempt should be made to secure reorders once a course of dealing has been established. Reorders are more profitable than initial orders, because the selling costs are usually high trying to find new customers, but reorders become a matter of routine. For example, each packet of stationery or some other product may contain near the end a reorder card which reminds the customer that the stock is nearly exhausted and it is time to place a further order. Similarly a circular may remind the customer, or even a phone call may elicit an order. The customer may say 'Oh well, send me the same as before, then!' and the representative has a useful order for very little effort.

Sales stationery

The Sales Manager should have a full range of prepared stationery designed to give good control of all representatives. Prepared material saves staff time, adds punch to any presentation made to customers and ensures adequate follow-up of all sales opportunities. For example, it is usual to draw up before each sales conference a loose-leaf collection of polythene wallets each showing at a single opening the publicity material, illustrations, prices and terms of sale of a product handled by the representatives. The whole book will be produced to the customer, who may very well take it over and flick through the pages, often quite quickly, because it is obvious certain lines are of no interest to that particular customer. However, the customer will stop and ponder pages of greater interest, and may say to the rep – 'Yes, I'll try six of Number 491' or something like that. The rep has a pre-printed order form ready and jots down the number required; holds forth if necessary about a particular new line, or an old line offered on more favourable terms (perhaps to clear stock) etc. At the end the order form, already completed with the name and address of the firm before the representative even started the call, and now containing details of the items required, has only to be presented to the customer for signature and the interview can be terminated and the order sent to Head Office.

Every interview will be reported – partly to prove that the representative is making the calls he/she is supposed to make, but also to give useful details to the Sales Manager. What day and time the call was made; who was actually seen; what the customer's attitude was – friendly or critical; any opinion he/she expressed on particular products; any comment he/she made on prices. Was any reference made to competitors? Were any rival goods displayed or featured, etc?

Many representatives are provided with suitcases which are designed specially to hold sales stationery, and further supplies of forms, brochures, gifts, etc. are provided in a backup pack which is renewed as supplies approach exhaustion. Small gifts are often provided for customers – for example calendars, note pads, pencils, ballpoint pens, telephone memo pads, etc. They are a useful way of getting advertising material into regular use – each page of a memo pad having the supplier's name, address and telephone number prominently displayed, for example.

The remuneration of sales staff

How to reward sales staff is always a difficult problem. The new salesperson has little knowledge of the product, no contact with an existing band of customers, little chance of repeat orders unless he/she is taking over an existing territory and if rewarded with commission on sales only is unlikely to make a living, and will leave. Some sort of basic salary is usually provided, increased by a commission on all sales made (or perhaps on calls made whether a sale resulted or not). The established salesperson usually earns far more than the basic salary and in some cases earns a quite unjustified huge salary. For example, if a product is so well designed and so appropriate for today's needs that it sells itself, the salesperson may get a high commission which should rightfully go to the design staff in Research and Development, or the Production Department. A scale of commission may therefore be graded – with a high reward for the first few items sold, but a lesser reward for the next batch, and a smaller reward for all further sales. The high commission on the first batch of sales encourages the new entrant, but as the product gains in popularity and it gets easier to find the customers, and the orders received increase in size, the scale is cut back to reflect the smaller sales effort needed.

13.5 The Advertising Department

Advertising takes many forms, and serves many purposes. While most advertising will be aimed at bringing a particular product or range of products before the public, other advertising with well-established companies is merely concerned with bringing the company's brand name before the public and reinforcing in the public's mind the company's image as a leading firm in its field.

Some advertising is **informative advertising**, aimed at explaining the uses of a product, the services it provides, the colours, shapes and sizes available and the prices payable. In a busy world we cannot find out about products ourselves and everyone welcomes this sort of informative advertising. Other advertising is **persuasive advertising**, attempting to sway us into trying a product. Such advertising can be tedious and a great waste of everyone's time, as for example, the endless advertising of soap powders and other materials on television. Where the brands are all very similar, and no real advantage is gained by preferring one to another, it is a waste of time and money to advertise them repeatedly. All the costs of this type of advertising have to be included in the price of the product, and they are made unnecessarily expensive by this type of excessive advertising. The Monopolies and Mergers Commission has investigated such advertising, and ruled against its excessive use, notably by the 'washing powder' manufacturers. Only three companies control the entire industry, and they were ordered to reduce their expenditure on this type of advertising by 40 per cent.

Some advertising is '**collective advertising**', which is commonly used in franchising. A franchise is a system of spreading a prosperous business, based on a good idea, to every corner of the land by allowing other people to share the procedure. Thus we find pizza parlours, fried chicken restaurants, picture framers, locksmiths, print shops, launderettes, travel agencies, etc. setting up in every town and village using the ideas of the franchisor and very often paying considerable sums for the franchise. The franchise agreement usually provides that a certain amount of advertising, both national and local, will be done by the franchisor for the benefit of the franchisees, who will gain from the extra business obtained.

Advertising is a very expensive business, and the costs can be prohibitive for many small firms. Some idea of prices can be gathered from the following list.

- Local newspaper – (25,000 circulation) £500 for a full page.
- National newspaper – (400,000 circulation) £10,000 full page.
- Popular daily (4 million circulation) £25,000 full page.
- Local radio – 60 seconds off peak £500.
- Local radio – 60 seconds peak listening £1,000.
- Television – 30 seconds off peak £5,000.
- Television – 30 seconds peak £30,000.

For many small businesses a local appeal is probably sufficient – since national advertising would produce more orders than the business could supply – and local mail shots and leafleting would probably bring an appropriate level of response.

The Advertising Department must solve the following problems:

1   What is the best way to bring our products before the public?
2   Does each product need separate publicity or is it possible to market the whole range? The more general our marketing the more likely we are to miss sales on a particular product, but where the needs of customers may vary a small catalogue may in fact be the best solution since each customer should find in it the model or style that appeals to him/her.
3   Which is the best media outlet for each product?
4   What is the timing of the publicity campaign to be? Television promotion brings a flood of enquiries to local retailers as soon as the advertising starts. Retailers and wholesalers must be alerted weeks before so that they have time to place orders and take delivery of the goods, before the public begin to demand the product. A great deal of planning goes into each advertising campaign, and success is dependent upon the sequence of operations being right.

The marketing mix

The marketing of a product usually involves a variety of activities and promotions, aimed at the various groups that we expect to be interested in our product. The approach may be different to different groups and even the packaging may be varied. Thus a standard product may be retailed to one group in a relatively cheap packaging and at a reasonable price. Other groups may be charged a higher price for the product in a better quality packaging and with cosmetic changes which make it appear different. We all know of ranges of cars which are basically the same product but different models have different features to attract customers whose needs are different. Some want an estate vehicle, some a saloon, some a sports model and so on. Similar considerations apply to almost all products – clothing, footwear, consumer durables, hi-fi equipment, cameras.

The different approaches call for a mixture of advertising, brochures, special offers, free gifts, competitions, after-sales follow-up and servicing, etc. The variety of approaches is called by the general term of 'the marketing mix'.

The Advertising Manager will devise a programme which will enable the company to have the utmost impact upon the market, depending upon the size of the company, its range of products, the target markets which have been identified and the wide variety of activities, which will be necessary to achieve the company's objectives. The term 'marketing mix' refers to this mixture of activities, each of which must be successfully pursued if the company's strategy is to succeed. We cannot usually attack all targets at once, and the returns from sales achieved in one particular project will be used to finance the next programme elsewhere. A product which will eventually sell nationwide may be started with a launch in East Anglia, or the West Midlands, or some other reasonably compact area where the impact made by television and press advertising, leaflet campaigns, etc. can be fairly easily achieved, measured and satisfied. The total marketing plan may consist of a repeated series of programmes in such local areas, each extension of the plan being more effectively managed as experience is gained, snags are overcome, etc. Figure 13.2 shows a typical range of activities.

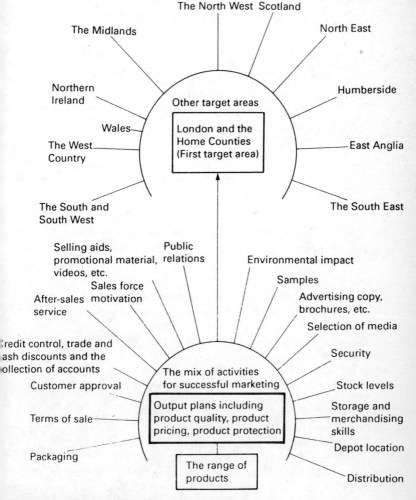

Figure 13.2 The marketing plan

13.6   Physical distribution management

Physical distribution management is concerned with the whole process of moving goods from the point of production to the point of consumption, across the gaps which separate producers from consumers. These are the 'geographical gap', and the 'time gap'. The geographical gap has to be bridged by transport of one sort or another, the time gap has to be bridged by merchandising skills of one sort or another.

Bridging the transport gap

The chief considerations with various types of transport may be listed as follows:

Road haulage
- It is door to door.
- It can be under our own supervision at all times if we use 'own transport' or 'contract hire' in which the contractor undertakes to carry all our goods for us.
- It is flexible – a road closed or a broken down vehicle is no real problem.
- Security and proof of delivery are fairly simple matters, and under our personal control if we take proper measures (cab radios etc.).
- Packing may be saved because goods are in our personal care.

But
- The loads are relatively small (44 tonnes at the most).
- Prompt discharge is essential if the lorries are to be used intensively.
- Running costs are relatively high (especially drivers' wages – compared with a train where one driver takes thirty or forty waggons).
- Pilfering is always possible and hijacking of whole loads not unknown.
- If we use 'hire and reward' vehicles we lose the personal control, though this is compensated by the professional care of the road haulier.

Rail haulage
- It is fast when it is actually on the move, 300–400 kilometres per day is about the usual.
- It is excellent for long journeys, but in the UK few journeys are over 200 miles, which is the minimum distance for really econ-

omical rail haulage. European freight tends to be rail freight
because of the long distances. The Channel Tunnel (Euro-tunnel)
will open soon, and should transfer much of UK European freight
traffic to rail.
- Train capacities are very large and company trains for coal, ore,
petroleum products, steel, etc. are very economical and efficient.

But

- Unless we have our own railway sidings it cannot be door-to-
door, and double handling is needed – i.e. a lorry has to be
loaded to bring the goods to the depot, then off-loaded onto the
train and the load then reloaded onto a final delivery vehicle at
destination. Even with containers this is all extra work, and
requires expensive installations such as overhead gantries that
can pick up a container from a lorry and move it across onto a rail
waggon, and vice versa.
- The railways are impersonal; delivery is not under our own
control; goods may wait in sidings or at depots where they are at
risk from theft or exposure to weather, temperature changes, etc.
- Packing costs are increased because of the need to crate goods
against every possible type of mishap, bad handling, etc.

Water transport
Water transport may be inland waterway, short-sea transport (across
to the continent and then on by road, rail or inland waterway) or
deep-sea transport. Deep-sea transport may be in general cargo
ships, but these days tends to be either bulk ships (for crude oil, ores,
packaged timber, etc.) or containerized traffic. The chief points are:

- Water transport can carry any type of cargo, to any weight – the
biggest VLCCs (very large crude carriers) can carry up to 500,000
tonnes of cargo.
- Loading and unloading is a highly mechanized streamlined operation which can turn a ship around in twelve hours.
- Freight costs are low, because of the large tonnages and twenty-
four-hour operations with relatively small numbers of crew.

But

- Water transport is relatively slow.
- It is subject to special hazards, such as the perils of the seas.
- It involves loading and unloading procedures at each end of the
sea voyage though on the short-sea routes this is a fairly simple
roll-on, roll-off operation.
- Packing has to be good quality, because of the rolling and
pitching to which ships are subject. Even containerized cargo

must be properly packed inside the container and restrained if the container is not absolutely full. This requires professional packing by stevedores who know how to ensure safe transits.

Air transport

Although there are specialist airfreighters which do not carry passengers but handle bulk cargoes such as flowers, fruit, market garden produce, electronic equipment, etc. the vast majority of air cargo still travels on passenger planes. The chief points are:

- Rapid delivery; even the Far East is only twenty-four hours away, and North American cargo is only a few hours away, either across the Atlantic or over the North Pole.
- Control is impersonal, but well organized because the time periods are short and delivery within 24–48 hours is possible.
- Lighter packing is acceptable.
- Insurance is cheap.
- Air transport is ideal for JIT operations. These are operations where a major manufacturer is supplied with components and spare parts 'just-in-time' before the factory runs out. JIT operations save warehousing and storage problems. The goods are used at once as they arrive.

But

- Freight rates are expensive; but these may be offset by cheaper packing.
- Fog does cause delays, and so does aircraft servicing because of the high safety requirements in air transport.
- Awkward loads are rarely carried by air, because the shape of the aircraft and its light construction makes it unsuitable for bulky objects, especially if they are heavy.

The range of facilities for handling goods today is very wide and capital intensive – in that a great deal of money has to be spent on them. For example, even wooden pallets are quite expensive (£5–£8) and large numbers of them are required so that forklift trucks can pick up a pallet load at a time. There are several types of forklift truck which can pick up goods and raise them not only off the ground but high enough to load onto lorries and onto shelves in warehouses. Turret forklift trucks can raise a pallet ten or twelve feet high and then turn to load the goods onto shelves in the narrow alleyways of a warehouse. Order picking lift trucks have a platform where the operator can stand and control the truck, as it not only moves along the gangway, but raises or lowers the operator to reach shelves where the goods required for a particular order are stored. Heavy duty lift trucks can lift a 32-ton container onto a lorry with a single lifting movement.

Bridging the time gap

Some goods do not deteriorate over time. They can simply be stored on shelves or in cupboards for use when required. Other items have a limited shelf life, while others are perishable (i.e. they must be used at once or they are wasted). In order to bridge the time gap it is necessary to know your merchandise. Does the product go bad; ripen; fade; melt; develop pests and funguses? Strawberries rot; pears ripen; garments fade; wheat overheats; butter must be refrigerated, etc. Every trade has its merchandising skills which new staff must learn if losses are to be avoided.

Besides the qualities of the merchandise the risks of storage and warehousing include the chances of pilfering, theft, burglary, fire, etc. Such risks are greatly increased when goods cannot be moved to the final consumer at once, but have to be stored until demand is strong enough. Security includes many aspects, of which we may list:

Prevention of opportunist theft
An opportunist theft is one where the thief seizes an opportunity that presents itself, and simply takes what can be obtained in a few seconds. Such things as front door security systems which prevent anyone entering a building until they have stated their business over an intercom system and the door-lock has been released to admit them, reduce opportunist theft. With vehicles drivers should always lock doors before going to make enquiries, and an open back of a lorry is always liable to opportunist theft. If a driver's mate is available he/she should guard the vehicle if left open during part-deliveries.

Gate control systems on warehouses and depots
Gate controls should be operated. This involves having an extra 'gate copy' added to the invoice. The exit from the premises is controlled by a barrier, where a gate-man stops all vehicles, takes the gate copy from the customer who is trying to leave, checks that only those goods on the list are actually being removed and raises the barrier to let the customer pass. For a full explanation of invoices see Chapter 15.

The 'inside-job'
This is the worst type of theft from depots and warehouses. This is where a member of staff is bribed (or perhaps recruited deliberately) to assist with a conspiracy to steal. The inside-person, knowing the layout of the depot and the best time to commit a burglary (i.e. when the warehouse is full) brings very heavy losses on the company concerned. Care must be taken when recruiting staff to take up references on all new personnel. Even when personnel are estab-

lished we must watch for personnel with problems (someone with an unmanageable mortgage or a member of staff who is betting heavily, or enjoying an excessive lifestyle). Such people are liable to be tempted into joining such conspiracies.

13.7 Export marketing

There are many reasons why export marketing should be an important part of every company's marketing effort. In the first place we live in a multinational world, where we need to import not only things we cannot grow (or make) ourselves, such as bananas and bamboo furniture, but many things we can make ourselves, but import to give a wider choice in our shops. We do not *need* to import Swiss watches, or Italian shoes, or German printing machinery or Japanese electronic equipment, but our quality of life would suffer if we did not. Second, export trade is wholesale trade, not retail trade. It is bulk trading, and may be much more profitable, even if it does involve extra expenses, because of the high volumes handled. We can often overcome the difficulties of exporting by using one of the channels of overseas trade where expert help is already available.

The chief channels of overseas trade may be listed as follows:

1 Export merchants.
2 Confirming houses.
3 Overseas agents.
4 Direct selling to overseas customers.
5 Overseas branch offices.
6 Overseas subsidiary companies.

A few words about each of these is desirable.

1 *Export merchants* A merchant is someone who buys goods on his own behalf, as principal, and sells them again at a profit. Such an export house may have customers abroad who have a specific requirement, or may be buying goods which they believe to be in demand in the countries they trade with. They are therefore taking on the costs both of transport and of bridging the time gaps (merchandising skills and warehousing, etc.). They will fix prices to the foreign customer in local currencies and as far as our business is concerned we are dealing with a home-based customer who will pay in sterling in the usual course of business.
2 *Confirming houses* A confirming house is one that obtains orders from overseas customers for goods of a particular type and quality, which they then obtain from the producer in the UK. By 'confirming' the order they make themselves liable for payment

when the goods are delivered to them for export, or they may be shipped or airfreighted direct in an agreed way. The confirming house thus assumes the responsibility for securing payment from the foreign customer, the exporter being paid at once.

3 *Overseas agents*   It is possible to appoint agents in foreign countries who will market your goods for you, using their existing sales base to display and advertise the product. This is often done 'on consignment', which means that each consignment is sold for the best price obtainable, the agent rendering an 'account sales' to show what the proceeds were. After deducting expenses and commission the agent sends a sight draft for the balance. It is usual for the agent to assume the risks of non-payment by the customer, since we have no means of judging his reliability, and if the agent does so he is entitled to an extra commission called a 'del credere' commission. 'Del credere' means 'in the belief that (the buyer is solvent)'.

4 *Direct selling to overseas customers*   This system requires the establishment of a full export department with representatives who travel abroad to make contact with potential customers. It is an effective way of doing business because of the strong personal links established with the customer, direct access by the customer for complaints and direct negotiation on prices. It does present difficulties – for example, language problems may arise and personal contacts are necessarily intermittent.

5 *Overseas branch offices*   Many overseas countries, particularly developing countries, are anxious to share in the advantages of international trade. They therefore welcome any system which sets up overseas branches using local personnel. By acquiring expertise in this way skills can be passed on which gradually raise the level of the developing country technically and commercially. Supervision by expatriate residents will be essential until local management can be trained up, and the interconnection with the parent company for training and updating conferences will be very valuable.

6 *Overseas subsidiary companies*   The ultimate stage of development is for an autonomous subsidiary company to be set up in the export market, with some agreed system for remitting profits to the parent company at intervals. Frequently, governmental agreement to this will be necessary, and it is essential to have a stable political framework with mutual advantages and mutual trust between the host country and the multinational enterprise.

Whichever of these methods is used the returns to the exporter will usually be satisfactory, because the extra expenses involved will be offset by the large size of the orders.

Incoterms 1990

Incoterms are international commercial terms which have been agreed at an international convention to be a satisfactory basis for trading between countries. If a trader specifies one of the thirteen incoterms the Courts of both countries (i.e. the exporter's country and the importer's country) will judge any dispute between the parties by referring to the definition laid down by the International Chamber of Commerce. The thirteen terms are abbreviated to three letter codes which can be easily displayed on any document. For example EXW means 'ex works', which means that the exporter does nothing but make the goods available at the factory gate. The foreign importer has to do everything else – which someone like the export merchant or the confirming house referred to earlier would be quite willing to do. By contrast DDP means 'delivered duty paid' in which case the exporter has to do everything – supply the goods, ship them to the foreign port, collect them at the foreign docks, pay any customs duty on entry and deliver them to the consignee. Obviously the price charged will be much higher for DDP than for EXW. The full list is:

EXW	Ex works
FCA	Free carrier
FAS	Free alongside ship
FOB	Free on board
CFR	Cost and freight
CIF	Cost, insurance, freight
CPT	Carriage paid to
CIP	Carriage and insurance paid
DAF	Delivered at frontier
DES	Delivered ex ship
DEQ	Delivered ex quay
DDU	Delivered duty unpaid
DDP	Delivered duty paid

Generally speaking we can see that the further down the list we go the more the exporter has to do. Three of the most common terms are explained more fully as follows:

1 *CFR* – cost and freight. The seller must pay the costs and the freight (freight is the carrier's reward for carrying as far as the port of destination) but the risk passes to the buyer as the goods cross the ship's rail in the port of shipment.
2 *CIF* – cost, insurance and freight. The seller is in the same position as in CFR but in addition has to provide marine insurance during the carriage. The risk passes to the buyer as the goods

cross the ship's rail, and the insurance then covers the buyer's risk.

3   *DDP* – delivered duty paid. This is the maximum commitment for the seller, and the minimum for the buyer. The seller delivers to the buyer after paying all the freight, insurance and handling costs including the duty on import to the country of destination. However, it is possible to deliver 'DDP exclusive of VAT and/or taxes'.

Notice that these 1990 terms are the only ones that should be used and terms like C and F (instead of CFR) and *franco domicile* 'free to the home of the importer' are obsolete and should not be used. For a full description of Incoterms 1990 see the official publication called *Guide to Incoterms* (available from the International Chamber of Commerce, 14 Belgrave Square, London SW1X 8PS (Tel: 071 823 2811). With this guide we can find what each party has to do under any particular term.

Obtaining payment in export trade

The chief worry of exporters is that they may not get paid, after all the efforts of manufacturing and exporting the goods. The chief worry of importers is that if they pay money in advance they may never receive the goods to which they are entitled. To overcome these difficulties several ways of ensuring that payment is received have been developed. There are five chief methods of payment, each of which has its own advantages and disadvantages. Dealing with them from the point of view of the safety of the exporter as regards payment they are:

1   Cash with order.
2   Confirmed (or unconfirmed) irrevocable documentary letter of credit.
3   Documents against payment.
4   Documents against acceptance.
5   Open Account.

A brief explanation of each of these is as follows.

1   *Cash with order*   The importer actually pays cash when he places the order. This is fine for the exporter, but costly and hazardous for the importer, whose capital is tied up well in advance of obtaining the goods. Only if a seller's market exists (say after a major war) and the importer wishes no barrier to stand in the way of receiving the goods, will he agree to this method. However, it might be used at other times if the sum was not great (for example, when foreign students send to the UK for textbooks).
2   *Confirmed (or unconfirmed) irrevocable letter of credit*   Since it is

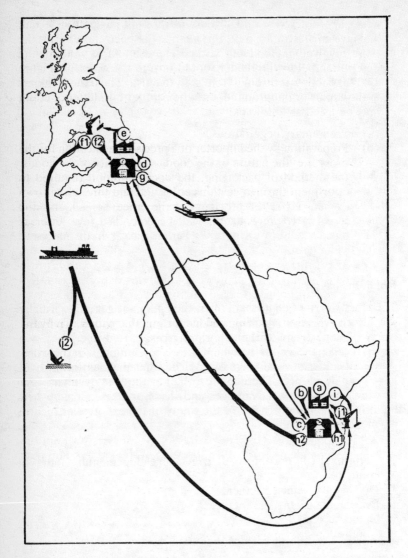

Figure 13.3   Exporting with a confirmed irrevocable letter of credit (reproduced by courtesy of Formecon Services Ltd)

Notes:

(a)   Importer requires UK goods.

(b)   Importer contacts his bank and arranges an irrevocable credit in favour of the exporter. He details the goods required and the arrangements the exporter must make re documentation, packaging, etc.

(c)   Foreign bank notifies UK correspondent bank about the matter and sends full details of letter of credit. In this case it asks UK bank to confirm credit.

necessary to describe one of these methods of payment in detail, and give an illustration of it, this method has been chosen. It is the most involved method of payment in use. After reading the description below the reader should turn to the diagram (Figure 13.3) and follow it through from start to finish. The basic elements in the export or import of goods to be paid for by a letter of credit may be listed as follows:

(a) Preliminary negotiations.
(b) Preparation by the importer of a precise specification for the order, i.e. the nature of the goods, the quality of the goods, the method of packaging, the documentation required to clear them through customs at his end and through his own exchange control procedures, the price agreed and the terms of trading. All this will be embodied in a letter of credit, to be sent to the exporter once a credit has been arranged.
(c) The arrangement of a credit by the importer with his own bank in his own country so that the exporter can feel confident he will be paid for the order if he complies with the terms laid down in the specification. The credit is usually irrevocable, which means that it cannot be withdrawn by the importer unless the exporter agrees.
(d) The notification by the importer's foreign bank of the existence of this credit to their correspondent bank in the UK. This correspondent bank may be asked to 'confirm' the credit, which means to honour it and pay the exporter when he has complied with the terms of the letter of credit. If the letter of credit is not confirmed – less satisfactory for the exporter – the UK bank will not pay the exporter until the documents have travelled out to the foreign bank and they transmit the funds to the UK bank.

(d) UK bank notifies the exporter that the credit is open by means of a 'letter of credit'. It also states that it confirms the credit.
(e) The exporter manufactures or obtains the goods, and ships them exactly as required in the letter of credit, receiving in return a bill of lading.
(f) (i) Goods set off on voyage.
     (ii) Exporter presents documents to bank.
(g) UK bank verifies that documents conform to letter of credit, and pays the exporter. It then passes the documents to the foreign bank.
(h) (i) Foreign bank checks documents and notifies importer.
     (ii) Foreign bank settles with UK bank.
(i) Importer collects bill of lading and if goods arrive safely collects them from port area.
(j) (i) If all is well transaction is completed and all parties are satisfied.
     (ii) If goods lost at sea importer claims on insurance policy.

(e)   The UK bank, having been notified of the existence of the credit, passes the letter of credit to the exporter, confirming it if requested to do so. This letter of credit is in effect a detailed export order for goods to be manufactured (or perhaps just purchased). Not only must the goods comply exactly with the terms of the letter of credit as to quality, price, etc., but the documentation must also comply (otherwise the bank will not release the credit in payment). The packaging and transportation must be as requested, insurance arranged (or details notified to the importer if he is insuring at his end), etc. Every detail must be correct, or we may find the cargo being rejected. Sometimes if the market has moved against the importer he may be only too happy to reject the consignment on a technicality.

(f)   The exporter now proceeds to make or obtain the goods, to pack them and document them and eventually he ships them as requested. He receives in return a shipped bill of lading, which proves they have actually been loaded on a named vessel. He has an insurance certificate (if the exporter was to insure) and other documents which he has prepared. These documents now represent the goods, which are on the high seas.

(g)   The exporter presents the documents to the bank. After checking everything against the detailed wording in the letter of credit the bank either pays the exporter (a confirmed credit) or acknowledges their correctness. The documents are then sent out to the foreign bank, who checks them again and, if satisfactory, releases the funds (an unconfirmed credit) so that the exporter can be paid by the UK bank.

(h)   The foreign bank now notifies the importer that his documents are available and when the ship comes in the importer presents the bill of lading to the master of the vessel who releases the export order into the importer's care.

(i)   A mutually beneficial contract has now been fulfilled; the exporter has been paid and the importer has the precise goods he ordered in mint condition. If they are not in mint condition he has an insurance policy to claim upon.

This involved process is illustrated in Figure 13.3.

3   *Documents against payment (D/P)*   With this method of payment an exporter who has received an order from an overseas customer arranges for documents of title to the goods to be released only against payment of a sight bill of exchange for their value. The goods are manufactured, packed and shipped, and the document of title (the bill of lading for sea transport) is presented to a

bank together with any other relevant documents, the invoice and the insurance certificate. Also attached is a bill of exchange payable at sight, which the bank will collect before releasing the documents to the importer. The UK bank sends the documents out by air mail (or perhaps by facsimile photocopying if the consignment is going by air) to a correspondent bank abroad. The correspondent bank calls in the importer and presents the bill of exchange. Upon payment the documents are released and the importer is able to collect his goods. The correspondent bank transmits the payment to the UK and the exporter's account is credited with the sum earned.

4 *Documents against acceptance (D/A)* With this method the procedure is very similar to 3 above but the bill of exchange is not a 'sight' bill but a 'usance' bill, one in which a period of credit is given to the importer. Instead of paying the bill before the documents are released he has only to accept the bill. This means that he signs his name on it to accept responsibility in due course when the bill becomes payable on the due date. The exporter is therefore giving the importer a limited period of credit. In due course the bill will be presented by the correspondent bank, and the funds transmitted for the exporter's benefit.

5 *Open account* Where a situation of complete trust exists between the two parties – for example, where the importer is known to be absolutely reliable or where the transaction is one between a holding company and its foreign subsidiary – the transactions are carried out on 'open account'. This means that the arrangements are exactly the same as with home trade, and statements are rendered periodically and paid according to the agreed arrangements.

13.8 Projects on marketing

1 Choose a particular good purchased by a large number of your fellow students or colleagues. Devise a list of questions which will discover which brand they use of the particular product and what motivates them to buy it. What shortcomings have they found about that brand, or other brands and what improvements would they effect if they could? From your information devise a specification for a rival product, and present it in the form of a proposal to a manufacturer to produce it. Refer in your proposal to the niche it might occupy in the range available in that field.
2 Using a local factory or service as the basis of your investigation carry out as deep a study as you can of the steps they take to market their output. Your enquiries should consider packaging, warehousing, distribution, inland and export marketing. If you

approach the firm directly make it clear that you are only interested from an educational viewpoint and that the report you write will not refer to them by name unless they wish it, but will relate to an imaginary company with a name you have invented.

3 Your employer has devised a package of supplies for use in schools and colleges. You can choose which area of activity you like from the following: science, business studies, foreign languages, mathematics, geography, history and religious studies. Initially there are five lines to be marketed at once, but a further five have also been investigated and are to be mentioned in the leaflet. You are asked to:
   (a) Decide on five products in your chosen field which have been developed.
   (b) Decide on five more to be mentioned as 'Coming Shortly'.
   (c) Draw up a leaflet to be based upon both sides of an A4 sheet of paper – you may fold it in any way you like – which:
        (i)   Tells lecturers and teachers about the products (illustrations will help).
        (ii)   Invites them to fill in an order form (think hard about what such an order form should have on it).
        (iii) tells them a little about your company (invent a name and address).

13.9   The new business and marketing

The proprietor of a new business faces the same sort of marketing problems as any other business but has fewer hands to work with and is often hindered by limited capital and time. Often the very commencement of the business depends upon some limited success in the marketing field, for banks do look for at least some initial promises by customers to take a product when it becomes available. A list of the things the budding entrepreneur must consider in the marketing field would be as follows:

1 Is my market clearly defined and fully known to me?
2 If not, it helps to define the trading area envisaged, both at the start and eventually; assuming some initial success.
3 What is the 'population' in this area – the word 'population' meaning not necessarily every man, woman and child, but the number of people likely to be interested in this product? How affluent are they, and what sort of expenditure could I look for on average?
4 How am I going to approach this population? Should I try a leaflet distribution, or a direct mailing or advertisements in the press (and if so which media outlet would be best)?

5 Can I locate any obvious main customers, and get advance promises to place orders, to help with any submission I need to make to bankers, etc. for financial assistance?
6 What is my supply position; can I buy or manufacture enough to meet the orders when they come in?
7 Can I find extra help if necessary to service the orders as they arrive and deal with any sudden rush as the campaign gathers speed.

13.10 Rapid revision

Answers		Questions	
	–	1	**What is marketing?**
1	It is a procedure by which goods and services to satisfy wants are offered to the general public, and moved across the geographical and time barriers which separate producers from consumers, so that services can be used and goods can be exchanged, passing into the possession of the consumers for a money consideration called the price.	2	**What are the elements of marketing?**
2	(a) The product, or range of products; (b) the price; (c) the promotion of the product; (d) the distribution of the product; (e) the final exchange with the customer; (f) the payment of the price.	3	**You are a young person in the Marketing Department. What do you need to know about the product?**
3	Everything! Its name, price, technical details, colour, size, relationship to other products, uses, advantages, disadvantages, weak spots, availability, etc.	4	**What do you need to know about its price?**
4	How much is it? Are any discounts given for bulk purchases? Are any discounts given for cash payment or prompt payment? Is VAT included in the price quoted? Are		

Answers	Questions
carriage and packing charges extra? Above all – don't concede discounts to a prospective customer without permission. Don't make binding contracts over the phone unless you have authority. Say 'Well, if you will send us a written order . . .'	**5 What is the sequence of events in making a sale?**
5 (a) We may start with a voluntary offer (an invitation to treat); (b) this leads to an enquiry; (c) the response to the enquiry may lead to an order; (d) we acknowledge the order; (e) we check out the details – stock position, credit-worthiness of the customer etc.; (f) we accept the order; (g) we purchase or manufacture the item; (h) we pack and dispatch it; (i) we invoice the customer; (j) after the goods arrive the customer checks them and eventually pays according to the agreed terms.	**6 What are the main types of advertising?**
6 Informative advertising and persuasive advertising. Collective advertising is advertising by franchisors to attract customers for the general body of franchisees.	**7 What is the marketing mix?**
7 It is the mix of activities concerned with the launch of a new product, or the extension of marketing activity into a new geographical area. It concerns the variety of measures to be used, and the provision of all the back-up facilities to reinforce the initial campaign and to follow up inquiries and fulfil orders.	**8 What is physical distribution management?**

Answers	*Questions*
8 It is the control of all the activities which move goods from the point of production to the final consumer. It involves mechanical handling, palletization and the creation of unit loads, containerization of cargoes, transport and distribution, warehousing, breaking of bulk, merchandising skills, order picking etc.	9 **What are the chief methods of exporting?**
9 (a) Sales to export merchants; (b) sales to confirming houses; (c) use of overseas agents; (d) direct selling to foreign customers; (e) overseas branches; (f) overseas subsidiaries (multinational operations)	10 **What are 'Incoterms 1990'?**
10 A set of thirteen internationally agreed terms for trading which have three-letter codes recognized worldwide. The most commonly used are EXW, FAS, FOB, CFR, CIF and DDP (a good student should be able to explain each of these).	11 **What are the five main methods of getting paid in international trade?**
11 (a) Cash with order; (b) letter of credit (confirmed or unconfirmed); (c) documents against payment; (d) documents against acceptance; (e) open account terms.	12 **Go over the test again until you are sure of all the answers. Then try the questions in Section 13.11 below.**

13.11 Questions on Chapter 13

1 What are the functions of the Marketing Director (a) in relation to the Board of Directors (b) in relation to his/her subordinates in the firm.
2 What considerations enter into the pricing of an article? Why is it

a common practice to restrict the rights of sales personnel to reduce the prices of goods when seeking orders from customers?

3 Write a piece of advertising material for any product you have purchased in the last few months and have considered good value for money.

4 Draw up a questionnaire to be used in asking people's opinions about television advertising.

5 Two brothers and their sister have gone into partnership to open a garden centre. Much of their custom will, they hope, be local but they also hope to attract customers with motor cars from a wider area. Suggest three types of advertising that might be effective for them, bearing in mind that they have a limited advertising budget. Describe the sort of marketing effort that is required in each of the methods you suggest.

6 Write short explanations (5–8 lines) of the following terms used in distribution:
   (a) Four-way pallet
   (b) Forklift truck
   (c) Loading bay
   (d) Refrigerated container
   (e) Overhead gantry
   (f) Turret truck

7 What is a JIT operation? How could a JIT operation save warehousing costs, storekeeping costs and mechanical handling costs?

8 What mode of transport would be the most satisfactory for each of the following, and why?
   (a) Jewellery from the UK to New Zealand.
   (b) Wool from New Zealand to Bradford.
   (c) Engineering components from Birmingham to Prague.
   (d) Cheese from Normandy to Frankfurt.
   (e) Flowers from the Azores to the UK.
   (f) Computers from New York to Nairobi.

9 What is the 'time gap' in distribution? What are the likely hazards in bridging the time gap for the following products being imported to the UK. If possible give more than one hazard for each project.
   (a) Australian beef.
   (b) Swiss watches.
   (c) Japanese electronic products.
   (d) Canadian wheat.
   (e) Californian fruit.
   (f) Colombian coffee.

10 Explain how a letter of credit works. To do this you need to explain:

(a) The foreign importer's actions to get the letter of credit on its way.
(b) The foreign banker's activity.
(c) The activities of the correspondent bank in the exporter's country.
(d) The exporter's activities up to the time the cargo is loaded on board ship (or aircraft).
(e) The chain of events after that.

14
Keeping the books of a business

14.1 Book-keeping records

If a business is to be successful we have to be able to keep proper
books of account, and follow the various activities in money terms
from start to finish. Many people are frightened away from self-
employment altogether because they feel the accounting aspects of a
business are too daunting. This is really quite a wrong attitude; there
are some simple systems which are so straightforward that anyone
can get the idea in half an hour, and start to keep their own books
straight away. There are computerized systems which will do all the
entries for you if you just tap in a few figures one at a time, and if you
do anything wrong the computer will usually stop and ask some user-
friendly question like 'Have you given me the correct information? I
need to know . . .'

A full system of book-keeping is called the double-entry system,
which is explained later in this chapter. Anyone can learn double-
entry book-keeping; it takes about a year to master the whole system
and no doubt many students using this textbook are already studying
the subject. Anyone who wants to study it at home should use the
companion volume to this one, *Book-keeping Made Simple*, by the
same author. It covers everything you need to know to run a small
business and to pass any elementary examinations in accounting.

Before looking at the simplest method, which is called the Simplex
System, and at double-entry book-keeping, we will first define
accounting.

Accounting is a set of systems for recording all the financial affairs of
a business so that we know the exact cost of everything we buy or
make, the overhead expenses we incur, the prices to charge to our
customers, the takings of the business, the money we owe and the
money we are owed, and the profits we have made in the course of
our business activity.

Three of the main subdivisions of accounting are financial accounting, cost accounting and management accounting. Financial accounting is concerned with the records of business transactions; with receipts and payments and whether business operations result in a profit or a loss. Cost accounting is concerned with the expenses incurred in the various cost centres of the business, and attempts to ensure correct pricing of contracts; to discover where actual costs differ from estimates, etc. Management accounting seeks to control not only the present pattern of business activities but the future pattern, charting the course ahead.

This is an elementary book, and we only need to know the simplest aspects of accounting, so let us begin by looking at the Simplex System.

14.2   The Simplex System

The Simplex System is a very clever way of keeping book-keeping records, especially suitable for very small businesses. What it offers you are fifty-two weekly pages, one for each week of the year, on which you can record all the receipts and payments as they occur. At the end of the week these records are carried to summaries at the back of the book, where they gradually build up quarterly totals, and finally a yearly total for all the receipts and payments in the year. These figures are then used to work out the profit (or loss) for the year, and a Balance Sheet showing the affairs of the business on the last day in the year. This weekly page is illustrated in Figure 14.1 (see pages 262–263). If you look at it carefully you will see it is in six main parts.

1 *The receipts section*   Every business receives money at regular (or irregular) intervals. Shops for example take cash over the counter, and many people pay by cheque or credit card. Other businesses get paid more rarely; farmers get a monthly 'milk' cheque for example and authors get paid at most twice a year – and some publishers only pay once a year. Whatever method of receipts applies to the particular business under consideration you enter the receipt of the funds on one of the 'Daily Takings' columns, on the day you receive the money. Other receipts are receipts which are not takings of the business – for example Figure 14.1 shows an enterprise allowance from the Government, a tax refund and a payment by a debtor.
2 *The paid to bank section*   This is a section where bank lodgements can be recorded on the day they are paid into the bank. Many firms pay in every day, but some pay in only once or twice a week.

RECEIPTS

Day/Date	Daily Gross Takings Cash Col 1	Cheques Col 2	Credit Cards Col 3	Other Receipts Col 4	Particulars	PAID TO BANK Cash Col 5	Cheques Col 6	Credit Cards Col 7	TOTAL Col 8
Sun : 2/4	186 27			80 00	ENT. ALLOW.				
Mon : 3/4	232 44	25 80	19 95	35 60	TAX REFUND			19 95	19 95
Tues : 4/4	256 26			5 48	DEBTOR P. SMITH	420 00	66 99		486 99
Wed : 5/4	112 27	12 64							
Thur : 6/4	299 95	19 74							
Fri : 7/4	364 24	26 34	41 05			520 00	58 72	41 05	619 77
Sat : 8/4	382 72	62 50	72 95						
Totals	1824 05	147 02	133 95	121 08		940 00	125 60	61 00	1126 60

PAYMENTS FOR BUSINESS STOCK

Date or Chq. No.	To Whom Paid	Amount Paid By Cash Col 9	By Cheque Col 10
3/4	J. CONLAN & SONS.	48 50	
3/4	J. BREWER & Co. LTD.		36 50
4/4	A. J. GOOD LTD.		136 95
5/4	J. BROWN & Co. LTD.	33 80	
7/4	F. LIVESEY & Co.	26 70	
7/4	A. NEWCOMBE		86 25

PAYMENTS OTHER THAN FOR STOCK

Nature of Payment	Amount Paid By Cash Col 11	By Cheque Col 12
Rent	35 00	
Rates		
Light and Heat		63 50
Carriage	9 45	
Postages £1·70 24p. £2·38	4 32	
Paper		27 46
Motor Expenses PETROL	16 12	
—do— REPAIRS		86 50
Travelling	7 32	
Cleaning	5 00	
Printing & Stationery		23 20
Repairs & Renewals		15 78
Insurance (Business)		
Advertising		
Telephone		
Sundries	1 05	
Wages (Employees)	65 75	

Inland Revenue (PAYE + NI)					27 96
Drawings of the Proprietor (see Note 4)			95 00		
Drawings – Partner 1					
Drawings – Partner 2					
Drawings – Partner 3					
Capital Items (see Note 3(1))					
—do—					
Totals			229 01		244 40

WEEKLY CASH REPORT

Cash in Hand (as counted) brought forward		6 46
Add { Gross Weekly Takings (Col 1 + Col 2 + Col 3)		2105 02
Other Receipts (Col 4)		121 08
Cash Drawn from Bank		
Total		2232 56
Deduct { Stock Payments (cash)(Col 9)	109 00	
Other Payments (cash)(Col 11)	229 01	
Amount paid to Bank (Col 8)	1126 60	
Total		1464 61
Cash Balance on books		767 95
Cash in hand (as counted) carr. fwd		767 60
Difference on books (+ or –)	—	35

Totals	109 00	259 60

WEEKLY BANK REPORT

Opening Balance brought forward		—	
Add { Total Paid to Bank during week (Col 8)		1343 56	
		1126 60	
Total		2470 16	
Cash drawn from bank	—		
Deduct { Stock Payments (Col 10)	259 60		
Other Payments (Col 12)	244 40		
Standing Orders/Direct Debits	—		
Bank and Interest Charges	—		
Total		504 00	
Closing Balance carried forward		1966 16	

Figure 14.1 The Simplex Weekly Page

3   *A payments for business stock section*   Here any purchases are
recorded. The word 'purchase' has a special meaning in accounts,
and means 'items purchased to be sold again at a later date', or
'items purchased to be embodied in the finished product to be
supplied to the customer at a later date'. Things like typewriters,
tills or furniture bought for use in the business are not 'purchases'
because there is no intention to sell them again. They are called
'capital items' or 'capital assets'.

4   *Payments other than for stock*   These are the overheads of the
business, but they also include the drawings of the proprietor(s)
and any capital items purchased. The Simplex System gives
traders a line for each of the commoner overhead expenses and a
few spare lines for any more-unusual item. Some people say when
they look at a Simplex Weekly Page – 'It looks very complicated'.
This is a mistake. When a system gives you a separate line for
every entry that is not complicated – it is easy. The complicated
paper to use is paper that is blank except for a lot of lines. If you
don't know what the lines mean you can't even start. If the lines
are all labelled and you can see exactly where everything goes it
makes it very simple.

5   *The Weekly Bank Report*   This is a section in which the bank
balance according to the books, is worked out each week. Of
course this may not be the actual balance at the bank, because the
bank does do things we don't know about (like charging bank
charges) but once a month when the trader receives a bank
statement the two figures will be reconciled, so that the trader
knows there is no error in his/her records.

6   *Weekly Cash Report*   This discovers the balance of cash in hand
according to the books. This should be the same as the 'cash in
hand as counted'. In this case it is 35 pence different which is
shown as a 'difference on books'.

With small traders the Inland Revenue takes the view that any
difference on books is almost certainly the proprietor's fault, and at
the end of the year the total will usually be treated as 'undisclosed
drawings'. It will be added to the drawings of the proprietor (and not
treated as a loss of the business). Drawings is the money the trader
takes out of the business for his/her own use. If money is missing from
the till the Inland Revenue will take it that the proprietor has it, and
will call it 'drawings', unless the trader can prove that it disappeared
as the result of a burglary (or theft by an employee who was
successfully prosecuted for theft).

Study Figure 14.1 carefully now, re-reading these notes as you do
so.

An exercise on the Simplex System

To help you try out the entries for the Weekly Page of the Simplex System a blank page for the Simplex D Book is given as Figure 14.2. The D stands for Schedule D, the tax system for small businesses. The page may be copied for educational purposes – do *not* write in this textbook unless it is your own copy. Better still, there is a package available free of charge to teachers and lecturers who wish to try out the system. The Simplex basic package enables all students to keep a month's records, for both financial accounts and VAT accounts, and draw up a set of Final Accounts at the end of the month. A complete answer book is provided. Those teachers and lecturers in the UK who are running courses in Business Studies, double-entry book-keeping or Enterprise Studies should apply on school or college letterhead, to G. P. Brogan Esq, George Vyner Ltd, Freepost, Holmfirth, Huddersfield HD7 1BR, stating the number of students they need to supply with materials.

An assignment on the Simplex Weekly Page

Although the best way to try out the Simplex System is to send for the basic package referred to, teachers who would like to try their classes out with a less testing assignment could use the blank Simplex Weekly Page reproduced in Figure 14.2. This may be photocopied for educational purposes. The students have to imagine they are running a small business where the financial events referred to happen in the sequence shown. If the example given in Figure 14.1 is followed students should have no difficulty in arriving at the correct totals for the week. These are given at the end of the exercise.

Exercise 14.1 on the Simplex Weekly Page

Jones is in business in the week commencing Sunday 13 April 19xx, which is week 15 of his financial year. The following events happen in the order shown. Make all necessary entries, total the various columns and work out the cash and bank balances according to the week's records, and the difference on books if any.

Sunday – closed. Cash in hand (as counted) £8.32 is brought forward, (see Weekly Cash Report), and his opening bank balance is £1,496.65 (see Weekly Bank Report).

Monday (a) R. Wall and Son are paid £42.75 by cheque (No. 129556) for business stock supplied; (b) Tom pays £2.50 postage on a parcel and £18.26 for petrol both in cash; (c) at the end of the day takings are found to be £386.54 in cash, £38.50 by cheque, and £30.00 by credit cards.

Week No. ___ Commencing: ___

RECEIPTS

Day/Date	Daily Gross Takings			Other Receipts Col 4	Particulars
	Cash Col 1	Cheques Col 2	Credit Cards Col 3		
Sun :					
Mon :					
Tues :					
Wed :					
Thur :					
Fri :					
Sat :					
Totals					

PAID TO BANK

Cash Col 5	Cheques Col 6	Credit Cards Col 7	TOTAL Col 8
Totals			

PAYMENTS FOR BUSINESS STOCK

Date or Chq. No.	To Whom Paid	Amount Paid	
		By Cash Col 9	By Cheque Col 10

PAYMENTS OTHER THAN FOR STOCK

Nature of Payment	Amount Paid	
	By Cash Col 11	By Cheque Col 12
Rent		
Rates		
Light and Heat		
Carriage		
Postages		
Paper		
Motor Expenses		
—do—		
Travelling		
Cleaning		
Printing & Stationery		
Repairs & Renewals		
Insurance (Business)		
Advertising		
Telephone		
Sundries		
Wages (Employees)		

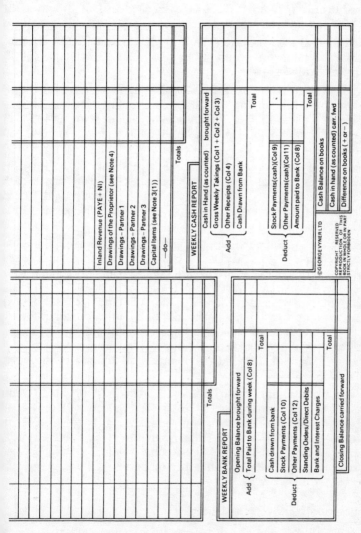

Totals

Inland Revenue (PAYE + NI)
Drawings of the Proprietor (see Note 4)
Drawings – Partner 1
Drawings – Partner 2
Drawings – Partner 3
Capital Items (see Note 3(1))
—do—

Totals

WEEKLY CASH REPORT

Cash in Hand (as counted)   brought forward
Add { Gross Weekly Takings (Col 1 + Col 2 + Col 3)
Other Receipts (Col 4)
Cash Drawn from Bank

Total

Deduct { Stock Payments (cash) (Col 9)
Other Payments (cash) (Col 11)
Amount paid to Bank (Col 8)

Total

Cash Balance on books

Cash in hand (as counted) carr. fwd
Difference on books (+ or –)

© GEORGE VYNER LTD

COPYRIGHT RESERVED.
REPRODUCTION OF THIS
BOOK IN WHOLE OR IN PART
STRICTLY FORBIDDEN

WEEKLY BANK REPORT

Opening Balance brought forward
Add { Total Paid to Bank during week (Col 8)

Total

Deduct { Cash drawn from bank
Stock Payments (Col 10)
Other Payments (Col 12)
Standing Orders/Direct Debits
Bank and Interest Charges

Total

Closing Balance carried forward

Figure 14.2 The blank Simplex Weekly Page (reproduced by courtesy of George Vyner Ltd – may be photocopied for educational purposes only)

Tuesday (a) Tom buys by cheque a capital item, a microwave oven for £286.50; (b) Tom receives £116.54 cheque as a VAT refund; (c) he pays £19.50 for advertising by cheque; (d) at the end of the day takings are found to be £564.00 cash, £173.80 by cheque and £68.50 by credit cards; (e) Tom banks £600 cash, cheques £155.04 and credit card £80.50 vouchers.

Wednesday (a) Pays postage in cash £1.90 and rent £280 by cheque; (b) the day's takings are found to be cash, £228.60, a cheque £28.45 and credit cards £42.60.

Thursday (a) Tom give his wife, whom he employs, wages of £84.00 cash and pays for printing £86.50 by cheque; (b) A. Khan & Sons supply stock worth £590.68 – Tom pays by cheque (No. 129560); (c) takings are found to be £376.65 cash, £196.80 by cheque and £427.50 by credit card.

Friday (a) Tom draws £100.00 for his personal use by cheque; (b) M. Kinder supplies fresh vegetables for resale – Tom pays in cash £47.50; (c) takings are £425.60 cash, £145.50 cheques and £95.55 credit cards; (d) Tom banks £950 cash, £373.80 in cheques and £520 credit card vouchers.

Saturday (a) A. Supplier supplies goods for resale £172.50 – Tom pays by cheque (No. 129561); (b) takings are found to be £792.84 cash, £384.60 cheques and credit card sales £347.60; (c) Tom pays for petrol £16.45 cash and wages to part-time helpers £92.50, in cash. *Note:* The cash in hand as counted at the end of the week (see below) includes not only cash but any cheques or credit cards still in the till and not as yet paid to bank. No bank standing orders, or interest charges apply this week, and no cash was drawn from the bank for shop use. The cash in hand (as counted) at the end of the week totalled £1,931.04.

Answers Total takings (cash) £2,774.23; (cheques) £967.65; (credit cards) £1,011.75. Grand total £4,753.63. Other receipts £116.54. Paid to bank £2,679.34. Payments for business stock (cash) £47.50 (cheques) £805.93. Payment other than for stock (cash £215.61 cheques £772.50. Balance on Bank Report c/fwd £2,597.56. Balance on Cash Report £1936.04. Difference on books – £5.

Business Studies students and Simplex

Simplex book-keeping is an excellent subject to introduce to Business Studies students. It is not very likely that any examiner is going to set a question on the Simplex system, but it is an excellent element in coursework and is even acceptable as a project. A student who has worked his/her way through the Simplex package has met a lot of book-keeping in the course of the journey, in a course which does not specifically require book-keeping, but by implication does. For example, the VAT element in Simplex really brings invoices, till rolls and credit notes to life, while the VAT return clarifies input tax and output tax better than any amount of talking. The coursework marks teachers and lecturers can award will be manifestly justified should the examiner call for the module to inspect the work done.

Finally, irrespective of examination work, the chief use of Simplex is to prepare those likely to take up self-employment for the real world that starts at 'Dawn on Day One' of their new business. From that moment documents begin to arrive, petty cash vouchers begin to collect and the full legal obligation of the business starts. Simplex will solve practically all the problems, for an outlay of about £5. It is difficult to imagine a more useful package to introduce to prospective entrepreneurs. They are offered a way to record receipts (sales or fees charged), and payments (whether for stock or overheads, or capital items) so that they can work out their profits for the year. Incidentally, in the process, they learn to keep both the VAT authorities and the Inland Revenue happy.

14.3   Double-entry book-keeping

Although on a Business Studies course we are not required to understand double-entry book-keeping fully, we can hardly hope to learn anything about business without meeting up with the term 'double-entry'. To see how the system works only needs us to study the illustration in Figure 14.3 (see page 270) and then to follow the brief description given in the sections which follow.

The system is divided into five parts:

1   Every transaction that takes place in business starts with an original document.
2   The documents are entered in **books of original entry** called 'Journals' or 'Day Books'.
3   The entries in the day books are transferred (posted) into the various parts of the **Ledger** which is the main book of account. Every page in the ledger is called an account.
4   From the accounts at the end of the month we can prepare a Trial Balance.
5   From the Trial Balance we can prepare a set of Final Accounts, in which we calculate the profit (or loss) made in the year. Study Figure 14.3 before reading the notes in the next section.

Figure 14.3 shows clearly how the double-entry system of book-keeping works. This method of keeping books so that business people can discover their exact financial position at any time is explained in the diagram, and the student should return to it regularly to discover

HOW DOUBLE-ENTRY BOOK-KEEPING WORKS

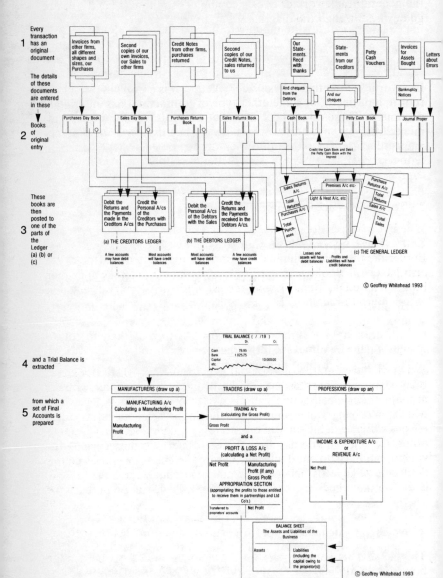

Figure 14.3   Double-entry book-keeping

how each section of his/her studies fits into the pattern of double entry.

At this stage let us take a very quick look at the diagram to pick up the general framework of book-keeping. The numbers (**1**) to (**5**) are guideways through the diagram.

1   The original documents

Every transaction that takes place, whether it is a purchase, a sale, a return, a payment, or some other type of transaction, has an original document. These documents are called invoices, credit notes, statements, receipts, petty cash vouchers, or they may be formal agreements like a hire-purchase document or a legal contract. Even mere letters of complaint require some action to be taken.

2   The books of original entry

When you have a document you first record it in a book of Original Entry. These books may be Journals – that is, Day Books – or Cash Books like the Four Column Cash Book or the Petty Cash Book. We also have Bill Books to record bills of exchange, and several other books. These Day Books keep a record of the documents received in chronological order, which is a useful record to have.

3   Posting the Day Books to the Ledger

When we have entered our original documents in the Day Books we then post the transactions into the Ledger, which is the main book of account. Every transaction will appear twice, because one account will be receiving value and another giving it. For this reason the entries will be a debit entry in one account and a credit entry in some other account. Hundreds, even thousands, of accounts may be involved, but if we do our double entry carefully the total entries on the debit side will exactly balance the total entries on the credit side. This is the way we check the books, by taking out a Trial Balance.

4   The Trial Balance

This is what its name implies, an attempt to discover whether the books really do balance. If they do not we know that someone has made a mistake somewhere, and we must discover it.

To take out a Trial Balance we must look at every account in our Ledger, and there may be thousands of them. Each account will be in one of three positions:

(a) It may have a debit balance outstanding.
(b) It may be clear, having no outstanding balance.
(c) It may have a credit balance outstanding.

We usually do a Trial Balance at least once a month, taking the opportunity to 'tidy up' accounts where we can, and bringing all the debit balances into a list of debit balances, and all the credit balances into a list of credit balances. These two columns of balances should come exactly equal, and we may conclude that if they do, it is fairly certain we have done our book-keeping well. The idea of the Trial Balance is the most important idea in book-keeping by the double-entry system.

5(a)   Final Accounts – The Manufacturing Account and the Trading Account

Different types of firms have different sets of Final Accounts. The most common type of organization is a trading organization, which buys goods for resale. Such a firm starts its Final Accounts with a Trading Account, in which we discover whether we are selling at a profit, or are making a loss. Before looking at the Trading Account we can see from the diagram that one type of organization – the manufacturing firm – has to work out first of all a Manufacturing Account. The Manufacturing Account consists of a record of all the costs incurred in manufacture, and these costs are then passed on to the Trading Account where they form part of the cost of sales. However, there is a technique for working out a Manufacturing Profit if we really wish to do so.

To return to the Trading Account, the figure for sales for the year is set against the cost of the sales (including the costs of manufacture in a manufacturing firm) to work out the overall profit – called in book-keeping the **gross profit**.

5(b)   Final Accounts – The Profit and Loss Account

In this second half of our Final Accounts we start with the gross profit and take away from it all overhead expenses. We add items of profit, such as commission or discounts received. This leads us to the clear profit or clean profit – called in book-keeping **net profit**. This net profit is the reward of the business person for his/her efforts.

With partnership enterprises and with limited companies, the net profit has to be shared out among the partners or shareholders. This is done in a section of the Profit and Loss Account called the **Appropriation Account**. We give the profit to the appropriate persons in the appropriate proportions according to the partnership agreement or the resolution passed at the annual general meeting of the company.

5(c) Final Accounts – Professional Firms, Clubs and Societies

Professional firms, dentists, doctors, lawyers, etc. and clubs and societies
do not use the term 'profit' for the results of their activities. Instead
they refer to 'revenues' and 'surpluses.' Such organizations are not
traders, and do not use Trading Accounts and Profit and Loss Accounts.
Instead they call their Final Accounts either **Income and Expenditure
Accounts** or simply **Revenue Accounts**.

5(d) The Balance Sheet

When we have prepared the Final Accounts, discovered the profit (or
loss) and allotted it to those entitled to receive (or suffer) it, we have
established what degree of success the business has achieved, and all
we need to do now is summarize the final position of the business by
drawing up a **Balance Sheet** which shows the assets and liabilities of
the firm.

14.4 Cash flow

One of the worrying things about the financial affairs of a business is
cash flow. We saw the ways in which cash flows in and out of a
business in Figure 11.2, but the problem is that flows are not even,
and at any time we may be faced with either a surplus of cash or a
shortage. Of course a surplus of cash is a happier situation than a
shortage, but even a surplus brings its problems. If a business has
plenty of cash there will soon be people suggesting ways of spending
it. Trade unions may put in claims for higher wages; departments may
press for larger spending budgets; new equipment may be called for
by other staff etc. Sometimes the extra cash will not really be
available at all, but only in hand, awaiting payment. Examples are
VAT money due to Customs and Excise and tax money due to the
Inland Revenue. It follows that real care must be taken to anticipate
cash flows, so that we know when a surplus will occur and when we
shall be short of cash and unable to meet all our obligations. The
usual thing is to arrange an overdraft, or if necessary a loan when a
shortage is going to occur, and to put cash away in a Deposit Account
when surplus funds are likely to be available.

To keep track of our cash flow we use a cash flow forecast, like the
one illustrated in Figure 14.4. This is reproduced from the Simplex D
Account Book, which, as mentioned earlier, is commonly used by
those starting out in business.

Having studied Figure 14.4 carefully we can see that the forecast
gives us a clear picture of the funds likely to become available and to
be needed in the month ahead. It is usual to roll the budget on from

CASHFLOW FORECAST

		MONTH 1		MONTH 2		MONTH 3		MONTH 4	
		Budget	Actual	Budget	Actual	Budget	Actual	Budget	Actual
1	Balance in hand (Cash and Bank)								
	RECEIPTS								
2	Daily Takings for month								
3	Debts collected								
4	Other receipts								
5	Loans arranged								
6	Extra capital contributed								
7	Total Receipts (add lines 2 to 6)								
8	Total Cash available (add lines 1 + 7)								
	PAYMENTS								
9	Business stock								
10	Rent & Rates								
11	Light & Heat								
12	Carriage & Postages								
13	Paper								
14	Motor Expenses								

	Travelling									
15	Travelling									
16	Cleaning									
17	Printing & Stationery									
18	Repairs & Renewals									
19	Insurance (Business)									
20	Advertising									
21	Telephone									
22	Wages (employees)									
23	Sundries									
24	Capital Items									
25	Loans Repaid									
26	Other external payments									
27	Total External Payments (add lines 9 to 26)									
28	Drawings – Proprietor or Partner 1									
29	„ Partner 2									
30	„ Partner 3									
31	Total Payments (add lines 27 to 30)									
32	Balance If line 8 > line 31, balance in Credit → carr. fwd. If line 31 > line 8, balance in (Deficit) →									

Note: The sign > means greater than.

Figure 14.4 A cash flow forecast (Notes to Figure 14.4 overleaf)

one month to the next, keeping about three months ahead of the actual date, so that we have advance warning of a likely shortage and time to see the bank manager and agree an overdraft figure. Certain things need thinking about as we prepare the budget. Some of them are:

1 *Sales* What sales are we likely to make in each month? For example, December is often a busy month, followed by a month (January) when trade falls away pretty seriously. Many firms run January sales to try to get what business is available. Few firms have steady trading throughout the year.

2 *Debts* Debts should, in theory, be paid up within thirty days in most trades, but some trades have a three-month credit period. This means goods sold in March are not paid for until June, and we have to survive until the money comes in. One firm in the author's experience landed a huge and profitable contract exporting manufactured goods for a leading manufacturer. Unfortunately they only paid three months after each consignment was shipped. By the time the first cheque came in the firm had overdrawn £3,000,000, and was utterly dependent on a friendly merchant bank to keep going.

Notes to Figure 14.4:

1 To draw up a cash flow forecast the trader first enters the month he/she starts to keep the forecast in the space provided at the top of the month column. The notes then read:

2 Fill in the total balance in hand (cash and bank) at the beginning of the month in line 1.

3 Fill in the 'Receipts' section (lines 2–6) with the money you hope to take this month and the debts you hope to collect this month. For example, invoices issued in January may not be payable until March.

4 The total estimated receipts (line 7) added to line 1 gives the estimated total cash available (line 8).

5 Now fill in the payments you expect to make for the months on lines 9–26. You can move across the page to enter a payment you know to be due in one of the months ahead (the full page shows twelve months) as soon as you know how much it is (e.g. a monthly HP payment could be entered right across the page).

6 When totalled these give the total expected payments to other businesses.

7 Now enter any drawings and find the total expected payments (line 31).

8 Take line 31 from line 8 to find your estimated cash balance at the end of the month. If it is a deficit (31 bigger than 8) take 8 from 31 and put a bracket round the figure to indicate a negative balance. Now arrange an overdraft to carry you over the bad period.

9 Carry the estimated balance to the start of the new month.

10 At the end of the month when you know the actual figures complete the 'actual' column to see how they compare.

11 If at all possible, practise **cash flow smoothing**. If you have a month where you have a lot to pay out try to rearrange your payments to spread them more evenly, e.g. arrange to pay your rates evenly over the year to avoid a big payment in any one month.

3   *Taxes*   Taxes have to be paid, either in January and June for sole traders and partnerships, or in January (in one lump sum) for companies. It is important to budget for this in the cash flow forecast.

4   *VAT*   VAT has to be paid quarterly. This must be budgeted for, as it may be a considerable sum, and it belongs to HM Customs, not us. We only collect tax for the Customs and Excise Department, and if we have used it for something else the penalties can be severe.

5   *Profits*   Profit distribution affects cash flows. Of course sole traders and partners usually draw what they need from week to week, or month to month, but at the end of the year they can draw out the rest of the profits if they wish – but only if the cash is available. Similarly shareholders can only be paid dividends if cash is available. If it is not the directors may decide to pass the dividend. This upsets the shareholders who may try to vote the Board of Directors out of office at the next Annual General Meeting. If a firm has made profits these profits should be available as cash. If they are not (because the cash has been spent on more stock, or more capital equipment) the business is said to be **overtrading** (expanding more than it really should be) and this may lead to disputes about the distribution of profits, and even to bankruptcy proceedings (if creditors cannot be paid).

6   *Wages*   Although we all want to be well paid, and management likes to have a reputation for fair treatment rather than miserly behaviour, all wage increases have to be budgeted for. Concessions cannot be made at the drop of a hat. A lightning strike called to compel management to concede a wage increase may only lead to the collapse of the company if there is no chance to save up the money for the increase. If management borrows the money it has to pay interest on the sum borrowed – rarely less than 15–18 per cent per annum these days.

Exercise 14.2   *Working out a cash flow forecast*

1   Peter Piper is setting up in business as a grocer. He will have £1,250 in the bank and £100 in cash on 1 July when he hopes to start. He hopes to take an average of £150 a day, (27 days in the month) in cash, and to do £1,000 a month with credit customers half of whom will pay within 30 days and half within 60 days. He will have an enterprise allowance of £40 per week. This is paid fortnightly and he expects two payments to fall in July only. He estimates initial stock will cost £1,000, followed by a further £250 each week (4½ weeks in July), rent is £56 per week (4½ weeks) and light and heat will not be paid for until September. Other costs include carriage £45 per month, cleaning £40 per month,

printing and stationery will cost £60 in July and insurance £120. He expects to pay £360 to part-time labour and to buy equipment worth £240. Work out his cash flow forecast for July and advise Peter of the wisdom of buying a second-hand motor vehicle he needs. There is a good one for £2,800 available, or an older model at £1250. Drawings will be at the rate of £100 per week (4½ weeks).

2 Peter has taken advice, since the motor vehicle seems to be essential, to ask his bank manager for a loan to start on 1 August. The loan is for £2,000, repayable at the rate of £104.60 per month, the first payment to be made in September. Work out a budget for August on the same terms as before except that the loan will become available and there will be no insurance to pay. Bank charges for arranging the loan will be £65.00. The car will be purchased at an agreed price of £2,750, but no other equipment will be purchased. Motor vehicle expenses of £98 (premium), £100 tax and £56 petrol will be payable in the month. There will again be only two enterprise allowance payments in the month. Other items are as before, but there will be no initial purchase of stock and the weekly stock purchases will rise to £300 per week for 4½ weeks. The balance at the start of August will, of course be the estimated balance at the end of July, as found when doing Exercise 1.

Answers to Exercise 14.2

Balance at the end of July = £1,868. Balance at end of August = £2,952.

14.5 The profits of a business

The chief purpose of being in business is to make a profit by the activities that are undertaken. This profit is the reward to the entrepreneur for all the work done, and the risks run. The profit belongs to those who showed enterprise, whether they are sole traders, partners or shareholders in a limited company. As there are many different types of business there is a different emphasis on the calculation of the profits. We can best illustrate these different attitudes by looking at the table shown as Table 14.1.

It is difficult to understand the affairs of any business unless we know the chief items included in any profit calculation and in this section we will take the simplest type of business, the trading organization, and consider the parts of its book-keeping which are concerned with working out the profits. We can then bring out some

Table 14.1 Different approaches to 'profit'

Manufacturers	Trading organizations	Professional people
Prepare (1) a Manufacturing Account, followed by (2) a Trading Account and (3) a Profit and Loss Account, and ending with a Balance Sheet	Prepare (1) a Trading Account followed by (2) a Profit and Loss Account and (3) a Balance Sheet	Prepare (1) an Income and Expenditure Account, followed by (2) a Balance Sheet *Note:* The Income and Expenditure Account may be called a Revenue Account

Notes:
1 A Manufacturing Account works out the costs of the goods manufactured, and we can also work out a manufacturing profit if we wish to do so.
2 The Trading Account works out the gross profit on trading. Gross profit means 'overall profit' before overhead expenses are deducted.
3 A Profit and Loss Account works out the 'net profit' or 'clean profit' after all overhead expenses have been deducted.
4 Professional people do not usually call their Profit and Loss Account by that name. Instead they call it an Income and Expenditure Account, or perhaps a Revenue Account. It still works out the profits of a business, but sensitive professions do not call them 'profits', but surpluses. Dentists do not say 'I made a profit on Mrs Smith's dentures' – but refer to the 'surplus' after expenditures have been deducted from the income of the practice.

of the things that we can learn from an appraisal of these accounts, which are called the Final Accounts of the business.

14.6   The Trial Balance of a trading business

The starting point for the Final Accounts of any business is the Trial Balance of the various parts of the ledger at the end of the last day of the financial year. The Trial Balance of an imaginary firm, Young Idea, a fashion boutique having a site inside a major shopping mall in a busy town centre reads as shown in Figure 14.5.

The one figure needed to work out the profits of the business which is not in the Trial Balance, is the closing stock figure. This is found by doing the stocktaking, an exercise in which all stocks are counted and valued at cost price, or net realizable value, whichever is the lower. Thus if an item in stock cost £20 it is valued at that figure, unless it has deteriorated while in stock and would now have to be sold at a price lower than original cost. In that case it is included in the stocktaking figure at this net realizable value. In this case the closing stock figure is found to be £19,130.

Trial Balance of 'Young Idea' as at 31 December 19xx

	Dr £	Cr £
Stock A/c (at start of year)	26,529	
Purchases A/c and Sales A/c	65,865	183,565
Sales Returns A/c and Purchases Returns A/c	2,565	264
Rent and Rates A/c	5,210	
Light and Heat A/c	846	
Carriage Outwards A/c	225	
Commission Received A/c		2,420
Discount Received A/c		1,256
Motor Expenses A/c	1,361	
Travelling A/c	281	
Cleaning A/c	1,475	
Printing and Stationery A/c	385	
Repairs and Renewals A/c	460	
Insurance A/c	120	
Advertising A/c	750	
Telephone Expenses A/c	1,125	
Wages A/c	39,785	
Land and Buildings A/c	45,000	
Plant and Machinery A/c	24,655	
Furntiure and Fittings A/c	8,725	
Motor Vehicles A/c	11,275	
Debtors and creditors	1,275	4,398
Cash at bank	5,948	
Cash in hand	327	
Capital A/c (M. Lawson – proprietor)		36,784
Mortgage A/c		30,000
Loan (from Bank) A/c		5,500
Drawings A/c	20,000	
	£264,187	264,187

Figure 14.5   The Trial Balance of 'Young Idea'

We can now proceed to draw up the Final Accounts, starting with the Trading Account, which is shown in Figure 14.6.

14.7 Final Accounts Part 1: The Trading Account

Consider the Trading Account given in Figure 14.6 of 'Young Idea', a fashion boutique having a site inside a major shopping mall in a busy town centre.

Trading Account of 'Young Idea', for year ended 31 December 19xx

	£	£		£
Opening Stock 1 January		26,529	Sales	183,565
Purchases	65,865		*Less* returns	2,565
Less returns	264		Net turnover	181,000
		65,601		
Total stock available		92,130		
Less closing stock		19,130		
Cost of stock sold		73,000		
Gross Profit (to Profit and Loss A/c)		108,000		
		£181,000		£181,000

Figure 14.6 The Trading Account of 'Young Idea'

Notes:

1 To find the profit we need to know how much we sold, and what the things that we sold cost us. Then sales − cost of stock sold = profit.

2 The sales are easy enough – the total of the takings for the year, but we did have a few returned items. The figure of £181,000 is the net sales figure, usually called the net turnover of the business.

3 What did we pay for these items? First we had some stock (valued at cost price) on the shelves and sales racks at the start of the year. We bought more (purchases) but returned a few items. When these purchases were added to the opening stock they gave us a total stock available in the year of £92,130. We still had £19,130 of stock (valued at cost price) on the shelves at the end of the year. What is not there, must have been sold (unless it was stolen by shoplifters). Anyway, we deduct this 'cost of stock sold' from the net turnover figure to find the profit made which is £108,000.

4 This sounds a good profit, but remember it is a *gross* profit – we haven't yet deducted the overhead expenses from it. When we do, we find the net profit. This is done in the Profit and Loss Account, as shown in Figure 14.7.

14.8   Final Accounts Part 2: The Profit and Loss Account

Profit and Loss Account of 'Young Idea' for year ending 31 December 19xx

	£		£
Rent and rates	5,210	Gross profit	108,000
Light and heat	846	Commission received	2,420
Carriage outwards	225	Discount received	1,256
Motor expenses	1,361		111,676
Travelling	281		
Cleaning	1,475		
Printing and stationery	385		
Repairs and renewals	460		
Insurance	120		
Advertising	750		
Telephone expenses	1,125		
Wages	39,785		
	52,023		
Net profit	59,653		
	£111,676		£111,676
		Net profit	£ 59,653

Figure 14.7   The Profit and Loss Account of 'Young Idea'

Notes:
1   The gross profit transferred from the Trading Account starts the Profit and Loss Account and one or two extra bits of profit – commission received and discount received are added to it.
2   Against these profits are set all the losses of the business, i.e. the expenses incurred during the year, to a total of £52,023.
3   The final result is that we have a net profit of £59,653.

14.9   Final Accounts Part 3: The Balance Sheet

The final part of the Final Accounts is to draw up a Balance Sheet of the business. It helps if we discuss a number of points about Balance Sheets before we actually draw one up. These points are:

1   The residue of the Trial Balance

The first thing to notice is that as each of the items used in the Trading Account and the Profit and Loss Account was transferred into these accounts, the balance on the account disappeared from the Trial Balance. For example, if we take the Opening Stock Account balance and debit it in the Trading Account we must credit the figure in the Stock Account, and as a result the Stock Account is cleared, and has no balance left on it. This happens to every account, and as they have no balances left they disappear from the Trial Balance. All we are left with is a small residue of the Trial Balance. We must look at this now.

Residue of the Trial Balance of Young Idea as at 31 December 19xx

	Dr £	Cr £
Land and Buildings A/c	45,000	
Plant and Machinery A/c	24,655	
Furniture and Fittings A/c	8,725	
Motor Vehicles A/c	11,275	
Debtors and creditors	1,275	4,398
Cash at bank	5,948	
Cash in hand	327	
Capital A/c		36,784
Mortgage A/c		30,000
Loan A/c		5,500
Stock A/c (at close of year)	19,130	
Profit and Loss A/c		59,653
Drawings A/c	20,000	
	£136,335	136,335

Notes:
1 The Stock Account appears again, because after it was cleared of the opening stock we then introduced the closing stock, a new asset of the business, valued at £19,130.
2 The other new account is the Profit and Loss Account itself, which has a credit balance of £59,653. This actually belongs to the proprietor, because the proprietor is entitled to all the profits.

2   The fixed assets

On a Balance Sheet the new assets now appear on the left-hand side, just as the assets do in the Trial Balance. You will often see them on the right-hand side, because this is the traditional way of recording them in the UK. Since the Companies Act, 1985 this is now incorrect, and we should show them on the correct, left-hand side.

Fixed assets are assets which last a long time, and are purchased for long-term use in the business. They are usually displayed in the order of permanence, with the most permanent asset (land and buildings) first.

3   The current assets

These are assets which do not last a long time, but turn into cash fairly quickly. They include stocks, investments held for the purposes of earning interest until the money they represent is required, and debtors (who we hope will pay in cash within thirty days). Cash at the bank and cash in hand are already in cash form.

4   The liabilities side

The longest-lasting liability of the business is the capital, because we never repay it until the business actually ceases to trade, when the proprietor (or more likely his/her heirs and successors) take the money back again. Long-term liabilities are ones that are repaid only over several years – such as mortgages or bank loans. Current liabilities are due for repayment in less than a year – which usually means creditors who are due to be paid in thirty days.

We are now ready to draw up the Balance Sheet of 'Young Idea'. This is shown in Figure 14.8.

Balance Sheet of 'Young Idea' as at 31 December 19xx

	£		£	£
Fixed assets				
Land and buildings	45,000	Capital at start of year		36,784
Plant and machinery	24,655	*Add* net profit	59,653	
Furniture and		*Less* drawings	20,000	
fittings	8,725			39,653
Motor vehicles	11,275			76,437
	89,655			
Current assets	£	*Long-term liabilities*		
Stock at close	19,130	Mortgage	30,000	
Debtors	1,275	Bank loan	5,500	
Cash at bank	5,948			35,500
Cash in hand	327	*Current liabilities*		
	26,680	Creditors		4,398
	£116,335			£116,335

Figure 14.8   The Balance Sheet of 'Young Idea'

Exercise 14.3   Simple Final Accounts exercises

Note: When attempting these exercises you will find them relatively easy if you just remember these points. Everything in business Final Accounts is either an asset, a liability, a loss or a profit. The assets and liabilities go in the Balance Sheet. The losses and profits go either in the Trading Account or the Profit and Loss Account. In these simple examples only six things go in the Trading Account – the opening stock, the closing stock, the purchases, the purchases returns (returns out), the sales and the sales returns (returns in). All other losses and profits go in the Profit and Loss Account. If you look at any item and decide where it is to go you will have no real difficulty in doing these exercises, especially if you look back to Figures 14.6, 14.7 and 14.8 to see the layout. The only item that appears twice is the closing stock, which not only goes in the Trading Account but also appears on the Balance Sheet as it is brought onto the books for the next year. (*For answers see page 289.*)

1   From the following particulars prepare the Trading Account of L. Sharp for the year ended 31 December 19xx: Sales £97,356; Purchases £35,275; Sales Returns £2,164; Purchases Returns £2,385; Stock 1 January £2,765; Stock 31 December £4,854.

2   From the following particulars prepare the Trading Account of M. Lowe for the year ended 31 December 19xx: Stock 1 January £4,279; Purchases £47,326; Purchases Returns £1,306; Sales £127,346; Sales Returns £2,263; Stock 31 December £7,359.

3   At 31 December 19xx, the Trial Balance of M. Clarke contained the following items:

	£
Stock at 1 January 19xx	12,785
Purchases	66,908
Sales	127,642
Returns outwards	5,195
Returns inwards	7,262

Clarke's stock at 31 December 19xx, was valued at £16,259. Prepare the Trading Account for the year ending 31 December 19xx.

4   From the following figures prepare T. Moore's Profit and Loss Account for the year ended 31 March 19xx.

	£
Gross profit	49,250
Discount allowed	725
Discount received	563
Bad debts	1,240
Rent and rates	4,540
Light and heat	1,256
Packing and delivery expenses	1,745
Commission received	894
Salaries	19,712

5   After the Trading Account had been prepared K. Spalding's Trial Balance contains the following items other than assets and liabilities. From them prepare his Profit and Loss Account for year ending 31 December 19xx.

	£
Gross trading profit	111,260
Salaries	43,515
Selling expenses	5,426
Packing materials	1,425
Rent etc.	4,846
Discount received	647
Discount allowed	443

6   From the following particulars prepare the Trading Account and then the Profit and Loss Account of R. McAdam, for the year ending 30 June 19xx.

	£
Stock at start of 1 July 19xx	21,760
Discount allowed	517
Insurance premiums	414
Salaries	29,426
Purchases	34,550
Returns outwards	512
Printing and stationery	825
Rent and rates	4,442
Sales	128,516
Returns inwards	1,516
General expenses	2,325
Telephone Account	825
Stock 30 June 19xx	1,585
Discount received	662
Interest paid on loans	430
Light and heat	1,124

7   Here is the Trial Balance of M. Shah's books. From it prepare his
Trading Account, Profit and Loss Account and Balance Sheet.

Trial Balance as at 31 December 19xx

	£	£
Stock at start	15,594	
Debtors and creditors	5,924	2,746
Freehold land and buildings	73,750	
Heavy goods vehicles	27,360	
Purchases and sales	146,742	312,385
Bad debts	390	
Motor vehicle expenses	4,175	
Office Repairs Account	495	
Returns – in and out	1,565	1,426
Fixtures and fittings	6,594	
Motor vans	11,625	
Office expenses	4,725	
Capital at 1 April last year		52,408
Mortgage		21,095
Drawings	19,750	
Salaries and commission	45,650	
Depreciation	4,250	
Carriage out	1,276	
Cash at bank	20,195	
	£390,060	390,060

Closing stock on 31 December 19xx £24,500.00

8 Here is the Trial Balance of M. Peacock's books on 31 December
19xx. You are asked to prepare the Trading Account, Profit and
Loss Account, and a Balance Sheet at this date for the year that
has just passed.

	Dr	Cr
Debtors and creditors	5,600	7,220
Plant and machinery	5,900	
Purchases and sales	48,200	143,000
Capital at 1 January 19xx		59,091
Premises	55,000	
Cash in hand	490	
Cash at bank	14,261	
Discounts allowed and received	550	1,460
Bad debts	540	
Motor vehicles	24,600	
Commission paid	1,200	
Insurance premium	512	
Office furniture	4,800	
Stock on 1 January 19xx	17,200	
Rent and rates	3,120	
Fees to lawyers for debt collection	180	
Returns – in and out	2,950	1,462
Office salaries	37,630	
Mortgage on premises		30,000
Drawings	19,500	
	£242,233	242,233

Stock at the end of December £15,254

9 Mark Coulsden is in business as a master tailor. On 31 December 19xx he takes out his Trial Balance as shown below. Prepare his Trading Account, Profit and Loss Account and Balance Sheet.

	Dr	Cr
Stock at 1 January 19xx	11,550	
Purchases and sales	48,200	135,500
Returns – in and out	1,225	1,341
Rent paid	5,620	
Carriage paid	240	
Office equipment	5,260	
Telephone expenses	1,246	
Premises	46,000	
Plant and machinery	30,800	
Motor vehicles	11,800	
Debtors and creditors	5,200	2,300
Office expenses	4,164	
Office salaries	27,200	
Commission paid	1,200	
Bad debts recovered		525
Mortgage on premises		28,800
Cash in hand	210	
Balance at bank	15,800	
Capital		64,749
Drawings	17,500	
	£233,215	233,215

Closing stock was valued at £17,176 on 31 December 19xx.

Answers to Exercise 14.3

1 Books of L. Sharp: gross profit £64,391, totals £95,192;   2 Books of M. Lowe: gross profit £82,143, totals £125,083;   3 Books of M. Clarke: gross profit £62,141, totals £120,380;   4 Books of T. Moore: net profit £21,489, totals £50,707;   5 Books of K. Spalding: net profit £56,252, totals £111,907;   6 Books of R. McAdam: gross profit £72,787, net profit £33,121;   7 Books of M. Shah: gross profit £174,410, net profit £113,449, fixed assets £119,329, current assets £50,619, capital at close of year £146,107, Balance Sheet totals £169,948;   8 Books of M. Peacock: gross profit £91,366, net profit £49,094, fixed assets £90,300, current assets £35,605, capital at close £88,685, Balance Sheet totals £125,905;   9 Books of Mark Coulsden: gross profit £93,042, net profit £53,897, fixed assets £93,860,

current assets £38,386, Balance Sheet totals £132,246, capital at close £101,146.

14.10   The role of accounting

Accounting serves several roles in business. First, it is a method of keeping track of all the financial affairs of the business in a very detailed way. Every transaction, however tiny, has to be recorded according to double-entry principles and by looking at the records we should be able to tell our cash position; our situation at the bank; how much we owe to every creditor and how much we are owed by every debtor. We should know what assets we own and what liabilities we owe, including that ultimate liability, the money the business owes to the owner of the business, on the Capital Account.

Second, accounting enables us to determine the profitability of the business. Although working out the profits at the end of the financial year is the most important of these calculations, because it is at that time that we are assessed for tax by the Inland Revenue Department, it is usual to work out **Interim Final Accounts** much more frequently, and most computerized systems could actually work out the profits for us at the end of every single day if we just pressed the right key. More likely we do it quarterly, or monthly at the very most.

Finally, one of the chief points about accounting is that it enables those who are charged with the duty of reporting back to the owners of the business, to give a good account of the business's affairs. Of course with sole traders and partners, who are usually in charge of their own books anyway the affairs of the business are well known, and reporting back is not such an important matter. It is a different thing with companies, which may have thousands of shareholders who are not entitled in law to see the books of the business and must rely on the Annual Report to see the state of affairs of the company in which they have invested. One major bank, in its Annual Report reveals as follows:

Total number of shareholders	106,361
of which: individuals	101,280
institutions investing the funds of other people (pensions etc.)	5,081
Total capital owned by shareholders	3,039 million
Total assets of the bank	42,400 million
of which, money belonging to customers is	38,114 million

Clearly the 106,361 shareholders could not all be allowed to look into the books, and many of them would not understand much of the records if they did, but there has to be some reporting back to the shareholders in an Annual Report. Any public company (not private companies) must publish an Annual Report, in a form laid down by the Companies Act, 1985. This is too difficult a subject for the present volume, but students should write to obtain a report from one or two famous companies and see how detailed and comprehensive these reports are.

14.11   The principles of accounting

Some of the principles on which accounting is based are worth mentioning here. They are:

1 *The concept of business entity*   A business is regarded as a separate entity. Its affairs are separate from those of the sole trader, partners or shareholders who actually own the business. The link between the business and the owners is the Capital Account, which shows how much, in the final analysis, the business owes to the owner of the business, or the owners if there are several of them.

2 *The prudence concept*   This holds that a business never counts a profit as being made until it has actually realized the profit, but it always takes a loss as soon as it occurs. That is why we value stock at cost price or net realizable value, whichever is the lower. We don't value it at selling price because that would be including a profit we had not yet realized.

3 *The going-concern concept*   If a business is going to continue in business we value the assets at their full value to the business as a going-concern. If the proprietors decide to discontinue the business we change the value of all the assets to what we can get if we sell them. Thus a cement works may be worth millions as a going-concern but if we decide to close it down it is hardly worth anything. Who wants kilns, and chalk hills, and mud banks. Very few people, and most of the machinery goes as scrap metal.

4 *The objectivity concept*   Accountants are supposed to view their businesses objectively (from the viewpoint of a disinterested outsider) not subjectively (from the viewpoint of a biased insider). What is this firm we are looking at really worth? How profitable is it compared with other firms? These are the sorts of questions accountants ask.

There are a number of other concepts which are most meaningful to those making a detailed study of double-entry accounting. Students who are really interested should see the companion volume to this one, *Book-keeping Made Simple*.

14.12   The interpretation of Final Accounts

When we look at a set of Final Accounts we need to be able to understand the facts behind the figures. What is the situation of the business and how successful is it? To do this we usually look at the figures in ratio form. A ratio is a quantitative relationship between two similar magnitudes which shows how many times one goes into the other, either integrally or fractionally. If profits have doubled this year, the ratio of this year's profit to last year's profit is 2:1.

The most important ratios to consider are:

1   The gross profit percentage.
2   The rate of stock turnover.
3   The net profit percentage.
4   Expense ratios.
5   The working capital ratio or 'current' ratio.
6   The 'acid-test' ratio or 'quick' ratio.
7   The return on capital employed.
8   The return on capital invested.

A short explanation of each of these is necessary.

14.13   The gross profit percentage

This is the percentage of gross profit that we make upon sales, or perhaps it is better to say 'upon net turnover'. The term net turnover means 'sales less returns', and the net turnover of the business is itself an important statistic about any enterprise. The formula for the gross profit percentage is therefore:

$$\text{Gross profit percentage} = \frac{\text{Gross profit}}{\text{Net turnover}} \times 100$$

Consider the Trading Account as shown in Figure 14.9.

Michael Smith
Trading Account for year ended 31 December 19xx

	£	£		£
Opening stock		14,500	Sales	127,900
Purchases	53,800		*Less* returns	5,400
Less returns	2,700		Net turnover	122,500
Net purchases		51,100		
Total stock				
available		65,600		
Less closing stock		18,200		
Cost of stock sold		47,400		
Gross profit		75,100		
		£122,500		£122,500

Figure 14.9   A Trading Account

The gross profit percentage on this Trading Account is:

$$\frac{\text{Gross profit}}{\text{Net turnover}} \times 100$$

$$= \frac{\text{£75,100}}{\text{£122,500}} \times 100$$

$$= \underline{\underline{61.3\%}}$$

Supposing the next year the firm does twice as much business? Would it need to make twice as many purchases? Would it expect to pay out twice as many expenses? Would it expect to make twice as much profit? Of course we cannot answer a 'yes' with absolute confidence to all these questions, but generally speaking the answer will be 'roughly yes'. If we sell twice as many goods we would expect to buy twice as many goods. For the sake of this argument we will assume that everything simply doubles. Next year the gross profit percentage works out as follows:

$$\frac{\text{Gross profit}}{\text{Net turnover}} \times 100$$

$$= \frac{\text{£150,200}}{\text{£245,000}} \times 100$$

$$= \underline{\underline{61.3\%}}$$

You will see that it is the same answer as we had before, and this is the vital thing about the gross profit percentage: it is a constant. It ought to come out the same every year providing our business is running in the same way. If the gross profit percentage has fallen during the year there must be some explanation. The most likely ones are:

1 The manager or staff are stealing the cash takings. This will reduce the sales figure and the profits will fall. The cash is being diverted into the manager's or someone else's pocket.
2 Perhaps someone is stealing the stock? One of the things about stocktaking is that it discovers losses of stock. A lower stock than we should have means a higher cost of sales figure and a lower gross profit. Who takes the stock home? Two pounds of sugar and a quarter of tea every night for a year makes quite a big hole in the stock. A very common practice of dishonest shop assistants is to help their friends to free goods. A packet of cigarettes to each boyfriend soon stops the gross profit percentage being constant.
3 If neither 1 nor 2 is the cause, stock might be getting lost in other ways. For instance, breakages due to clumsiness in the crockery department transfer some of the stock to the dustbin. Bad buying

of perishables has the same effect – we throw away the tomatoes that go bad, the cheese that gets stale, the cakes that go dry. If we don't actually throw them away we have to sell them cheaply and that still means the profit on them is lost.

4   Another type of bad buying, in the clothing and footwear trades especially, concerns the out-of-touch buyer who is behind the times and buys lines that have to be reduced in the sales because we cannot get rid of them in any other way. We have to keep our fashion buyers young in heart or their work will adversely affect the gross profit percentage.

5   A quite legitimate explanation for the falling gross profit percentage may be that the cost of goods to us has risen and we have been slow to pass this on to the public. It may be because we have poor control in our pricing department, or because competition from more efficient traders prevents us from raising prices. Sometimes governments regulate prices by law and force the trader to accept lower profit margins. A government tax may be levied but because of the demand in our particular market we may be unable to pass the tax on and must suffer it ourselves. The astute business manager will at least be ready with plans to recoup these losses as soon as the law, or the market situation, changes.

14.14   The rate of stock turnover

We have already seen that the turnover of a business is the final sales figure i.e. the sales less returns inwards. It is as the stock turns over that the business makes a profit, and the more frequently stock turns over the more profit we make. Other things being unchanged, if the rate of stock turnover is increased profits will rise. It may even be worth lowering prices, and thus selling at less profit per unit, if the turnover rises more than proportionately.

The rate of stock turnover is always expressed as a number. To say that the rate of stockturn is six means that the stock turns over six times in a year. Is this a good rate of stockturn or is it a poor one? We cannot possibly say until we know the product we are discussing. If a grocer turned over his stock of eggs six times a year they would be in stock for an average of two months each. This hardly makes them new-laid eggs by the time they are consumed. On the other hand, grand pianos tend to be a slow-moving line and do not deteriorate if kept in stock two months. Some classes of goods are very 'perishable', like newspapers, which must be turned over every day if they are to be sold at all.

Calculating the rate of stock turnover

Two formulae which give the same answer are:

1   Rate of stockturn $= \dfrac{\text{Cost of stock sold}}{\text{Average stock at cost price}}$

2   Rate of stockturn $= \dfrac{\text{Net turnover}}{\text{Average stock at sales price}}$

Use formula 1 for the moment. If you find the average stock, and divide it into the amount of stock sold at cost price, you will find out how often the stock turns over in each trading period.

The average stock is found by taking opening stock + closing stock and dividing by 2. If quarterly stock figures are available we can add up the four quarterly figures and divide by 4.

Using the Trading Account of Figure 14.9 we find that the average stock comes out to £16,350.

$$\frac{£14,500 + £18,200}{2} = \frac{£32,700}{2} = £16,350.$$

As the cost of stock sold is £47,400 it follows that

Rate of stockturn $= \dfrac{£47,400}{£16,350}$

$= \underline{\underline{2.9 \text{ times per year}}}$

Whether this is a good rate of stock turnover we cannot say unless we know the product being dealt in. It helps us form an opinion if we try to find how long the average item is in stock. This is found by dividing 2.9 into 12 months, or 52 weeks, or 365 days. Thus:

$$\frac{12}{2.9} = \underline{\underline{4.1 \text{ months}}}, \text{ or}$$

$$\frac{52}{2.9} = \underline{\underline{17.9 \text{ weeks}}}, \text{ or}$$

$$\frac{365}{2.9} = \underline{\underline{125.9 \text{ days}}}$$

It appears the average item is in stock for about four months. This would not seem a very good rate of stock turnover for most sorts of goods.

Exercise 14.4   *Gross profit percentage and rate of stock turnover*

1   Tom Pinch makes a gross profit of £17,256 on a net turnover of £86,280. What is his gross profit percentage?

2   Mail Pop sells a total of £245,000 compact discs and earns a gross profit of £83,300. What is their gross profit percentage?

3   A. Trader had in stock on 1 July 600 articles costing £12 each. During the month he bought 1800 more of these articles at the same price and sold 2020 at £20 each, of which 20 were returned. Draw up a statement showing the gross profit earned and express the gross profit as a percentage of the turnover.

4   On preparing the Trading Account of R. Lyons, a retailer, for the financial year ended 31 March 19xx, it was found that the ratio of gross profit to sales was 15 per cent, whereas for the previous financial year the corresponding ratio had been 25 per cent. State, with your reasons, whether or not the following may have contributed to cause the decline:

   (a)   The firm's telephone bill had doubled in the last month.

   (b)   The cost of a new delivery van had been included in the purchases for the year ended 31 March 19xx, and charged to Trading Account.

   (c)   The sales for the year ended 31 March 19xx, showed a decline compared with the previous year.

   (d)   In both years R. Lyons and his family had been supplied with goods from the shop but the value of these goods had not been recorded in the books of the business.

   (e)   On the last day of the financial year an employee was successfully convicted of dishonesty with regard to the theft of takings from the tills.

5   A. Brown has an average stock of £7,250 and his cost of stock sold in the year was £87,000. What was his rate of stock turnover?

6   Alexandra Kingston has an opening stock of £5,250 and a closing stock at the end of the year of £7,750. The cost of the stock sold in the year was £55,250.

   (a)   What was her rate of stock turnover?

   (b)   How many days was her average item of stock on the shelves before it sold? (Answer correct to the nearest day.)

7   A trader carries an average stock, valued at cost price, of £9,500 and turns this over five times per year. If he marks his stock up by 25 per cent on cost price, what is his gross profit for the year?

8   A trader carries an average stock valued at cost price of £15,500 and turns this over four times a year. If his mark-up is 20 per cent on cost, what is his gross profit for the year?

9   A retailer carries an average stock valued at cost price of £11,275. His rate of stockturn is 150, his average profit is 30 per

cent on cost, and his overheads and running expenses come to £350,000. What is his net profit for the year?

10 H.J. is in business as a retailer and during the year ended 31 December 19xx, the average value of his stock at cost price was £18,500. He turned this over nine times, at an average mark-up of 50 per cent. His fixed expenses were £29,500 and his variable expenses 10 per cent of the turnover. Calculate H.J.'s profit or loss for the year. (*Answers on page 307.*)

14.15 The net profit percentage and expense ratios

The net profit is the clear profit left after the office and selling expenses have been deducted from gross profit. If we wish to check on the efficiency of the office and sales side of our business, the ratio that gives us a clear picture of the trends shown is the net profit percentage. This is found by the formula:

$$\text{Net profit percentage} = \frac{\text{Net profit}}{\text{Turnover}} \times 100$$

Consider Figure 14.10, a Profit and Loss Account, which follows from the Trading Account in Figure 14.9.

Michael Smith
Profit and Loss Account for year ending 31 December 19xx

	£		£
Salaries	31,450	Gross profit	75,100
Light and heat	1,300	Commission received	4,180
Insurance	850	Rent received	3,250
Advertising	12,400		82,530
Depreciation	3,450		
Bad debts	650		
	50,100		
Net profit	32,430		
	£82,530		£82,530

Figure 14.10 A Profit and Loss Account

The net profit percentage here is calculated as follows:

$$\text{Net profit percentage} = \frac{\text{Net profit}}{\text{Turnover}} \times 100$$

$$= \frac{£32,430}{£122,500} \times 100$$

$$= 26.5\%$$

Once again we would expect the net profit percentage to be constant – that is, to remain roughly the same from year to year – provided we always prepare our Profit and Loss Account in the same way. It follows that any significant change in net profit percentage, say 3 per cent or more, would be investigated to discover the cause.

Suppose that last year the net profit percentage was 30 per cent and this year it has fallen to 26.5 per cent. This is a significant fall and we must find the reason.

What can have caused a fall in the net profit percentage?

If the gross profit percentage is steady but the net profit percentage has fallen the fault must lie in the expenses or profits shown on the Profit and Loss Account. We should examine each expense item carefully, working out an expense ratio to turnover, for this year and the previous year. This is quite simple and involves a calculation:

$$\text{Expense ratio} = \frac{\text{Expense}}{\text{Turnover}} \times 100$$

So for salaries it would be:

$$\frac{\text{Salaries}}{\text{Turnover}} \times 100$$

$$= \frac{£31,450}{£122,500} \times 100$$

$$= \underline{\underline{25.7\%}}$$

The ratio tells us that 25.7 per cent of all the money taken by selling our products is used up in paying salaries. By comparing this with the similar figure for the previous year we may discover some increase in expense. Perhaps the manager has taken on more staff than are really necessary? Similar expense ratios may reveal other causes of the change. Perhaps the advertising has been excessive? An increased advertising budget has not yielded proportionately higher sales. Perhaps insurance rates have risen, and have not been passed on to the consumer in higher prices? The profits on the credit side may show some falling off from the previous year. Have we received less commission than previously, or less rent? These will also affect net profit percentage.

When we discover the cause of the fall in net profit percentage we must take the necessary action to correct the profitability of the business. This means we must reduce the expenses that are soaring, or increase the receipts that have been declining. If such action is impossible, we must pass the increased cost on to the final consumer.

Exercise 14.5   Net profit percentage and expense ratios

1   Michael Petriades has a net profit of £47,256 on his business which has a turnover of £186,256. What is his net profit percentage?
2   Rose Glade Hotel has a net profit of £55,287 on a turnover during the year of £192,656. What is the net profit percentage?
3   In making a comparison between two successive years of his business, R. Rogers notices the following matters:

	Year 1	Year 2
	£	£
Turnover	165,000	185,000
Gross profit	65,900	77,560
Net profit	28,800	31,600

Present these two sets of results in such a way as to make a comparison, and state any conclusions you can draw.

4   M. Smith presents you with the following data about his business. In Year 2 he had appointed a dynamic young manager who has produced the increase in turnover shown. Comment upon these results, and on the manager's performance.

	Year 1	Year 2
	£	£
Turnover	127,000	168,000
Gross profit	45,500	68,500
Net profit	28,250	31,000

5   In Year 1 Brown's turnover was £165,000 and the following items appeared in his Profit and Loss Account, amongst others:

Occupation expenses	£2,300
Heat and light	£500
Telephone expenses	£725

In Year 2 Brown's turnover, under a new manager, had risen to £225,000 but net profit percentage was down by 3 per cent. The above expenses had changed as follows:

Occupation expenses	£3,600
Heat and light	£725
Telephone expenses	£2,430

Comment on the possible causes of the fall in net profit percentage, offering support for your answers where possible from the calculation of helpful ratios.

6   In Year 1 Green's turnover was £185,000 and the following items appeared in his Profit and Loss Account, amongst others:

Salaries	£36,250
Rent and rates	£5,924
Advertising	£4,265

In Year 2 Green's turnover, under a new manager, had risen to £365,000 but net profit percentage was down by 3 per cent. The above expenses had changed as follows:

Salaries   £69,716
Rent and rates   £12,650
Advertising   £12,785

Comment on the possible causes of the fall in net profit percentage, offering support for your answers where possible from the calculation of helpful ratios.

14.16   The interpretation of the Balance Sheet

Consider the Balance Sheet shown in Figure 14.11, which follows on from Figures 14.9 and 14.10.

Michael Smith
Balance Sheet as at 31 December 19xx

Fixed assets	£		Capital	£	£
Land and buildings	65,000		At start		115,900
Plant and machinery	45,524		*Add* net profit	32,430	
Furniture and fittings	13,260		*Less* drawings	18,500	
Motor vehicles	19,056				13,930
	142,840		Net worth of the business		129,830
Current assets	£		Long-term liabilities		
Stock at close	18,200		Mortgage		30,000
Sundry debtors	4,254		Current liabilities		
Bank	1,326		Sundry creditors		7,202
Cash	412				
		24,192			
		£167,032			£167,032

Figure 14.11   A Balance Sheet for appraisal

Balance Sheets are not always well presented and the ratios which may be found from the Balance Sheet require the accountant to use figures which appear only when the Balance Sheet is in good style. These figures, which have been referred to in Section 14.8, are as follows:

1 *Current assets*   Those assets which are held in the business with a view to their conversion into cash in the ordinary course of the firm's profit-making activities.

2 *Fixed assets* Those assets which are retained in the firm for use by the proprietor and his/her employees, because they permanently increase the profit-making capacity of the business.

3 *Net assets* In many sets of published accounts the current liabilities are brought over to the assets side of the Balance Sheet and deducted from the current assets. This gives the *net current assets*, also called the 'working capital' (see below). When the net current assets are added to the fixed assets they give the *net assets*, i.e. the total assets less the current liabilities. The net assets represents all the assets purchased by the firm, using its long-term funds (capital and profits ploughed back, plus any long-term borrowing).

4 *Current liabilities* Those liabilities which will fall due for payment fairly quickly, and certainly within less than one year.

5 *Long-term liabilities* Those liabilities which will not fall due immediately, but which will be repaid over an agreed period greater than one year.

6 *Capital* The net worth of the business to the owner of the business; that portion of the owner's wealth which he/she has invested in the business either originally or by leaving past profits to accumulate in the service of the firm.

Figure 14.11 shows a typical Balance Sheet which will serve as a basis for the discussion. By careful consideration of this Balance Sheet and the ratios described below the reader may learn more phrases which are commonly used in business to help in the interpretation of Final Accounts. A mastery of these terms enables an accountant to make sound judgments about businesses whose affairs are under consideration. The new terms are:

1 *Fixed capital* This is capital tied up in fixed assets (which are shown on the assets side). In the case of Smith the fixed capital is £142,840. The significance of fixed capital is that it is sunk into the business and cannot be regained without seriously affecting the conduct of the business. If Smith tries to realize this fixed capital by selling motor vehicles or plant and machinery, the distribution or production of the firm's products will be hampered. If he tries to sell the premises he will be out in the street.

2 *Floating capital or circulating capital* This is capital tied up in current assets (also shown on the assets side). These can be realized more easily and without interfering with the conduct of the business; indeed, that is what we are in business for – to turn over stock and make profits as the stock turns into cash.

3 *Liquid capital* The term 'liquid' in economic matters means 'in cash form'. The liquid capital is that portion of the assets that are available as cash, or near cash. In this case it is £5,992, the total of cash, bank moneys and debtors.

4 *Working capital*   This is the most important of these four terms –
one of the most vital concepts in business. It is that portion of the
capital invested in the business which is left to run the business
after providing the fixed capital. Once a firm has bought its
premises, plant and machinery, etc., it still needs working capital
to run the business, to pay wages and sundry expenses. One might
really say that having met all the capital expenditure one still
needs funds for revenue expenditure. The £24,192 that Smith has
left after paying for his fixed assets is clearly something to do with
working capital, but the real way to find working capital is as
follows:

Working capital = current assets − current liabilities
$$= £24,192 − £7,202$$
$$= £16,990$$

5 *External liabilities*   These are liabilities owed to persons outside
the business, and that means both current liabilities and long-term
liabilities, in this case £37,202.
6 *Capital owned*   This is the net worth of the business, the value of
the business to the owner of the business. In this case it is
£129,830.
7 *Capital employed*   This is a very important figure. It can be
defined in a number of different ways, but for our purposes we
will define it as the long-term capital employed in the business.
This means we will disregard the current liabilities, and only count
the net worth of the business, and the long-term liabilities, in this
case the mortgage. However, we have to adjust the net worth
figure because, although the original capital has been employed
all the year, the increase in net worth (£13,930) has only been
available during the year, and if we assume it accumulated evenly
we can only say half the figure was employed for the full year.
This means the capital employed was really £115,900 + £6,965 +
£30,000 = £152,865.

We must now turn to consider each of the ratios which can be
found from the Balance Sheet.

1   The working capital ratio (or current ratio)

One of the problems many businesses face is running short of
working capital. Working capital is the money we have left over to
work the business after we have purchased the fixed assets. The
danger is that we might not be able to pay our creditors in any
particular month. Our current assets must be large enough to pay our
current liabilities.

The working capital ratio shows the relationship between current
assets and current liabilities. Ideally a business should be able to meet

all its current liabilities without hesitation. The ratio is therefore:

Working capital ratio = $\dfrac{\text{current assets}}{\text{current liabilities}}$

In the case of Smith's Balance Sheet this works out to:

$\dfrac{\pounds24,192}{\pounds7,202} = 3.4 \text{ times}$

What is a reasonably safe working capital ratio? It is generally agreed that 2:1 is a desirable working capital ratio. This means that the external debts can be met twice over from the available current assets.

Clearly Smith has plenty of working capital, for he can pay his current liabilities three times over.

So important is working capital considered to be that many accountants prefer to show the figure on the Balance Sheet itself. This is done by bringing the current liabilities over to the assets side of the Balance Sheet and deducting them. This leaves a 'net current assets' figure only (sometimes called a 'net working capital' figure) to be added in with the fixed assets.

2 The liquid capital ratio, acid-test ratio or quick ratio

Even if the working capital ratio is adequate it can sometimes be unsatisfactory if the majority of the current assets are in stock, an illiquid asset. We cannot pay our creditors with stock, and so the acid-test of solvency is given by those assets which can *quickly* be turned into cash. There are cash itself, money in the bank, investments and debtors (who have a legal obligation to pay). The quick ratio, liquid capital ratio, or acid-test ratio is found by the formula:

Liquid capital ratio = $\dfrac{\text{current assets} - \text{stock}}{\text{current liabilities}}$

$= \dfrac{5,992}{7,202} = 0.83 \text{ times}$

The name 'acid-test ratio' is used to show that this is the critical test of solvency. Can the firm, with its present cash and debtors (due to pay within the month) meet its current liabilities (due for payment within the month)? This is very interesting because it shows how weak this firm is as far as liquid assets go. Most of its current assets are stock.

The minimum acid-test ratio is 1:1, which means that a firm can pay its immediate debts at once from its immediately available assets.

3   The return on capital employed

The general formula for finding the return on capital employed is:

$$\frac{\text{Profit}}{\text{Capital employed}} \times 100$$

For our purposes at this level of study we have defined capital as the long-term capital employed which includes the original capital, plus half the increase and the mortgage. To find the ratio, return on capital employed, we must therefore include the 'profit' earned by both these sums of capital. This means the word 'profit' covers not only the profit earned £32,430 but also the interest paid on the mortgage in the year, which we will say our records show as £2,700. Therefore:

$$\begin{aligned}
\text{Return on capital employed} &= \frac{\text{Profit}}{\text{Capital employed}} \times 100 \\
&= \frac{£32,430 + £2,700}{£152,865} \times 100 \\
&= \frac{£35,130}{£152,865} \times 100 \\
&= \underline{\underline{23.0\%}}
\end{aligned}$$

The return on capital employed is used to compare one business with another. It tells us how efficiently this business is using its capital, and enables us to compare it with other businesses in the same industry, or in other industries.

4   The return on capital invested

When a business proprietor wishes to assess whether it is worthwhile being in business it is usual to find the return on capital invested at the start of the year. This would be worked out from the profit earned in the year, but it is usual to adjust this profit in two ways, to make the figures more meaningful. The two adjustments are as follows:

(a)   The proprietor of a small business would in normal events take a job with some firm if he/she were not self-employed. In judging how far it is profitable to be in business the entrepreneur might well feel that a substantial sum for loss of wages in some other opportunity should be deducted from the profit figure (the return being earned from self-employment). This is what economists call the 'opportunity cost' of self-employment.

(b)   Similarly, if the capital were not tied up in this business it could be earning a suitable dividend from a building society or other investment. The entrepreneur might therefore discover the true reward for being in business in the following way:

Profit − (Loss of earnings in some other employment and loss of interest on capital not invested elsewhere)

Such a formula reduces the profit to the point where it shows only the net benefit from being self-employed. Suppose that Smith, in the Balance Sheet shown in Figure 14.10 could have earned £12,500 employed by someone else, and could also have earned 8 per cent interest on his capital at the start of the year just by leaving it in a Building Society Investment Account.

$$\text{This means the opportunity cost} = £12,500 + \frac{£115,900 \times 8}{100}$$

$$= £12,500 + £9,272$$

$$= \underline{\underline{£21,772}}$$

Then:

$$\text{Return on capital invested} = \frac{\text{net profit} - \text{opportunity cost}}{\text{capital invested at start of year}} \times 100$$

$$= \frac{£32,430 - £21,772}{£115,900} \times 100$$

$$= \frac{£10,658}{£115,900} \times 100$$

$$= \underline{\underline{9.2\%}}$$

The actual extra return he is getting on his capital invested is 9.2 per cent, which does not seem an enormous amount, but it is £10,658 more in the year, and then – don't forget – there are the non-monetary satisfactions.

Exercise 14.6   *The interpretation of a Balance Sheet*

1   Define the following terms:
    (a)   Working capital
    (b)   Current assets
    (c)   Current liabilities
    (d)   Fixed assets
    Why is it important to distinguish each of these items clearly?
2   (a)   What do you understand by the term 'working capital'?

(b) State, with reasons, whether the following transactions would increase or decrease the working capital of a business; or would they have no real effect?
(i) Machinery no longer required is sold for cash, £1,250.
(ii) £2,000 is paid for a lorry.
(iii) £500 is received from a trade debtor.
(iv) Stock costing £200 is sold on credit to a customer for £250.
(v) Stock is exchanged for office furniture £160.

3 From the Balance Sheet of R. Chalmers given below you are asked to state, or calculate:
(a) The fixed assets total.
(b) The current assets total.
(c) The net working capital.
(d) The working capital ratio (correct to one decimal place).
(e) The acid-test ratio (correct to one decimal place).
(f) The net worth of the business to the owner of the business, at the end of the year.
(g) The return on capital employed (given that interest on the mortgage has been paid in the year of £1,750).
(h) The return on capital invested at the start of the year given that Chalmers could have earned £9,500 in employment elsewhere and his capital could have earned 10 per cent in a high-interest Deposit Account.

R. Chalmers
Balance Sheet as at 31 December 19xx

Fixed assets	£	Capital	£	£
Land and buildings	63,250	At start		86,500
Plant and machinery	27,550	Add net profit	29,250	
Furniture and fittings	8,750	Less drawings	11,095	
Motor vehicles	9,580			18,155
	109,130			104,655
Current Assets	£	Long-term liabilities		
Stock at close	12,250	Mortgage		20,000
Sundry debtors	1,260	Current liabilities		
Bank	4,925	Sundry creditors		3,285
Cash	375			
	18,810			
	£127,940			£127,940

4 From the Balance Sheet of New Enterprise given below you are asked to state:
(a) The fixed assets total.
(b) The current assets total.
(c) The net working capital.

(d)   The working capital ratio (correct to one decimal place).

(e)   The acid-test ratio (correct to one decimal place).

(f)   The net worth of the business to the owner at 31 December 19xx.

(g)   The return on capital employed in the business, given that the mortgage interest paid in the year was £3,250 and the interest paid on the loan was £1,896.

(h)   The return on capital invested at the start of the year, given that D. Smith could have earned £12,500 in employment elsewhere and his capital could have earned 10 per cent interest in a Building Society.

New Enterprise (Proprietor D. Smith)
Balance Sheet as at 31 December 19xx

Fixed assets	£	*Capital*	£	£
Land and buildings	72,500	At start of year		79,930
Plant and machinery	39,500	*Add* net profit	37,853	
Furniture and fittings	12,285	*Less* drawings	23,250	
Motor vehicles	11,785			14,603
	136,070			94,533
Current assets	£	*Long-term liabilities*	£	
Stock at close	14,956	Mortgage	36,500	
Sundry debtors	3,872	Loan from bank	15,800	
Bank	1,215			52,300
Cash	615	*Current liabilities*		
	20,658	Creditors		9,895
	£156,728			£156,728

Answers to exercises on the interpretation of Final Accounts

Exercise 14.4

1 20 per cent;   2 34 per cent;   3 Gross profit = £16,000; gross profit percentage = 40 per cent.   4 (a) No – the telephone bill does not affect the Trading Account; (b) Yes – a capital item has been mistakenly called 'purchases'. It would cause a fall in gross profit percentage; (c) No – the volume of sales does not affect the ratio; (d) Yes – both the years will be affected, but if they took home more this year than last year it could explain part of the fall in gross profit percentage; (e) Yes – theft from the tills definitely affects the gross profit percentage.   5 12 times a year.   6 (a) 8.5 times a year; (b) 43 days.   7 £11,875.   8 £12,400.   9 £157,375.   10 Net profit was £28,775. (Note: gross profit was £83,250 (nine times £9,250). Turnover was nine times £27,750 so variable expenses were £24,975 (10 per cent of £249,750).)

Exercise 14.5
1 25.4 per cent.   2 28.7 per cent.   3 Gross profit percentage rose
from 39.9 per cent to 41.9 per cent; net profit percentage fell from
17.5 per cent to 17.1 per cent. Although in absolute terms all the
figures for turnover, gross profit and net profit were up on the
previous year, the ratios show that the final net profit was actually
smaller as a percentage of turnover, and therefore not particularly
good.   4 Gross profit percentage rose from 35.8 per cent to 40.8 per
cent. Net profit percentage fell from 22.2 per cent to 18.5 per cent. It
is clear that although the dynamic young manager has pushed up
turnover considerably and seemed to be getting better margins on the
actual trading, the overhead expenses had increased so that they
largely ate into the higher profits being made, and the final results
were therefore relatively disappointing.   5 Expenses ratios changed
as follows:

	%	%
Occupation expenses	1.39	1.6
Heat and light	0.30	0.32
Telephone expenses	0.44	1.08

Telephone expenses increases have had the biggest impact on profitability, but there may be other expense items that have also had an
impact, but they are not available to us for comment.
6 Expense ratios changed as follows:

	%	%
Salaries	19.59	19.10
Rent and rates	3.20	3.47
Advertising	2.31	3.50

Both rent and rates and advertising caused some reduction in the net
profit percentage, but not the full amount and there must be other
expenses which have risen more than proportionately to the increased turnover.

Exercise 14.6
1 See text.   2 (a) See text; (b)(i) Increase, (ii) decrease, (iii) no
change – the debtor has ceased to be a debtor and we have cash
instead, (iv) increase of £50, (v) decrease.   3 (a) £109,130,
(b) £18,810, (c) £15,525, (d) 5.7, (e) 2.0, (f) £104,655, (g) 26.8 per
cent, (h) 12.8 per cent;   4 (a) £136,070, (b) £20,658, (c) £10,763,
(d) 2.1, (e) 0.6, (f) £94,533, (g) 30.8 per cent, (h) 21.7 per cent.

14.17   Rapid revision

Answers		Questions	
	–	**1**	**What is accounting?**
1	It is a set of systems for recording all the financial affairs of a business so we know the exact cost of everything we buy or make, the overhead expenses we incur, the prices to charge our customers, the takings of the business, the money we owe and the money we are owed, and the profits we have made in the course of our business activity.	**2**	**If you were just starting out in business what would be the best system to use?**
2	The Simplex System – because it is a very simple short-cut on double-entry book-keeping.	**3**	**What is double-entry book-keeping?**
3	It is a full system of book-keeping, in which all transactions are recorded to show both actions that take place, one account giving value and another account receiving value.	**4**	**What is the chief book of account?**
4	The ledger, every page of which is called an account. Today the ledger need not be a book – it can be a memory bank in a computer. If so it is usually divided into three chief parts, a Debtors Ledger, a Creditors Ledger and a General Ledger.	**5**	**What are the three classes of accounts?**
5	Personal accounts, nominal accounts and real accounts.	**6**	**Suggest four names of personal accounts.**
6	They will either be debtors or creditors Tom Smith Account; Mary Jones Account; Brown and Green Account; The Taff Vale Steelworks PLC Account.	**7**	**Suggest four nominal accounts.**

310   *Business Studies*

Answers	Questions
7 They will either be profits of the business or losses of the business. Rent Received Account; Fees Received Account; Telephone Expenses Account; Salaries Account.	8 **Suggest four real accounts.**
8 They will be assets of the business. Cash Account; Motor Vehicles Account; Premises Account; Furniture and Fittings Account.	9 **What other books are there besides the ledger?**
9 (a) The Cash Book; (b) the Petty Cash Book; (c) the Journal Proper; (d) the Purchases Day Book) (e) the Sales Day Book; (f) the Purchases Returns Book and (g) the Sales Returns Book.	10 **Where are the profits of a business worked out?**
10 The manufacturing profit (if any) in the Manufacturing Account; the gross profit in the Trading Account and the net profit in the Profit and Loss Account.	11 **What is a Balance Sheet?**
11 It is a snapshot picture of the affairs of a business, at a given moment in time, showing the assets owned, and the liabilities owed. The usual moment to draw up a Balance Sheet is the last moment of the last day of the financial year, to show what the old year is passing over to the new year, in the way of assets and liabilities.	12 **Go over the test again until you are sure of all the answers.**

15
Business documentation

15.1 Introduction to business documents

Documentation is essential to business activity. A document is the easiest way to establish a relationship between businesses and the easiest way to link parts of a business one with another. A document can give instructions; signal the start or the end of any particular activity; acknowledge the payment of money, etc. Although today we often hear the word 'systems' used to refer to computerized activities all the original systems of business were paper systems, which triggered off various activities. Most computerized systems are based upon the earlier paper systems, and merely carry out the same activities more rapidly and, perhaps, more thoroughly.

Those starting out in business need a thorough grounding in business documents, and in this chapter we shall study the following:

1 Invoices, including delivery notes and advice notes
2 Credit notes
3 Debit notes
4 Statements
5 Receipts
6 Petty cash vouchers
7 Deeds
8 Master documents
9 Bills of lading

There are many more we could study, but these will be enough for the present.

15.2 The invoice

An invoice is a business document which is made out whenever one person sells goods or supplies services to another. It can be used in the courts of law as evidence of a contract for the sale of goods or the provision of services. It is made out by the person selling the goods, and will always have at least two copies. In the majority of businesses it will have rather more copies, four or five, and in some businesses even more than that. Since the various copies go to different people to trigger off different activities it is common for the copies to be different colours – white, yellow, blue, green and pink being the commonest colours chosen. Since invoices have to repeat the information on each copy it is necessary to have some method of reproducing the typing – and this involves either feeding carbon paper between the sheets or having the invoices made up in multi-part sets with carbon paper arranged to reprint the information on the next page down. Some computerized systems will print off the copies required individually. In this chapter we will refer to a four-part set, as shown in Figure 15.1.

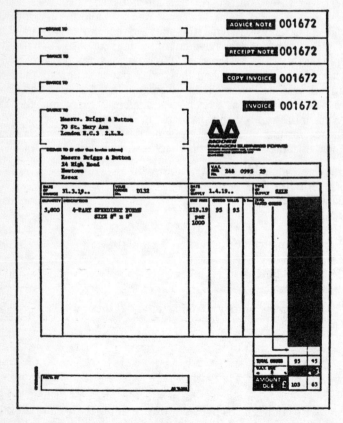

Figure 15.1   A four-copy invoice system

The layout of an invoice

To fulfil its legal function as evidence of a contract of sale, an invoice must have the following information:

1 The names and addresses of both the parties to the transaction.
2 The date of the sale, or supply of services.
3 An exact description of goods, with quantity and unit price, and details of the trade discount (if any) given. If the invoice refers to services it will describe the services rendered.
4 In the UK it must give details of the VAT charged as it becomes a tax invoice for VAT purposes. It will also show the supplier's VAT Registration Number.
5 It may give the terms on which the goods are sold or services supplied e.g. discount and credit period. The words 'Terms Net' mean no discount is allowed. The words 'Prompt Settlement' mean no credit period is allowed.

Lastly, many firms write 'E & O E' on the bottom of the invoice. These letters means 'Errors and Omissions Excepted'. If an error or omission has been made, the firm selling the goods may put it right. In English law written evidence may not be varied by oral evidence so that if an invoice were presented in the courts it could not be said orally: But my Lord, that was a mistake.' However, the words 'E & E O' written on the invoice would permit this to be done. In fact this has been tested in the Courts. In the case of Webster *v.* Cecil (1861) it was held that a genuine slip of the pen could be corrected so that the phrase 'E & O E' is not really necessary, but is often still seen.

You may see an invoice bearing a phrase reading: 'Title in the goods described on this invoice does not pass to the buyer until the invoice is paid in full.' This is a clause called a 'Romalpa Clause' named after one of the parties in a famous legal case. The point is worth mentioning. When one person sells goods to another the property (right of ownership) in the goods usually passes at the moment when the sale is agreed, even though the goods may be delivered later, and the money payment may also be made at a later date. Suppose the buyer has received the goods but goes bankrupt and does not pay. A receiver will be appointed by the Court to take charge of all the bankrupt's possessions and sell them, and this will include any goods the property in which has passed to the buyer, although in fact he/she has not paid for them. This is clearly unfair to the unpaid seller. By putting in a Romalpa Clause on the invoice, the seller makes it clear to the customer (and everyone else, including the receiver and the Court) that the goods are not the buyer's property until paid for in full. The seller, on hearing that the buyer is bankrupt, will call and collect the goods, which are still the seller's property in law.

What happens to the four copies? They are used as follows:

1 *Top copy*   This is sent by post or by hand to the person buying the goods, who enters it in the Purchases Day Book (a purchases invoice). It is then kept as the purchaser's copy of the contract of sale, or supply of services.

2 *Second copy*   This is the seller's Sales Day Book copy. It is kept by the seller, entered in the Sales Day Book, and then filed to be kept as the seller's copy of the contract of sale.

3 *Third and fourth copies*   These are sent together to the Stores Department of the seller, where the storekeeper takes the goods out of store. The third copy, often called the **Delivery Note**, is given to the driver to take with him to the buyer's warehouse, where he presents it with the parcel of goods and gets a signature on it to prove that the goods arrived safely. This copy is then taken back by the driver to the storekeeper and is filed in the store after being entered in the Stores Record Book. The fourth copy is wrapped up in the parcel before it is given to the driver. It is often called the **Advice Note** and it enables the buyer's storekeeper to check the contents of the parcel and record the stores that have just arrived in the Stores Record Book.

Sometimes there is a Representative's Copy, which is sent to the commercial traveller who took the order. He/she is then able to prove to the buyer that the firm has handled the sale in a proper manner and can remind the customer what was ordered. This may save a great deal of time because the buyer may say 'All right, repeat that order will you.'

As mentioned in Chapter 13, see page 245, there may be a 'gate copy' instead of an advice note where customers are buying goods at such places as do-it-yourself shops. This copy is kept by the gateman after he has checked the goods leaving the premises.

How long do we keep an invoice

Usually for six years. Under the Limitation Act, 1980 an action in the Courts on a simple contract cannot begin more than six years after the contract was made. If we keep our invoices for six years the chance of the invoice being needed as legal evidence disappears. Many firms get rid of their old invoices by shredding them into packing material.

Value Added Tax and invoices

The VAT regulations give the invoice a special status as a tax invoice, for all traders who are registered for VAT, whether voluntarily or compulsorily (because their turnover exceeds £45,000 a year). The invoice must show the tax charged (currently at a standard rate of $17\frac{1}{2}$ per cent) unless the goods are zero-rated items such as food, or children's clothes, etc. The tax on the invoice becomes the **output tax** of the seller, which he/she has collected on behalf of Customs and Excise, and for which account must be made, usually once a quarter.

The tax increases the bill to the customer, who pays the extra money when the bill is paid, but if the customer is a registered business the proprietor is allowed to deduct the tax as **input tax** when he/she in turn settles the VAT Account with Customs and Excise. The actual arrangement is:

Output tax − input tax = tax payable

Since output tax will nearly always be greater than input tax (because output tax is based on a trader's selling prices, but input tax is based on the trader's cost prices), the trader will finish up paying a balance of money to Customs and Excise Department. The only traders to whom this does not apply are traders in zero-rated items, who may buy items on which they have paid input tax, but cannot collect any output tax because they only sell zero-rated items. For such traders output tax will be zero and input tax may be quite a large sum, so that Customs and Excise owe the trader money. To save hardship zero-rated traders reclaim this every month.

A final point is that where a trader does not issue sales invoices, because trading is cash trading (for example an ordinary shopkeeper) the cash takings in the tills includes tax which the trader has collected. The output tax element of this money has to be found by what is called a 'Special Retailer's Scheme Calculation'. There are twelve different methods. A typical quarterly VAT account is shown in Figure 15.2.

15.3 The credit note

We must expect in the course of business that some of our customers will return goods for valid reasons. A purchaser is not entitled to return something just because he has changed his mind about having it; but occasionally we may oblige a client by accepting this type of return. The usual reasons for returning goods are:

1 The purchaser holds that the goods are unsatisfactory for some reason, e.g. wrong colour; wrong size; not up to sample; not up to specification; imperfectly finished; damaged in transit, etc.
2 The purchaser is entitled by contract to return goods, for instance goods sent on approval.

In these circumstances the document used is the credit note.

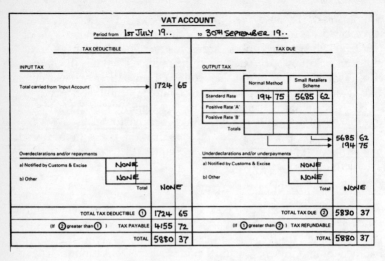

Figure 15.2   A VAT Account from a retailer, showing the tax due (courtesy of George Vyner Ltd, Huddersfield)

Definition

A credit note is a business document made out whenever one person returns goods to another. It is usually printed in red, to distinguish it from an invoice, and like an invoice, is made out by the seller of the goods, who is now receiving them back again. Usually there are only two copies.

The credit note should show:

1   The names and addresses of both parties to the transaction.
2   An exact description of the goods being returned.
3   The unit price, the number and the total value of the goods returned.

Other reasons for sending a credit note

1   *Allowances*   Sometimes goods that are unsatisfactory for some reason are not returned because of the inconvenience and cost. A piece of furniture that has been damaged by rain in transport may only need repolishing. The purchaser may be perfectly prepared to have this repolishing carried out by one of his own employees, provided the seller will make him an allowance to cover the cost. This will be done by sending a credit note for the agreed amount. This is called an allowance.
2   *Overcharges for goods*   Sometimes a typing error, or a mis-casting, or some other slip results in a customer being over-

CREDIT NOTE

Messrs Brewis and Jeffrey,	No. 7864
Cherrydown,	RIDER & Co. Ltd.
Newtown,	High Street
Essex.	London, W.C.2.

DATE   20th May   19..   REP.   M. TYLER.

No.	Description	Code	Pub. Price	Trade Discount	
3	Dining Chairs (damaged in transit)		1·50	—	4·50

Figure 15.3   A credit note – the original document for returns
(*Note:* Credit notes are almost always printed in red, but some computerized notes may be in black)

charged for goods. All invoices should be checked when they arrive and if an item has been overcharged, or the goods have been sent at full price when some trade discount had been promised, the matter should be taken up at once with the supplier. Suppose a typewriter valued at £300.00 was invoiced at £3,000.00. Clearly a credit note for £2,700 will be required to correct the overcharge.

Credit notes may therefore be sent for three reasons:

1   To credit a debtor with returns.
2   To credit a debtor with an allowance.
3   To credit a debtor to correct an overcharge.

In each case the crediting of the debtor's account reduces his/her debt to us, and thus takes account of the returns, allowance or overcharge, whichever it may be.

15.4   The debit note

A debit note is a document which is made out by the seller whenever the purchaser has been undercharged on an invoice, or when the seller wishes to make some charge on a debtor which increases the debtor's debt. It may also be made out by the purchaser whenever he/

she returns goods. It then advises the creditor what goods are being returned, and invites the seller to send a credit note (see Section 15.3 above).

Suppose that an invoice has been sent to a purchaser of a type-writer valued at £300.00, but by mistake the typist has typed £30.00 as the purchase price. Clearly the seller will want to correct this under-charge, but another invoice would not be appropriate since no 'goods' are being delivered. A debit note for £270.00 treated exactly like an invoice and put through the Day Books in exactly the same way as an invoice will put this matter right. In the same way charges for carriage, or insurance, which were not known at the time the invoice was made out, could be charged to the debtor by means of a debit note.

15.5   Statements

A statement is a business document which is sent out, almost always monthly, showing the balance outstanding on a customer's account and inviting them to pay it. The full name for a statement would be **Statement of Account**. First let us be clear that one can only expect to receive a statement if one has entered into an arrangement with a supplier to trade on 'monthly account' terms. A great many of the things we buy are 'one-off' purchases from firms with whom we do not have regular account terms, and we shall receive an invoice which says: 'Please pay on this invoice, by return of post.'

Where we do trade on monthly account terms (sometimes called 'open account' terms) we do not pay on the individual invoices, but wait for the monthly statement. Some firms send out statements on the last day of the month, but this makes a considerable amount of work in the last few days of the month. Many large firms send out statements on what is called '**cyclical billing**' – that is they send out about 5 per cent of statements every working day. Thus one firm might get its statement on the 8th of every month, while another would get its statement on the 19th of the month. One major credit card company has 8 million customers, and sends each one a state-ment every month. That is 400,000 statements every day. There are two advantages to cyclical billing:

1   It spreads the work evenly over the month.
2   The cash flows in evenly over the month. Getting some cash in every day is always a happy event for any firm.

There are two kinds of statements:

1   An 'account rendered' statement.
2   A computerized statement, or one prepared from simultaneous record systems.

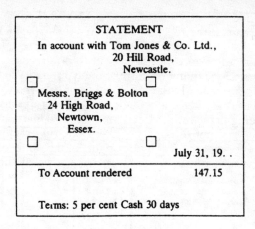

STATEMENT

In account with Tom Jones & Co. Ltd.,
20 Hill Road,
Newcastle.

Messrs. Briggs & Bolton
24 High Road,
Newtown,
Essex.

July 31, 19. .

To Account rendered	147.15

Terms: 5 per cent Cash 30 days

Figure 15.4   A simple 'account rendered' statement

An 'account rendered' statement is shown in Figure 15.4. It has no real details – only the amount owing. The words 'To account rendered' mean: 'We have sent you invoices, debit notes and credit notes during the last month which, if you check back on them, show that you owe us £147.15. Would you please send this amount now.'

Actually Figure 15.4 shows them that if they pay within thirty days they can deduct 5 per cent for cash discount. Most firms would make quite sure they did this.

Computerized statements and simultaneous records statements

Many firms today are using computerized forms of book-keeping. There are many such systems. The statement shown in Figure 15.5 is printed by kind permission of British Olivetti Limited. You will notice that it does not just contain the words 'To account rendered' but instead contains details of all payments by the debtor and of goods sent to him and items returned by him. This is because under computerized book-keeping the statement is printed automatically from the entire data file for the month concerned. At electronic speeds it is no trouble for the computer to give all the details. Most firms use some system of cyclical billing, as explained above.

Some small firms do not use a computerized system but instead use simultaneous records systems. Two of the main firms producing such systems are Kalamazoo, a Birmingham-based firm, and Safeguard Business Systems, of Crewe. Since these systems work by producing three records simultaneously – the statement, the ledger card and the Sales Day Book record – they have all the details on the statement as each invoice, credit note or debit note is entered. Therefore, they produce a statement which, although handwritten is rather similar to

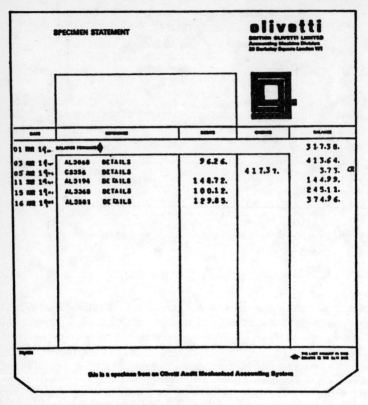

Figure 15.5   A computerized statement

the computerized statement shown in Figure 15.5. The Safeguard 3 in 1 System, with the statement uppermost is illustrated in Figure 15.6.

15.6   Receipts

Receipts are rarely asked for these days, because under the Cheques Act, 1957 Parliament declared that a paid cheque (i.e. one stamped by a bank to say it had been paid) constituted a receipt in law. At that time banks always returned all paid cheques to the customer, so that the payer eventually got the cheque back stamped paid. Today banks do not usually return cheques, though they will if a customer insists, but they make a charge for the trouble of picking them all out from the mass of cheques being handled. Otherwise the banks archive the cheques, for some time at the branch and then elsewhere, for the six years required under the Limitation Act, 1980.

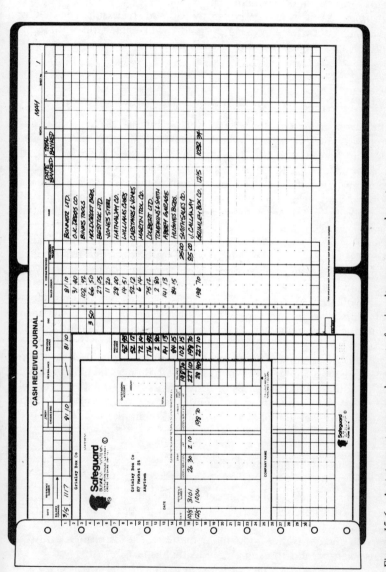

Figure 15.6 A statement prepared as part of a simultaneous records system

Today anyone paying cash will usually request a receipt and anyone paying by cheque may also demand a receipt if they really want some proof of payment. The receipt is usually either a gummed receipt torn out from a carbon copy pad and stuck on to the invoice, or it may just be a rubber stamp – paid – with a place for the date, the amount and if necessary the cheque number.

15.7 Petty cash vouchers

The words 'to vouch' mean 'to certify the honesty of'. When money is spent it is always essential to have some piece of paper which vouches for the honesty of the transaction. Wherever possible a petty cash voucher should come from outside the business (an external voucher). Thus if the office junior is sent to buy string, or sealing wax or even sandwiches for a visitor it is usual to say: 'And ask for a bill, or a till receipt.' This becomes the petty cash voucher, and the petty cashier will clip the till receipt to a piece of paper, give it a number from the page in the Petty Cash Book where it is entered, and file it away. Where a petty cash voucher cannot be obtained from outside (for example railway tickets are collected at the end of a journey and therefore cannot be used as petty cash vouchers) an internal petty cash voucher is produced. This states the amount that has to be reimbursed to the employee who is claiming the petty cash, and is signed by the manager or other supervisor who authorized the expenditure.

Although dishonesty with petty cash might seem a trivial matter police records show that 60 per cent of all offences leading to officers being called to the premises of firms are associated with this type of petty offence. Students might ponder the unpleasant results of succumbing to such temptations, and avoid them like the plague.

15.8 Formal documents (deeds)

Deeds are formal legal documents which deal with important matters such as the purchase and sale of landed property, the relationship between partners, the formal apprenticeship of young people in certain ancient trades and similar matters. They are often drawn up by solicitors, and the signatures to them must be witnessed by two witnesses. Where a contract is made in this formal way it is possible for a legal action to be commenced on it up to twelve years after the contract was made – which is twice the normal six-year period for ordinary contracts. We need not concern ourselves too much with these formal documents, but it is important to know what they are.

White — Customer's copy
Buff — Store copy

Customer's receipt for cash purchase

(U.K.) V.A.T. Registration No. 232 5555 75
(R.I.) V.A.T. Registration No. 8/K/56287

Ref. No. 728149

Store address stamp

F. W. WOOLWORTH P.L.C.

19-24 Sidney Street
Cambridge OB2 3H1

Sales receipt   Date 14 July 19..

Qty.	Item Group like rated items together	Unit S.P.	V.A.T. %	Incl. V.A.T. £	p
6	100 Watt Light bulbs	75p		4	50
1	Candle Lamp	7·95		7	95
1	13 Amp plug	1·15		1	15

Received with thanks   R.T.

Total £ 13 60

Complete this section only if requested by customer	Totals excl. V.A.T. £	p	V.A.T. %	Amount of V.A.T. £	p	Totals incl. V.A.T. £	p
			Zero				
Totals							

Customer's name   G. M. Whitehead

Address   2174 Camside

Cambridge

S.75 (V.A.T.) – 11/80

Figure 15.7   An external petty cash voucher

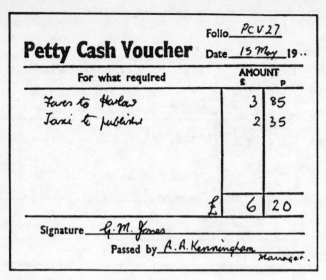

Figure 15.8 An internal petty cash voucher

Almost invariably any matter pertaining to a deed will be handled by a firm's solicitors, and legal advice would be taken about it.

15.9 Documents used in banking

The most usual documents used in day-to-day banking are the cheque and the paying-in slip, but it is helpful to give attention to bills of exchange first, because they are the original document used in banking, of which the cheque is just a specialized version – indeed the definition of a cheque is given in the Bills of Exchange Act, 1882 as: 'A cheque is a bill of exchange, drawn on a banker, payable on demand.'

Bills of exchange

Bills of exchange are still widely used in the UK by firms and companies wishing to obtain finance (trade bills) and by banks who not only issue bills on their own behalf (bank bills) but also add their names to the bills of ordinary firms to make them more respectable, the bank agreeing to honour the bill if the drawer or acceptor of the bill fail to honour it.

A bill of exchange is a method of payment used between businesses which has certain advantages over other methods of payment. It has a very precise definition in the Bills of Exchange Act, 1882. An

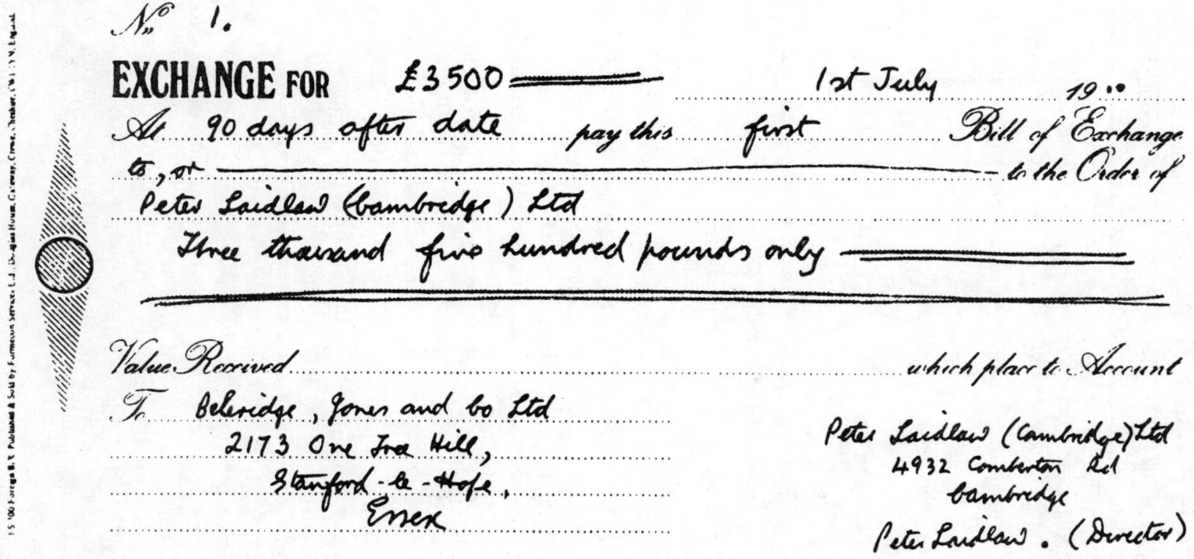

No. 1.

EXCHANGE FOR £3500 ——————

1st July 19..

At 90 days after date pay this first Bill of Exchange

to, at Peter Laidlaw (Cambridge) Ltd

—— to the Order of

Three thousand five hundred pounds only ——————

Value Received

To Beldridge, Jones and Co. Ltd
2173 Ore Fox Hill,
Stanford-a-Hope,
Essex.

which place to Account

Peter Laidlaw (Cambridge) Ltd
4932 Comberton Rd
Cambridge

Peter Laidlaw. (Director)

Figure 15.9 An inland bill of exchange

illustration of a bill of exchange is given in Figure 15.9, and will be explained later. It is best first to read the definition and the text that follows. The definition is:

> A bill of exchange is an unconditional order in writing, addressed by one person to another, signed by the person giving it, requiring the person to whom it is addressed to pay on demand or at a fixed or determinable future time a sum certain in money to or to the order of a specified person, or to bearer. (Bills of Exchange Act, 1882)

The following points will help your understanding of the definition:

1 The one who writes out the order to pay is called the **drawer**.
2 The one who is drawn upon (i.e. ordered to pay) is called the **drawee**.
3 Later this person (the drawee) may 'accept' the bill. This is a special use of the word 'accept' because it means 'accept the obligation to pay expressed in the bill'. If I accept the duty to pay I write 'accepted' across the face of the bill and sign it (even just signing my name on it will do). From that time on I am known as the **acceptor** of the bill and have absolute liability on it; I must honour the bill on the due date. If I dishonour it that is an utterly disgraceful act and may lead to bankruptcy (unless I make other arrangements).
4 The amount of money must be absolutely clear – '**a sum certain**': this is not the same as 'a certain sum'. For example, I cannot make out a bill requiring someone to pay the value of my horse Dobbin. That is an uncertain sum. It must say 'three thousand pounds' or 'four hundred pounds'.
5 The time must be either fixed or at least determinable. For example, '90 days after date' is determinable if the bill is dated 1 July. It is 29 September.
6 The person who is entitled to be paid is called the **payee**, but it is usually the same person as the drawer, since – as we shall see – it is usually the drawer who is supplying goods to the value of the bill, and wants to be paid for them. If the drawer decides he wants the acceptor to pay someone else he can always order him to pay that person by endorsing the bill (writing on the back of it) 'pay J. Smith' or whoever it is. That is why the definition says '**to pay to or to the order of a specified person**'.
7 A bill can be made payable to bearer but this is risky, since any finder of the bill, or any thief, could claim the money and the acceptor would be free of debt if he paid the wrong person, even if that person had no right to the bill.

Now read the definition again. Then study Figure 15.9 carefully, using the following notes to help you understand the figure and how it fits the definition:

1   The drawer of the bill is Peter Laidlaw, a director of Peter Laidlaw (Cambridge) Ltd.
2   The drawees are Beleridge, Jones and Co. Ltd. They have not yet accepted the bill, and so have no liability on it at all at present.
3   The bill is an unconditional order in writing. It says 'Pay three thousand five hundred pounds to Peter Laidlaw (Cambridge) Ltd.' It does not add 'provided you are in funds at the time' or any other condition. It just says 'Pay!'
4   It is addressed by one person (Peter Laidlaw) to another Beleridge, Jones and Co. Ltd) and is signed by the person giving it (Peter Laidlaw).
5   The date is determinable; it is 90 days after 1 July, which is 29 September 19xx.
6   The sum of money is certain; it is three thousand five hundred pounds.
7   The bill is payable to, or to the order of, Peter Laidlaw (Cambridge) Ltd.

How bills of exchange promote business activity
It is very important to understand how bills of exchange work. The process is illustrated in Figure 15.10(a) and (b). First note the following points:

1   A person who wishes to buy goods but has no money may agree to accept a bill of exchange drawn at some future date for the full value of the order he wishes to place. Let us suppose this is £3,500 of furniture from a furniture manufacturer, Peter Laidlaw (Cambridge) Ltd, and that ninety days' credit is agreed.
2   The drawer draws a bill for £3,500 on the customer (the drawee) who accepts it (thus becoming the acceptor of the bill) and returns it to the drawer. The drawer delivers the goods and has a ninety-day bill for £3,500 instead. He can either keep the bill and present it on the due date or he can cash it straight away, as explained below.
3   When a drawee 'accepts' a bill and acknowledges the obligation in it he is bound by law – in the most solemn way – to honour the bill on the due date. If he is a reputable person the bill is as good as money, and any bank will discount it. There is a special kind of bank that does little else but discount bills of exchange; it is called a discount house. What it will do is cash the bill by giving the drawer the **present value** of the bill. This is the face value less interest at an agreed rate for the number of days it has to run. So the drawer who discounts the bill with the bank gets less than the face value; in other words, a discount is deducted by the bank or discount house.
4   The bill is endorsed by the drawer with a signed and dated order

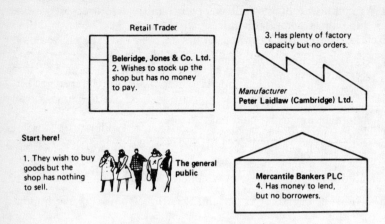

Figure 15.10(a)   Trading inactivity before the use of a bill of exchange

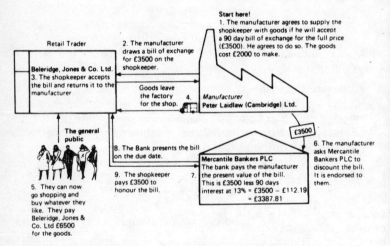

Figure 15.10(b)   Active trading under the use of a bill of exchange

to pay the bank. The bank is now the 'holder in due course' of the bill, and owns it, having given value for it.

5   On the due date the bank will present the bill to the acceptor, who honours it by paying the full value. The bank has earned the amount of interest it deducted when it discounted the bill, and the 'loan' it made to the drawer has been paid in full. Where does the acceptor get the money to honour the bill? The answer is that he has had ninety days to sell the furniture at a profit, and can therefore honour the bill and have something left over for himself.

We can now follow what is happening in the two diagrams. Figure 15.10(a) illustrates trading inactivity before the use of a bill of exchange. Note the following:

1 Business cannot proceed because the retail trader has nothing to sell and no money to buy stock.
2 What is needed is a mechanism by which the retailer can order supplies without paying for them at once, but which enables the manufacturer to be paid immediately.
3 Since a bill of exchange from a reputable trader is almost as good as money it will be as acceptable to a bank as money. They have plenty of money to lend out to reliable customers, so they do not mind oiling the wheels of commerce by advancing money to the holder of a bill of exchange.

Now look at Figure 15.10(b), which illustrates active trading under the influence of a bill of exchange. The following notes indicate how everyone finished up after the various activities sparked off by the drawing of this bill of exchange:

1 The manufacturer (Laidlaw) sold goods costing £2,000 for £3,500, but actually only realized £3,387.81 after discounting charges. Profit: £1,387.81.
2 The shopkeeper (Beleridge) sold goods costing £3,500 for £6,500. Profit: £3,000.
3 Mercantile Bankers PLC loaned £3,387.81 for ninety days and earned £112.19. This is actually 13.4 per cent interest.
4 The general public enjoyed the pleasures of the consumer society – comfortable furniture costing £6,500.

Foreign bills of exchange, as their name implies, are used in internatonal trade. Their use is referred to in Chapter 13 (see page 252) in '**documents against payment**' and '**documents against acceptance**' arrangements. In the first of these the documents which will enable a foreign importer to claim his/her goods from a ship at the port of destination are flown out to a foreign banker accompanied by a sight bill of exchange. This type of bill of exchange is payable on sight. The foreign importer pays the bill to the banker and is given the documents so that he/she can go to the port and collect the goods on arrival.

With 'documents against acceptance' the foreign customer is given time to pay. The bill is not a sight bill, but a usance bill, one where time is given to pay, as in the inland bill of exchange shown in Figure 15.9.

The foreign importer merely accepts the bill of exchange and is handed the documents needed to claim the goods from the port on arrival. The foreign bank may send the bill to the exporter's country, or, if instructed to do so, retains it for presentation on the due date.

The foreign importer honours the bill on the due date, and the money is sent by the foreign bank electronically to the exporter, through the banking network (it being credited in the exporter's account).

The conclusion is that bills of exchange are a useful instrument to encourage business activity, and are mutually beneficial to all parties as long as no difficulties arise and the bill is honoured on the due date.

It will be clear from these illustrations that banks have a useful part to play in discounting bills of exchange and thus advancing cash to suppliers who are waiting for payment. Generally speaking banks will discount inland bills of exchange that have only six months or less to run. The essence of the bill of exchange system is that it is financing real trade; in other words, the acceptor of the bill will eventually be able to honour it out of the proceeds of the business activity which the bill helped to finance. Be clear also that the bill of exchange can be rediscounted as often as is necessary in the interval between acceptance and honour on the due date. The bank that discounts it for the supplier may pass it on to a discount house in due course, and the final holder in due course will present it on the due date. The supplier will never see the bill again unless it is dishonoured, when it will quickly return to him to honour. As the first endorser he is absolutely liable on it, and must honour it if the acceptor does not. He will then take up with the acceptor the dishonour of the bill, and if necessary will sue him for the money. Dishonour of a bill is a serious matter and can lead to bankruptcy.

Cheques

Cheques have been described in detail in Chapter 11 (see page 193).

Paying-in slips and bank giro credits

Paying-in slips are available on the counters of most banks for the convenience of customers who wish to pay cash or cheques into their bank accounts. More conveniently, the banks issue books of paying in slips which are personalized – i.e. they have the customer's name printed on each slip and they have the account details encoded on the paying-in slip in MICR style. MICR stands for 'Magnetic Ink Character Recognition'. The bank's computer can read the characters instantly and since the paying-in slip is encoded as soon as the money and cheques are paid in with the amount of the deposit the computer at once knows which account is to be credited and with how much. The customer's account can therefore be updated in a few thousandths of a second.

The bank giro credit slip is very similar, but it is used when the money has to be paid, not into the account of the branch's customer

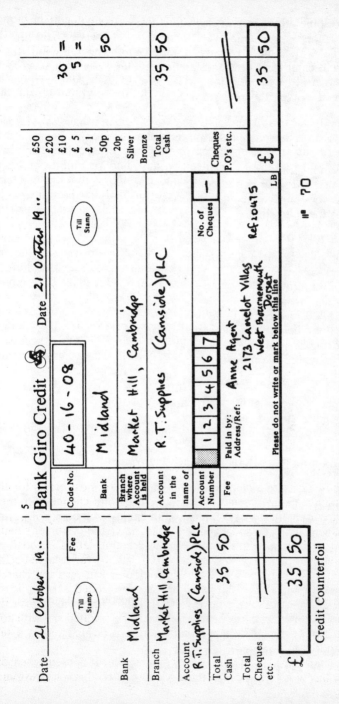

Figure 15.11 A bank giro credit slip for mail-order payments

but into some other account elsewhere. For example, many firms pay wages in this way to employees banking at all sorts of banks in all sorts of towns. Similarly many 'home agents' who sell goods from mail order catalogues to friends and neighbours, pay the money they collect over the counter for the credit of the mail-order house concerned. A typical bank giro credit slip is shown in Figure 15.11.

15.10   Export documents: the master document

International trade is the most important section of documentation work since a very large number of forms are required by the various parties who engage in and supervise overseas trade. A full list includes the following:

Commercial forms

- Acknowledgement of order
- Works order
- Proforma invoice
- Export invoice
- Certified invoices as to value
- Certified invoices as to country of origin
- Packing lists
- Despatch advice note

Transportation and shipping

- Export cargo shipping instructions
- Standard shipping note
- Dangerous goods note
- Bills of lading
- CMR note (for international road movements)
- CIM note (for international rail movements)
- Certificate of shipment
- Airway bill
- The single administrative document (SAD) (for H.M. Customs)
- Bank documentary collection form
- Bills of exchange

To prepare such documents, and make sure they are all correct for any particular export transaction is not easy. Many years ago a movement to simplify international trade procedures was started, and an international convention agreed as follows:

1 That all documents should be on A4 stationery (or on documents which could form part of an A4 page).
2 That the A4 page should be divided up into areas called 'fields' and that every form would have the same information in the same

field. This means that even a person who does not speak the language in which the form is written can find the information he requires so long as he knows which part of the form it is written in.

3 Of course not every form needs every bit of information, and if it does not require a particular box the place is left blank on that form and is said to be 'at free disposal'. That means that the shipping company, airline etc. can use the box for any purpose it likes – for example it might carry other information not required officially but useful to the operator concerned. It might even carry an advertisement or something like that.

The UK representative at the international conventions is the SITPRO Board. This officially accredited body is the Simpler Trade Procedures Board, which is based at Venture House, 29 Glasshouse Street, London W1R 5RG (Tel. 071 287 3525). Their publication *Topform* includes illustrations of all the official designs for export forms and is absolutely authoritative on all such matters – revised as new designs are introduced.

More important perhaps, is the SITPRO master document, from which almost all forms can be prepared. This is illustrated in Figure 15.12, and should be studied carefully. The procedure is that the master document is completed carefully, checked and double-checked to ensure complete accuracy. Thus the exporter's name and address should be carefully checked for correctness (since even a single incorrect letter may lead to some Customs Office somewhere in the world refusing to allow the goods to move). All the other documents are then printed from the master document, with a mask inserted where necessary to shield off information not required on any particular form. Once printed there is no need to check any document – if the master was right the copies made from it are bound to be correct. Imagine how easy it would be to have errors if all the documents were typed by hand by copy typists.

Study the master document carefully now.

Aligned series

Where documents are arranged in the SITPRO manner, with every field of the A4 sheet of paper designated to carry one piece of information, which will appear in that same spot on every document, it is said to be an **aligned series**. Every document can be run off from a master document but they will not all appear alike, because the master document's framework is printed in 'drop-out-blue', which is a colour that the photocopier cannot see. The result is that if a bill of lading is fed into the copier, or an insurance certificate, or a standard shipping note, the information on the master document will appear in the spaces where it is required, but that is all. Material not required is

MASTER DOCUMENT

Exporter No.

Invoice no.

Customs reference/status

Invoice date

Carrier's bkg. no.

Exporter's reference

Buyer's reference

Forwarder's reference

Consignee

Buyer

Freight forwarder

Country of despatch

Carrier

Country of destination code

Country of origin

Country of final destination

Other UK transport details

Terms of delivery and payment

Vessel/flight no. and date

Port/airport of loading

Port/airport of discharge

Place of delivery

Insured value

EUR 1 or C. of O. remarks

DANGEROUS GOODS: Refer to IMDG, ADR, IATA, CIM and UK regulations as appropriate and specify: proper shipping name; hazard class; UN no.; flashpoint °C

Shipping marks; container number

Number and kind of packages; description of goods *

Item no.

Commodity code

Quantity 2

Gross weight (kg)

Cube (m^3)

Procedure

Net weight (kg)

FOB value (£)

Summary declaration/previous document

LIMIT OF SAD BOX 31 ▷

Commodity code

Quantity 2

Gross weight (kg)

Cube (m^3)

Procedure

Net weight (kg)

FOB value (£)

Summary declaration/previous document

Commodity code

Quantity 2

Gross weight (kg)

Cube (m^3)

Procedure

Net weight (kg)

FOB value (£)

Summary declaration/previous document

Identification of warehouse

FREE DISPOSAL

Invoice total (state currency)

Total gross wt (kg)

Total cube (m^3)

Freight payable at

Signatory's company and telephone number

Number of bills of lading

Original Copy

Name of signatory

Place and date

Signature

Figure 15.12 The SITPRO master document (courtesy of the SITPRO Board and Formecon Services Ltd, Crewe)

masked off – with a different mask for each document. An export order might have:

1   A commercial invoice (eight copies)
2   A bill of lading (three copies)
3   A certificate of origin (four copies)
4   A standard shipping note (four copies)
5   A bank documentary collection form (two copies) – and so on

All will be run off by the master document, and all will read exactly the same because errors cannot be made in the copying process.

15.11   Formfill – an electronic form filler

Imagine an export consignment in which we need twenty copies of an invoice, three bills of lading, and forty other assorted documents. Imagine also that if even one letter overlaps into another box on the master document it will cause trouble (because in the masking process that letter will be sure to be masked off on some form). We clearly need to be careful in typing our master. Fortunately help is available with a computerized system called Formfill. This software is produced by Formecon Services Ltd, Gateway, Crewe CW1 1YN. Schools and colleges with computer facilities might like to consider ordering the package, which does the following things.

● Streamlines exporting to every country in the world.
● Enables you to complete export/shipping documents very simply by computer.
● Contains all the latest design forms (including SAD – the Single Administrative Document).
● Shortlists the forms you might need appropriate to the particular country of destination.
● Lets you select which documents to complete, just one or more, per shipment.
● Displays on the screen each form in 'live' format as you call them up for completion.
● Allows you to choose, in any order, which boxes to complete.
● Each box 'zooms-in' to full size for entry of your particular data.
● Has a 'help' facility to give you an explanation of the information required in every box.
● Means you only complete each different box heading once. The software repeats the data on every form where required reducing keyboard time and improving accuracy.
● Automatically completes the shipment forms selected, through your computer printer (including multipart sets).

The simplicity of this system is marvellous. For example, the exporter's name and address appears on every form. The whole form appears on the screen, but by means of a 'mouse', an electronic cursor device, we can call up any particular box to appear by itself. This removes the form from the screen and replaces it with the 'exporter' box. We type in the exporter's name and address, check it carefully and when we are satisfied return it to its place on the screen. It shrinks down to a tiny size, much too small to read, while we call up the next box we wish to complete. From now on, every form we print will have the exporter's name and address on it, full size, without any work from us, and when all the forms are printed the whole electronic master document will be filed away in the computer's memory.

The databank on which the Formfill system depends is able to store in its memory every detail of every country's export requirements, and can be kept up to date by **update disks**, which are fed into the computer to delete changed items and insert the revised information.

15.12   Bills of lading

The bill of lading has been chosen to represent the many documents used in overseas trade, and prepared by the SITPRO master document method. Lading refers to the loading of goods on board a ship and a bill of lading is a list of the packages loaded on board for a particular exporter. The bill has three functions:

1   It is a receipt for the goods shipped on board.
2   It is evidence of the contract of affreightment between the shipper (the exporter) and the shipowner.
3   It is the document of title to the goods. The bill of lading represents the goods while they are on the high seas. If I sell you a bill of lading it transfers the ownership of the goods listed on the bill to you, wherever they are on the high seas. When the goods arrive you can collect the goods from the master of the vessel on presentation of the bill of lading to him/her.

One example of a bill of lading is illustrated in Figure 15.13. It is a house bill of lading issued by a freight forwarder. Note that there is a place for the master of the vessel, or his representative, the freight forwarder, to sign the bill as proof that the goods have been shipped on board.

Export documentation is an involved subject because of the wide variety of modes of transport used, and the different requirements of various countries. A reference book such as *Croner's Reference Book for Exporters* is absolutely essential, unless a databank such as the Formfill service referred to earlier is available. Croner's

© SITPRO 1987

HOUSE BILL OF LADING

Shipper *(hereinafter called the Shipper)*		B/Lading number	Customs reference/status
			Shipper's reference
			Forwarder's reference

Consignee

Notify party and address

Other UK transport details

Conveyance	Point of loading
Point of discharge	Destination

Shipping marks; container number	Number and kind of packages; description of goods	Gross weight (kg)	Cube (m³)

SHIPPED by or RECEIVED for shipment from in apparent good order and condition, except as noted in the Particulars.
Contents, weight, value and measurement according to sender's declaration.
This house Bill of Lading shall have effect subject to our Trading Conditions.

IN WITNESS whereof the Undersigned have signed the number of Bills of Lading shown all of this tenor and date. One Bill of Lading, duly endorsed, is to be given up in exchange for the goods or for a delivery order for same upon which the other bills of lading contained in the set shall be void.

Freight payable at

Number of original Bills of Lading

For particulars of delivery apply with this Bill of Lading to

Place and date of issue

Signature

Format approved by the Institute of Freight Forwarders Ltd

Form No 800   Published and Sold by FORMECON SERVICES Ltd. Gateway, Crewe CW1 1YN   Tel. 0270 500800

SITPRO Approved Licensee No. 21

Figure 15.13 A bill of lading

reference books are available from Croner House, 173 London Road, Kingston-on-Thames, Surrey KT2 6SR.

15.13   Projects on documentation

1   Collecting documents

It is not easy to collect documents because they are vital parts of everyone's business and no one is prepared to give them up. Some firms will, if asked, donate documents which are about to be shredded (because they are more than six years old) to bona fide educational establishments, but it is almost impossible to obtain current documents except from ordinary households. For this reason it is worth making a class collection of the more common documents, with each student able to bring in one or two. Firms can be approached for specimen documents, but they will usually want to be assured that they are made useless by having the word 'specimen' stamped right across them. A rubber stamp of this sort is relatively inexpensive and a useful classroom asset.

2   Designing an invoice

The design of stationery is very important, because:

1   There are legal overtones to all stationery – certain details must appear by law on certain documents.
2   The document usually has a commercial function to peform – for instance an invoice is evidence of the sale of goods or the supply of services and needs to name both parties to the transaction when it is finally completed.
3   The document also has internal functions, for example it may be used to extract statistical information, accounting information, etc.

The assignment is to design an invoice which is attactive, clear and appropriate for the needs of the firm chosen. This may be entirely of your choice or it may make use of the details given below. Where a series of question marks appears you are invited to make up a number to save conflicting with real numbers (for example telephone numbers).

1   The company is East Anglia Transport (Tadlow) Ltd
2   Its address is 1024, Arrington Road, Tadlow, Cambridgeshire CB32 9PQ
3   The VAT No. is ???/????/???
4   The telephone number is (????) ?????
5   The fax number is (????) ??????
6   The telex number is ?-???. (The answerback code is EATRA.)

7 You need a place for the date, the invoice number and the customer's account no.
8 The company registration number is Registered in England No. ??? ????
9 You need details on the invoice for:

    (a) The catalogue number of the articles.
    (b) The description of the goods.
    (c) The quantity.
    (d) The unit price.
    (e) The total value.
    (f) The VAT rate.
    (g) The VAT amount.
    (h) Suitable totals.

You need a passage to the effect that all goods are supplied under the company's Standard Terms and Conditions, a copy of which has already been supplied to the customer. It should also state that claims must be notified in writing within three days (and a note on a delivery note is not regarded as notification). Non-arrival of goods is to be notified within twenty-eight days of despatch date (as shown on the invoice – for which you need a box reading 'date and time of dispatch').

15.14 Rapid revision

Answers	Questions
–	**1 What is an invoice?**
1 A business document which is made out whenever one person supplies goods or provides services to another.	**2 How many copies are there?**
2 Usually four, a top copy for the customer to be their purchases invoice, a second copy for the seller (as a sales invoice), a delivery note for the driver who delivers the goods and an advice note to pack with the goods. There may also be a representative's copy and possibly a gate copy.	**3 What is a debit note?**

Answers	Questions
3 A document very much like an invoice to notify a customer of an undercharge on an invoice, or some ancillary charge for transport, packing etc. not known at the time of invoicing. (*Note:* It is also used to notify a supplier that you are returning goods.)	4 **What is a credit note?**
4 It is a business document which is made out when one person returns goods to another and is usually printed in red. It is made out by the original supplier to acknowledge the return of goods. A credit note is also used to notify an allowance off the original supply price for such things as damage in transit.	5 **What is a statement?**
5 A business document sent out monthly to 'open account' customers requesting payment of the outstanding balance on an account. It may offer a settlement discount for prompt settlement.	6 **What is a receipt?**
6 An acknowledgement of payment made. Today the vast majority of payments are made by cheque and the Cheques Act, 1957 says that a paid cheque is a receipt.	7 **What is a bill of exchange?**
7 It is an unconditional order in writing . . . (you will find the rest on page 326). It is well worth learning this important and difficult definition by heart!	8 **Why is export documentation so difficult?**
8 Because of the widespread controls operated by customs authorities and national governments around the world. Documentation is required to	

Answers	Questions
prove the authenticity of cargoes moving across frontiers, and to prevent smuggling, improper financial transactions, drug smuggling, etc.	**9 What body in the UK seeks to make export documentation easier?**
9 The SITPRO Board (The Simpler Trade Procedures Board).	**10 How is export documentation usually prepared?**
10 From master documents designed by SITPRO.	**11 What is Formfill?**
11 A set of electronic software for completing export forms using the computer's ability to store information for box after box on the form, and print it out on every document that requires the information. It is available from Formecon Services Ltd, Crewe.	**12 What are the three functions of the bill of lading?**
12 (a) It is a receipt for goods, shipped on board a vessel; (b) it is evidence of the contract of carriage; (c) it is the document of title to the goods listed, which can transfer ownership of the goods from one trader to another while they are on the high seas.	**13 Go over the test again until you are sure of all the answers. Then try the questions in Section 15.15 below.**

15.15 Questions on Chapter 15

1 What use would be made of the following copies of an invoice:
   (a) The top copy
   (b) The second (Day Book) copy
   (c) The delivery note
   (d) The advice note
   (e) A representative's copy
   (f) A gate copy
2 What is an aligned series of documents? What is the advantage of such a series in the export trade?

3 Explain why a bill of exchange can promote business activity, by describing how A. Retailer can obtain supplies for the Christmas festival without paying for them until February.
4 What is the importance of a paid cheque?
5 What is a deed? What special rules apply to matters which are arranged formally in this way?
6 Give three reasons why A might send the credit note to B. Would it increase B's debt to A, or decrease it? Explain why.
7 Explain the term 'documents against payment' by referring to Abdul Ajakaiye of Nigeria, who has ordered manufactured goods from Electronics Ltd but does not wish to pay until the goods concerned arrive in Lagos.
8 Explain the term 'documents against acceptance' by referring to Albert Akintunde, of Mombasa, who has ordered goods from Manufacturers (UK) Ltd which he will supply to the Government of Kenya, but cannot pay until the Kenyan Government pay him on the contract date 120 days after arrival of the goods in Mombasa.

Part Four
People in Business

16
Personnel and business

16.1 People and personnel

Everyone who approaches the end of a school or college course starts
to worry about a job. Will I find employment when my course comes
to an end? What skills and attributes do I need to obtain employment
and have the courses I have pursued been the right ones to fit me for
the world of work? We are all people, and we all need jobs, but are
we suitable as 'personnel' for the various types of organization –
firms, companies, government departments, etc. – which require
human resources. There is a subtle difference between people and
'personnel'. We can understand this difference most easily if we look
at a simple definition of the department charged with finding staff in
every business – the Personnel Department.

*The Personnel Department is a department charged with the duty of
obtaining for any organization such human resources as it needs in all
its various departments, with the necessary skills, abilities and experience to keep the business in good heart for the conceivable future.*

Notice that the business does not just want people – it wants people
with the right sort of skills, qualifications and experience. Of course,
the younger a person is the less skills, qualifications and experience
he or she has. In that case what we are looking for is the potential to
develop skills and qualifications in the years ahead. Examination
results are a help in this respect, because they show a person's
potential for progress in learning the practical skills, and acquiring
the specialist qualifications that will be needed in the years ahead.
Thus people who go into banking will usually have only a very limited
knowledge of banking – they have to learn all their banking skills
'in-house' on specialist training courses once they are employed.
They will, after a year or so, master their banking theory and become
an ACIB (Associate of the Chartered Institute of Bankers) and
eventually achieve even higher grades of membership of that important professional body. Remember, academic qualifications are
only an introduction to business life; the real qualifications come

when we obtain professional qualifications in the profession or industry we join when we take employment.

16.2   The working environment

Except in the very smallest firms the working environment is one in which a number of teams of people with different skills and abilities are working together to create goods and services to satisfy human 'wants'. Sometmes they work well together and sometimes they are found to be uncooperative, with petty rivalries and personal differences interfering with the smooth operations which are so desirable if goods and services are to be produced easily and economically. Even a single employee can create a bad atmosphere in a department, and disrupt the general effort to an alarming extent. One pupil once told the author of the present book 'I hope to be a small *clog* in a big machine when I leave college' – an ambition it is all too easy to achieve. One of the worst jobs a Personnel Officer ever has to do is to find some way of removing a person who disrupts the organization because he/she lacks some skill, or the good manners to cooperate with other members of the team, or has some personality defect which makes him/her difficult to work with.

It is important for each new employee, and particularly each new young employee, to approach the new job with a positive, cheerful and optimistic attitude. Where am I going to fit into this organization? What post would I eventually like to fill, and what do I have to do to start making my way up the ladder that leads to this position? You should start early to work towards full professional qualifications in the trade or industry concerned – taking such chances as are offered to you to acquire skills and knowledge which will help your progress. Even if the first job proves to be a poor choice for you personally there are many general skills you can acquire even in an unsatisfactory position. Working to make yourself indispensable in every job you undertake, however humdrum, is never a waste of time. The person who gains most is you!

16.3   The employee as an individual

Every employee is an individual, with a need to achieve through his/her work the fulfilments which the working side of one's life should realize. We are not wage-slaves, and if we are treated as wage-slaves we shall do our best to escape to a more agreeable environment. Naturally when we are young we have much to learn, and must expect to be told many things which are in the best interest of ourselves, our fellow workers and the firm or company which employs us. As we gain experience and qualifications we expect to make more of a mark in the company, to acquire status through promotion and recognition of the vital part we are beginning to play in the success of the company.

Not everyone is the same, or has the same needs. Some have family circumstances which prevent them pursuing the fullest success in their employment situation; they are content if they earn a good wage or salary for the work done, and can leave work at the end of the day without a backward glance. A larger proportion of employees have at least some element of ambition. It has been found that the chief needs of most employees are for the four satisfactions illustrated in Figure 16.1 – self-realization, self-esteem, status and the respect of peer groups.

1 *Self-realization* This involves the gradual advance in skills and knowledge which turns a young and unsure person into a confident, knowledgeable person. It usually involves some sort of success – successful control of a particular type or area of work, success in acquiring professional qualifications, etc. Self-realization cannot be achieved in a day or a month. We gradually begin to appreciate that we are enjoying work, are becoming self-confident and are 'holding the job down' in a satisfactory way.

2 *Self-esteem* This results from self-realization. We appreciate our own value. We feel more confident, are pleased with our own success, look forward to growing responsibility and enjoy quiet self-satisfaction. The danger is that one might become too self-confident and self-assertive.

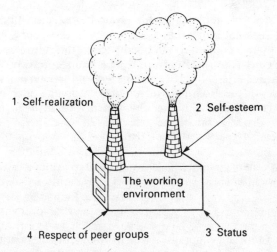

Figure 16.1 The needs of the individual

3 *Status* This is conferred by promotion and recognition from above. It may include designation as supervisor, head of section, etc. It often brings special rights and privileges, such as pension rights, perquisites (perks) such as the right to a company car, etc.
4 *Respect of peer groups* The word 'peer' means 'person of the same rank as ourselves'. Generally speaking, people like to have the respect of their peers. It is a sign that we have made progress and achieved a certain status, but without taking unfair advantage of anyone in the process. The respect of one's peers can only be achieved by genuine hard work and merit, not by luck, or by unscrupulous behaviour.

16.4 The employee as a member of a group

Although the employee's individuality is important, the needs he/she has to achieve self-realization have to be achieved within a working environment where the employee is one of a group, or rather several groups. Thus a young employee joining, say, the Despatch Department of a mail-order firm as a junior packer will have a small circle of packers with whom he/she works, but will also be part of the larger Despatch Department and then part of the mail-order company. A pattern of loyalties will no doubt develop, most closely linked to the immediate group which surrounds the young employee, but gradually extending to larger groupings as the employee concerned becomes better known.

Formal groupings in business

The word 'formal' implies that the group has been set up in a legal way. This does not imply that there is any necessity for solicitors or other legal persons but only an obedience to the rules laid down by the management, or the Board in the case of a company. A formal grouping arises originally as a result of a resolution moved, seconded and passed by the Board to set up the grouping concerned. This would of course apply to the department in which an employee works, but also to some of the groupings in which he/she operates. For example, if appointed to a Health and Safety Committee, or a Welfare Committee, or a Joint Consultative Committee between unions and management these would all be formal, interdepartmental committees.

Informal groupings in business

Besides the formal groupings of the working environment there are informal groupings, clubs, societies, sports associations, etc. Since these informal groupings go across departments they give the young employee a knowledge of other departments, leading personalities, etc. All this is useful and broadening. The Personnel Officer or his assistants play a considerable role in these informal clubs, societies and committees, and encourage young staff to get involved and develop their personal interests and social skills.

16.5 The Personnel Officer's day

No two days are exactly alike in personnel work, because there are many things to do and some idea of their variety is helpful to anyone seeking to understand the Personnel Officer's approach to appointing new staff. The general layout of the Personnel Department and the matters it must take into account are shown in Figure 16.2. Study this diagram carefully now.

We could imagine a typical day as follows:

8.45 a.m.   Arrival at work. Consideration of important mail items. Dictation of immediate responses so far as possible. Delegation of other items as casework to suitable staff. Consideration of diary for the day.

9.30 a.m.   Interviews for junior appointments of school-leavers. Six to be interviewed by a panel of three staff. Decisions, letters of appointment and letters of regret.

11.00 a.m.   Disciplinary procedure meeting at factory site over horseplay resulting in accident. Staff representatives present. Final warning issued.

1.00 p.m.   Lunch with Managing Director to discuss possible redundancy situation at depot in East Anglia. Alternative approaches for finding new work discussed.

2.00 p.m.   Read and sign letters dictated earlier. Further dictation re casework and approaches for new work discussed at lunchtime.

3.00 p.m.   School appointment – careers opportunities for school-leavers – video presentation and 'Question and Answer' session.

4.30 p.m.   Sign correspondence dictated earlier. Discussion of casework progress with senior staff. Drafting of report to Board about 'in-house' training over the past year and plans for extension in year ahead.

5.45 p.m.   Departure.

16.6 The types of work available

Work may be classified in many ways. There are millions of jobs waiting to be done and thousands of different ways of doing them. It

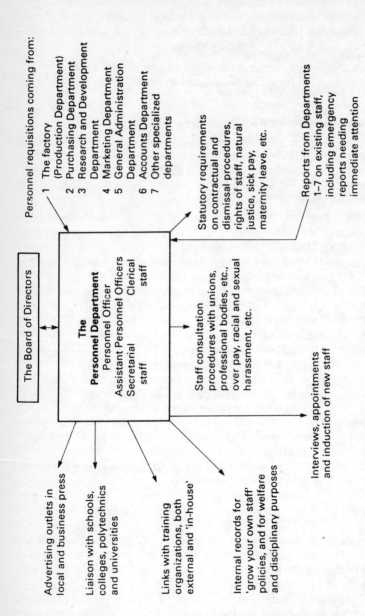

Personnel requisitions coming from:

1 The factory (Production Department)
2 Purchasing Department
3 Research and Development Department
4 Marketing Department
5 General Administration Department
6 Accounts Department
7 Other specialized departments

The Board of Directors

The Personnel Department
Personnel Officer
Assistant Personnel Officers
Secretarial staff   Clerical staff

Statutory requirements on contractual and dismissal procedures, rights of staff, natural justice, sick pay, maternity leave, etc.

Reports from Departments 1–7 on existing staff, including emergency reports needing immediate attention

Staff consultation procedures with unions, professional bodies, etc., over pay, racial and sexual harassment, etc.

Advertising outlets in local and business press

Liaison with schools, colleges, polytechnics and universities

Links with training organizations, both external and 'in-house'

Internal records for 'grow your own staff' policies, and for welfare and disciplinary purposes

Interviews, appointments and induction of new staff

Figure 16.2 The duties and interests of the Personnel Department

is impossible to draw up a chart showing all the jobs available and the best way to develop an understanding of the broad categories of work is to consider some key words usually used in describing jobs. We will think about the following key terms.

1 Skilled work and unskilled work.
2 Industrial work, commercial work and professional work.
3 Core work, contract work and casual work.

Skilled and unskilled work

Unskilled work is the sort of work which anyone of reasonable intelligence, and free from physical disability, can do with a short introductory explanation of what is required. The term is rather unfair, in that many people doing so-called 'unskilled' work are in fact extremely skilful and quickly develop not only the sort of physique needed to do the job well and quickly but also many clever ways of organizing the work to make it less burdensome. Such work may appeal particularly to those with outside commitments and interests apart from the job, who simply wish to earn a good income. Some people cannot be totally dedicated to their employment because of family circumstances, and a job which is undemanding, and can be forgotten after working hours, is ideal. The vast majority of manufacturing processes require this type of work, and those to whom such work appeals can usually find employment.

Skilled work requires more training than just a few minutes of explanation. There are many types of skilled work, but they nearly always require a nice mixture of theory and practice. For example, the engineer needs to understand materials, processes, tools, stresses and strains, and many other theoretical aspects, but in putting them into practice he/she also needs skills which cannot be mastered at a single attempt, but need repeated practice. The competent secretary usually needs several months to become fluent at secretarial skills, and the surgeon may need several years before complete mastery of a particular type of operation is achieved.

Industrial work, commercial work and professional work

In fact all these types of work may be done in the same building and even in the same room, but they are useful broad descriptions of work. *Industrial work* implies factory work, or site work of some sort. There is an enormous range of such activities, and they may be skilled, semi-skilled or unskilled. They often require more physical labour than commercial work and professional work, but as they are usually backed by an array of power tools, lifting and handling devices, conveyors and elevators, etc., they may still be within the capacities of almost everyone. Indeed many disabled people do industrial jobs, with tools and equipment specially adapted to meet their particular needs.

Commercial work is work in the fields of trade, banking, insurance, transport and communications. We saw in Part One of this book that modern methods of production produce enormous outputs of goods which come pouring off production lines. We have to clear them out of the way at once or the production lines will be jammed, and this means immediate transport to depots and warehouses where goods can be stored until the market demands them. Marketing activities are a huge part of commercial work, and so are the invoicing and accounting services which ensure payment is received for supplies.

Professional work is work performed by key staff who have achieved membership of one of the professional bodies which operate at the very highest level in all walks of life. We think of doctors, dentists, solicitors and accountants as typical professional people, but there are many, many more. For example, there are many different types of scientists at the same level, chemists, physicists, hydrologists, biologists, etc. There are many commercial bodies, such as the Institute of Purchasing and Supply, the Institute of Personnel Management, the Chartered Institute of Marketing and the Institute of Freight Forwarders. All these bodies lay down strict codes of conduct for their members; set difficult entry qualifications so that members have to pass a succession of examinations and also have several years of practical experience before full membership is achieved. You can join any of these organizations, for a membership fee of – say – £20, but you only become a student member. When you have acquired both the examination qualifications and the experience to be a credit to the Institute of your choice, you will become a full member. The terms vary. Some are called Associates, for example one becomes an Associate of the Chartered Institute of Bankers. Others use the term 'Graduate', as for example Graduate of the Chartered Institute of Transport. Higher than the graduate level are 'Fellows' and similar designations. One reaches such levels by virtue of senior management positions successfully held over several years, or as a result of some singular service to the whole industry which the Institute considers deserves recognition.

Core work, contract work and casual work

This division of work into core work, contract work and casual work is a relatively new description of the work situation in many companies today. The essential work of the company is done by a core of highly-skilled and highly-experienced key members of staff. They are highly prized, highly expensive and companies do their best not to lose them to other firms. They are paid well, are expected to show absolute dedication to the company, are on call day and night, and lead extremely stressful lives. There are not too many of them in any company, not nearly enough to do all the work that has to be done.

Who does this work then? The answer is that a great deal of it is contracted out to freelance self-employed people who are not employees, but are paid by the job. We have all seen on television Red Adair, the oil trouble-shooter, flying in to put out a blazing oil rig, and cap the well. Not all jobs are so spectacular, but all sorts of routine or trouble-shooting jobs are contracted out in this way. For example, if a cosmetic firm wants to send out free samples to potential customers it finds a small firm willing to do the work for an agreed fee. Self-employment in this way offers many opportunities, but the 'safe' life of an employee, with pension schemes and social clubs, and regular pay packets is not available.

The third class of work is designated 'casual work' but not in the old-fasioned way in which that term was used. The workers are employees, but they are not expected to rise through the ranks of the company and become the managing director one fine day. They can, and do, behave more casually. They want flexi-hours (i.e. if they want to take an hour off to go shopping, or to the dentist or the doctor, they can take it). Such people do all the routine work and they need looking after if management is to encourage enough loyalty to keep them working as a team. They have skills, and energy, and ability which need encouraging. They need status, and the esteem of peer-groups just as much as any other employee. What they may need, but do not get, is the security of long-term staff membership with a clear career structure. This is replaced by good wages, merit and loyalty ratings and the freedom to leave when they want to because they are in no sense wedded to that particular job, or that particular company.

16.7   The functions of the Personnel Department

We may list the functions of the Personnel Department as follows:

1   To secure staff, as explained earlier, with all the necessary skills and experience required for all departments of the business. This requires the drawing-up of a personnel policy for the organization, the preparation of job specifications, advertising for staff, reviewing all applications and drawing up shortlists for interview, interviewing and selecting the best applicants and formally appointing them.

2   The induction of new staff in a proper manner, so that they are aware of their duties and responsibilities; the possible dangers in their new employment, the standards of behaviour required,

health and safety aspects and remuneration (wages and salaries).

3   To ensure compliance with the law in all aspects as far as employment is concerned; the Health and Safety at Work Act, the Payment of Wages Act, Employment Law, etc. This may require training activities to meet legal requirements, the keeping of written records, etc.

4   Participation in matters relating to wage claims, redundancy schemes, joint consultation about working conditions and any similar matters relating to labour relations, unfair dismissal, sexual or racial harassment, etc.

5   All aspects of disciplinary matters, improper or irresponsible behaviour, warning staff where necessary and dismissal of staff in a proper manner in accordance with the principles of natural justice. These are (a) that it is essential to hear both sides in any dispute and (b) that no one may be a judge in his own case. Thus if a supervisor is in dispute with an employee the matter must be decided by a third person of management level and not be decided by the supervisor who is a party to the dispute.

6   Whenever a redundancy situation arises due to a change in the fortunes of the business, so that, in order to save the entire business some part of it must be closed down, a proper scheme must be prepared; those to be made redundant must be given adequate warning and if retraining to redeploy staff is needed a suitable training scheme must be drawn up. The pensions arrangements for staff forced into early retirement must be made and the Personnel Officer will play a leading part.

7   Various types of welfare arrangements may be made, especially where such events as bereavements, industrial injuries or nervous breakdowns occur.

8   A comprehensive set of records must be kept on employees so that their progress, rates of pay, promotion etc. can be monitored and they can be helped to acquire further skills and qualifications which will ensure adequate replacements for all ranks of staff are available within the organization.

Points to remember

- The difference between people and personnel is that personnel have the necessary abilities, aptitudes, qualifications and experience to be of use to a firm or company, whereas the broad generality of people may not have such qualities.
- The working environment is a place where teams of people are working in cooperation to produce some useful good or service. It is essential to fit into this environment as smoothly as possible.
- What we hope to achieve in the working environment are the four essential satisfactions – self-realization, self-esteem, status and the respect of peer groups.

- A formal grouping in business is one set up by management under its rules of procedure. An informal grouping is one set up as a voluntary association of members for social, sporting or recreational purposes, or for some sort of welfare activity of an unofficial nature.
- The Personnel Department has very widespread activities which include the general responsibility to find staff of such abilities and experience as are necessary for all departments; to induct and train them and monitor their progress over the years as they move up through the organization.

16.8 Project on the work of the Personnel Department

Taking your local newspaper as the source of your material, make a collection of ten display advertisements offering employment in local firms. From these advertisements draw up (a) a list of the advertisers; (b) the types of position offered; (c) the qualifications required; (d) the salary scale mentioned (if any); (e) the suggested method for following up the advertisement; (f) the closing date (if any) specified.

Present your project in the form of a table showing the names of the advertisers down the left-hand side and the various points (a)–(f) across the page. Indicate which of the jobs you could apply for (if any), in a final column.

16.9 Rapid revision

Answers		*Questions*	
–		**1**	**What is the Personnel Department?**
1	It is a department charged with the duty of obtaining for a firm or company such human resources as it needs in all its various departments, so that it is never starved of people with the necessary skills, qualifications, abilities and expertise.	**2**	**What is the working environment?**
2	It is the total climate that surrounds us in the working situation – our colleagues, supervisors, working situation and the formal and informal groupings to which we belong.	**3**	**What are the needs of employees within this environment?**

Answers	Questions
3 To achieve self-realization, self-esteem, status and the respect of peer groups (people at the same level as ourselves).	4 **List the functions of the Personnel Office.**
4 (a) To recruit staff; (b) to train them and develop them; (c) to devise a personnel policy for the firm; (d) to devise job descriptions, advertise posts, vet applications and interview prospective employees; (e) to ensure compliance with the law about employment practices, health and safety at work, payment of wages, etc.; (f) to join in industrial relations activities, joint consultation and wage negotiations; (g) to assist with disciplinary matters, warnings to staff, dismissal procedures, redundancy schemes, etc.; (h) to assist with welfare arrangements, especially after industrial accidents, etc.; (i) to keep comprehensive records on all personnel matters.	5 **Go over the test again until you are sure of all the answers. Then try the questions in Section 16.10 below.**

16.10   Questions on Chapter 16

1   Write the text of an advertisement for an employment opportunity in any firm with which you are familiar. Give a description of the job concerned, the salary payable, the qualifications required and the deadline for applications. Invite applicants to write to you, as Personnel Officer of the firm concerned.

2   A firm employs the following personnel: A Managing Director to whom the Factory Manager, the Accountant and the Marketing Manager report. Each of the four senior executives has a secretary. There are three other managers:

   (a)   Personnel, with a staff of one shorthand-typist and two clerks.

   (b)   Public Relations with a staff of one shorthand-typist and two clerks.

    (c)   The Administration Officer, with a staff of three filing clerks, three copy-typists and two wages clerks.

The Personnel Manager reports direct to the Managing Director.

The Public Relations Manager reports to the Factory Manager.

The Administrative Officer reports to the Accountant.

Make out an organization chart, showing clearly the lines of authority.

3   (a)   Design a record card for use in a Personnel Department, with provision for the following information:

Employee's name	Date left
Employee's address	Date of birth
Department	Education and qualifications
Date joined	Job title – with several lines to allow for promotion
	Salary – with several lines, the first of which reads 'At start'

Fill in the relevant information as for a junior clerk.

    (b)   What means can you suggest for quick recognition of cards of a particular department?

4   What is meant by each of the following terms:

    (a)   Status

    (b)   A formal grouping

    (c)   Induction of new staff

    (d)   Unskilled labour

5   'A Personnel Officer is not solely concerned with the welfare of employees!' What is the Personnel Officer's chief concern in any firm?

17
Recruitment of staff

17.1 The avenues for recruitment

Recruitment presents a number of problems. Not only has the Personnel Officer to find people of the right quality, knowledge and experience, but it is essential to do so at the least cost, and in line with legal and social restraints imposed by a variety of Acts of Parliament. Before considering the avenues of recruitment we must consider these aspects.

Cost

An average display advertisement in a large circulation national newspaper costs several hundred pounds. A similar advertisement in a local evening newspaper may cost as much as £100. A small classified advertisement costs between £20 and £35. If we use a local employment agency to find us staff of a particular type we can expect it to cost us at least one week's pay for that member of staff and if the person concerned is at all skilled, for example a fashion designer, it would be nearer one month's pay, perhaps as much as £2,000. Such agencies do save the Personnel Officer a great deal of time and expense, for much of the preliminary work of selection is done in the agency, and only one or two high-flyers are actually interviewed for the position. Certainly the costs are high if this method of recruitment is used.

Probably the cheapest way of recruiting staff is to ask existing staff who know of friends or relatives in need of a job to give their names and addresses to the Personnel Department, or bring them along one evening for an interview. There are no costs associated with this type of recruitment, and the existing employees without knowing it perhaps, do a good deal of the selection process. For example, an existing employee is not likely to introduce a person who is a known troublemaker, or who has personality defects which make him/her unable to work and succeed in that kind of firm or company. The existing employees will have the possibility of adverse repercussions on their own careers in mind when they propose a new member of staff. Equally the new members of staff will have a sense of loyalty to the person proposing them and will be keen to avoid embarrassing them in any way. The trouble is that there are racial and sexual overtones to this method of recruitment.

Racial and sexual balance in personnel

The UK has undergone some important changes in recent years, particularly the increased number of citizens from the Caribbean, Africa and Asia. Another change is the greater part played by women in the labour force and their needs for equality of opportunity. The trouble with asking staff to introduce relatives and friends for employment is that these introductions will tend to be biased, both as to ethnic origin and sex, towards the status quo. Thus those at present employing predominantly white staff will tend to be introduced to applicants who are also white, and male staff are more likely to introduce a male friend when expansion occurs, rather than to think of female staff seeking to break into a new area of work, previously largely staffed by males. The adoption of such a recruitment policy could even be viewed officially as a form of veiled discrimination, if it results in the personnel of any firm not corresponding in pattern to the overall ethnic pattern of the community, or the overall sexual pattern within a profession or trade. In some industries it might be desirable to have a bias in favour of underemployed groups to redress the adverse balance in employment within a firm or company.

17.2 Personnel requisitions

The recruitment of a new member of staff starts when a supervisor or manager somewhere in a firm completes a personnel requisition form and submits it either to his/her superior or to the Personnel Department. The form used may have been designed 'in-house', but one or two companies do specialize in drawing up forms for other people to use, and the personnel forms used in this book are provided by Formecon Services Ltd, Gateway, Crewe CW1 1YN. Figure 17.1 shows the personnel requisition form from this series. It serves two purposes. First it requires the department that needs an extra employee to give all the information necessary so that a suitable advertisement can be drawn up giving the qualifications and experience required. The form draws out from the manager seeking to appoint staff both the job description (we must be able to tell applicants exactly what we want them to do) and the person specification (we don't want to appoint someone who is totally unsuitable).

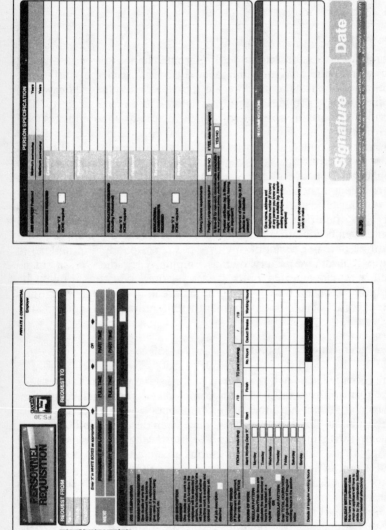

Figure 17.1 A personnel requisition form (courtesy of Formecon Services Ltd)

The second use of the form is to serve as the original document for the Personnel Department in its attempt to fill the position. A completed personnel requisition form enables the whole process to start up. Consider the illustrated form in Figure 17.1 now.

17.3 Job descriptions

Part of the procedure for filling in a personnel requisition form is the drawing-up of a suitable job description. Actually job descriptions have more than one function. When we first decide to appoint someone to a particular post we must have a clear idea of the work required and a job description is the management's attempt to describe as clearly as possible the type of work an employee will be required to do. However, we cannot specify in detail every type of task to be performed, and new tasks arise all the time. It is, therefore, wise to include in the job description some phrases which require the employee to be generally cooperative and helpful in any type of work assigned to him/her. One of the worst things from an employer's point of view is to have staff down tools and say 'I'm not doing that, it's not my job.' Such phrases as 'and will cooperate with Mrs X at busy times with mail shots and other publicity' draw attention to the need to play a full role in the department.

Equally it is unsatisfactory to an employee to be suddenly burdened with a number of tasks which were not envisaged as being within the classes of work that would be required when employment began. Some firms therefore, when job descriptions are under review, ask the employee to fill in a job description form too. This will include all the work that the employee is called upon to perform. It can be used as a basis for discussion with the member of staff and for comparison with the job description as drawn up by management. It will soon be clear that some areas of work are not included on one of the forms. These will be the subject of negotiation. For example, management may want the employee to take on an extra task, and it may be a matter for debate as to whether the time is available to do it. Equally management may detect that the employee has been burdened with work that some other member of staff should be doing. Some people love to delegate their work to others and have an easier life as a result. Correction of such unfair behaviour resolves the difficulty.

Job descriptions are not only used when recruiting staff, but once prepared are on file as valuable reference points for a number of activities. For example:

1 They may be used at the periodical review of an employee's work, when merit awards and pay increases are under consideration.

Both the member of staff and his/her supervisor may be asked to comment on the employee's performance and whether the full job description is being carried out.

2 They are useful when training replacement staff. It is always essential to have staff trained to take over another person's work at a moment's notice. Holidays, sickness, promotions, staff giving notice, retirement and premature deaths cause vacancies all the time. The job description enables staff to be trained up to take over aspects of other people's work and thus ease all such difficulties.

3 In any dispute with a member of staff the job description is the reference point for judging performance. If performance is poor this is made quite clear, in writing. An employee will then have a chance to correct his/her performance, and failure to do so may lead to dismissal. An employee who alleges unfair dismissal will find it less easy to succeed at an industrial tribunal in the face of several clear warnings in writing.

Listed below are some of the headings on a typical job description form. The layout of the form gives enough space for each of these points to be fully explained.

1 *Job titles* A good job title accurately conveys the nature of the work the jobholder is required to perform.

2 *Purpose of the job* A brief outline of the main reasons why this job is needed by the employer.

3 *Job location* This states where the job is principally located, whether travel forms a part of the job, and details of any territory for which the jobholder is responsible.

4 *Responsibilities* A description of those aspects of the job which require judgement, common sense and the use of personal technical skill(s), qualifications, etc., e.g. negotiating prices or making personal decisions regarding health and safety, directing the work of others, etc.

5 *Duties* Details of the fundamental tasks which the jobholder must do, for example, operating a machine, taking sales orders, etc. Since most jobs involve a wide range of duties it may not be practical to list them all here. This box concludes with the words 'The employee must also perform any other duties the employer might reasonably expect.'

6 *Authority and discretion* The limits of the jobholder's authority should be defined under this title, making clear, particularly in financial terms, the level at which expenditure requires approval from a supervisor.

7 *Liaison* Many jobs involve direct and indirect contact with other people and this requires a description as to the scope of contact

(including persons other than employees), whom the jobholder supervises and to whom the jobholder is responsible.

8 *Targets* With some jobs the provision of work targets or 'goals' are a useful addition to the job description. These may relate to quantity (e.g. sales or production levels) or quality (e.g. reject rate).

9 *Conditions* Many jobs have special conditions attached such as requirement for the jobholder to be mobile or to have colour vision. Such conditions should be described in this section.

17.4 Advertising the vacancy

With all this information the Personnel Department can set about finding the required member of staff. Obvious sources are:

1 *Existing staff* Have we someone in a declining area of work for whom this new post would be a promotion, or an acceptable sideways step to avoid future redundancy? If so, we approach him/her.

2 *Applicants on a waiting list* Sometimes we interview several applicants for a job when we can only appoint one, and quite good people have to be rejected. This is naturally a disappointment, and we may soften the blow by offering to put them on a waiting list. If such a person is suitable for the new post that has arisen it is a cheap solution to a recruitment problem to telephone them or write to them and invite them to a further interview.

3 *The local Job Centre and Careers Service* Many firms and companies use local Job Centres and Careers Service offices as a source of recruitment. These services help unemployed people and school leavers find jobs and they are therefore logical organizations to approach for staff. They usually make no charge to the firm for low-level staff, but there is a higher-level register for skilled staff where some charge may be made to the organization seeking an employee. Even so, this is an economical way to find staff.

4 *Local employment agencies* Many Personnel Officers use the services of a local employment agency to save time and trouble when finding new staff. If a sound relationship can be built up with such an agency all that is needed is for a copy of the employment requisition to be passed through to the agency which will then do all that is necessary. For example, it might already have such a person on its books seeking employment. It might know of someone of the right calibre doing a temporary job elsewhere, who would become available in a very short time. If it has no such person on its books it could go ahead and advertise

the post in a manner it knows to be appropriate. Look at any evening, daily or Sunday newspaper and you will find such advertisements from agencies acting for a major client. They often include such phrases as 'The company concerned is a small company who want someone who can offer a wide range of secretarial and communication skills.' Note that as the company is not itself named, it will not be bothered by hundreds of applications, many of them from totally unsuitable people. The agency will sort out the suitable applicants and submit only those with a good chance of being selected.

5   *Advertising the post*   If this is not done by an outside agency the Personnel Department will draw up an advertisement appropriate to the situation. It is usual to give the following information:

(a)   The name of the firm or company.
(b)   A brief outline of its work, and its situation in the industry.
(c)   A brief job description and the qualifications hoped for from applicants.
(d)   Some idea of the salary payable, or at least a reference to the fact that the salary is negotiable.
(e)   Details of how to apply and address for all correspondence. In urgent situations a telephone number, and named contact, may be given to encourage applicants to phone for an informal discussion.
(f)   A coded insertion in the address (for example Dept ES) may enable the advertiser to identify which advertisement produced the response. For example the reference ES may indicate *Evening Standard*. This is useful in choosing newspapers for future advertisements.

A typical advertisement is given in Figure 17.2.

Points to remember

●   When seeking to recruit staff it is essential to keep costs as low as possible and to recruit on a fair basis so that allegations of racial or sexual discrimination cannot be made against the firm or company.
●   Managers who require staff complete a personnel requisition form which is sent to the Personnel Department. It gives a job description and person specification (i.e. a list of the characteristics we would like him/her to have if an applicant was to be perfect for the job).
●   A job description is a detailed description of the duties and general activities an employee would be expected to perform. It assists the Personnel Department to recruit a suitable person, and

Mowbray Car Hire Services

PART TIME
MD's SECRETARY

We are a rapidly growing National Car Hire Company. Our MD is in his office about 3 days a week and needs a secretary on these days. The successful applicant will be a competent typist, able to take shorthand and to use (or willing to learn) word processing using Word Star Software.

We are shortly moving from our offices in Blewbury to purpose-built premises in Reading, and the successful applicant will be expected to move with us. Hours by arrangement but to cover periods 9.30am–4pm on 3 days a week.

Applications in writing to: Mrs P. Grant, Dept OT, Mowbray Car Hire Services Ltd, Main Road, Blewbury, Oxon OX11 9QD or ring for informal discussion on (0235) 000 000.

Figure 17.2 A typical advertisement for recruiting staff

also serves for the future as a reference point for deciding whether the employee's performance is adequate.

17.5 Job applications

Every job application has two or three stages, and each is in the form of a business letter. It is therefore desirable to write in a style which is acceptable to businesses, although of course a responsible firm will answer any letter, whatever its form. You are seeking to impress them with your suitability as an employee, and the ability to write a good letter, in proper business style, is a basic qualification. The layout required is explained in Section 17.7 below. First let us consider the stages in job applications. These are:

1 A brief letter requesting an application form for a post you have seen advertised.

2   A covering letter, to cover the return of the application form.
3   A letter acknowledging the receipt of an invitation to an interview and confirming your intention to attend.
4   A letter acknowledging the receipt of a letter of appointment, and confirming your intention to commence employment as requested.
5   Alternatively, a letter expressing your disappointment at not being selected and asking that your name be borne in mind should a further vacancy occur, or should the person actually selected not take up the appointment.

As an alternative to 1 and 2 above, we could have a letter written to a firm whose activities we are interested in and which we should like to work for, although so far as we are aware no vacancy exists at present. This is a slightly more adventurous activity than the routine application, but it does have the advantage that it is probably the only application the firm will be receiving and the person who deals with staffing will therefore give it undivided attention.

This group of letters seems a fairly daunting prospect, but once you have written a rough draft for each they will soon become routine, and will present few problems, except the rather tedious chore of writing them out each time they are required. Don't get depressed about this. You have to keep at it with cheerful enthusiasm. A draft is a rough guide both to the layout and the content of a letter, which you will then adapt to suit the particular letter you are writing.

17.6   The materials for regular letter writing

Sadly, you have to speculate before you can accumulate, and setting yourself up to write regularly for jobs requires a basic organization and the expenditure of a few pounds. You need the following things:

1   Some plain white A4 bond paper – which you can buy from any stationer. If you are hopeless at writing on plain paper and keeping the lines neat some firms do sell a pad with the first page ruled with thick black lines. You place this *under* the first sheet and the lines show through well enough for you to see them as your write your letters. If you don't find this in a shop use a ruler and a black ball point pen to rule up one page in this way and use it every time you write a letter.
2   Two sizes of envelopes – A5 and A4. You may prefer to get white ones, but brown ones are cheaper and will probably be adequate. Buy about fifty A5 envelopes (210 × 148 mm) and about ten A4 envelopes (297 × 210 mm). These are best for sending in application forms, which are usually A4 size.
3   A couple of black ballpoint pens. 'Medium' pens are better than fine point pens, and black is essential. Many firms copy letters and

application forms so that each member of an interviewing panel can have a copy, and black on white paper gives the best copies. Lots of copying machines cannot 'see' blue – so writing job applications in blue ballpoint pen is a positive disadvantage. Don't do it!

4 A supply of first class stamps. Never send anything second class. With a first class stamp you are practically guaranteed next day delivery.

5 You need to keep a record of all job applications, and this is best done in a lever arch file. They cost about £1.50 at any good stationers.

6 A box of treasury tags is extremely helpful, and only costs about 50 pence at any good stationers. They are invaluable for keeping papers together, but you do need a tiny punch to punch a hole in the corner of the paper. Two-hole punches can also be obtained very cheaply.

7 Finally, writing your own name and address is one of the really boring things about job applications, especially if you enclose stamped addressed envelopes for replies. You may like to spend the very small sum required to get 1000 addressed labels printed by a specialist firm. The usual cost is about £2–£3 for the smallest labels and £10 for large ones. They are a great time saver and well worth the money if you can afford it. There are many firms offering these address labels, but one such firm is Able-label Department, Steepleprint Ltd, Earls Barton, Northampton NN6 0LS. The price is at present £3.25 for 1000 labels, but this is subject to small increases in line with inflation.

17.7 The layout of a business letter

To illustrate the layout of a business letter we have a number of specimen letters to suit each of the job application letters listed in 17.5 above. Opposite each letter is a list of the points you should know about the layout of the letter. These specimen letters can be used as a rough draft for letters of the type concerned which you yourself need to write.

Letter No. 1:   Requesting an application form

This letter appears on page 368 as Figure 17.3. Read it now, and then read the notes below.

Using this letter as a rough draft
If you are using this letter as a rough draft you will appreciate that you have to change each part of the letter to the correct wording for yourself, the addressee, the job you are applying for and your own

Peter Bracey,
10 Wildflower Walk,
Peartree Way,
Newtown,
Herts.,
ST3 5PQ

The Personnel Officer,
Higgins White Tile Co. Ltd,
24 Eastern Way,
Countrytown,
Herts.,
ST1 3DT

27 October 19xx

My ref: Job application
No. 5

Dear Sir,

Trainee Planning Clerk – Hertfordshire Times –
27 October 19xx

Would you kindly send me the application form and job description referred to in today's advertisement in the Hertfordshire Times.

I am a school leaver with examination qualifications in English, Maths, Technical Drawing and Woodwork, with a strong practical bent – for example I am a 'scooter' driver and do all my own maintenance. I therefore feel that you would find me suitable for a post of this type.

I enclose a s.a.e. for reply, and thank you for your help.

Yours faithfully,

Peter Bracey.

Figure 17.3   A draft letter requesting an application form

Notes:
1   The sender's address appears in the top right-hand corner. This could be a stuck-on address label. If you use one of these, stick it on carefully with the sides of the label parallel to the top and sides of the paper.
2   The date is important – and in this case it lets them know you are writing at once, immediately after seeing the advertisement.
3   You don't have to put a reference but it is helpful to you – you are going to keep a record of all your job applications in a lever arch file. Replies will come in at all sorts of different times and it helps to have a clear reference.

qualifications. Make sure you spell all the words correctly and keep your personal details brief, because you will have plenty of time to give them the full details when you complete the application form.

Addressing the envelope
There are two styles of addressing an envelope – the fully blocked style – chiefly used by typists because it is more economical of typing time, and the open style usually used when writing by hand. In this style the lines do not begin directly below one another, but start slightly towards the right of the line above. These two examples are shown in Figures 17.4 and 17.5.

Keeping a record of letters sent
There is a strong case for keeping a copy of all letters sent, and of all the details that led you to write the letter in the first place. The trouble is that when one receives replies or invitations to interviews, several weeks may have elapsed and you may not remember which firm you wrote to and which job you applied for. Keep as full a record as you can – for example cut out the advertisements you reply to and file them away with your copy letters. It may be necessary to buy a pad of carbon paper from a stationery shop and use this to take a carbon copy each time you write or type a letter. If you are using a home computer, print off two copies, one for them and one for your records.

---

4 The address on the left-hand side is called the 'inside address'. It lets everyone know to whom the letter is being sent, so that the envelope in which it arrived can be discarded.
5 The words 'Dear Sir' are called the 'salutation', or greeting. If the advertisement gives the name of a female Personnel Officer (Mrs J. Baker) the internal address would read Mrs J. Baker, Personnel Officer, and the salutation would be 'Dear Madam'.
6 The underlined section below the salutation is called the 'subject heading'. Every business letter starts with a subject heading especially if it is only mentioning one topic, as in this case.
7 The first paragraph of the letter is the key sentence – it tells the reader the whole point of the letter – 'Please may I have the application form'.
8 The second paragraph is just a brief mention of your qualifications, to give them some idea that it is worth while considering you. You are obviously young (and therefore suitable for a trainee), you have a technical background which might be helpful to someone planning kitchens and bathrooms (where tiles are chiefly used).
9 The phrase 'Yours faithfully' is called the 'complimentary close' and is a polite way of ending a letter to someone you do not know personally or professionally.
10 If you are typing a letter, always type your name and then sign above it. If you are writing your name, sign it legibly and *not* with an illegible flourish.

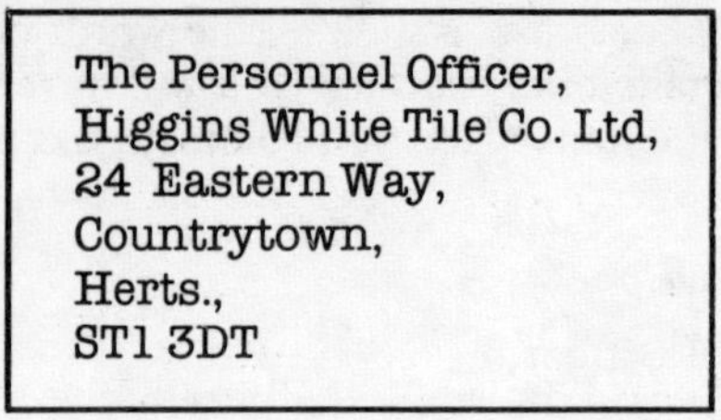

```
The Personnel Officer,
Higgins White Tile Co. Ltd,
24 Eastern Way,
Countrytown,
Herts.,
ST1 3DT
```

Figure 17.4   An envelope typed in fully blocked style

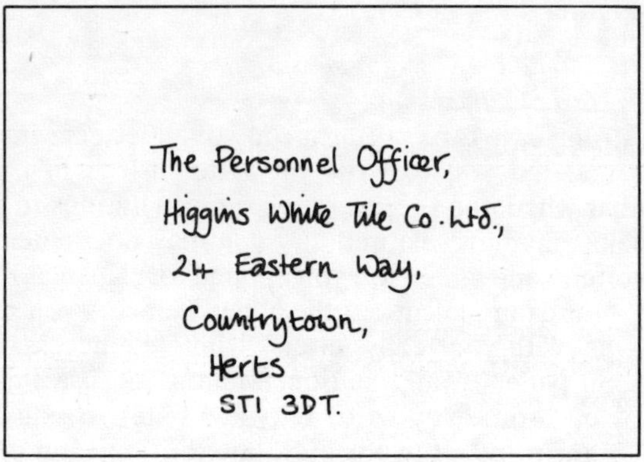

```
The Personnel Officer,
Higgins White Tile Co. Ltd,
24 Eastern Way,
Countrytown,
Herts
ST1 3DT.
```

Figure 17.5   An envelope in handwritten style

Letter No. 2:   Returning an application form (see Figure 17.6)

Our second letter is again a brief letter to cover the return of an application form. The following points are of interest:

1   Firms are frequently busy and may have to deal with many applications so that it is impossible to acknowledge their safe arrival. If you want to know that your application has been received safely you can enclose a stamped addressed envelope for return of a slip of paper, as indicated in Figure 17.6. This is particularly easy to do if you have plenty of labels made out to yourself. This brief addition to your letter is easily torn off and returned to you – provided you have remembered to enclose that stamped addressed envelope.
2   If you enclose any items it is helpful to put a list of the items at the bottom left-hand corner, starting with the word Enclosures (or Enc). As you put the letter into the envelope you check that the enclosures are included as well. You can clip the items together with a treasury tag if you wish.

Peter Bracey,
10 Wildflower Walk,
Peartree Way,
Newtown,
Herts.,
ST3 5PQ

The Personnel Officer,
Higgins White Tile Co. Ltd,
24 Eastern Way,
Countrytown,
Herts.,
ST1 3DT

3 November 19xx

My ref: Job application
No. 5

Dear Sir,

Completed Application Form – Trainee Planning Clerk

My completed application form for this post is
enclosed. I hope you will find it satisfactory and will be
kind enough to grant me an interview.

Would you please acknowledge its safe receipt by
returning the slip at the bottom of this letter in the
enclosed s.a.e.

Thanking you for your courtesy, and I hope to hear
from you in due course.

Yours faithfully,

Enclosures: Peter Bracey.
1 Completed application form
2 SAE for acknowledgement

- -

Higgins White Tile Co. Ltd,
24 Eastern Way,
Countrytown,
Date: . . . .   Herts., ST1 3DT

We acknowledge receipt of your application form, which
is receiving attention.

Signed . . . .

Figure 17.6   Returning an application form

Letter No. 3:   Acknowledging an invitation to an interview
                   (see Figure 17.7)

Note that this is a brief letter, which is only intended to confirm that
their invitation has arrived and that you will put in an appearance as
requested. If you do not acknowledge such an invitation it leaves the
firm concerned just a little bit uncertain as to whether you received
the letter and will actually appear. Many applicants fail to turn up as
requested, because in the meantime they have accepted another post,
or on reflection feel the job they applied for is for some reason
unsuitable. It goes without saying that such applicants bring the
school or college from which they are applying into a certain amount
of disrepute. There may be three or four quite important members of
staff acting as an interview panel and they will not be pleased to be
treated so casually. If you acknowledge the invitation you will rise in
the estimation of the Personnel Officer, since it is clear you know how

---

Peter Bracey,
10 Wildflower Walk,
Peartree Way,
Newtown,
Herts.,
ST3 5PQ

The Personnel Officer,
Higgins White Tile Co. Ltd,   9 November 19xx
24 Eastern Way,
Countrytown,   My ref: Job application
Herts.,   No. 5
ST1 3DT

Dear Sir,

               Interview 17 November 19xx 10.30 am —
                         Eastern Way offices

       Thank you very much for inviting me to an
interview at the time and place shown above. I confirm
that I shall attend, and will bring my original certificates
as requested.

                                      Yours faithfully,

                                      Peter Bracey.

Figure 17.7   A letter acknowledging an invitation to be interviewed

to behave in a business situation and appreciate their courtesy in inviting you to attend the interview panel.

Letter No. 4: Acknowledging a letter of appointment
(see Figure 17.8)

A letter of appointment should always be acknowledged, if only because it makes a binding contract between you and the employer. In law a contract consists of three parts, an offer, the acceptance of the offer by the offeree (the one to whom the offer was made) and valuable consideration. Valuable consideration means that the offer, or the acceptance, is one where money (or some other valuable)

The Personnel Officer,
Higgins White Tile Co. Ltd,
24 Eastern Way,
Countrytown,
Herts.,
ST1 3DT

Peter Bracey,
10 Wildflower Walk,
Peartree Way,
Newtown,
Herts.,
ST3 5PQ

21 November 19xx

My ref: Job application
No. 5

Dear Sir,

Letter of appointment – to commence work on
3 January 19xx

Thank you very much for the letter of appointment received today, after my interview on 17 November. I confirm that I shall start work as requested on 3 January and that my parents have agreed to equip me with the specialist tools and drawing instruments etc., specified in your technician's list. I look forward to joining the company, and appreciate this opportunity to become an apprentice technician.

Yours faithfully,

Peter Bracey.

Figure 17.8 Acknowledging a letter of appointment

forms part of the bargain being made. If a firm sends you a letter of appointment this is an offer to appoint you as their employee on certain terms laid out in the letter. These term usually include some statement about the salary payable, which is the valuable consideration offered. All you have to do to accept the position offered is to acknowledge the offer made and express your willingness to commence work as suggested. A formal contract of employment will be offered later – the law allows a short period before the formal contract is offered so that it becomes clear that both parties are satisfied with the arrangement. New employees may find the work so different from what they imagined that they want to end the arrangement very quickly, and it would be a waste of time and money for an official contract of employment to be drawn up in that situation.

Letter No. 5:   A letter expressing disappointment

If you receive a letter from a prospective employer which regrets that a post cannot be offered to you, the tone of the letter may reveal how close you came to being the chosen candidate. If it appears that only some minor matter prevented you being selected, and if the position is one that you really feel keen about, it is often a good idea to put your disappointment to them in writing. For a variety of reasons the chosen candidate may in fact not take up the post offered. For example, an excellent candidate may get offers from several firms or companies and can only accept one. Often a candidate who does well at an interview may decide that the interviewing panel did less well – leading him/her to conclude that the job is less desirable than he/she first thought. A disappointed candidate who expressed a keen desire to take up a post may well find it is not too late after all. Figure 17.9 suggests a typical letter of this sort.

17.8   Curriculum vitae

When applying for jobs for which an application form is not required, or when applying to a firm or company speculatively to ask if they have a vacancy it is usual to enclose a *curriculum vitae*, which is often abbreviated to 'CV'. The words mean 'the course of my life'. The CV gives a brief account of your qualifications and achievements to date. You should draw up a CV to fit your own particular circumstances. It is best to get it typed, and run off half a dozen copies at the local copy centre. It does need updating from time to time as you acquire further qualifications and experience. In a period when you are actively applying for jobs always keep a few CVs available so that you do not delay an application for lack of a CV to enclose.

A typical wording is shown in Figure 17.10.

Peter Bracey,
10 Wildflower Walk,
Peartree Way,
Newtown,
Herts.,
ST3 5PQ

The Personnel Officer,
Higgins White Tile Co. Ltd,
24 Eastern Way,
Countrytown,
Herts.,
ST1 3DT

22 November 19xx

My ref: Job application
No. 5

Dear Sir,

Failure at interview
(Your letter dated 20 November 19xx)

It was extremely disappointing to receive your
letter today in which you inform me that you are unable
to take me on as a Trainee Planning Clerk. I felt that the
interview went fairly well, despite the fact that one or two
of the other candidates had better academic qualifications
than myself. My hope was that I could compensate by my
enthusiasm and my practical bent for these shortcomings
in the qualification field.

Is there any chance please that you could put me on
a waiting list, or allow me to apply again next Summer
when I shall have completed my examinations? I did feel
that the job seemed a most appropriate one for me, and I
would not like to start looking elsewhere if there is any
chance of being reconsidered. If that is a possibility
perhaps you could let me know which further
examination passes would weigh more heavily in my
favour at a further interview. There are several months
still before the examinations, and a real effort in such
subjects might enable me to improve my chances. Any
guidance you can give me would be much appreciated.

Yours faithfully,

Peter Bracey.

Figure 17.9 A letter expressing disappointment

Curriculum vitae

Name: Julietta Debotista

Address: 2742 High St, Chadwell St Mary, Grays, Essex

Telephone No.:   (0375) 975924

Marital status: Single

Date of birth: 3 November 19xx

Education: (i)   St Olave's Secondary School
             (ii)   Grays Tertiary College
             (iii)   Thurrock Technical College

Qualifications: GCSE   Maths (E); English (B); History (C); Biology (B); French (C); German (C); Creative Arts (B); Music (B).

             A Levels   Business Studies (D); French (C); General Studies (C).

Current course: Accounting Technicians' Course

Employment experience: Part-time posts in a number of shops. Employment training course and holiday work (keyboard operating) Helpful Bank PLC.

Non-vocational interests: Swimming, rock-climbing, singing (Youth choir), orchestra.

Posts of responsibility: Member of Student Union Recreational Committee, Thurrock Technical College.

Figure 17.10   A curriculum vitae

17.9   Testimonials and references

A testimonial is a certificate of character, conduct and qualifications, issued by an employer, head teacher, careers teacher, or other person in a position of responsibility. It usually takes the form of a letter, given to the person whose character etc., is being described, so that he/she may show it to anyone when applying for a job, or for membership of an organization, club, etc. It is of general interest, not related to any particular future employment or suitability for a named post. It often begins:

'To whom it may concern'

for it is likely to be presented to almost anyone. It then continues by stating that the person who signed it does know the person named in the testimonial, and believes them to be of good character, honest, industrious, etc.

There are many occasions when a student needs such a testimonial, and it is always difficult if a student cannot find anyone to provide one. It is as important to establish a good name as any other qualification on earth. 'Who steals my purse steals trash . . . But he that filches from me my good name robs me of that which not enriches him, and makes me poor indeed', says Iago in Shakespeare's play *Othello*. It is always desirable at the end of any period of work, whether it is part-time or full-time, or at the end of any position of responsibility, to ask the person in charge if they would write you a testimonial. You never know when such a written recognition of your character will be helpful.

Sometimes a person asked for a testimonial in this way may well reply 'Well, I could of course do so, but I think it would be better if you used my name as a referee.' This means that in any application for employment or where a character reference is needed you may give the person's name, address and telephone number. This is very helpful, but there is one point worth knowing. A referee asked to give an opinion about you is in a situation called 'qualified privilege'. In law this means that anything written or said to someone who asks the referee for an opinion is privileged – and cannot be the subject of legal action. The referee is entitled to say what he/she believes is the truth about you, and you cannot complain if your bad points are mentioned as well as your favourable points.

17.10 Interviews: the firm's or company's viewpoint

In this chapter we are viewing recruitment from two aspects – the firm's point of view and the point of view of the applicant for employment. Taking the firm's or company's point of view first, the aim is to fill whatever vacancies are available with suitable people who will stay with the firm for some considerable time and thus recoup the expenses involved in recruiting them, and solve the firm's personnel problems. The applicants' qualifications, experience and skill will be of paramount importance, but their long-term aspirations and aims are almost equally important. If we take them on, and induct them properly, and teach them everything they need to know, will they stay with us? Will they regard the firm's advancement as being as important to them as their own advancement? Naturally a firm cannot expect a lifetime dedication to the firm, but they are looking for a reasonable span of service reflecting the grade of post being offered, and they do hope that the 'Man/Girl Friday' of today will be the supervisor of five years hence and the Managing Director twenty-five years hence. (A Man/Girl Friday is a popular advertising phrase meaning – like Robinson Crusoe's friend on the desert island – a generally helpful person who can turn his/her hand to anything that is required.)

Preparing for the interview

Generally speaking we begin by preparing a shortlist of the best applicants and taking up references about them. We may make telephone enquiries about them and if so it is helpful to use a Pre-employment Telephone Enquiry Form as we make the call. This helps us ask the correct questions, without overlooking anything, and gives us a little space to jot down notes on each point. Often a tone in the former employer's voice will convey as much as the words said – he/she may be cheerfully enthusiastic or gloomily hesitant.

When calling for a written reference it is usual to include details of the post for which the applicant is applying and a stamped addressed envelope for reply. We are asking the referee not only for an opinion of the applicant's general ability and integrity, but also for an opinion of his/her suitability for the post we have in mind. A person may be perfectly honest and upright but still have little prospects of being successful at the job proposed.

All the information collected about a candidate should be collated before the interview and if necessary duplicated to give everyone on the interview panel a copy. If this is too expensive a member of the personnel staff might draw up a digest of the most important points and make this available for all the panel before the meeting so that they can look through the details.

The interview itself

Interviews are becoming more and more formal affairs these days, because all sorts of problems can arise if racial or sexual discrimination can be held to have been practised at the interview. It is therefore essential to have more than one person present if at all possible, and for a written record to be kept. To this end a small panel is usually appointed to interview candidates, and some division of the questioning is usually devised. Thus the Head of Department where the applicant hopes to work might enquire about qualifications, experience and skills, while the Personnel Officer asks about

long-term aims and ambitions, and a third person asks about family
and health background, etc. The aim is to give the candidate an
opportunity to express his/her opinions, expectations etc., not to
merely answer 'yes' or 'no'. Thus a question 'Did you get a Grade B
in Maths? calls for a 'Yes' or 'No' answer, but a sentence like 'There is
a good deal of Mathematics in this type of job – how do you feel
about Mathematics?' is likely to reveal quite a lot about the candidate's mathematical background. He/she may wax enthusiastic, or be
hesitant, or confess to a weakness in Mathematics, but an intention to
study the subject now its importance has been pointed out.

Remember, especially when interviewing top-quality candidates,
that the panel is being interviewed too. An unfriendly or un-
sympathetic interview will seriously prejudice the applicant against
the firm, and may lose the organization a potentially promising
employee. It is usual to include at the end of an interview the
question 'If we do decide to offer you an appointment will you accept
the offer?' This gives the applicant who has already decided against
the firm or company the chance to indicate, however hesitantly, that
other offers may be more attractive, while an applicant who responds
enthusiastically may influence the panel in his/her selection.

17.11 Interviews: the applicant's viewpoint

An applicant for employment should prepare for an interview as
thoroughly as the panel who are conducting the interview. One can
usually anticipate most of the questions that will be asked and there is
a lot to be said for preparing a written answer to those which seem to
be particularly important. 'Writing maketh an exact man' said one
philosopher, and to set down in writing what you feel about any
subject cannot but improve your performance at any interview. Of
course the subjects that spring to mind vary with every job, so it is
difficult to pinpoint examples. Some questions that occur most often
are these:

'What do you think you can bring to this company?'

This gives you an opportunity to list your skills, your experience and
your interests. It may enable you to show how deeply you have
thought about the company itself and its markets. You might suggest
that it appears to be going in certain directions and you could say
which of these directions particularly interests you. You might comment on present products, and related areas where you envisage
developments could take place. You might only be able to offer a
sincere commitment to routine activities and express the hope that
you would gain experience and find a field, at present unknown to

you, where you could usefully pull your weight in the general interests of the company. A young and inexperienced person must offer enthusiasm and hard work with some idea of the areas that interest him/her.

'Where do you see yourself in fifteen years time?'

One applicant who answered this question by saying 'Doing your job?' to the Managing Director who asked it was not as favourably received as perhaps he had hoped, but the other members of the panel enjoyed the response. Such a question gives you a chance to air your understanding of the various levels of work. For example most people, given fifteen years, can reach full professional status in any industry, with the qualifications and experience to become full members of the professional body, whatever it is. A list of professional bodies is given in the Appendix of this book, with their names and addresses. You might like to look through this list and see which institutes have some appeal to you. It gives a useful subject of discussion to suggest that one of these institutes is the sort of professional body for which you would seek to qualify, and a letter addressed to the institute concerned will bring you a number of brochures about student membership. Remember though, that the term student does not mean merely an academic student, but someone gaining experience in the industry while studying part-time or by correspondence.

'What interests you about this post for which you are applying?'

Here you have a much more limited field to expand upon. The post may be a relatively low-level position. You should express your confidence in your ability to perform it. Think through the likely tasks you will have to perform and from your knowledge and limited past experience justify your claim to hold the job down and do it well. Then go on to expand upon the opportunities you hope it will lead to in the future. Any job is simply a foot in the door – you don't know until you get in what other opportunities it will lead to but you should be able to envisage two or three avenues you would not mind exploring. Think these avenues through – because it is a favourite ploy of interviewers to lead you on and on until they have marched you up to the frontiers of your knowledge. Make sure you can take them at least some way up the career ladder in each direction and then say 'Well, that's really as far as I've gone in thinking about these opportunities but I am sure there is still more to come. I want to reach a sound performance level whatever avenue the company points me down. I've got wide interests and feel sure the opportunities will come if I prove myself in this particular position.'

A common conclusion to an interview is to ask the applicant if he/she has any questions for the panel. Think up one or two questions which you could ask at this point, avoiding questions which have already been dealt with in the interview, for example, salary, working hours, etc. There may be special requirements that you want them to meet; for example some examination or other event you need to attend; some travel facility or accommodation facility you are hoping they can assist with. A question about training, educational needs, etc., may be appropriate. If you feel very satisfied with the interview and there is nothing further you need to know, say so and say how much you have appreciated the interview and hope for a successful outcome.

17.12 Inducting a new member of staff

New members of staff have to be inducted into the firm or company. The first day of employment is an important day for the new recruit, and may well be remembered all his/her life. It is important to make the day memorable by a formal welcome, which looks optimistically forward to a long and mutually beneficial association. At the same time the induction period is one which has legal overtones, since it establishes in great detail the contractual relationship between the two parties (employer and employee) and also the duties of care between the parties. For example, the employer has a duty to ensure a safe system of work, and a duty to pay the agreed wage or salary. Equally, the employee has a duty to perform the work agreed in a proper manner, to behave in a proper way, to be punctual, regular in attendance, solicitous of the employer's business interests, etc.

The best plan is to follow a list of induction activities such as the one illustrated in Figure 17.11. It lists all the employer's expectations and requirements covering the everyday working procedures and deals with various aspects of health, safety, transport, protective clothing, etc. It is an NCR (no carbon required) two-part set, which enables both employer and employee to retain a signed copy at the end of the induction period, as proof that the employee acknowledges that the range of points listed has been covered. This becomes part of the employee's records and will be retained on file. Thus if the induction checklist includes reference to a no-smoking rule in a part of the plant where fire is a particular hazard, an employee later found to be recklessly disregarding the rule could be warned for this behaviour, and could not deny being made aware of the danger.

An induction meeting usually ends with the new staff being given a tour of the departments, where some of the key staff can be introduced and perhaps allowed to make a few points about the work of their departments.

Figure 17.11 An induction checklist (courtesy of Formecon Services Ltd, Crewe)

17.13 A project about recruitment

(a) Make a collection from local and national newspapers of advertisements about jobs that would be appropriate for your group. (b) Select one advertisement. Drawing names from a hat at random, select one of your group to be the applicant for this advertisement and three people to form the interview panel. Repeat this with another advertisement until everyone in the group has a part to play, either as an applicant or a panel member. (c) With the applicants working on their own, and the panel members in groups of three, do some preliminary work in preparation for the interview. (d) In turn, playing the roles you have been assigned, conduct the interviews. (e) Critically appraise the performances of the parties, suggesting positive improvements in the approach or attitude displayed.

17.14 Rapid revision

Answers	*Questions*
–	**1 What is a personnel requisition?**
1 It is a request from a head of department to the Personnel Officer asking him/her to recruit, or arrange the transfer from elsewhere in the company, of a suitable person to perform a particular job.	**2 What does the requisition do?**
2 (a) It lists all the details of the person required, including not only the skills but the desirable personal qualities for the post; (b) it often includes a full job description; (c) it then becomes the basic mechanism for recruiting the person required.	**3 What points need to be noted when drawing up a job description?**
3 (a) A clear idea of the work to be performed; (b) a general proviso that a cooperative attitude re other duties will be expected; (c) some idea of the level of the	

Answers	Questions
job – for comparison with other functions; (d) the authority and discretion of the jobholder; (e) the degree of liaison with other staff; (f) any special conditions.	**4 When is the job description used?**
4 (a) During the recruitment process; (b) at regrading and merit-rating reviews of an employee's progress; (c) at times of reappraisal for industrial relations and pay bargaining.	**5 What are the general principles in letter-writing related to jobs?**
5 (a) Keep the letter reasonably formal, rather than personal; (b) use a subject-heading line to pinpoint the nature of the letter; (c) give references and dates of earlier correspondence; (d) make your points as lucidly as possible in short paragraphs; (e) take copies of all letters if possible.	**6 What is a CV?**
6 A curriculum vitae – which means 'the course of my life' and gives a brief account of a person's qualifications and experience.	**7 What is a testimonial?**
7 An open letter bearing witness to a person's character and qualifications, which may be shown to anyone interested.	**8 What is a referee?**
8 A person who has consented to the use of his/her name, address and telephone number for the purpose of giving written or oral information about a former employee or acquaintance.	**9 How should an employer approach an interview with a potential employee?**
9 (a) In as well-informed a manner as possible, after reading any correspondence, application forms, etc.; (b) after taking up references; (c) with other	**10 How should the applicant approach an interview?**

Answers	Questions
members of a panel to ensure absence of bias; (d) with prepared questions which give the applicant a chance to unfold his/her ideas.	

| 10 (a) As well prepared as possible; (b) learn what you can about the company's products, services, etc.; (c) decide what part you can play in the company and envisage your future development; (d) think through any reservations you have (and seek reassurance about them if necessary). | 11 **What is induction?** |

| 11 It is the process of settling a new person into a firm, and clarifying any problems. The company wants to lay down certain ground rules; emphasize health, safety, employment rules, etc. The employee wants to be informed about his/her duties, rights and privileges. | 12 **Go over the test again until you are sure of all the answers. Then try the questions in Section 17.15 below.** |

17.15 Questions on Chapter 17

1 The Roman Valley Employment Agency advertises a vacancy with a client which particularly appeals to you. Write a letter asking for the application form. You may invent your own 'job' to suit your personal interests. The agency's address is 20 High St, Localtown NE7 2DP.

2 The Personnel Officer and the applicant for a position have totally different attitudes to a vacancy. Explain these different attitudes.

3 Draw up a CV for yourself giving full details of your qualifications, experience, etc. If you have not yet achieved any qualifications give details of the subjects you are studying and your particular interests.

4 Write a testimonial for your best friend mentioning his/her strengths and weaknesses. In your letter refer to both personal characteristics and scholastic and vocational skills and abilities.

5 (a) Invent five questions to ask an applicant at an interview.

You may choose any career area (job specification) you like.

(b) Now invent three questions the applicant might ask the interviewing panel (but do not refer to either wages, hours of duty or holidays – since we can assume these will have been mentioned at the interview already).

6 When inducting a new member of staff into a firm the Personnel Officer might touch on many matters of importance to both new members of staff and the firm or company. List fifteen points that spring to mind which a Personnel Officer might raise.

7 Write a letter expressing your disappointment after failing to be appointed to a post on which you had particularly set your heart.

18
Incentives in employment

18.1 Why people work

An old jocular remark says:

We go to work, to get the cash, to buy the food, to get the strength, to go to work, to get the etc., etc.

While it is true that to some extent work is a bit of a treadmill, it is also a way of achieving status, self-esteem and the esteem of one's peer groups. For those who see the world as a vast collection of economies, all interwoven and with their own specialist contributions to make to the produce and output of the world, work is no real problem. There are an infinite variety of jobs; one may do one thing for a few years and then change to something else; it only takes about three years to master almost any job and with the economy developing so fast some methods of production are bound to go out of use and be replaced by new technologies. If we keep young in outlook, and keep our enthusiasm about the world in which we live, we shall always find somewhere to work usefully.

Why do people work? First – we work because, as Karl Marx did say, most of us have nothing else to sell but our labour power, and that is the way we earn our bread and butter. The other resources available to mankind – land and capital are in short supply. In the UK William the Conqueror seized all the land and infeudated it to lesser men, barons and earls and knights. A few of their descendants still own some of it, and other parcels of land have come into the hands of ordinary people. Often by the end of our lives most of us at least own a home and fifty feet square of garden, but with 55 million of us land is in short supply. Similarly capital, while it is more abundant than it used to be, is in short supply too. 'Labour we can all supply – if we are willing.' Every mouth that comes into the world has two hands to work for it.

Second, we work in a particular job because that is something that appeals to us relative to other jobs that are available. Most of us still choose the work we will do – we just don't look at jobs that don't appeal to us. We may have a little difficulty in getting the right education, or the right training, or the right experience but you can get almost anything you want if you just work single-mindedly towards it. Business Studies students are better placed than most for there are so many different jobs going, and almost any job is good experience for other jobs. The young despatch rider working as a courier in the London traffic finishes up running an insurance office because he has the right experience (after all those accidents).

18.2   Incentives for young people

The financial incentive

The first incentive to a school or college leaver is the job itself and the financial reward that comes from it. One has to strike a balance between a sensible appraisal of one's own knowledge and ability, and willingness to work, against the value to the firm or company that your work will achieve. Like any other contract the contract of employment has to be mutually beneficial. If you are manifestly putting more into the job than you are getting out of it you will leave sooner or later. If you are manifestly not worth what they are having to pay you they will find some excuse to terminate the employment sooner or later too. Whatever the starting rate of pay, do the job to the very best of your ability, and prove to yourself that they are getting value for money. Then ask for a rise. Do not be afraid to explain that you have worked hard and you do like the job (or are prepared to put up with its drawbacks) but that you do feel a rise is in order – or at least you want them to know that you are looking for a reassessment of your salary when an appropriate time comes round.

Besides pay, which is the most vital element, the other things young people need are training, qualifications and a reasonably pleasant working environment.

The training incentive

Every young person needs training, and the need arises at all levels. A formal programme of training is probably best, and we might note the following stages:

1 *Induction training*   This has already been mentioned. It involves introducing the new employee to the layout of the firm; the chief departments and the work they do; the potential hazards and difficulties; the rules of conduct, etc. This is followed by stage 2.
2 *Job training*   The new employee has to be introduced to the department in which he/she will work; the variety of activities

performed in the working day and the best way of performing them. Each job has its routine; its system of operations. We shall understand the job better if we know why things are done in a certain way – and what sort of results follow from them. For example, some jobs produce an output – an actual product. Others may be maintenance jobs – they do not produce any output but they prevent breakdowns which otherwise would interfere with output. Other jobs exist for safety reasons – to prevent fires, asbestosis, dust explosions, etc. Many powders are highly explosive even if they have no connection with explosive substances – for example flour, sugar and many chemicals. A recent devastating fire on the London Underground was largely due to poor maintenance and the accumulation of fluff and dust, in circumstances where fire might easily occur. On-the-job training teaches about the employee's immediate present post. Once the employee has settled in the training incentive moves to a higher level.

3   *Advancement training*   Once an employee has settled in, new horizons have to be opened up before him/her. The employee's horizon should be enlarged within the firm, but in an outward-looking way towards the whole industry. Thus the young banker will move up from a routine level to a higher, more specialist level. Eventually it will be to a level where the bank which is the actual employer is seen as only a part of the general banking field, set in its environment of the whole banking industry. This process must take several years – but the long vista of 'advancement' training is part of the incentive package management devises to reduce labour turnover, train up staff for higher level posts and keep staff loyal and cooperative. Some advancement training is 'in-house' training, where we learn the specialist aspects of our own company's procedures and activities. Other training may be day or evening release to technical colleges and specialist training seminars for particularly complex matters – for example such courses are often arranged to deal with new legislation and similar developments.

4   *Full professional qualification*   The ultimate result of 'advancement' training should be full professional qualification and membership of the appropriate professional body for the industry concerned. You take up 'student membership' by registering as a student of the professional body, and you start to study the theory behind your industry at the same time as you learn the practical affairs of the industry in your employment. One philosopher said

'Theory, without practice, is barren
Practice, without theory, is blind'

Professional people learn both the theory and practice of their jobs. Most professional bodies will not accept students until they actually take employment in the industry, because while the theoretician is, we hope, someone who understands and knows about an industry, they cannot possibly get a true understanding of what is involved unless they are in the industry. You cannot be a freight-forwarder if you've never stuffed a container, or a member of the Chartered Insurance Institute if you've never processed a claim. Every Business Studies student should see full professional qualification as the true aim of his/her studies.

The working environment

The third area of incentives for young people is in the general nature of the working environment. This should be reasonably democratic, with a cheerful, optimistic and enthusiastic approach to the work in hand. This will be enhanced if the company's whole approach is one of service to the public, and to the community in general, while at the same time there is a proper recognition of the worth of staff. Management should lead by example rather than autocratically; the supervisor should not be just a taskmaster.

An excessively profit-orientated attitude reduces the quality of life within the firm, especially if it is accompanied by detailed work-measurement and the achievement of 'norms' of output (which are often drawn up without allowances being made for interruptions that inevitably occur in complex industrial and commercial organizations).

An agreeable working environment depends a great deal upon the working situation – heating; lighting; ventilation; absence of draughts; acoustic controls to reduce noise; ergonomically-designed furniture; a full range of other working facilities, etc. If a range of sports facilities, social events, canteen facilities and creche facilities are available these will contribute to the wellbeing of staff, and may encourage job applications and reduce labour turnover. These incentives of course cost money, but their cost is offset to some extent by reduced recruitment costs, and by losses due to staff conflicts and uncooperative behaviour (which can be a feature of firms and companies where such incentives are not available). Students should be aware that many companies today are 'management satisfying' companies. Whereas the sole trader or partnership business under the personal supervision of the proprietor is usually profit-orientated to a very considerable extent, and this would also be the case with many family-run limited companies. The public limited company is often not driven by the profit motive to the same degree. The shareholders who own the company and are entitled to the profits do not have the same degree of influence over the company, and the management is virtually independent of them. Many of the shareholders are more interested in capital gains than in distributed profit, though they usually expect a reasonable dividend each half year. The directors, therefore, are free to run the business in such a way that they make reasonable profits, but also arrange affairs to avoid excessive aggravation in the industrial process. This means that staff can be paid reasonable salaries for reasonable efforts, and funds can be made available for improving the working environment – without looking too closely at the return an improved environment brings. The policy is to keep management and staff satisfied with their lot, because in the end that is the most profitable way to work. There are critics of this approach, but it does not necessarily follow that staff who are well paid and well cared for necessarily become 'fat cats'. Quite the reverse. They may be more loyal, and more resourceful to keep their families enjoying the prosperity to which they have become accustomed.

18.3   Incentive packages for older staff

At the very highest level it is usual to offer incentive packages to older staff, especially those who are invited in from other firms where they are already well-established and earning good salaries. We need not dwell too fully on such matters in an introductory book like this but the following elements may well enter into such a package.

1   An attractive salary scale, including financial benefits associated with results achieved – for example sales turnover, profitability of the whole enterprise, productivity, bonuses, etc.
2   Assistance with housing, health insurance and pension funds.
3   The provision of a company car, and the use of other company facilities (holiday accommodation etc.).

All such benefits in kind are now taxable to some extent at least, being given a notional value by the Inland Revenue Authorities which is counted as extra income and subject to tax. The popular name for such incentives is 'perks' – which is a corruption of the word 'perquisites' – a payment over and above the ordinary wage or salary. In medieval times, when money wages were less than they are today and a guinea a year was a common reward, the perks were often more important than the pay. For example, servants were allowed to take home to their families what was left over from a meal, and the children of harvest workers went 'gleaning' in the fields to collect ears of wheat that had escaped the sickles, or grains that had fallen to the ground during the gathering process.

Points to remember

• The chief incentive to work is the reward earned by working, which enables us to purchase a balanced basket of goods and services, according to our personal tastes and scale of values, for ourselves and our families.

- The second incentive in employment for young people is the chance to acquire skills and experience which will eventually make us secure and prosperous.
- The stages of acquiring security and prosperity are (a) job training, (b) advancement training, (c) full professional qualification.
- The other incentive to employment is the provision of a satisfactory and agreeable working environment. There are many factors which enter into an agreeable working environment – temperature, ventilation, furniture etc., and if a range of social and recreational facilities is also available this will promote labour stability and reduce labour turnover.
- More senior staff may be attracted by incentive packages which include besides an excellent salary structure such perks as help with accommodation, health care, pension funds and the provision of a company car.

18.4   Calculating gross wages

The traditional way of recording hours of work for hourly-paid workers was by 'clocking in and clocking out'. A timing device is placed at the factory gate with clock cards arranged in racks on either side of the clock. An employee entering the factory takes his card from the 'out' rack, puts it into the clock to be stamped and replaces it in the 'in' rack. The result is a clock card similar to the one shown in Figure 18.1. Today sophisticated electronic devices may be used instead of a mechanical clock.

Example

An employee works $47\frac{1}{2}$ hours per week, of which $7\frac{1}{2}$ hours was overtime at time and a half. His rate of pay is £1.85 per hour. What is his gross wage?

$$\text{Total hours payable} = 47\frac{1}{2} + (\frac{1}{2} \text{ of } 7\frac{1}{2})$$
$$= 47\frac{1}{2} + 3\frac{3}{4}$$
$$= 51\frac{1}{4} \text{ hours.}$$

Gross pay = $51\frac{1}{4} \times$ £1.85

$$
\begin{array}{r}
51.25 \\
1.85 \\
\hline
256\ 25 \\
4100\ 00 \\
5125\ 00 \\
\hline
94.81\ 25 \\
\hline
\end{array}
$$

$$= £94.81$$

Name: J. Gardner					
Clock No. 278					
Week No. 1		Commencing	4 April		
Day		In Out	*Less* Lunch-time	Hours worked	Overtime payable
Mon.	a.m.	08.00	$\frac{1}{2}$	$8\frac{1}{2}$	$\frac{1}{4}$
	p.m.	17.00			
Tue.	a.m.	07.59	$\frac{1}{2}$	$8\frac{1}{2}$	$\frac{1}{4}$
	p.m.	17.00			
Wed.	a.m.	08.00	$\frac{1}{2}$	$9\frac{1}{2}$	$\frac{3}{4}$
	p.m.	18.00			
Thur.	a.m.	07.30	$\frac{1}{2}$	$10\frac{1}{2}$	$1\frac{1}{4}$
	p.m.	18.30			
Fri.	a.m.	08.14	$\frac{1}{2}$	$8\frac{1}{4}$	$\frac{1}{8}$
	p.m.	17.00			
Sat.	a.m.	08.00	$\frac{1}{2}$	$8\frac{1}{2}$	$8\frac{1}{2}$
	p.m.	17.00			
Sun.	a.m.	09.00	–	$3\frac{1}{2}$	$3\frac{1}{2}$
	p.m.	12.30			
Overtime rates	Total			$57\frac{1}{4}$	$14\frac{5}{8}$
Weekdays $1\frac{1}{2}$	Add overtime			$14\frac{5}{8}$	
Weekends 2					
	Hours payable			$71\frac{7}{8}$	

Figure 18.1 A clock card

Notes:
1 A normal working day is eight hours.
2 Employees clock in and out only once a day, but half an hour is deducted for meals which are taken in the canteen.
3 Since overtime is at time and a half on weekdays, overtime is calculated by paying the employee for any extra time and overtime equal to half the extra time.
4 At weekends, when overtime is at double-time, the employee is paid for the hours worked and overtime for that number of hours as well.
5 Clock hours are calculated to the nearest quarter of an hour.

18.5   The Simplex Wages System

The Simplex Wages System is a very simple system for the small business which does not employ many staff – there is in fact room for up to twenty-eight employees in the book. The system is illustrated in Figure 18.2, and the notes opposite the illustration explain the chief points.

18.6   The Kalamazoo Wages System

Some three million people in the UK alone are paid their wages weekly or monthly using the Kalamazoo Wages System. This system is an example of **simultaneous records**, a system which avoids copying errors by preparing several sets of records simultaneously using carbon or NCR (no carbon required) paper. A few words of explanation are helpful. To keep proper records of wages three things are required.

1   A **pay advice note** which shows the employee exactly how the pay has been calculated. This is used to make up the wage packet, and enables the employee to check the pay on receipt. Sometimes the packet has small holes in it so that coins can be counted, and the notes can be checked, before opening the packet. Alternatively, if the wages are paid into a bank account the wages slip is the only item in the wage packet, and advises the employee how the wage has been calculated.
2   A **payroll** which lists all payments made for the week or month, and which is the firm's record in a special looseleaf binder.
3   An individual **employee's record card**, which lists all the employee's pay for the year. In any query about pay we can produce this record to discuss it with the employee. We do not want to produce the payroll, for this would enable the employee to see what other staff earn.

In the Kalamazoo system a flat board, called a **copywriter** is used as a backing sheet as shown in Figure 18.3. It has a row of studs at the top over which the various documents can be placed. First comes a set of ten wages advice notes. On top of this is placed the NCR coated payroll form. Then the individual's record card is placed over the top of the payroll form. The week's pay is then entered on the record card. Naturally the entry is copied onto the payroll form and the advice note because of the NCR coating. When the entry is complete the wages clerk takes the next employee's record card, and positions it over the next clean column on the payroll – a few studs up from the previous entry. The perforations in the forms can be seen in Figure

18.3 and in Figure 18.4. Figure 18.3 shows how the system works. The final result is a full set of records, (1), (2) and (3) as explained above. A pay advice note is shown in detail in Figure 18.4.

Statutory sick pay (SSP) and statutory maternity pay (SMP)

These two recent developments in wages payments reflect the anxiety of Governments to streamline procedures which, while actually part of the social security system, could in fact be more easily handled by employers. The fact is that employers are collecting, in tax and national insurance contributions, very considerable sums of Government money. The Government was, by contrast, engaged in paying out many small payments to the same people (employees) when circumstances required it, for sickness pay and maternity allowances. The logical thing was to require employers to pay out these sums of money on the Government's behalf, and reclaim it by deduction from the tax and national insurance contributions. The details of the SSP and SMP systems need not concern us here. The fact is that employees who are ill become entitled to sick pay, and women who become pregnant and leave work temporarily during the confinement period, are entitled to maternity pay. They now find the sums due to them included in their wage packets, and do not have to claim these allowances separately from a Government agency. They are paid as part of their working situation.

18.7 Commission

Commission is money paid as a reward for services which bears a simple percentage relationship to the value of business transacted. Many agents are rewarded by a commission, perhaps 5 per cent of the value of the deal arranged. Many salespeople are paid a basic salary which by itself would not enable the employee to enjoy a very good standard of living, but this is supplemented by a commission related to the sales made.

The following types of commission are used:

1 *Straight commission*   The reward is based on a simple percentage rate of the value of the sales made or business transacted.
2 *Graduated commission*   The reward is graduated, either in increasing steps or decreasing steps. Thus an agent might earn 10 per cent on the first £5,000, 5 per cent on the next £5,000 and 2½ per cent thereafter. The bigger commission at the start encourages the agent to set out in business.
3 *Volume commissions and value commissions*   Volume commissions are paid on the number of articles sold (£10 per machine,

Week Ending _____ Week No _____

NAME		Earnings for Week + Overtime 1	Statutory Sick Pay (S.S.P.) 2	Statutory Maternity Pay (S.M.P.) 3	Total Pay for Week (Col 1 + 2 + 3) 4	Less Allowable Charity Gifts 5	Less Company Pension Scheme 6	Taxable Pay (Col 4-5-6) 7	Employees Deductions — Tax 8	Employees Deductions — National Insurance 9	10	Total Deductions (Col 8 + 9 + 10 + 11)	Net Cash Wage (Col 7-11) 12	Employer's National Insurance 13	Employees Contributions at Contra Out Rate 14
J. STOKES	1	185 80	47 20	-	233 00	-	12 40	220 60	40 77	21 01		61 78	158 82	24 40	-
A. JONES	2	100 00	-	-	100 00	-	4 95	95 05	11 34	9 04		20 38	74 67	9 04	-
B. SEWELL	3	79 00	-	-	79 00	-	-	79 00	14 85	-		14 85	64 15	5 56	
F. SMYTH (MRS)	4	100 00	-	-	132 85	-	-	132 85	23 22	11 92		35 14	97 71	11 92	
	5			32 85											
	6														
	7														
	8														
	9														
	10														
	11														
	27														
	28														
Total		464 80	47 20	32 85	544 85	-	17 35	527 50	90 18	41 97		132 15	395 35	50 92	-

All figures shown are merely for example purposes. Actual deductions should be made by reference to current information from the Inland Revenue and Department of Health and Social Security.

Figure 18.2 The Simplex Wages Book

Notes:

1. The names of the employees are written down the side of the page. Each week when the page is turned over the list of names is still visible.
2. In Column 1 we record the gross pay – which is the earnings for the week and the overtime due.
3. If the employer has to pay any statutory sick pay (SSP) (see Section 18.5) it is added to the pay at this point in Column 2.
4. Similarly any statutory maternity pay (SMP) is added at Column 3. This gives the total pay for the week in Column 4.
5. Certain charitable contributions and company pension contributions are tax free, and these are deducted in Columns 5 and 6 to give the Taxable Pay in Column 7.
6. By using the Tax Tables A and B provided by the Inland Revenue Authorities to all employers it is now possible to work out the tax payable (Column 8) and by using the tables provided by the Department of Social Security the National Insurance Contributions (Column 9).
7. This results in the total deductions shown in Column 11.
8. By taking Column 11 from Column 7 we get the net cash wage, which the employee will find in the wage packet with a wage slip showing the calculation.
9. Finally the employer's contribution to National Insurance is listed in Column 13.
10. Note, that the tax due, and the National Insurance contributions must be accounted for each month and paid to the Inland Revenue, but any SSP and SMP payments in the month may be deducted. The system is very simple and very inexpensive.

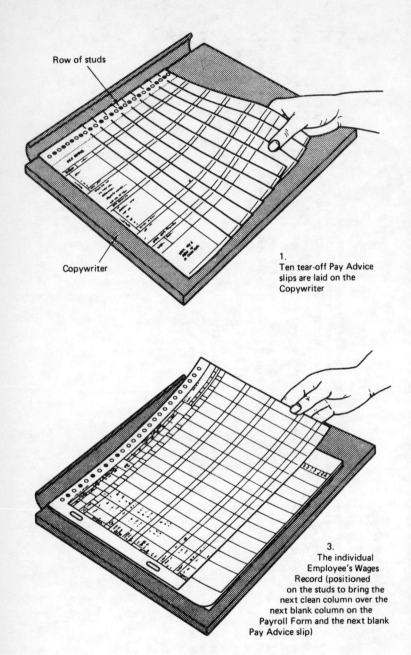

Row of studs

Copywriter

1.
Ten tear-off Pay Advice slips are laid on the Copywriter

3.
The individual Employee's Wages Record (positioned on the studs to bring the next clean column over the next blank column on the Payroll Form and the next blank Pay Advice slip)

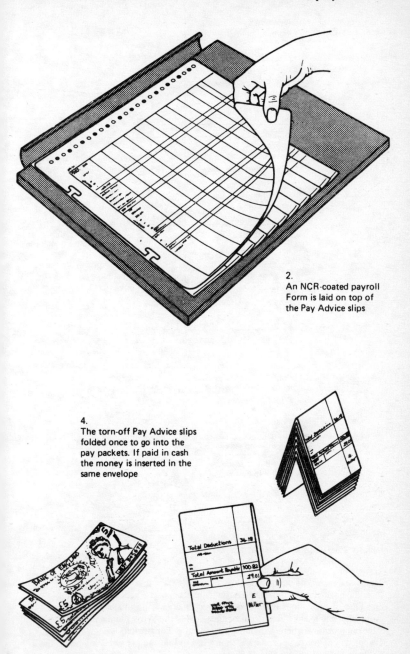

2.
An NCR-coated payroll
Form is laid on top of
the Pay Advice slips

4.
The torn-off Pay Advice slips
folded once to go into the
pay packets. If paid in cash
the money is inserted in the
same envelope

Figure 18.3 The Kalamazoo Wages System (reproduced by courtesy of Kalamazoo Ltd)

Pay Advice

Week or Month No.	Date
'14	10/7

Earnings

Details

A	92 24
B	5 00
C	
D	
E	
SSP	37 76
SMP	- -
Gross Pay	135 00
Superannuation	
Gross Pay less Superannuation	135 00
Gross Pay to Date for Tax Purposes	2 085 00
Tax Free Pay	985 18
Taxable Pay to Date	1,099 82
Tax Due to Date	246 73
Tax Refund	- -

Deductions

Tax	18 56
• N.I. Contribution (Employee)	12 19
1 Xmas Fund	- 75
2 Trade Union	1 00
3	
4	
5	
Total Deductions	32 50
Net Pay	102 50
F Lodging allowance	21 00
Total Amount Payable	123 50
N.I. Contribution (Employer)	12 19
N.I. Total (Employer and Employee)	24 38
G	
• Contracted Out cntb. incl. above	
Earn. on which E'ees. cntb. pybl.	135 00
Earn. on which E'ees. cntb. at CO. rate pybl.	

Your Pay is made up as shown above

Miller
K.E.

Figure 18.4   A Kalamazoo wages advice slip

Notes:

1 The week or month number is shown and the date it commences.
2 There are six lines for types of earning, such as basic wage, overtime, commission, etc. One of these lines is for statutory sick pay (SSP) and another is for statutory maternity pay (SMP). The total of these gives the gross pay.
3 Superannuation is then deducted, because it is not taxable.
4 The gross pay for tax purposes is then used to find the tax payable – using the Tax Tables provided by the Inland Revenue.
5 The deductions are then listed, which gives the net pay.
6 There are then two lines for any additions to net pay – such as refunds of tax overpaid or expenses incurred. This gives the total amount payable.

for example). Where a whole range of items is being sold this is inconvenient and it is better to base the commission on the total value of the goods sold.

Calculations on commission

Straight commission is very simple to calculate. It is merely a percentage rate of the value of business transacted.

Example
An employee is paid a basic wage of £50 per week plus a commission of 5 per cent of sales. In week 23 of the financial year he makes sales of £950. What is his gross pay for the week?

$$\text{Commission} = 5\% \text{ of } 950$$
$$= \tfrac{1}{20} \times £950$$
$$= \frac{£95}{2} \qquad \text{(cancelling by 10)}$$
$$= \underline{\underline{£47.50}}$$

$$\text{Therefore gross pay} = £50 + £47.50$$
$$= \underline{\underline{£97.50}}$$

With **graduated commission** the commission payable is made up of two or more parts. A cut-off point is laid down for each rate of commission payable.

Example
An employee is paid a basic salary of £60 per week, followed by a commission of 2½ per cent on the first £1,000 of sales and 5 per cent thereafter. What will she earn in a week when sales total £4,700?

$$\text{Commission on the first } £1,000 = 2\tfrac{1}{2}\% \text{ of } £1,000$$
$$= \tfrac{1}{40} \times £1,000$$
$$= \underline{\underline{£25}}$$

$$\text{Commission on the balance} = 5\% \text{ of } £3,700$$
$$= \tfrac{1}{20} \times £3,700$$
$$= \underline{\underline{£185}}$$

$$\text{Gross pay} = £60 + £25 + £185$$
$$= \underline{\underline{£270}}$$

7 The employer who also needs to know what the total cost was for National Insurance – in this case the employer has to pay £12.19 making £24.38 in all.
8 Two useful systems for statutory sick pay and statutory maternity pay are available from Formecon Services Ltd, Gateway, Crewe CW1 1YN.

18.8   Bonus schemes and other forms of remuneration

There are many methods of paying wages and salaries besides time rates – so much per hour, per week or per month. Some of these schemes are complicated, having been arrived at after long hours of negotiation between trade unions and management. The general idea behind all of them is that the wage or salary payable should reflect to some extent not only the presence of the employee going about his/her ordinary work, but also the positive contribution made to productivity. Thus a skilled, efficient worker who turns out a lot of product should be rewarded better than an unskilled, inefficient employee. It is often difficult to decide such incentive payments – for example the fast worker on a lathe or other machine may actually be dependent on a whole team of people who feed work to him/her and clear the production lines after output has been achieved. Sometimes 'team bonuses' are used to pay according to the output of the team, with an agreed method of sharing the bonus among the team members.

The chief ways of arranging payments are time rates, piece rates, individual bonus schemes and team bonus schemes.

Time rates

Time rates are used for most jobs where (a) a young person is learning the trade or (b) it is difficult to measure the work achieved (as in oil refinery work where the process of refining crude oil goes on without the employee being able to do very much at all to influence productivity). The time worked is measured on some sort of clock card or electronic register of time, and the time worked multiplied by the hourly rate of pay plus any special allowance for overtime, Sunday working, unsocial hours, etc. gives the payment due. Other staff may be paid a weekly wage, or a monthly salary, and there are few, if any, extra payments.

The trouble with such methods is that there is no real incentive to work harder – the 'self-starter' does more than his/her fair share of work, and is 'underpaid', the lazy member of staff gets away with an unsatisfactory performance and is really overpaid.

Piece rates

Piece work is payment by the piece produced, irrespective of the time taken. Thus a slow worker, or a person new to the trade, might only turn out a few items and earn a low wage, whereas the skilled worker produces a larger output and makes an excellent pay packet each week. The system is open to abuse, because the poorest workers may find it difficult to manage on their low pay, and others may rush the work to such an extent that 'rejected work' results (often sold as 'seconds'). There has to be some sort of quality control and – on the other hand – workers may find that they cannot earn as much as they hoped because machines break down, or materials are in short supply, etc. An excessively harsh piece rate system is often called a 'sweat-shop', with employees seriously overworked trying to produce enough units of output to make a decent wage. Trade unions in the last fifty years have done much to improve the work of these in such trades as the clothing industry and light manufacturing, so that sweat-shops are not as common as formerly. An improved method of payment is **piece-work with guaranteed day rates**. This pays an employee a guaranteed wage per day, or week, but also an agreed rate per unit produced. If the output achieved pushes the wage above the guaranteed rate the employee is paid the extra – if the output is low the worker cannot earn less than the guaranteed weekly wage.

Individual bonus schemes (often called premium bonus schemes)

The general idea is that all jobs are given an estimated time, and a worker gets a guaranteed rate of pay per hour for the job. If high levels of output are achieved, and the job is done in a shorter time, the worker gets a share of the time saved, usually 50 per cent.

Suppose a job is timed to take 60 hours, but the worker actually does it in 40 hours. The worker will be paid for 40 hours work, but will get a bonus of 50 per cent of the time saved. 50 per cent of 20 hours is 10 hours, so the worker who has done 40 hours work is paid for 50 hours. If wages are £3 an hour, the normal wage would be £120 (40 × £3) but the bonus would bring in another £30, raising the pay to £150 in all.

Group bonus schemes

Similar to the above, but taking account of the work of a whole team, the bonus will be calculated for the group, and then shared among them in some fair way. Details of such schemes are too complex for a book of this sort, but the chief point to realize is that the arrangement is mutually beneficial – the employees get more pay but the employer gets a reduced cost of labour per unit of output (because – using the example mentioned above – a unit designed to take 60 hours of work actually only cost the employer 50 hours of work and was actually finished in 40 hours making it easier to meet deadlines on the delivery of finished goods – always a help in any industry).

18.9   A project on wages

It is very instructive, especially from the point of view of career choice, to know what people earn. Unfortunately few people will reveal their true earnings (except to the Income Tax Inspector). It is therefore worthwhile to make a systematic study of newspaper advertisements and specialist magazines (such as the science press, the accountancy press, insurance and banking papers, etc.). Start to build up a class collection of wage and salary scales and put them into alphabetical order. For comparison purposes it is best to change all hourly rates of pay to a weekly wage based on a 40-hour week. Thus an office junior at £2.35 per hour would be given as earning £94.00 per week.

Where the wage paid is given monthly (it may be called a salary) show it as a monthly figure. Reduce all earnings given at an annual figure (many advertisements read £17,500 p.a. and car) to a monthly figure by dividing by twelve. An interesting point here is that there is no difference in law between wages and salaries. The word salary actually comes from the Latin word *salarium*, meaning salt-money (an extra payment made to soldiers on campaigns in Africa, to enable them to buy salt – or as one joker put it – the original sweated labour).

Include any reference to perks such as the use of a car, in your final list of salaries payable.

Present your project as a short report on the earnings of such classes of workers as you can find details about. Do not forget that all such wages are gross wages, from which deductions for tax and National Insurance contributions will be made, to leave a final 'net pay'.

18.10   Rapid revision

Answers	Questions
–	**1 We go to work, to get the cash, . . . (continue)**
1 . . . to buy the food, to get the strength, to go to work, etc.	**2 What are the basic resources of mankind?**
2 Land, labour and capital – the factors of production.	**3 What is special about labour?**

Answers	Questions
3 It is the human factor. We can nearly all offer labour as our contribution to the production of the world.	**4 What are the rewards of labour?**
4 Wages (or salaries), status, self-esteem and the esteem of others (but particularly our peers).	**5 What are 'peers'?**
5 People of the same level as ourselves. It is a fact that we care little for the high and mighty, or for those below us, but we do like to be recognized by our equals as worthy and upright people.	**6 What are the stages of training?**
6 (a) Induction training; (b) job training; (c) advancement training; (d) full professional training.	**7 What factors contribute to a satisfactory working environment?**
7 (a) The actual physical environment – furniture, equipment, temperature, humidity, ventilation, etc; (b) the supervisory element – democratic workplaces are more pleasant than authoritarian ones – managers and supervisors should lead by example rather than precept.	**8 What are wages?**
8 The reward paid to labour.	**9 What are the chief methods of rewarding labour?**
9 (a) Time rates (per hour, per week or per month); (b) piece rates (per unit of output); (c) commission (for sales staff).	**10 What is a bonus system?**
10 A system which rewards employees for special efforts and increased productivity. It gives them a share of the time saved if	

Answers	Questions
they work faster than the agreed rate, the extra payment for this time being the bonus.	**11** **What is the Simplex Wages System?**
11 A very simple wages system for small firms which keeps track not only of the wages paid, deductions made, etc., but also of the moneys paid over to the Inland Revenue authorities.	**12** **What is the Kalamazoo Wages System?**
12 A widely used wages system which is a simultaneous records system. The three records required (a) payroll; (b) the individual's pay record and (c) the wages slip or advice note are all produced at once, using NCR paper.	**13** **What is the real advantage of the Kalamazoo System, apart from the fact that the three records are all produced at one writing?**
13 The individual's pay record is on a separate sheet, and can be discussed quite freely without the employee seeing what other people earn.	**14** **Go over the test again, until you are sure of all the answers. Then try the questions in Section 18.11 below.**

18.11   Questions on Chapter 18

1   Calculate the gross pay for the ten members of staff whose clock records show hours of work as follows. All staff work a normal week of 40 hours, and overtime is paid at time and a half (answer correct to nearest penny).

	Name	Hours worked	Extra hours payable	Rate of pay
(a)	Mr Black	47½	?	£2.70
(b)	Mr Gray	45	?	£2.65
(c)	Mr White	40	–	£2.30
(d)	Mrs Green	49	?	£2.50
(e)	Miss Brown	48½	?	£1.80
(f)	Miss Smith	44½	?	£2.10

Name	Hours worked	Extra hours payable	Rate of pay
(g) Miss Plumber	40	–	£2.30
(h) Mr Baker	62	?	£3.95
(i) Mr Cook	65½	?	£3.60
(j) Mrs Barber	48½	?	£3.55

2   Calculate the gross pay for the ten members of staff whose clock records show hours of work as follows. All staff work a 37½-hour week. Overtime is calculated at time and a half on week days and double time at weekends. (Calculations correct to the nearest penny.)

Name	Hours worked	Of which weekend working was	Extra hours payable	Rate of pay
(a) Mr A	37½	–	–	£3.95
(b) Mr B	42½	–	?	£3.80
(c) Mrs C	37½	–	–	£2.85
(d) Mrs D	46	4	?	£1.95
(e) Miss E	45½	4	?	£2.45
(f) Miss F	51	7	?	£2.75
(g) Mr G	53	7	?	£3.60
(h) Mr H	47	4	?	£3.30
(i) Mrs I	46½	–	?	£3.95
(j) Mr J	39½	–	?	£4.20

3   Calculate the commission payable to an agent on the following deals:

(a)	10% on £7250	(b)	10% on £5,335.50
(c)	5% on £485	(d)	5% on £1,850
(e)	2½% on £7,640	(f)	2½% on £19,800
(g)	1% on £175,500	(h)	1% on £1 million
(i)	½% on £2,420,000	(j)	¼% on £80 million

4   A salesforce is remunerated by a basic salary of £120 for which each salesperson is expected to achieve a certain quota of sales which reflects the area in which he or she works. After this quota has been achieved each unit sold brings in a commission of £4.50. Calculate the gross pay of each of the employees listed below.

Name	Quota (in units)	Actual sales (in units)
(a) Mr A	25	29
(b) Mr R	15	27
(c) Mr T	18	32
(d) Mr W	30	58
(e) Mr Y	36	84

5 Sales staff in a store earn a basic monthly salary plus graduated commission related to the sales made and taking account of the department in which they work. What will each of the following staff earn?

	Basic salary	Rate of initial commission	Limit	Higher rate of commission	Sales in month
(a)	£120	1%	£5,000	5%	£8,800
(b)	£135	2%	£8,000	5%	£9,200
(c)	£140	2%	£10,000	5%	£12,700
(d)	£150	2½%	£15,000	10%	£17,200
(e)	£160	2½%	£15,000	10%	£16,900

6 An auctioneer is paid an attendance fee of £10, and then takes a commission of 5 per cent on the first £350 of goods sold, and 10 per cent thereafter. Sales total £722. What was his total fee?

7 An auctioneer is paid an attendance fee of £50, and then takes a commission of 2½ per cent on the first £850 of goods sold, and 5 per cent thereafter. Sales total £8,250. What was his total fee?

8 A commission agent takes 1 per cent of the first £25,000 of sales arranged, and ¼ per cent thereafter. If he sells altogether £282,500 of goods, what was his total commission?

9 A commission agent takes 2 per cent of the first £20,000 of sales arranged, and ½ per cent thereafter. If he sells altogether £175,580 of goods what was his total commission?

10 These exercises are based on the Kalamazoo Wages System.
(*Note:* To complete a full set of Kalamazoo wages records it is essential to have the correct stationery and invent imaginary names, code numbers, etc. Schools and colleges wishing to purchase such stationery should approach the Education Department of Kalamazoo Ltd, Mill Lane, Northfield, Birmingham B31 2RW. For the purpose of the exercises below it is suggested that pay advice notes similar to Figure 18.4 should be ruled up.)
Complete wages advice notes for the four employees A.B.; C.D.; E.F. and G.H., whose pay details are as shown in the following table.

	1 A.B.	2 C.D.	3 E.F.	4 G.H.
Week	1	7	9	16
Date	12.4.19..	24.5.19..	7.6.19..	26.7.19..
Earnings A	66.50	122.50	79.80	84.60
Earnings B	4.55	3.80	17.24	16.60
Earnings C (SSP)	37.40		37.40	
Earnings D (SMP)				
Gross pay	?	?	?	?
Superannuation	3.55	6.32	4.85	5.06

	1 A.B.	2 C.D.	3 E.F.	4 G.H.
Gross pay for tax purposes	?	?	?	?
Gross pay to date for tax purposes	? *(Note:* It is week 1)	836.50	902.60	1582.50
Free pay	26.15	189.70	297.90	553.60
Taxable pay to date	?	?	?	?
Tax due to date	12.30	193.80	181.20	308.40
Tax paid up to last week	–	202.90	166.70	291.20
Tax	?	? *(careful)*	?	?
NI Contribution	5.23	9.30	7.14	7.21
Charity	0.25	0.15	0.15	0.20
Total deductions	?	?	?	?
Net pay	?	?	?	?
Refunds (if any)	?	?	?	?
Total amount payable	?	?	?	?
NI contribution (employer)	9.25	16.44	12.63	13.17
NI total	?	?	?	?

Answers to Questions on Chapter 18

1 (a) £138.38; (b) £125.88; (c) £92; (d) £133.75; (e) £94.95; (f) £98.18; (g) £92.00; (h) £288.35; (i) £281.70; (j) £187.26.
2 (a) £148.12; (b) £171; (c) £106.88; (d) £101.89; (e) £126.18; (f) £168.44; (g) £231.30; (h) £177.38; (i) £201.45; (j) £170.10.
3 (a) £725; (b) £533.55; (c) £24.25; (d) £92.50; (e) £191; (f) £495; (g) £1,755; (h) £10,000; (i) £12,100; (j) £200,000.
4 (a) £138; (b) £174; (c) £183; (d) £246; (e) £336.
5 (a) £360; (b) £355; (c) £475; (d) £745; (e) £725.
6 £64.70.
7 £441.25.
8 £893.75.
9 £1,117.90.

10

	1 A.B. £	2 C.D. £	3 E.F. £	4 G.H. £
Gross pay	108.45	126.30	134.44	101.20
Gross pay for tax purposes	104.90	119.98	129.59	96.14
Gross pay to date for tax	104.90	As given	As given	As given
Taxable pay to date	78.75	646.80	604.70	1,028.90

	1 A.B.	*2 C.D.*	*3 E.F.*	*4 G.H*
	£	£	£	£
Tax	12.30	9.10 (refund)	14.50	17.20
Total deductions	17.78	9.45	21.79	24.61
Net pay	87.12	110.53	107.80	71.53
Refunds	–	9.10	–	–
Total payable	87.12	119.63	107.80	71.53
NI Employer's	9.25	16.44	12.63	13.17
NI Contributions	14.48	25.74	19.77	20.38

19
Communication in business

19.1 The meaning of communication

Communication has many meanings. Basically it means maintaining links with other people for the purpose of passing news and information from one party to another. This is obviously of great importance in business, where instructions like 'Start up production!' 'Stop production!' 'Withdraw all chocolate bars from the shelves' and a million more pieces of information have to be passed every day. We must have links – by telephone, telex, computerized data-links etc. Indeed many people think of communication as largely being pieces of apparatus that can put us in touch with other people.

A more subtle meaning of 'communication' is concerned with 'understanding'. Personnel Officers have to be good communicators, because they have many things to explain to many people, at all sorts of levels. Quite often a senior Board member may make a statement to lower level personnel which is almost completely unintelligible to them. He/she may use words they don't understand or deal with matters they are not interested in because he/she is avoiding the real problem and what is being said is brushed aside as irrelevant. 'He is not communicating' we say – by which we mean that the statement made does not elicit any real response from these addressed. In this respect, to be able to promote understanding, everyone with any sort of authority needs to be a good communicator. The Head of Department with his/her staff; the supervisor with his/her shopfloor workers; the craftsman with his/her apprentices. One Managing Director turned the performance of his factory round with a can of white paint and a clear piece of floor. At the end of a shift he counted the completed machines and painted 5 on the floor. The next shift saw it, as they came in and at the end of the shift told the Managing Director to make it a 6. Within a week they were in double figures and within a month they were up to 35 a shift. They had got the message – without a word being said.

Communication is important in every business. We have to be able to get in touch with people. Many firms depend for all their orders on the telephone system. For example, perishable foods – like dairy products – are delivered against orders phoned through by shopkeepers who have a copy of the order form and simply say 'Twelve of Number 5, three of Number 18, twenty of Number 24', and so on. With computerized links we can book an airline ticket, or a hotel room, or a holiday, in a matter of minutes. The computer is making important decisions for us in millionths of a second. 'Yes – you can have a window seat, on Flight BA521, and I can book it for you Y/N.' A touch on the Y key will book the seat, reduce the number of places on that aircraft for future applicants and start arrangements for printing tickets, etc. as necessary.

19.2   The pattern of business communication

Communication can be divided into two parts – spoken communication and written communication. These two major sections can then be subdivided into **mass media communication** in which we address the widest possible public audience and **personal communication** in which we have a more limited audience, often just a single individual.

Figure 19.1 shows in diagrammatic form the various ways of addressing these audiences. Note that as far as spoken communication is concerned we can divide the personal approaches into two parts – **face-to-face communication** and **telephone links**. With written communication the types of link are divided into **internal links** (within the firm or company) and **external links** to customers, suppliers and interested parties. Some of these external links are telecommunication links. Study Figure 19.1 now, and the detailed descriptions of some of these methods of communication given in Sections 19.3–19.7 below.

19.3   Spoken personal communication

The effectiveness of face-to-face communication lies in its impact, which is direct and personal. If the speaker is knowledgeable, with a carefully thought out message lucidly expressed, and the audience is attentive, the information should be conveyed satisfactorily. No doubt there are many occasions when this is so, but we can all think of occasions when communication between the parties has been less than perfect. It is not unknown for those seeking to impart information to begin speaking before the audience is attentive; to mumble their presentation so that some people in the audience cannot hear

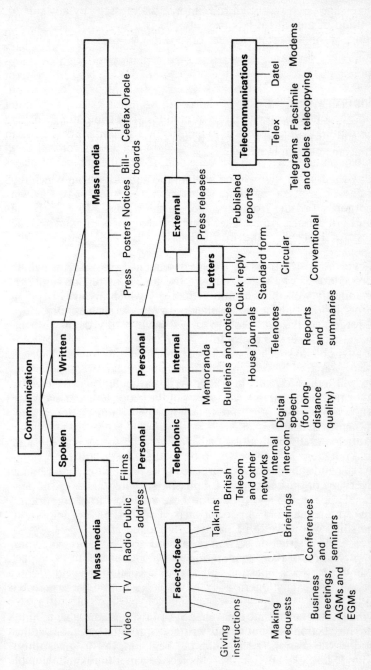

Figure 19.1 The pattern of business communication today

the message anyway; to fail to reinforce the message by any sort of repetition of the salient features, etc.

Some of the important aspects of face-to-face communication may be listed as follows:

Giving instructions

The essential point about instructions is that you are laying down rules and procedures for a particular aspect of work, or set of circumstances. You must:

1   Lay them down clearly and explain the authority from which the rules or procedures come. This could be the speaker's own authority (arising from the office he/she holds). More likely the authority comes from higher up in the chain of command and the task of conveying the instructions has been delegated to the speaker.

2   Give the instructions in a logical sequence, so that the whole procedure can be visualized by those under instruction, and it is manifestly well thought out. A delivery which involves hopping around from one idea to another, with phrases such as 'Oh before I forget, at the end etc.' when we have hardly dealt with the beginning is sure to be confusing. To keep the sequence logical it is advisable to speak from a list of subheadings or topics which has been prepared beforehand and marshalled in a correct sequence.

3   It will reinforce the instructions if particular people can be allocated responsibility for aspects of the procedure and everyone knows who they are and to whom they should turn in any difficulty that arises.

4   Anticipate any difficulties that may arise so far as you can and make it clear how these are to be met if they do arise.

5   At the end summarize the purpose of the procedures, and remind everyone of the key points. Emphasize such matters as dress, personal appearance and conduct if these are likely to be important; give the names and important facts about VIPs (very important persons) who have to be particularly looked after.

6   Leave the instruction session on a good note by expressing your appreciation of their cooperation and help.

7   Allow time for a question and answer session at the end in case people have any queries, or have suggestions which may be helpful.

8   Finally, whenever time beforehand permits, it is advisable to have the instructions set out in typewritten form to be given out at the end of the session (rather than the beginning). This gives those who do not take notes a physical piece of paper to remind them of

the salient points. It also covers the instructions for anyone who was absent – a copy can be inserted into their pigeon-hole or in-tray to ensure they are informed about the matter.

Briefings and meetings

All sorts of business meetings take place, some of them formal, following well-known procedures for the conduct of meetings. Others may be less formal. For example, a briefing is part of a public relations exercise which gives the general press and the trade press information about a particular event. It might be about the resignation of a director, or a threatened takeover. It might relate to a prosecution of a company, or the directors of a company. It might be about a defective product, or some other cause for public concern. A briefing does not usually permit lengthy discussion of the matter, though it would be usual to answer factual questions from the floor of the briefing room to make sure the reporters and others understand the problem and the action taken. Such statements are today the usual way to lower public concern on any matter, and we see them every day on our television screens.

Talk-ins

Talk-ins are an opportunity for anyone in a company or a department to air their views on a particular problem, or make suggestions which they feel will be helpful. They usually take the form of a statement on behalf of management at some level – it may be departmental or it may be higher than that. This statement is then thrown open to discussion, and although it would be for the chairperson to conduct the meeting in an orderly manner, so that everyone does not talk at once, it would be usual to let everyone have their say, and perhaps the most voluble people would get their chance early in the discussion. Not everything said by someone who is voluble is necessarily valuable, and other speakers may in the end make more useful points. The whole idea of a talk-in is that all views should be expressed and the most useful contributions will be noted down and tried out. One might, for example, at the end of a talk-in appoint a small committee to go into the various ideas in more detail and make positive recommendations to solve the problem. Such a committee is often called an **ad hoc committee**. The words mean 'arranged for a special purpose', to distinguish them from **standing committees** (such as a Welfare Committee, or a Health and Safety at Work committee). Standing committees last a very long time and meet several times a year to review the matters they are charged to study.

AGMs and EGMs

As far as companies are concerned Annual General Meetings (AGMs) are required by the Companies Act, 1985. The directors must send out notices to all shareholders and it would be usual to include the Annual Report of the company including the accounts, the Directors' Report and the Auditors' Report. The directors' recommendations about any dividend to be declared are included in the report, or if it is not proposed to declare any dividend some explanation would be given. The recommendation has to be approved by the members at the AGM before any distribution can take place.

An extraordinary general meeting (EGM) is called whenever a member requests it – provided he/she has the support of 10 per cent of the shareholders. Such a requisition must state the reason for calling the meeting – which usually means a matter of great concern to the company and possibly of concern to the general public. The directors must then call the EGM within twenty-one days.

Seminars and conferences

Seminars and conferences are a very important part of face-to-face communication, because they deal with aspects of business which are of major importance at the present time. Conferences tend to be discussions of major developments which are about to take place, or which people feel should be brought about. They are very often of an international character – such topics as world trade, Third World debt, acid rain, river pollution, etc. are the sort of topics conferences are organized about. Seminars tend to be at a lower level, and deal not only with current problems but with the endlessly recurring problems of business life in general, for which we are constantly needing to train and retrain staff.

For example, export documentation is a topic that constantly has to be relearned as new methods come into use. What was once typed out laboriously in an export office is now passed through as electronic data by DTI (direct trader input) from the exporter's office to HM Customs, to arrange passage of the goods through the ports. A typical seminar programme is shown below. It is clear that it covers a great many aspects of export documentation. It is reproduced by courtesy of Croner Conferences and Training, Croner House, London Road, Kingston upon Thames, Surrey KT2 6SR.

Understanding export documentation

This seminar is designed to dispel the mystique which surrounds export documentation by teaching staff about each document, its format and function. The seminar is suitable for personnel at any level and from any department – Sales, Shipping or Finance – who are in any way concerned with the paperwork necessary to effect a smooth and professional export transaction. A basic working knowledge of the mechanics of exporting would be useful for those attending. Practical exercises will be used throughout. The programme will cover:

- The main problems concerning the exporter.
- Terms of delivery (with reference to INCOTERMS 1990) and their effect on the paperwork involved.
- A close consideration of the costing sheet.
- The chronology of an export transaction.
- *'Sales' documentation:*
  Enquiry, order, contract, works orders, pro-forma and commercial invoices, packing lists etc., pre-shipment inspection, import and export licences.
- *'Financial' documentation:*
  A *very brief* consideration of the bill of exchange, letters of credit and the marine insurance policy or certificate.
- *'Shipping' documentation:*
  Consignment notes B/L, CMR, CIM, AWB, CTD.
- *Official documentation:*
  Consideration of the documentation required by H. M. Customs, particularly after the creation of the Single Market in the European Community, including the new arrangements for VAT on goods purchased and sold to EC firms and citizens.

19.4 The telephone system

The telephone was invented by Alexander Graham Bell, a teacher of the deaf, in 1876. It is a device that has changed the world. It gives instantaneous communication around the world, and in the next few years will provide colour television pictures of one's caller so that the parties will be not only involved in direct personal conversation but will be able to see one another as well and discuss documents and charts even though they are ten thousand miles apart.

It is a popular misconception that using the telephone is expensive. Actually it is one of the cheapest means of communication, if properly used. For example, to send a typewritten letter to someone costs most firms about £5. It isn't just the price of the stamp, but the precious time spent in dictating the letter, getting it typed, the headed notepaper, the printed envelope, etc. On a routine matter – like raising a query with a supplier – which can often be answered in five seconds, the telephone call will cost far less. Credit card companies, wishing to check American credit cards presented in Europe by travellers can phone America, check the entire file of stolen

American credit cards and confirm that the credit card they are holding is genuine, in about six seconds, at a cost of about eight pence. The speed at which telephone systems work is breathtaking.

'If properly used' is an important phrase. Very few people use the telephone properly. The basic rules are:

- Never let a telephone ring. It doesn't matter what you are doing, lift the phone and answer it. It may be an emergency – lots of calls are! It may be a customer with a £1 million order! It may be an irate customer with a complaint, in which case we don't want to add to his/her irritation by leading the caller to think that nobody cares enough even to pick up the phone.
- Don't say 'Hello', announce yourself! 'Laver Electronics, Whitehead speaking; may I help you?'
- Never be smart, witty at a customer's expense, or unhelpful over the telephone. Be courteous, polite and efficient.
- Keep a pencil and paper handy at all times. Take a message if you can't deal with the matter yourself and make sure it reaches the person concerned and that you have all the details they will need to deal with the query. The obvious ones are the caller's name, company, code and telephone number. It helps to know the nature of the query, because some are more urgent than others. A query about a package being flown out that day to Tokyo is more urgent than a query about a lost invoice or credit note. Sometimes a note about the best time to call back is helpful. Put the date and time on the message you take, so the eventual

```
        Telephone  Message Form
                        Date..............
                        Time..............
 Caller's name..........................
 Address................................
 Telephone No. ............ Ext. No. ........

 Message for..............................
 Message: ...............................
 ......................................
 ......................................
 ......................................
 ......................................
 ......................................
 ......................................

        Message taken by....................
```

Figure 19.2   A useful telephone message pad

recipient knows when it was received. Put your name on it so they know whom to contact if there is any query.
- Close the call with a recapitulation of the points you have noted down and a promise to relay the information to the person concerned.

Figure 19.2 shows a useful telephone message pad. You can purchase similar pads from any stationer's shop, or you can type up a suitable design yourself and run off some copies on a plain paper copying machine.

Telephone systems

Telephone systems can be as simple or as complex as the user requires. Generally speaking it is helpful to have a reasonably sophisticated system. Even the sole trader can have one of the latest 'Inphones' – with a number of useful facilities that are 'in' at the time of writing. For example you may have:

1 *Last number redial* So often when we call a number, and most numbers have at least nine digits, these days, we find it is engaged. A telephone that remembers the last number dialled, and will redial it on touching a single key, is a great help.
2 *Number memories* Some phones have four, and some ten memories where you can record the numbers you most frequently call. They can then be dialled automatically by pressing just two keys to select the number you require.
3 *Notepad memory* These record a number as you are given it by directory enquiries or some outside caller. When you replace the receiver the number is ready to dial, and on lifting the receiver and pressing a simple key the numbers on the 'notepad' will be dialled automatically.
4 *Cordless phones* These are radio-telephones with a very limited range – about 100 metres. They enable a sole trader who is working way from the phone to take the portable part away to the workplace. Any incoming call will be transmitted to the portable part, and any number dialled by the sole trader on the portable part will be transmitted in the opposite direction.
5 *Number display* Some phones show a number display of the number dialled. Any mis-dial will be obvious to the sender who can break off the call and start again.

More sophisticated systems

Many firms and companies need a full network of internal and external facilities and a system can be tailormade to fit anyone's needs exactly. Some of the common facilities in use are as follows:

1   *Multi-extension and multi-line systems*   We can have as many
    extensions as we like, and as many lines as we like. A line is an
    outside link to the general telephone system. Suppose a company
    has ten outside lines but fifty extensions. Any one of the fifty
    extensions can obtain an outside line (usually by dialling 9). Of
    course if all the ten lines were busy the engaged tone would be
    heard, but usually one of the lines will be clear. The lines are
    interconnected so that if one is busy the call is switched to the next
    or the next if necessary.
2   *Multi-operator systems*   Some systems avoid the need for a
    telephone operator by switching calls through to any extension.
    The person who answers the extension can redirect a call from his
    her extension to any other extension. In this way everyone is a
    telephone operator and calls are only one step away from the
    desired point of contact.
3   *'Follow-me-anywhere' calls*   An extension-user is about to leave
    his/her own desk and go to see a colleague. By keying in the
    colleague's number an incoming call will be diverted. Similarly if
    the extension-user is leaving the building calls can be diverted to a
    secretary or a colleague who has agreed to handle them.
4   *'Hold' keys*   If a caller phones in with a query it may be helpful to
    discuss a point with a colleague before answering the query. If the
    telephone has a 'hold' button the outside caller will be held on a
    security line (unable to hear the second conversation taking
    place). When the point has been resolved the extension-user can
    go back to the outside caller and answer the query. This is cheaper
    than having to ring back to the caller, for it is the caller who pays
    for the call.
5   *'Trunk-call barring'*   Some extensions can be barred from
    making outside calls altogether, or they may be barred from
    anything but local calls. This prevents mis-use of the telephone
    system.
6   *'Call logging'*   Abuse of the telephone system can be avoided by
    logging all calls i.e. keeping a written log of all calls made. The
    general administration officer will then check the print-out to see
    whether the numbers are business or private numbers, and will
    instruct the petty cashier to collect the charges from staff who
    made private calls.

There are many more services available. They are relatively inexpensive, and are paid for with a quarterly rental fee, so the initial
cost is not great – just an installation charge.

19.5   Analogue and digital systems

Traditional telephone systems are called analogue systems. They
work from the waveform created by human speech at one end, which

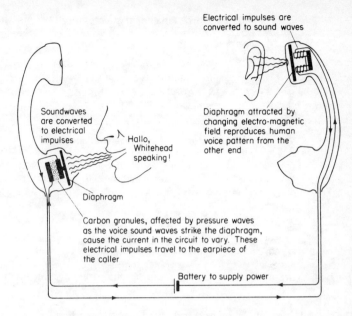

Figure 19.3   The principle of the traditional telephone

Notes:
1   The human voice makes sound waves which strike the diaphragm of the microphone in the telephone handset.
2   The pressure waves cause the diaphragm alternately to compress and release the carbon granules behind it. This alternately increases and decreases the flow of current in the circuit passing through the telephone network to the earpiece of the caller's handset.
3   In the earpiece the current is led around an electro-magnet which becomes more or less magnetized as the current varies. The strong current attacts the earpiece diaphragm strongly – the weaker current releases the diaphragm.
4   This movement of the diaphragm imitates the movement of the human voice box miles away which is causing the current to vary, and we hear the same sounds the speaker is making.

is transmitted along a wire to the receiver's telephone where the wave pattern is turned back again into a sound wave that can be picked up by the receiver's ear. This is illustrated in Figure 19.3 and explained in the notes below it.

The trouble with the traditional system is that the wave pattern of speech produced at the caller's end becomes weaker and weaker the farther it travels, and distortions in the cables make it difficult to pick out the signal easily, because of background noise. The more modern system is to send the message in digital form, that is to say as a series of numbers. The two parts of Figure 19.4 show what happens.

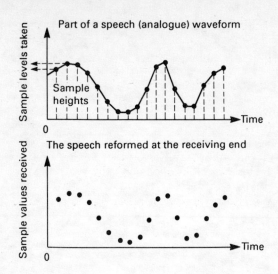

Figure 19.4 Turning an analogue wave into a digital stream of information

Notes:
1 The original voice pattern can be seen as a wave in the top half of the diagram.
2 The size of the wave can be measured at any given moment by measuring how far it is from the two axes which meet at 0. Thus the position of any part of the wave can be stated by measuring its height above the horizontal axis and its distance from the vertical axis.
3 This is actually done every 125 millionths of a second, in other words 8000 times every second.
4 If these millions of measurements are then sent over a first-class quality line as a 'bitstream' i.e. a stream of data in computerized form, they can be used to reassemble the wave at its destination so accurately that the speech produced in the earpiece is clear and free of background noise. It is possible to have 'dedicated' lines, always available for your exclusive use. This is particularly useful for television companies, press agencies, etc.
5 The actual device for turning the analogue speech into a pulsed code of measurements is called a **modem**. This stands for modulator-demodulator. To modulate is to vary the frequency or pitch of the human voice. The modem measures the pitch of the voice, converts it into a machine language which can be transmitted, transmits it and then turns the resulting set of measurements into a wave again.
6 The use of the modem not only enables one conversation to be sent, but up to 2000 conversations can be sent on a single cable, or in radio form to a satellite in space, without getting them mixed up. This requires 140 million bits of information to be sent every second. It is difficult to imagine such huge movements of data.

19.6 Telephone answering machines and paging devices

Telephone answering machines are now relatively cheap (less than £100) and can be purchased from a wide variety of outlets. They do need a special device called a jack to be fitted by Telecom engineers, but this is relatively inexpensive. Most machines can now be accessed remotely, in other words you can call them from anywhere in the world and get them to play your messages back to you – though with some models the playback wipes the machine clear and you only get one chance to listen to the message. The playback can be voice-activated, in other words the machine will not play back for other people, only if your voice matches the silence-speech pattern the machine recognizes.

Many people misunderstand the telephone answering machine. 'I won't have one' they say 'because I don't often get important messages.' This overlooks the fact that what you need to know, usually, is that no one has been trying to get you. If the machine has no message on it, that too is information. You can get down to work straight away knowing that no one is pressuring you for anything. Some machines have a paging device which will page you when a message comes in. The paging device warns you that someone has left a message – and so long as you have not been paged there is no need to contact the machine.

Paging devices

A paging device takes its name from the pageboy in nineteenth century hotels who would go through the lobbies calling 'Message for Mr Jones please; Message for Mr Jones.' Today the radio paging device will find anyone within a designated area. There is a **tone page** in which you hear an audible tone to attract your attention. A **silent page**, which is worn on the wrist vibrates to attract your attention. This is useful in hospitals at night, or in noisy situations where the tone page might not be heard. The **display page** and the **message master** give written messages which can be read from a screen – which can be illuminated if lighting is poor. Many small businesses find a paging device a great help. For example, a sole trader (say a plumber) who is out on a job can be kept in touch with a display page or a message master and can go on to an emergency job as soon as possible – rather than ringing back to the office to find out if anyone has phoned in with an emergency request. A message master will take up to ten different messages of thirty characters each. Thus 'Bailey; 10 King Street; pipe burst' would be all that was needed.

Points to remember

- Communication has many meanings. It can mean the passing of information from one person or group to another person or group. Its deepest meaning is a 'meeting of minds' where the ideas conveyed are fully appreciated by the other party, with all the implications that follow from the basic ideas conveyed.

- Communications can be divided into spoken and written communication. The spoken word can be conveyed by mass media means, or personally – either in a face-to-face situation or by telephone.
- Written communication can be by mass media means, or personally either by internal messages or external correspondence and electronic messages.
- In face-to-face communication we should be well prepared. We should speak calmly and in a logical sequence; anticipate difficulties and deal with them in the course of the explanation, briefing, etc. and we should repeat and emphasize special points to ensure the fullest understanding by those present.
- Telephonic communication is relatively inexpensive and as sophisticated a system as is economic should be provided. Such a system can provide numerous facilities, including long-distance speech and data transmission through high-quality, dedicated lines.

19.7   Exercises on spoken personal communication

1   Five members of the class put their names into a hat and the numbers 1–5 in another hat. One name and one number are then drawn out to allocate one of the following five subjects to each. The selected person then envisages a plan of action to make the arrangements called for, and gives them, as a set of instructions to the class. Usually not more than two such sets of instructions can be given in a single lesson period. The class then comments upon the effectiveness of his/her communication. The five subjects are:

(a)   A visit to the institution you work for – or attend if it is an educational establishment – by a leading personality from either the Royal Family, or some centre of government.
(b)   An open day for the general public to be organized by the institution or establishment as in (a) above.
(c)   A charitable event run for your favourite charity.
(d)   An advertising campaign is expected to bring in requests for sample cosmetics manufactured by your firm. Arrangements are required to deal with this flood of requests (each enclosing 50 pence in stamps).
(e)   A traffic survey is to be carried out on a particular stretch of road in the locality – to find out how much traffic it is carrying in peak hours (7.30–9.30 a.m. and 4.30–6.00 p.m.).

Note: When criticizing the performance of each student you might like to consider the following points:

(a) Did the speaker appear confident about the arrangements made and give the impression of being in control of the situation?

(b) Did he/she speak clearly, so that all could hear?

(c) Was the coverage logical, with each set of events being explained lucidly?

(d) Were any markers laid down for the staff – i.e. individuals appointed to look after certain aspects; telephone numbers to ring in an emergency, etc?

(e) Were possible difficulties anticipated and suggestions made for how to deal with them?

(f) How would you rate the speaker's performance on a scale of 1–10?

2 *Answering the telephone* – put the names of three girls from the class, in a hat, and the names of three boys in another hat. Pick out one of each to form a team to play the roles shown below. Pick two more teams in the same way.

Situation

A female customer is calling to complain about the non-arrival of goods promised for delivery yesterday, although she had taken a day off work to wait in for the delivery. She is extremely upset and complains that Mr Johnson had promised her delivery faithfully by lunchtime yesterday. The male member of the team is answering the telephone and knows nothing about the order but this is not surprising since he works in the Buying Department and the Sales Department is in another building twenty miles away. He has never heard of Mr Johnson, but he does know the principles for answering the telephone mentioned earlier in this chapter. Allow the three teams to take it in turn to play the roles of customer and representative of the firm. At the end of each call assess the representative's telephone answering technique, especially from the following viewpoints.

(a) Did the representative use a pleasant, clear speaking voice at all times.

(b) Did he keep calm and deal with the caller in a courteous and pleasant way.

(c) Did he answer the call in a proper manner at the very start of the conversation.

(d) Did he help the situation by dealing with the matter in a positive way, which helped the situation improve, rather than making it worse.

(e) Was the solution he found for the problem a good one, and what would he need to do after the call had finished to solve the problem completely.

19.8   Mass media communication

We live in a world where the 'media' – meaning those who have the opportunity to use mass media techniques – can reach audiences of every type with effortless ease. Radio and television convey information to huge audiences around the nation and the world. The best way to sell any product is to present it on television or local radio, and the surest way to obtain an order is to tell the retailer that the product will be featured in his/her area in the coming weeks. Films and videos are another way of reaching large audiences, and public address systems, while more localized, have a part to play too. Ceefax and Oracle are two teletext services which offer a wide range of information to those who have a teletext television set.

19.9   Written communication: internal

Much communication is in written form. It has the advantage that it tends to be more reliable than oral communication; it is in permanent form and can always be presented in Court if any dispute arises between the parties about what the actual relationship between them was. Of course, not everyone succeeds in a letter or memo in saying exactly what they meant to say, but the Courts will pay great attention to written evidence, and will almost always uphold it. If the writer did not say exactly what he/she meant to say so much the worse for him/her. Today written communication can pass electronically from place to place and cross the world in seconds. Known as e-mail (electronic mail), it can be queued electronically if an executive is away from his/her desk. Documents can also be sent electronically, arriving anywhere in the world in about 20 seconds, and error-free.

Figure 19.1 shows the main types of written communication, which can be subdivided into mass media forms and personal forms. The mass media forms include the use of the press, both for news items and advertising. These have been referred to earlier (see Chapter 13), especially the part played by the specialist business press. Other forms of mass media are posters, billboards and public notices. Students should note that such public notices are subject to planning controls and other restrictions. It is an offence to 'fly-post', in other words display notices in public places without permission. Such displays lower the quality of life because they are unsightly and usually disfiguring.

Internal written communications includes the following forms:

Memos

A memo (short for memorandum) is a note to help the memory. At one time they were regarded as informal reminders, and were not

---

Memo from Tom Brown   Telephone: Usual Extension 121
Date 31.7.19xx
To Malcolm Shah, Production Department   Time 09.30

An overnight telex from Batangas says that the pump
which is already on order and due for despatch by sea on
Friday is urgently needed. Can we air freight it out to
Manila today. Will you take steps to get it crated and I will
look after the office side and let you know flight times. Via
Hong Kong seems the quickest way. Liaise with me at
once if there is any problem. Top priority on this please.

Thanks
Tom

Figure 19.5   An internal memo

signed, but today it is common to have memo forms printed, or even
in three-part sets of NCR paper. With such a set the person initiating
the memo writes a message on the top half of the page, tears off the
top copy and retains it. The second and third copies go to the person
addressed (who writes an answer on the second copy, tears it off and
retains it and sends the third copy – which now bears the initial
enquiry and the response – back to the original sender. Such a system
is very straightforward.

Although a memo is meant to be brief, it must be intelligible. Do
not say so little that the person it is addressed to cannot understand it.
Figure 19.5 shows a typical memo.

House journals

House journals are increasingly used in large organizations as a way
of keeping everyone informed about the affairs of the company. It
does much to promote understanding and goodwill within the organization if management regularly features future plans, upturns and
downturns in trade, profitability, return on capital invested, etc. Less
formal items include 'news' features about staff, promotions, retire-
ments, activities of a social or recreational nature, etc. With desktop
publishing, in-house printing and similar facilities available to many
firms the house journal can be an attractive and informative link
between departments, plants, depots and other centres of activity. It
requires not only some specialized input from those organizing the
actual production of the journal but also a wider group of interested
people feeding information and news to the editorial staff. Students
should know that this kind of activity, which is not something that

everyone is prepared to take on, can have useful side-benefits if it is responsibly done. Not only does it draw those who help to the attention of senior staff, but it enables them to get to know everyone in the organization and everything that is going on. It is always helpful to an ambitious person to know colleagues in other departments and their future programmes and plans. It is easy then to act in such a way as to advance the desired programme and avoid or reduce undesirable activities.

Telenotes

A telenote is a drawing board device which is linked into the telephone network by a transceiver which can both receive and transmit electronic messages. The telenote device enables a person at one end to draw something on the telenote drawing board, and have it instantly transmitted to a colleague at the other end, where the same drawing or diagram appears. Thus fashion garments, electrical circuits and similar matters can be discussed over the telephone with both parties able to see the other's ideas.

Reports and summaries

Much of business proceeds along fairly formal lines with a set pattern of activities, which gradually develops a coherent proposal on which a Boardroom discussion can take place. We might imagine the following scenario:

1   A has an idea and sketches it out for B.
2   B considers it and sends it back to A with a suggestion or two that might be an improvement on the original.
3   They agree that A should write a preliminary proposal about it for Boardroom consideration.
4   The Board agrees to set up a small ad hoc committee to go into the details and report back.
5   The committee's report at a later date leads to a decision by the Board to proceed with a prototype model of the device concerned, and a budget of £10,000 for the work.
6   An evaluation of the prototype is submitted in a further report which leads to the Board's decision to market the new product.

This rather lengthy and formal procedure ensures that an idea is given serious consideration, is properly evaluated and reported upon and, if it survives the critical appraisal, becomes a viable and worthwhile part of a company's activities.

The layout of a report is as follows:

1   State the subject of the report, and who authorized it to be prepared.

2 Give the names of the parties involved in preparing it.
3 Outline the problem and the measures taken to resolve it.
4 Make recommendations, in a really detailed way, suggesting what future policy should be, and the likely outcomes if the proposed policy is accepted and pursued.

19.10 External written communication

When we deal with other firms and companies communication is largely by correspondence of one form or another, but this is a situation which is likely to change in the years ahead as computerization reduces correspondence. A number of major developments are under way to produce the paperless office, replacing the typewritten letter with EDI – electronic data interchange. Already one Act of Parliament specifies that information about export movements need not exist in documentary form, but may exist only in the memory of a computer, provided both parties in the contract can actually obtain the information on their screens at will – in other words know how to access the computer's memory and call up the information they want. Customs entries (a vital procedure for registering the movements of goods across frontiers) can be entered by certain firms electronically instead of in document form. All such systems are part of the **information technology** – the classification, storage and retrieval of information through electronic devices.

Ordinary correspondence has been to some extent discussed in Chapter 17. A few further points are dealt with below.

Quick-reply or standard-form letters

Many letters are prepared in a standard form, because the same sort of questions constantly arise or need to be asked. For example, the Department of Inland Revenue often hears in one way or another (for example by reading advertisements in the local press) that a new business has set up which is not apparently on its books. They therefore send out a standard letter which asks such questions as the following on the left hand side of the paper and leaves a space on the right hand side for a quick reply.

	Questions		*Answer*
1	When was the business called 'The Fisherman's Restaurant' first opened?	1	
2	Who owns this business?	2	
3	Is the business a sole trader's business, or a partnership, or a limited company? etc.	3	

```
To...............          From The Cashier's Department,
                                  Gracechurch Ltd,
                                  12795 London Way
                                     EC1 3PB


Dear............,

     Your cheque has had to be returned herewith because
(please see line marked X below)

1   It has not been dated .........
2   It has no signature .........
3   The alteration has not been initialled .........
4   It has only the words filled in; the amount in figures
    has not been completed . X ......
5   It has only the figures filled in; the amount in words
    has not been completed .........
6   The amount in words and the amount in figures are
    not the same .........
7   The word 'pounds' has been left out after the amount
    in pounds .........
8   The payee's name has not been inserted .........

     Would you please correct this error and return the
cheque in the enclosed envelope, which requires a stamp.
     Thanking you in anticipation.

                              T. Goddard
                              Chief Cashier
```

Figure 19.6   A standard letter from the Cashier's Department

A similar sort of standard letter is shown in Figure 19.6.

Today many electronic typewriters have memories, and standard paragraphs can be stored in the memory (usually up to about twenty paragraphs). A busy department where the same queries arrive repeatedly might therefore save time by answering a letter by standard paragraphs. Suppose a letter arrives asking a question about the Simplex System of Accounting, referred to earlier. The manager might simply write on the letter, 1,3,17. When the secretary answers the letter he/she types the address of the addressee and the salutation, and then calls up Paragraph 1, which reads:

Thank you for your letter to the Simplex Advice Bureau, asking for help with your problem. We are always happy to answer queries like this.

The secretary then calls up Paragraph 3, which reads:

The method of entering Enterprise Allowances is explained on our Difficulty sheet No. 4 – 'How to enter Enterprise Allowances', a copy of which is enclosed.

The secretary then calls up Paragraph 17, which reads:
I do hope this solves your problem, and we wish you every success with your new business.

Yours faithfully

pp Brian Senior

(Dictated by Mr Senior and signed in his absence)

The secretary can handle the whole thing, with a minimum of typing because the memory types each paragraph automatically.

Circulars

Circulars are letters addressed to a wide variety of people (but these days with a memory typewriter they can be personalized – the computer feeding in a personal salutation and address from the memory bank). They are chiefly used for advertising – in what is called a mailshot. One firm of the author's acquaintance regularly sends out mailshots of 250,000, the postage alone costing about £15,000 despite generous discounts from the Post Office.

The problem with circulars is to prevent them becoming 'junk mail', which is thrown into the wastepaper basket as soon as it is received. The list of addressees must be people who are genuinely interested in the product or service being offered, and the margin of profit on the product or service must be reasonably high so that one success pays for many failures.

A mailshot is only as good as the responses you get and the follow-up you provide to turn an inquiry into a sale.

Press releases and published reports

A press release is a circularized letter sent to all press outlets likely to be interested, featuring a new development or a new product or some happy event – such as a 'golden disc' award in the record industry or an anniversary of the formation of a firm or company. It may be a speech which is of significant importance by the Chairman of the Board. In that case an 'embargo' time is put on the press release to prevent publication before the chairman has delivered it. The press release enables the journal's editor to get the speech typeset, and think up a good headline, but the actual appearance of the speech will be postponed until after the embargo is lifted.

Many reports are published, and a charge may be made for them. Others are free, and may be sent out automatically (for example company reports are sent out to shareholders at the end of the financial year). Others may be sent out on request as, for example, when an important conference is oversubscribed and some interested people are unable to attend. On request they will be sent a conference report, including the text of all the major speeches.

19.11   External written telecommunications

The most important communication developments have been in telecommunications, particularly international telecommunications. The chief element in these advances is the use of digital bitstreams of data – as described in Section 19.5 above, over glass fibre cables and radio waves to satellites. The biggest advance is the facsimile copying (FAXing) of documents as a stream of information which can be reassembled at the other end into an exact copy of the document, whether it is typewritten material, drawings and plans etc. So powerful is the system that even television pictures can be sent so that video conferencing circuits around the world can be set up. Thus if a one-hour session is booked all those interested parties in a project can not only discuss it in the comfort of their own offices, but can show their diagrams, plans and charts. Think how much better that is than choosing one person to go to the conference and hoping he/she can convey what was said in a proper, unbiased way on return. No waiting about in airports, or wasted time in hotels. Simply invite everyone to come to their appropriate head office, depot or plant and they can all hear, see and participate in an international video-conference.

The telex, fax, datel and modem facilities now available have this feature in common; they get through every time. If you call at an office you may be faced by a receptionist who will not let you see the person you wish to see. If you telephone, the operator or secretary may be adept at filtering off unwanted calls. With a telex, fax or computerized service the message you send will get through. You can send electronic mail to hundreds of addresses at once, and it will all get through. One team of two salesmen calls on 1000 customers a week and never leaves the office. By using 'call free of charge' lines in international trade it is possible to break right through the barriers to reach your customers direct. Few foreign customers want to phone internationally at their own expense – it costs about £1 a minute. But that is not expensive compared with the cost of sending a salesperson abroad. Suppose it costs £600 airfare and £150 a day to send a salesperson to a foreign country. Suppose also that a ten-minute call will answer all the foreign customer's questions and a £10 fax charge arises from sending him/her a document. At about £20 a customer for these charges you can deal with thirty customers for the airfare, and another 100 customers for a fortnight's hotel expenses. Telecommunications, if properly used are a cheap way of doing business.

The chief methods in use from British Telecom are:

1 *International direct dialling*   Firms have a direct phone link to colleagues, suppliers and customers in 190 countries.
2 *International 0800*   Firms can tell their customers to dial them free of charge from abroad – the 0800 system charges the call to the person called, or charges the foreign customer only for a local call and the balance to the person called.
3 International telex   This service gets written messages direct to over 200 countries right into the firm called. The answerback code tells you that you are connected and can pass your message – when the message ends the answerback code confirms that it was all received. With Telex Plus the depression of a single button will send the message to 1000 locations.
4 *Bureaufax and telex bureaux*   These are available for use by all those who do not have a fax or telex machine, and also may be used by firms who wish to send a message to any number of destinations while leaving their own equipment free for other business.
5 *Translation bureaux*   These will translate documents, conversations and business meetings conducted over the telephone.
6 *International video-conferencing*   This has been described above.
7 *Datel Service*   This enables files of data to be passed over the telephone network to 100 countries.
8 *Digital private circuits*   These provide totally private circuits for telephones, fax, data and video communication. It is also possible, through 'Leaseline', to have the same private circuits to 100 nations around the world.

Managing the network

A network is an interconnected pattern of communications which links computers to computers. A LAN (local area network) is a series of terminals connected to each other (e.g. within an office) and able to communicate with one another and with computerized facilities. Thus they might share not only a computer, but printers, microfilm equipment, etc. A good example is their use in banking, where a branch can contact (a) all its own accounts, to which it has direct access and is on-line, with instantaneous update; (b) Head Office, with whom it has direct access, but chiefly updates its affairs at the close of the working day; (c) one or more computer bureaux to whom it feeds information at the end of a working day to update such matters as the balances on all accounts (for access by ATMs asked to dispense cash) etc.

On an international basis a network could put Head Office in touch with branches and depots around the world. Such a network might be able to access computers around the world with large specialized databases (such as financial, medical or scientific data). One such system is called DIANE (Direct Access Information Network for Europe). British Telecom will not only help firms to set up a network but will manage the network for them, through its subsidiary Primex International Private Networks, offering twenty-four hours maintenance, power back-up and network management.

Access to networks is gained by a twelve-number code, which acts as a user-identifier. The user can now access any database in the network, use its programs, copy its information and take advantage of all the services offered. The extent of the use is monitored, and a bill is sent to the customer. The system works on a worldwide basis, but is particularly widely used in North America and Europe.

19.12   Information technology

Information technology is any sort of technology which enables us to receive information from a computerized source, giving instantaneous access to stored data. It may be of a localized nature (such as the accounting information of a particular firm) or more widespread – like the networks described in the previous paragraph. Common examples of information technology are the systems used in travel agencies for booking holidays, hotel accommodation, aircraft seats, etc. Similarly hospital appointments, freight space on ships, meals at fast-food counters, prices on the Stock Exchange, etc. are all specialized aspects of IT (information technology).

Some of these systems are called 'Expert Systems' by which we mean a system that has been programmed with all the knowledge that is available in a particular field, such as medicine, or astronomy, or economics. The caller might call up the medical system, outline the symptoms a patient was showing and the computer, by cross-checking and referencing its body of data, would diagnose the illness, or the likely illnesses, that might cause these symptoms.

Telemetry is a system of measuring data and alerting operators to emergency situations. For example rivers can be monitored to show the level of oxygen in the river to prevent fish kills; oxygen being bubbled into the river if the sensor detects a danger level. Overheating in grain stores, or atomic plants, and tidal levels which might indicate possible flooding can be detected in the same way.

19.13   The computerization of communication

The last twenty-five years has seen the most wonderful development of all in communication, the development of computerized communication. Computerization has already been referred (see Chapter 13) but its communication aspects deserve special mention because they are so spectacular. It is the use of **on-line computerization** which is so effective in the communication field.

Many activities for which we use computers are not particularly urgent, and so long as we allot them a time when the computer can perform the activity there is no absolute urgency for them to be done at once. For example, the payroll of a company which pays its employees monthly only has to be done once in the month. All the details required except the month's current figures for hours worked etc. are in the computer already, in the backing store. The programs are also in the backing store and can be loaded into the central processor in a few seconds. So long as we supply the details for this month – hours worked, changes (if any) in rates of pay etc. – we can run the program at any time of the day or night. All the information is off-line except for the short while the program is being run.

With on-line systems we have a system where anyone, at any time, can go into the computer and get information out of it. Actually the computer can only deal with one enquiry at a time, but because it works so fast it appears to anyone contacting the computer that it is responding immediately. An on-line system is said to be operating in **real-time**, that is the person has access to the computer at the very moment that he/she applies to the computer for information. The computer takes instant command of the situation and will do whatever is requested, making such decisions as are necessary. For example – suppose there are 10,000 bank machines (automated teller machines) in the streets outside banks in the UK. Suppose at any given moment there are 8000 of them being used by customers. The machines are on-line to a major bank computer which knows the state of every account in the bank as it was at 5.00 p.m. the night before. The 8000 people are all asking for money, all at the same time. The computer compares each request, one at a time, with the bank balance in the account the previous night. If there is enough money in the account it releases the money to the customer. If there is not it prints out a slip saying – 'Sorry – insufficient funds available – contact your branch for assistance.' The 8000 people do not realize they have been in a queue 8000 people long, because the computer works very fast, at about 12 mips. MIPS stand for millions of instructions per second, and bank computers work at about 12 million instructions per second. Each customer requires quite a few instructions, but even 8000 people can be dealt with in a few seconds at these fantastic speeds.

A similar sort of situation is used in rapid-transmit real-time railway systems. The computer runs the railway. It knows where every train is in the system, and lets them go, or holds them up, so that the line is used to its fullest capacity, and at the highest possible speed with no chance of a crash. The communication between the computer and the trains is made in millionths of a second. Similarly, in booking hotel accommodation, or airline tickets a real-time system is used so that anyone coming on-line to book a hotel room or an airline ticket is in an orderly queue. There are people all over the country calling in to get from the computer a display about any aircraft or hotel. The full details are displayed on a screen while the travel agent discusses the arrangements with the customer. As each seat or room is booked the computer updates itself to show that there are less seats or rooms available. Finally, when the plane or hotel is full the computer shuts out any further enquiries with a 'Fully booked' signal.

19.14   Projects on communcation in business

1   Using any firm you are familiar with, or if you are not at work using the school or college you work in, describe the communications network within it. Your project will take the form of a report which answers most of the following questions:

   (a)   Who is the most senior person in the firm or institution?
   (b)   Who are the other senior people, the Board, or the Governing Body or whatever it may be?
   (c)   Roughly how many subordinate people are there in lesser positions and how are they subdivided (into departments, branches, etc.)?
   (d)   How does (a) above communicate with (b) above?
   (e)   How do (a) and (b) communicate with (c)?
   (f)   Describe the services available including: (i) external telephone; (ii) internal telephone; (iii) intercom or loudspeaker calling system; (iv) house journal; (v) noticeboards; (vi) telex; (vii) fax; (viii) datel or similar services.
   (g)   How successful is the system in your opinion and is the morale in the organization good, with everyone well-informed about the organization's affairs?

2   Buildem and Lettem are estate agents who handle properties for a large number of clients, both as regards the purchase and sale of property and the letting of property. Outline methods for dealing with the information required to carry out these activities, so that suitable properties could be located for various customers.

19.15 Rapid revision

Answers		Questions	
	–	1	**What is communication?**
1	It is the passing of information from one person to another, either directly or by such devices as telephonic communication, intercom, correspondence, etc.	2	**When is a person not a good communicator?**
2	When the message he/she is trying to deliver is not understood, or not listened to by the other party by reason of boredom, antipathy to the speaker or distrust of him/her.	3	**What are the main subdivisions of communication?**
3	Spoken communication and written communication. Each of these can then be subdivided into personal communication and mass media communication.	4	**What are the mass media methods of spoken communication?**
4	Radio, television, video, public address and films.	5	**What are the mass media methods of written communication?**
5	Press, posters, noticeboards, billboards, Ceefax and Oracle.	6	**How is personal spoken communication subdivided?**
6	Into face-to-face communication and telephonic communication.	7	**What are the six ways of face-to-face communication?**
7	(a) Giving instructions; (b) making requests; (c) briefings; (d) talk-ins; (e) business meetings, especially AGMs and EGMs; (f) conferences and seminars.	8	**What are the main branches of telephonic communication?**

Answers	Questions
8 (a) Public telephone services of British Telecom and others; (b) internal intercom; (c) digital transmission (for high quality, long-distance calls and video-conferencing).	**9 What are the chief forms of personal communication in writing within an organization?**
9 (a) Memos; (b) bulletins; (c) notices; (d) house journals; (e) telenotes; (f) reports and summaries.	**10 And with outside organizations?**
10 (a) Correspondence, including standard form letters, quick reply letters and circulars; (b) press releases; (c) published reports.	**11 What is IT?**
11 Information technology – it is any sort of technology which enables the user to receive information from a computerized source, giving instantaneous access to stored data.	**12 What is a LAN?**
12 A local area network. It is a series of terminals linked with one another, usually through a Head Office, enabling all of them to contact one or more central computers; to share databases, etc. Examples are in banking, travel agency work, estate agency work, etc.	**13 What is the wider meaning of a network?**
13 It means a system which permits authorized users to gain entry to other organizations' computers, through a twelve-number user – identifier.	**14 What is an 'expert system'?**
14 A system where a computer has been programmed with an entire body of expertise – for example medical knowledge, legal knowledge etc. The applicant to	

Answers	Questions
	15 What is telemetry?
the expert system can pose a problem and the computer will sift through all the information and come up with a possible solution. For example, in police work, it might print out a list of known criminals who could crack the kind of safe described.	
15 Automatic transmission of data to a point where action can be taken to solve a problem, for example the low level of oxygen in a river; the overheating of a spaceman's suit, etc.	**16 Go over the test again until you are sure of all the answers. Then try the questions in Section 19.16 below.**

19.16 Questions on Chapter 19

1 Devise a blank memo form for use in your business to be run off by the local print shop in pads of fifty copies each. Make sure you have room for the sender's name, department, telephone number and extension, and for the destination addressee and his/her department. The date and time, and a 'Please reply by' section should also be part of the heading to the form. The message section should be at least two-thirds of the page.

2 You have noticed that an order for numerous items to be delivered by Friday includes an item which the customer has already been told cannot be available until next Monday. Write a memo to Tom Larkin in the Sales Department from your position in the Despatch Department asking if the whole load can wait until Monday as the customer's address is on the very limit of the driver's round and a double delivery will cost about £8 extra.

3 Tell Jill Peters, in the Order Processing Department, of a phone call you have had from Liz Scott to say that the recent order she sent for 2 packs of 200 millilitre skin moisturizer should have read 20 (twenty) packs. Will she please increase the order accordingly. Ask her to acknowledge that this has been done. You work in the Customer Liaison Department.

4 Ask Mike Dawson, the foreman in the Computer Assembly Department, to phone Roy Chalmers at Mervo-Products PLC about a Securicor Delivery he is expecting. It has been hijacked;

but if he moves quickly they can divert other supplies (but there will be a 5 per cent increase in price). Is this OK?

5   Devise a quick reply form to be used in an office to which students are constantly applying for help with financial grants to meet emergency situations. Use your imagination about the sort of information a bursar dispensing funds would need to know.

6   What is the difference between analogue and digital transmission of speech over the telephone? Explain in detail.

7   What is a local area network? How could it help a retail outlet in the travel and tourism industry?

8   What are (a) video conferencing and (b) bureaufax facilities.

9   Phone 0800 400 436. What is an 0800 number, and how does it work. (The number given is British Telecom's 0800 number for firms needing to know about services that will boost their sales and profits.)

10   What is the difference between an AGM and an EGM? How would those called to such meetings be summoned to attend, if they wished to know about the affairs of their company?

20
Employer–employee relationships

20.1 Nature of the relationship

The relationship between employers and employees has always been a difficult area of discussion since there are countless different relationships in millions and millions of firms and companies around the world. If we try to draw conclusions about such relationships we are likely to find that there are many exceptions to the general rules we have specified. It is perhaps most helpful to describe the extreme points of view, knowing that most actual situations will be somewhere between the two.

The strictly economic view is that labour is just another resource, a factor of production, which entrepreneurs will use best without any sentiment or consideration of the personal nature of the worker as a private person with his/her own rights and needs. From this point of view the position of the entrepreneur is one of complete freedom to 'hire and fire' as he/she thinks fit. The entrepreneur will mix together the factors – land, labour and capital – in the optimum way to get the best results, and maximize the profits of the enterprise. He/she will pay the worker as little a reward as possible (because the rewards paid to the workers eat into the profits available at the end of the accounting period). Profit is a residue that is left over after all the other factors have had their rewards, so it is obvious there is less profit left if wages are raised.

The opposite point of view would be a situation where the entrepreneur had such a close relationship with the employee that under no circumstances would the employee be dismissed, and once formed the employer–employee relationship would be indissoluble. One can imagine that situation in certain circumstances, as where a man employs his wife, or a wife employs her husband, or where the employee is the son or daughter of the proprietor of a firm. It is more difficult to imagine in a non-personal relationship, though we do hear of Japanese companies where the employee can look forward to a lifetime's service in the same company. Bearing in mind how technology changes and how people change as they grow older, it is difficult to imagine that many people would want to stay in the same job for a working lifetime.

In any case, even where the relationship is a friendly and considerate one at all times there does come a time when the economic facts of life make a totally considerate attitude impossible. Business fluctuates, and the labour force has to be reduced. Proprietors die, and their heirs are 'not the man their father was'. Personalities clash and people are made scapegoats for some failure of policy or strategy. In America the phrase 'I'll have to let you go' is used, which is a more face-saving expression than 'You're sacked'.

The more general situation may perhaps be described in the following way:

1   Generally speaking, and certainly at the start of a relationship both parties view the relationship as a long-term one. The employer undertakes to employ the employee, to provide a safe system of work as required by law, to pay an agreed scale of remuneration, to provide a framework of considerate welfare arrangements appropriate to an employment situation (for example not to dismiss the employee just because he/she becomes sick) etc. The employee in return undertakes to attend punctually and regularly, to perform such work as is required, to behave in a proper manner both towards the employer and fellow employees and to be as solicitous of the firm's well-being as of his/her own well-being.

2   At the same time there is an underlying recognition that no employment situation is really permanent. The employer is entitled to dismiss the employee in certain circumstances, such as dishonesty, gross negligence, immorality etc. The employer is entitled to terminate the employment in certain circumstances, such as where a redundancy situation arises due to changes in the economy; competition prevents the continuance of the business; etc. In such situations the employee will be treated in a proper manner no doubt, but the job will come to an end sooner or later. Equally the employee is entitled to give notice and leave the employment. There may be many reasons why an employee decides to do this, but to the extent that it is always a possibility the employer–employee relationship cannot be regarded as completely stable and permanent.

The employer–employee relationship is an important relationship in law. In its most ancient form it is known as the master–servant relationship, and much of employment law as it exists today is based upon the ancient law of master and servant. Superimposed upon this ancient code we have modern enactments about such important matters as the payment of wages, industrial relations law, contracts of employment, etc. These enactments together with the old common law about master and servant, give employees certain rights.

We may divide these rights into two areas – the personal rights of employees and the collective rights of employees.

20.2 The personal rights of employees

The personal rights are embodied in an Act called the Employment Protection (Consolidation) Act, 1978, but as this Act has been amended by one or two Acts subsequently we usually say 'as amended' when we refer to the 1978 Act. These rights are:

- A right to a written statement or a written contract of employment.
- Rights which take effect when notice of dismissal is given, including a right to a written statement giving the reasons for dismissal.
- A right to complain to an industrial tribunal if unfairly dismissed.

Each of these must now be explained.

A written statement or contract of employment

An employee who works more than seventeen hours a week must be provided with either a written statement of the terms of the employment or a written contract of employment, not later than thirteen weeks after starting work. The reason for the delay is that some people change jobs very soon after taking employment, when they find the work is not what they had hoped for. It would be a waste of time to enter into a formal arrangement if the employee was unlikely to settle.

The statement or contract must:

1 Identify both parties – the employer and the employee.
2 State the date when the employment began.
3 If the employment is for a fixed period state the date when it will come to an end.
4 State the rate of pay, the way pay is worked out and the pay period (an hour, a week or a month being the usual periods).
5 State the normal hours of work, and any special rules about working hours.
6 Explain what happens regarding holidays, sick pay, absence during injuries, etc.
7 Give details of any pension scheme, and whether the employee is contracted out of the State Pension Scheme.
8 State the length of notice required on either side.
9 State the employee's job designation.

It must include a note of any disciplinary rules affecting the employee and refer to any Code of Practice on Disciplinary Behaviour that exists in the organization. It must also make it clear to whom the employee may complain if wrongly disciplined – usually a person such as the Personnel Officer.

Itemized pay statements

Employers must give employees on or before pay day an itemized pay statement showing the gross amount of wages or salary, any variable deductions and details of the way they are calculated, the net pay receivable and any other details about the method of payment, etc. Where these arrangements fall into a steady pattern the details need not be given on every occasion, but may be replaced by a statement at intervals showing the aggregate deductions made.

Summary dismissal

Note that a person may be summarily dismissed – without notice or pay in lieu of notice, for gross misconduct. Gross misconduct is conduct that goes to the root of the contract of employment – for example theft of money or goods and behaviour endangering other employees or the whole business.

Rights after notice or dismissal

During notice an employee who works normally is entitled to normal pay. If no work is provided and an employee is willing to work he/she is entitled to a week's pay for each week of notice. A dismissed employee who has worked more than six months is entitled to a written statement of dismissal giving the reasons, within fourteen days of requesting it. If the statement is untrue in any way the dismissed person may make a complaint to an industrial tribunal.

Unfair dismissal

Dismissal is always an unpleasant event, certainly for the employee and often for the employer as well. If dismissal is unfair it not only arouses great resentment in the employee, but in his/her workmates and many strikes have been caused by the unfair dismissal of an employee. Employment law now holds that an employee has the right not to be unfairly dismissed, though in its present state this only applies to employees who have been employed for at least two years. An employee is dismissed in law, if:

1   The employer terminates his/her contract, with or without notice, or

2   he/she is employed under a fixed-term contract and at the end of one fixed term a new contract is not offered, or
3   if he/she is constructively dismissed. Constructive dismissal occurs when the employer breaches the terms or conditions of employment so seriously that the employee is entitled to leave, and can claim that the only reason for leaving was the bad attitude of the employer.

What is 'unfair'? We can best answer that by saying what is fair. A fair dismissal is one where:

1   The employee is incapable of, or not qualified, to perform the work and this can include poor health.
2   The employee's conduct is bad, and makes his/her employment disadvantageous.
3   There is no work to do – in other words the employee is redundant in the present situation.
4   Legal reasons prevent the employment continuing – for example an employee driver has been deprived of his/her driving licence for some reason.

If the employer can prove that one of these situations covers the dismissal then the dismissal will be deemed fair by the tribunal. If not, the employee who has been dismissed will be given compensation (or the employer may agree to take the employee back).

Even if the employer can prove fair dismissal, the manner in which the dismissal occurred may be unfair. For example, in a redundancy situation was the choice of this particular employee for redundancy fair? If others are being kept on there may be an element of unfair selection. The laws of natural justice are sometimes infringed. These laws say:

1   In any dispute both parties must be heard. If an employee had no chance to defend himself/herself that is unfair.
2   No man may be a judge in his own case. Thus if a manager who has dismissed the employee does not let some third party of similar (or higher) rank hear the employee's appeal, it is unfair. The manager cannot be both a party to a dispute and the judge who decides what is fair.

20.3   The history of industrial relations

Since the earliest days of the industrial revolution, which is generally held to have started in the year AD 1760, labour has tried to organize and secure the workers a fair reward for their work. Unionization reached its peak, perhaps, in the great Labour administrations of the 1960s and 1970s – there has been some decline in the strength of labour organizations since then, but no real lowering in the living standards achieved. The history of trade unions is interesting and still has some bearing on industrial relations today.

The stages of their development may be listed as follows:

1   The development of 'craft' unions of skilled men, whose work was essential to production in the early days of the industrial system. They were concerned not only to win better wages and conditions from their employers but also to erect barriers against entry by less-skilled men (to avoid the dilution of labour). The development of these craft unions was the main development up to about AD 1880.

2   Later the 'mass' unions developed to represent semi-skilled and unskilled employees in major industries. Focal points for this type of union were the transport industries; the railwaymen, the seamen, the port employees and – later – road haulage staff playing a prominent part. Some industries were more difficult to organize – for example, the retail trade and the garment trades consisted of many small firms, where it was difficult to arrange concerted action to compel employers to concede improvements in wages and conditions.

3   The growing band of 'management men' sought to organize in a rather different way. By forming professional bodies grouped around a particular form of expertise they created powerful pressure groups. The impact of these groups in securing a high standard of living for members was all the more effective because under the new system they were replacing the self-made entrepreneurs of earlier eras and consequently could be vocal in the most effective place – the boardrooms of the limited companies which employed them.

4   In the period between the wars and directly after the Second World War white collar unions developed to represent the mass of clerical workers, bank employees, etc.

5   These developments still left a large body of labour disorganized and ill-represented. Their battle was won on the political field, in the name of justice and fair play in an egalitarian society. Many of this last group work in low-paid public sector fields where there is no opportunity to win concessions at the expense of consumers. With more than half the nation's wealth being spent on services of this type the pressure to hold down wages in these areas is intense. Well may the hospital worker point to the injustice of his rewards compared with (less-skilled) employees in many industrial and commercial occupations. The withdrawal of labour in such areas is seen to be a blow at the very fabric of our way of life, hitting as it does the sick, the infirm, the socially deprived, etc. Such action is a measure of the desperation of public-sector workers, who

cannot compel an adequate concession by the ordinary processes of negotiation and arbitration.

What organizations are there, and what do they seek to do?

If we look at some typical organizations we shall perhaps be able to see what they are, and what they seek to do for their members.

The craft unions

These are the traditional representatives of skilled workers. They won their rights in the course of Victorian progress in industrial relations, as capitalist society broadened to embrace all the wealth-creating forces in society. The power of the landed aristocracy declined, the society where the squire, the parson and the doctor reigned supreme was replaced by one where engineers, scientists, financiers, merchants, importers, exporters and transport organizers became more important. These people rose from the ranks of labour to become a broad middle class – educated, skilled and knowledgeable. They were not all captains of industry but aspired to some level of management. Their unions were numerous, and relatively small and exclusive. The Engineers Union, the Boiler-makers, the Amalgamated Society of Locomotive Engineers and Firemen, the Electricians, the Woodworkers, etc. Members qualified for membership by apprenticeship and were (and still are) keen to maintain differentials (i.e. higher wages than less skilled employees).

The industrial unions

Although the members of the craft unions occupied key positions in industry, there was a broader band of working people in industry who could not aspire to membership of the craft unions. They saw the progress the craft unions had made and sought to organize themselves on an industry-wide basis. Such unions as the National Union of Railwaymen, the National Union of Mineworkers, the unions in the cotton and woollen industries, the National Union of Seamen and similar groups became very powerful. Their strength lay in their ability to bring industry to a standstill if they were not fairly treated. Young people today can scarcely believe how little people earned in those days. In 1912 the dockers' cry as they launched a nationwide strike was:

'Eight hours work, eight hours play
Eight hours sleep and eight bob a day.'

For those too young to remember what a 'bob' is, eight bob a day was 40 new pence a day, or £2.20 for a 5½ day week. They didn't get it, and the strike was broken.

In 1941 the author of this book asked one farm labourer in Yorkshire how much he earned. 'Ten shillings a week (50 pence today) and a pig a year.' The pig was a six-week old pig, which the labourer's wife fattened on potato peelings and scraps from the kitchen. Even in 1962 the wage of a London docker was only £12 a week; if he could find a ship to unload.

General trade unions

The growth of the general trade union is the big advance in trade unionism in the twentieth century. The largest and most representative of this group is the Transport and General Workers Union (the TGWU). For this union 'transport' really means road transport. The trouble with road transport is that it is easy to enter the industry, or it was in 1920. Anyone could buy a lorry or a bus and set up as an owner driver. It was a difficult industry to organize, with many small firms employing low-paid workers. For strength the unions gathered into it many other groups of low-paid workers and has certainly improved the lot of its members greatly – helped by political changes, and the more sympathetic attitude of Labour Governments. Today other general trade unions, like NUPE, The National Union of Public Employees, are doing similar, very essential work in ensuring that their groups of relatively low-paid workers are fairly represented in wage bargaining.

The most powerful body in trade unionism is the Trade Union Congress, which meets annually as a forum to debate union affairs, and whose permanent secretariat is the most powerful and vocal spokesman the Trade Union Movement can offer when matters of public interest require a trade union voice to be heard.

Professional associations

Professional bodies do not always regard themselves as 'trade unions', but their organizations aimed at fostering the professionalism of their particular groups within industry are certainly akin to trade unions. They are not perhaps so closely identified with wage bargaining as trade unions, though they all act as pressure groups to ensure proper rewards for their members, but their members are very vocal and well-educated and can often negotiate for their salaries individually. Almost every student of Business Studies will one day become a member of the professional body in the field he/she finally selects as the best career for him/her. Such bodies as the Chartered Institute of Bankers, the Chartered Institute of Transport, the Chartered Accountants, etc. are prestigious bodies recognized worldwide as influential spokesmen for their industries. They are not just interested in pay – that is taken for granted. Their chief interests are in the professionalism that is displayed in the industry they serve; its status in the economy; its responsiveness to the needs of the nation and the international community and their members' situations within the private and public sectors of their own national economies.

The 1980s have seen a great contraction of trade union powers, and massive changes in legislation to restrict the powers of the unions, which, rightly or wrongly, were blamed for much of the troubles of the UK economy in the 1970s. The 1970s were certainly a time of confrontation in industrial relations, and the confrontations persisted into the 1980s with a year-long miners' strike. The whole essence of Conservative policy was the introduction of 'supply-side measures' – measures to increase the output of goods and services by raising productivity, abandoning 'smokestack' industries (smokestacks were the symbol of Victorian production methods) and the introduction of new technologies into every level of industry. Supply-side measures are measures designated to make markets work better, and the markets referred to are the markets for factors – land, labour and capital. As far as labour is concerned the restrictive practices of some unions were brought to an end by a combination of legislation to reduce the powers of the unions by requiring secret ballots before strikes could be called, an end to 'closed-shop' arrangements, etc. and resolute refusal by the Government to give in to industrial action which had to be paid for by the Treasury in increased pay awards. Companies which were facing financial problems due to excessive wage concessions were not taken over by any sort of nationalized body, as they had been in the 1970s but were allowed to fail, or be taken over by more rigorous management.

At the same time, surprisingly enough, the actual rights of workers were restated rather than eroded, to give employees rights known as 'collective rights'.

20.4 The collective rights of employees

The collective rights are:

1 To be a member of a union and take part in its activities.
2 To refuse to join a union compulsorily.
3 To refuse to pay any penalty or make a contribution to charity instead of becoming a member of a trade union.
4 Not to be excluded from union membership if that is a condition of employment because a union membership agreement operates.
5 A right to paid time off work to perform industrial relations duties if appointed an official of the union.
6 A right to time off without pay to attend meetings of the union (but industrial action itself is not included).

7   A right to a separate ballot at the place of work if industrial action is called for by the union.
8   A right not to be disciplined unjustifiably by the union.

A recent Act, the Employment Act, 1988 appoints a **Commissioner for the Rights of Trade Union Members**, who may give legal advice and aid to a trade unionist bringing an action against his/her union.

The restatement of these rights is important, because if there is any infringement of them it is possible to complain to an Industrial Tribunal and considerable compensation may be obtainable (up to about £20,000).

20.5   Trade unions and employers' organizations

The Employment Protection Act, 1975 as amended, defines trade unions and employer's organizations, and appoints an authority, the **Certification Officer** to keep a list of all such organizations.

Trade unions are defined as organizations which consist wholly or mainly of workers of one or more descriptions, and whose principal purposes include collective bargaining on behalf of their members. Trade unions and employers' organizations must keep accounting records which are properly audited, and submit annual returns to the Certification Officer. They must observe all rules and regulations about membership, amalgamations, changes of name etc., and must keep rule books available for public inspection.

The Advisory, Conciliation and Arbitration Service (ACAS)

This service was set up on a statutory basis and its powers and duties include:

1   Offering conciliation and other assistance to settle any trade dispute.
2   Providing conciliation officers to help settle complaints made to industrial tribunals.
3   Referring matters in dispute to arbitration or to the Central Arbitration Committee (CAC).
4   Offering advice to employers, employers' associations, workers and trade unions on industrial relations and employment policies and publishing general advice, including suggested Codes of Practice or Codes of Conduct.

Today ACAS's activities are frequently featured on our television news programmes. They are active in almost every dispute and seek to keep the industrial relations situation as cool as possible and work towards conciliation rather than confrontation.

Organizations of employers

Employers have always banded together in associations of one sort or another, and if the organization is concerned with regulating the relationships between employers and employees as an important part of its activities it is regarded as an 'Employer's Association' for the purpose of the Trade Union and Labour Relations Act, 1974, and the Employment Protection Act, 1979 as amended. Such an association acquires special status under the Acts, and is capable of suing and being sued in the courts in its own name.

There are many employers' organizations. They exist not only to form a meeting ground for employers where problems of mutual interest may be discussed, but to represent employers generally in the economic and political fields. They may act as pressure groups to ensure that Parliament is appraised of the views of any industry in matters where legislation may be planned. They may promote desirable practices from the point of view of safety, hazardous materials and movements of cargo, etc.

One of the most famous is the CBI – the Confederation of British Industry – a body which is active in representing industry in political and economic discussions at home and abroad. Its viewpoints are lucidly expressed by a team of well-qualified and experienced spokespersons at many levels.

One of the elements in the legislation is that the employer has a duty to reveal to the trade union representatives (when they recognize any union) such information about the organization as the trade union might need to represent its members properly. This is a very important duty as far as the trade unions are concerned since without information about such matters as profitability, payroll numbers, labour turnover etc. it is difficult for them to judge what is a 'fair' claim for their members.

ACAS has issued a Code of Practice on this duty of disclosure which includes the following points:

1 The employer should release information which is in his/her possession to trade union representatives if they request it, unless it is against national security, or was given to the employer in confidence, or its disclosure would do substantial injury to the company (for example from competitors). If this is not done the trade union may apply to the Central Arbitration Committee to hear the matter.
2 The most likely headings under which disclosure might be demanded are (a) pay and benefits; (b) conditions of service; (c) manpower; (d) productivity and performance; and (e) financial costs and benefits, profits, etc.
3 Trade unions should not ask for the disclosure of information which would affect the company's competitive position.

4   Information should be requested and provided early in any negotiations so that discussions when held are realistic and based upon correct knowledge of the employer's situation.

20.6   Implications for the firm of industrial relations policies

Although the industrial relations problem is one of the most daunting problems firms face, it is a nettle that has to be grasped. The following checklist of points is worth considering and may give the reader some ideas about weaknesses in his or her own firm:

1   Is the communication between management and employees good in each section of the firm? Do employees know with whom to raise a complaint, and how the complaint will proceed? Managements are often quick to detect their own needs and to take steps to reshuffle staff arrangements to solve any problems. Are they equally quick to detect, or better still anticipate, the needs of staff at all levels?

2   Are all managers clear that they will be responsible for keeping an ever-open door in their own fields of responsibility? They must know that even the most imposing doors of top managers can be opened at once on any sort of major problem.

3   To many employees the immediate superior is often an insurmountable problem, and this can cause much frustration. Is there a safety-valve procedure for the employee who feels particularly aggrieved, and unable to get his/her grievance aired? This could perhaps be a special feature of six-monthly or annual personnel appraisals. A member of staff who is asked particularly about problems or grievances on the clear understanding that it is his/her right to have such problems aired and investigated, is less likely to cause troubles than one whose problems have been 'bottled up' for months, or even years, on end.

4   The best way to keep one's ear to the ground is for top management to have frequent contacts with staff at all levels, both formal meetings and informal meetings. A 'suggestions box' is another way to get the odd grievance aired. This type of contact is particularly important when other firms are in difficulties in the area or in the industry.

5   Employees who are called out for a national strike frequently do so with mixed feelings and are anxious about the impact of strike action upon both their pockets and their prospects. Confrontation with their own management is often not part of the dispute. In such circumstances a low-key, sympathetic approach may secure many advantages, such as the right of office staff to cross picket lines, agreement to allow safety (and, even more important,

maintenance) staff to work on so that whatever time is lost will be made up all the more easily after the dispute is settled. Provision of reasonable picketing facilities will often be appreciated, and contacts with both organizers and actual pickets should be maintained by all key staff. This will often hold at bay the more volatile activists and minimize tension with all ranks. The subsequent return to work should be openly discussed and procedures planned in the best interests of customers, staff and company (in that order). What is good for the customers and the staff will probably be best for the firm anyway in the long run. An *ad hoc* committee for monitoring the disruption to production and making plans for recovery afterwards, attended by leading strikers in return for a contribution to strike funds, may even be a possibility. This type of cooperation will do much to reduce bitterness.

6 Inevitably hardship arises in strikes. There are those who maintain that strikers should suffer the full rigours of their own action, and they may have a point. At the same time, especially in a national strike where the workers are obliged by reasons of solidarity to come out even though they are less than fully enthusiastic, adequate aid should be available to prevent real hardship. A special welfare fund may be available, or advance wages may be paid to those in real difficulties.

7 Every encouragement should be given to shop stewards and similar leading personalities in the unions in a firm to improve their education and training in business. This is particularly true in the field of Economics and Accountancy. A shop steward who can read and understand a set of final accounts is likely to be a moderating influence in the union rather than the reverse, and special additions to the accounts which bring out the proportions of cash flowing to workers, shareholders, etc., are likely to encourage realistic (rather than exorbitant) wage claims.

Above all, management and trade union sides should recognize that in the end the business has to go on if jobs are to be preserved and the prosperity of all maintained. There is no point in either side winning Pyrrhic victories. (King Pyrrhus, congratulated on his victory over the Romans in 279 BC, looked at the thousands of his best men dead on the field of battle and said 'One more such victory and we are all undone'.)

20.7 A project on industrial relations

During any school or college year certain industrial disputes are bound to arise and hit the headlines, both locally and nationally. It is difficult to study such events in real depth by the whole class, and the best thing is to appoint two members of the class for each major strike who will start a scrap book on it using the reports in one or two major national or local papers. The strike should be studied from the following points of view:

1   What were the chief causes of the strike – what was it all about?
2   Were ballots held before strike action took place and what were the actual results of the ballot?
3   How did the strike develop – what was the history of the strike? Was ACAS or any other body called in? If the strike is local, regular liaison with pickets to discover their feelings may be helpful in bringing out the true feelings of the rank and file members.
4   What was the actual result of the strike? Did either side win, and was it a real or a Pyrrhic victory.

The two class members should compile a written report on the strike and present it to the class as part of the industrial relations aspects of the syllabus.

20.8   Rapid revision

Answers	Questions
–	**1 What was the early approach of industrialists to labour?**
1 That labour was just another resource, like raw materials, or land, that could be used or not used, as economic circumstances dictated.	**2 How do we characterize this approach?**
2 As a 'hire and fire' attitude. The employer has the right to hire people and fire people, as he/she wishes.	**3 What is special about labour?**
3 It is the human factor, and as such needs more consideration than the other factors – land and capital.	**4 What is the dilemma of both employers and employees?**

Answers	Questions
4 That while both expect that a contract of employment is a long-term arrangement, in fact in the last resort they know it may end at any time, either because the employee gives notice to the employer, or because economic circumstances make it impossible for the employer to keep the employment going (situations of redundancy).	**5 What are the personal rights of employees?**
5 (a) The right to a written contract of employment; (b) the right to an itemized pay statement; (c) the right to a written statement giving the reasons for dismissal; (d) the right to complain to an industrial tribunal if unfairly dismissed.	**6 What are the essential elements of a contract of employment?**
6 It must identify both parties; (b) it must state the date the employment began and give the job designation; (c) it must state the rate of pay, the method of calculation of pay and the pay period; (d) it must state the normal hours of work and any special rules about working hours; (e) it must explain about holidays, sick pay, absence during injuries etc; (f) it must give any special disciplinary rules and the name of the person to whom complaint should be made about any improper disciplining.	**7 What are the collective rights of employees?**
7 (a) The right to belong to a trade union; (b) the right to refuse to join a union compulsorily; (c) the right not to be refused membership if membership is a condition of employment; (d) the right to time off without pay to	

Answers	Questions
attend meetings; (e) the right if elected to office in the union to time off with pay to deal with union matters; (f) the right to a ballot at the place of work if a strike is called.	**8 What are the chief types of trade unions?**
8 (a) Craft unions (for skilled trades); (b) industrial unions representing less-skilled trades in the major industries; (c) general trade unions (representing large groups of workers in widespread (often service) occupations; (d) professional associations (of high level managerial staff in the key industries).	**9 What are employers' organizations?**
9 Combinations of employers to represent the employers in all matters of political and economic affairs where the views of industry and management should be heard.	**10 What is the CBI?**
10 The Confederation of British Industry – the most prestigious of all employers' organizations and industry's most powerful pressure group on economic affairs.	**11 What is the TUC?**
11 The Trade Union Congress – the permanent organization which speaks on behalf of trade unions in all matters that arise.	**12 What is ACAS?**
12 The Advisory, Conciliation and Arbitration Service. It is a statutory body which offers conciliation services to both sides in industry, to assist in resolving disputes before they lead to strikes and the disruption of production.	**13 Go over the test again until you are sure of all the answers. Then try the questions in Section 20.9 below.**

20.9   Questions on Chapter 20

1   'Labour is just another resource which is available to entrepreneurs seeking to produce goods and services.' Comment on this statement and say whether in your opinion, there is anything 'special' about labour.

2   What is a trade union? What is an employer's organization? What are their aims?

3   What might be the effect of a round of wage negotiations on (a) the price of the goods supplied by the firm concerned; (b) the profit of the firm; and (c) the investment in new machinery etc., in the following period?

4   What would you regard as sound bases for good industrial relations? How may such a system be instituted and maintained?

5   Assess the importance of industrial relations to the economic performance of industry. How may good industrial relations be fostered?

6   'The minister has asked the parties to this potential dispute to meet at the premises of ACAS, to see if any solution can be found to the problem before the matter deteriorates into industrial strife.' What might ACAS do to help avert strikes?

Part Five
Aiding and Controlling
Business Activity

21
Aiding business activity

21.1　Why aid business activity?

Business activity creates wealth, by which we mean an abundance of goods and services. Since everyone is interested in prosperity, and wishes to share in whatever wealth is created, it stands to reason that any help that can be given should be given to someone prepared to start a factory, dig a mine, drill for oil, plant a forest or do any other wealth-creating thing. Since it is often when businesses are trying to start up, or are still very small, that they have the greatest difficulty, more help from central government and local government bodies is usually given to small firms. The trouble is that while they are still small those who have capital to invest (the institutional investors) hesitate to risk lending them capital. It needs someone in an official capacity, with funds provided by the taxpayer or the local ratepayers, to 'prime the pump'.

'Priming the pump' is an expression that is widely used for an initial injection of capital. It goes back to some of the early pumps, which would not pump water up until some water had been poured into them to get the mechanism working properly. The last thing everyone who pumped some water up did at the end was to pump up one extra bucketful before they finished pumping so that next time the pump was needed there was water to prime the pump. In the same way we often cannot produce any wealth unless we have some initial finance to prime the pump and get the business started.

Sometimes official aid is given without any requirement to return the money given, even if the business proves wildly successful. In other cases the help may take the form of an interest-free loan, while others may include an element of interest but at a relatively low rate – less than the rate charged by the banks and finance houses. All sorts of schemes have been tried, and some of them have been proved very successful. Less successful schemes are discontinued after a time and new schemes are tried. For that reason it is helpful to liaise with your local Small Firms Service office (see your local telephone directory) for details of current schemes, as new schemes may be added at any time. Some of the ways of helping business activity are given in the sections that follow.

The main areas of aid are:

1   Financial help of various sorts.
2   Help with premises.
3   Training facilities.
4   Special schemes for young people.
5   Advisory services.
6   Advice about exports.

21.2   The Start-up (Enterprise) Allowance Scheme

This scheme has been very successful and 600,000 people have benefited from it since it was set up. The number of self-employed people has risen in fourteen years (1979–93) by 1 million, to 3 million. The scheme pays those who are genuinely unemployed (i.e. unemployed for more than eight weeks) and who would like to set up in business, the sum of £45 per week for 12 weeks, then £35 for 12 weeks and then £25 for a further 12 weeks. If a husband and wife are both unemployed and they set up in partnership they each get the allowance. Cynics might say that since an unemployed person would be getting more than £45 in social security payments anyway the scheme is largely a way of doctoring the unemployment statistics. The scheme does not only involve a money payment, but quite a lot of helpful advice and back-up from the Enterprise Council, from bank managers, etc. The psychological impact is large too. Instead of being one of the unemployed one becomes self-employed. A person who sets up as a small company (and you can buy one off the shelf for £120) becomes a 'company director' overnight. While the status of a company director is often exaggerated, and not every company director is a millionaire, the morale of a person who is unemployed one day and a company director the next is often infinitely greater than the same person would have displayed if re-employed in a dead-end job.

The scheme is subject to some control by the Enterprise Council. The idea proposed, whatever it is, has to be discussed with a counsellor from the Enterprise Council and if it is considered viable the Start-up Allowance will be arranged. The applicant must have a capital of £1,000 (£2,000 if a married couple are involved). This is no problem really, because any bank will usually make this available to be repaid at about £53 a month as the business starts to earn money. Many people, as soon as they get the Start-up Allowance, repay the money borrowed unless they really need it for their business. A self-employed window cleaner with a ladder, a bucket and two clean rags does not need £1,000 capital and simply repays it.

Of course some businesses do fail, but the scheme reveals that about 60 per cent of them do keep going after the end of the first year when the Start-up Allowance ceases, and some of those who fail find that it is easier to get a job after they have been in self-employment for a year. Perhaps, knowing how hard it is to get going in business, they are more appreciative of their new employment, and consequently are less likely to be made redundant. Contact for this scheme begins through the local Jobcentre.

21.3   The Loan Guarantee Scheme

Sometimes a scheme which appears desirable and viable needs more capital than the small business can supply but the institutional investors hesitate to provide the capital because the trader or partners have no track record of proven business ability, and no assets worth mentioning as security for the loan. The **Loan Guarantee Scheme** is a government scheme to guarantee 70 per cent of the loan (85 per cent in some urban renewal programmes for the decaying inner cities). The government charges a small premium for insurance of the guaranteed part of the loan, to provide a pool of money from which those loans that are not repaid will be financed.

Loans can go up as high as £100,000, and must be based upon a sound business plan and a detailed outline of what is proposed. The bank making the loan then submits the plan as an approved scheme and in due course the guarantee is issued and the business can begin its expansion programme. Those wishing to get such a loan apply to any local bank.

21.4   The Business Expansion Scheme

This is a scheme designed to benefit people who have money to invest but who hesitate to lend it to smaller businesses because they cannot risk the large sum involved or feel that it will not be possible to earn a reasonable return on the investment. Such people are usually paying taxes, and often have sufficiently large incomes to be paying tax at the higher rate, which is at the time of writing 40 per cent. Under the scheme an investor who agrees to take ordinary shares in an unquoted trading company (that is a company that is not a public limited company with shares quoted on the Stock Exchange) is allowed to treat the sum invested as a payment out of current income, and not liable to tax. Thus an investor who invested £25,000 in such a company would save 40 per cent of this (£10,000) in tax. The investor would therefore get a £25,000 investment for only £15,000. This is a considerable inducement to the investor, and since the shareholding would be in ordinary shares it might be part of the arrangement for the investor to join the Board of the company and play some role in managing it and helping it to become successful. Those who are interested in investing in this way approach their local tax inspector for advice.

21.5   Nationalized industries' 'Aid to Small Businesses' schemes

The Coal Board and British Steel have set up special agencies to assist businesses to start up in areas where redundancies are making miners and steelworkers unemployed. The aid takes several different forms – for example cheap rate loans for at least some part of the start-up costs; assistance with premises and workshops; financial advice and training in business skills.

21.6   Premises

Although most business premises are provided by the private sector, and most estate agents have specialist staff who deal with commercial property, there are a number of other sources which may provide cheaper premises especially for new enterprises. Most local authorities are doing a good deal to help new firms find premises. Many of these are special developments of new property – empty shells in some cases waiting to be fitted out to the requirements of any firm that becomes interested. Such an arrangement is of course very useful – the new enterprise gets a place designed to meet its own special needs, often with an option to expand further if this becomes necessary.

Other local authority premises may be renovated buildings which have outlived the use of the original proprietors and are taken over by the authority to be turned into reasonably equipped, but relatively cheap, business premises. The advantage usually is that the authority will see to repairs, general maintenance and security matters, and the new business can get on with its own affairs so long as it abides by the terms of its contract with the local authority. As local authorities want to encourage employment in their areas the terms in the contract are rarely onerous, and every encouragement is given to the new business.

Another body which is very active in this field is the Rural Development Commission, a new name for a well-established body now embodied within it called COSIRA, the Council for Small

Industries in Rural Areas. One of its important activities is building small workshops and similar premises to encourage small businesses, and draw back into the countryside some of those people who in earlier times moved out to take work in the cities. It brings together local authorities, the Commission itself and a body called English Estates which is a government agency formed to finance industrial and commercial development in areas where the private sector hesitates to invest. It offers many different types of property, but the small units are run very flexibly – in other words people can take the property on very short leases (three months) so that if their idea is not successful they can simply give three months' notice to leave the premises. Some of the properties available are craft homes, where a workshop and domestic accommodation are linked to give the small craft business easy and cheap premises where they can meet local needs – for example tourist interests.

21.7 Training facilities

The UK is one of the best places in the world to get business training. There is a local college within reach of almost every person in the country. The important thing to realize is that the type of training required is not school-based, or academically-based through the universities, although of course many schools do run Business Studies courses, and so does almost every university. This is especially true now that the vast majority of polytechnics have been redesignated as universities. The polytechnics were previously the top level of this parallel stream of training running alongside the academic stream. This stream is the Further Education system which operates at all levels – from training the sort of person who missed out completely at school for one reason or another, and needs to start at a very basic level right from the start, up to people taking top-level professional qualifications. Another aspect of this alternative stream is that it operates in three ways – full-time studies, part-time day release studies and evening studies. It can also put on specialist courses in-house for firms who want special training programmes devised tailor-made to their requirements. If you need sound business training after leaving school and do not wish to go on to university seek out this less academic route at your local technical college, college of further education or poly-technic. The subjects taught will still be rigorous and demanding, but they will be slightly more practical and work-orientated. The BTEC courses, run by the Business and Technician Education Council lead on to full educational qualifications in their own right, but also give you entry to the professional examinations of all the professional bodies. The Youth Training Scheme makes extensive use of technical college facilities but also makes use of other 'trainers' for various schemes in particular trades.

Self-employment training

A certain amount of self-employment training takes place at the technical colleges and polytechnics already referred to, but there are also courses run by various Local Enterprise Agencies, the Small Firms Service, the Training Agency etc. For example, there is a Business Enterprise Programme which offers seven days of basic training covering the skills needed to set up and run a small business. This is offered by the Training Agency whose address may be found in every local telephone directory. They also offer a Management Extension Programme for unemployed managers and executives which includes a placement in a host firm to develop a particular aspect of the business, under supervision. There is also a Graduate Gateway Programme to encourage graduates to consider a business career. Business Growth Training is a further area, which offers part-time courses on expansion strategies for growing firms.

21.8 Special schemes for young people

There are a number of schemes aimed particularly at helping young people. The most prestigious perhaps is the Prince's Youth Business Trust, which provides finance (by grants and loans), workshop space, training and general counselling for young people – defined as being persons under twenty-six years of age. The Trust works through regional coordinators and the name of your local coordinator can be found by phoning London on 071 262 340.

Another similar nationwide network is the 'Livewire' organization sponsored by Shell UK Ltd which has a counsellor in every county and deals with enquiries from young people under twenty-six years of age wishing to create their own work. Leaflets are available from local Jobcentres, or you can dial 091 261 5584 for the name and address of your local counsellor.

'Head Start in Business' is a scheme run by the Industrial Society from its Enterprise Unit at the Industrial Society, Robert Hyde House, 48 Bryanston Square, London W1H 2LN (Telephone 071 262 2401). The actual courses are run from Brent Business Venture Ltd, 177a Cricklewood Broadway, London NW2 3HI. The courses cover all aspects of self-employment, legal matters, production, marketing, employing people, book-keeping etc.

Instant Muscle is a similar organization which operates nationwide. Its aim is to assist people who wish to start up small businesses by providing professional business counselling, advice and training. This is with particular reference to the unemployed, the inexperienced and those needing a significant level of individual assistance and support.

About half of its participants have no academic qualifications but Instant Muscle's experience has proved over the years that this need not debar individuals, who have the necessary enthusiasm, diligence and initiative from running successful businesses.

21.9 Support for export activities

Export activities are often misunderstood. Many business people think that because export customers are far away and there are extra costs in reaching them and in providing special packaging and foreign language cartons etc. that it must be difficult to make a profit. They forget that overseas trade usually results in large orders, and that dealing with things in bulk is more economical. The government is keen to encourage business people to start exporting and provides a good deal of help and encouragement. The Department of Trade and Industry runs helpful services like the Export Market Information Centre, in London which provides a great deal of information on export markets.

This information is available in most local area offices of the Department of Trade and Industry by computer links. There is also a computerized Export Intelligence Service which gives advance warnings of export opportunities in all countries around the world. Other services include Technical Help for Exporters, run from the British Standards Institute in Milton Keynes, which can solve all sorts of technical problems – like voltages in use in different countries, electrical systems, etc. There is also a 'New Products from Britain' publicity service which will help business people assess the commercial viability of a product or service in an overseas market.

21.10 Useful publications

There are a number of useful publications which teachers, lecturers and students should obtain. Some are official publications, from such bodies as the Department of Employment and the Central Office of Information. Others are funded by major organizations as part of their general enterprise activity. The names of official publications do change from time to time as policies change and it may be necessary to write and ask for current literature in the enterprise field. Some of the present titles are:

- *Services for Small Businesses* – from the Department of Employment, either at local offices or at Caxton House, Tothill Street, London SW1.

- *In Business Now* – from the Department of Trade and Industry, 7th Floor, Bridge Place, 88–9 Eccleston Square, London SW1V 1PT (Telephone 071 215 0802).
- *The Small Business Digest* – National Westminster Bank PLC, 3rd Floor, Fenchurch Exchange, 8 Fenchurch Place, London EC3M 4PB.
- *Business in the Community Magazine* – 227A City Road, London EC1V 1LX.

21.11   A project on aid for business activities

Although there is a great deal of aid available for those wishing to set up their own businesses the agencies concerned are busy dealing with genuine applicants for help and cannot provide masses of literature for every student of Business Studies. It is, therefore, best if materials about aid for business activity are requested officially by staff and made available for student use.

The likely agencies besides those already mentioned, are the local unit of the Small Firms Service (see your local telephone directory) and the local branches of the major banks, most of which now have small business advisers. Staff should also obtain some information from the local enterprise agency – there is one in nearly all districts.

Based on such materials the following projects should present little difficulty.

1 Robert Midgeley and his wife Ann are both unemployed in an area where there is little prospect of employment for Robert, who is unskilled and has previously been employed as a caretaker and odd-job man. His wife has experience as a cook and has been hoping for a vacancy at the local hospital, but none has arisen. Robert is a driver and they live in an area near a busy main road with much traffic. They are considering setting up a roadside café. What would be involved in such a project, and is there any help available? Draw up a business plan and a description of the help that might be available.

2 Peter Lark has a good job with a graphics designer but does not get enough work of the type he most likes – which is cartoon style illustration. He is considering setting up on his own, and has been promised one firm order by a national newspaper of £100 per week for a 'four illustrations only' comic strip featuring a space-woman visitor from another planet – the series to last six months with a possible extension to one year. Draw up a business plan and an account of the help that might be available.

3 Heavy Removals Ltd is a subsidiary of Macro PLC, and was taken over three years ago. Since that time it has been starved of capital by the new owners who are now in financial difficulties anyway – chiefly due to large borrowings during their expansion period. The chief staff in Heavy Removals Ltd think they could buy out the company from Macro PLC for £22 million. They can raise £2 million from their own resources and a further £500,000 from drivers and other staff who also dislike working for Macro PLC. What sort of help is available to such a 'management buyout?'

21.12 Rapid revision

Answers	Questions
–	**1 Who provides help for enterprising people?**
1 Banks and other financial institutions will provide a great deal of help but in areas where there are serious problems (areas that used to be called depressed) it is usually official agencies set up by central government, local government or the European Community.	**2 How does this sort of agency work?**
2 (a) The government provides funds to set up a basic organization; (b) it also persuades leading personalities to take some part in the work, and prosperous firms to second one or two members of staff to act as advisers, consultants, etc. (c) funds are made available either officially or through some link with a bank or other financial body to 'prime the pump'.	**3 What does 'prime the pump' mean?**
3 It means 'to get things going'. The government expects some projects to fail but hopes the successful ones will restore prosperity to previously depressed areas.	**4 What is the Start-up Allowance Scheme?**

Answers	Questions
4 A scheme to give £40 a week to any unemployed person for one year (£80 to a married couple if both are genuinely unemployed) to help them set up in business.	5 **What is the Loan Guarantee Scheme?**
5 A government scheme to encourage banks to lend to more risky projects by guaranteeing 70 per cent of any loan (85 per cent in urban renewal programmes). Loans can be as large as £100,000 and must be based on a sound business plan.	6 **What is the Business Expansion Scheme?**
6 A scheme which allows those who have good incomes, and are prepared to invest cash in a new enterprise or an expanding enterprise, to count the investment as a business expense and therefore subject to tax relief. Thus at 40 per cent tax rate an investment of £10,000 would save £4,000 tax and effectively only cost £6,000.	7 **Why is training an aid to enterprise?**
7 Because training is more work-orientated than other educational activities, and may be of direct benefit to a budding entrepreneur in two ways: (a) it may teach particular trade skills; (b) it may teach business and management skills.	8 **Why is export activity often more profitable than home trade?**
8 Because it is wholesale – not retail. The orders are bigger, and therefore there is a large profit element, only some of which is needed to cover the extra expenses involved.	9 **Go over the test again until you are sure of all the answers. Then try the questions in Section 21.13 below.**

21.13   Questions on Chapter 21

1   Why do government agencies work best in reviving areas depressed by the collapse of older industries?
2   Suggest five reasons why an unemployed person might do well to consider self-employment.
3   'It is unlikely, lad, that you will ever earn enough to own a car of your own,' – schoolteacher to sixteen-year-old school-leaver. 'Not a bad set of wheels, Sir, don't you think,' – the same school-leaver, at nineteen, celebrating his first million by buying a Rolls-Royce, and featuring in a television programme about the rebuilding of Sheffield. Why should a school 'failure' do so well?
4   Magenta Ltd supply dyes to the clothing industry in their own home country but have never considered export trade. What outlets are open to them to export their products and where might they get help and advice?
5   Draw up a list of professional advisers whose help might be required by a person going into business. What services would each be able to offer. In your answer refer particularly to (a) premises; (b) business structure; (c) book-keeping and accounts and; (d) marketing.

22
Controlling business activity

22.1 The need for controls

Although governments want to encourage business activity as much as possible so that a high standard of living can be enjoyed by its citizens, they cannot allow completely free enterprise. In the early days of the capital system, from about 1760–1880 the doctrine of 'laissez faire' applied. 'Laissez-faire' means 'leave things alone to work themselves out', in other words: 'Don't try to control business, leave entrepreneurs free to enrich themselves and they will eventually enrich us all.' It was a fine theory, and to some extent it worked as far as the creation of wealth was concerned, but it had some very serious side effects. In those days the area around Birmingham became known as the 'Black Country', because the smoke and fumes turned buildings black with grime. Industrial injuries were common, and industrial diseases such as silicosis and bronchitis were rife. The countryside was scarred with slagheaps and rubbish tips, and the rivers became so polluted that fish could not live in them. One ancient writer records that when the Romans came to Britain they found the rivers so full of fish that you could just take them out of the streams without any need for fishing – yet after fifty years of uncontrolled capitalism there were rivers with no single living thing in them. This is still true of some of our rivers even today.

What happens when you have uncontrolled business activity is that a great many costs – especially environmental costs – are left to be borne by the general public. These costs are called '**social costs**'. They have to be borne by society generally, instead of by the entrepreneur as a business cost. They may be in the form of air pollution – harmful gases not being cleared from factory waste gases before being re-leased into the atmosphere. They may be in river pollution – liquids containing dangerous chemicals (heavy metals like lead and arsenic etc.) being released into rivers. They may be in the form of employee illness – respiratory problems, poisoning, industrial in-juries and deaths and today, cancerous diseases caused by excessive atomic exposure during work, or by such accidents as the Chernobyl disaster. The latter accident reminds us that it is not just capitalism that is at fault. The worst examples of pollution today are in the former Communist countries, precisely because public opinion has been stifled for seventy years and unable to control plant managers concerned with output, and prepared to disregard social costs.

Probably social costs will always continue to some extent to be unloaded upon the community, but in every aspect of production, distribution and exchange we should seek to control business activity, and ensure industry carries the full costs of production. Equally there may be many methods of working which are against the public interest. Controls are necessary to prevent fraud, and various sorts of cheating such as the adulteration of food, mis-descriptions of the quality of materials used in manufacture, false price-marking etc. Many manufactured items are poorly designed, and such problems as the collapse of prams and pushchairs, dangerous children's cots, unsafe electrical appliances etc., need to be checked by procedural methods – for example banning the sale of products, suspension of sale until modifications are put in hand and the recall of dangerous items.

22.2   Private costs and social costs

It is not an easy thing to distinguish private costs from social costs. For example, most of us have cars, and bear the cost of our petrol as a private cost. We cannot use the car without belching forth exhaust gases, and those who live near a busy main road will know that these exhaust gases spoil the environment for us. They make it impossible to sit in the garden – children may be brain damaged by the lead where motorists have not changed to unleaded petrol, etc. The brain-damaged child bears as a social cost what the motorist does not bear as a private cost – because if all motorists used catalytic converters on their exhaust systems the most serious effects could be avoided. In many states in the USA the law requires exhaust gases to be below certain harmful levels and if a vehicle is tested and is found to be outside the limits the motorist must put the work in hand before the vehicle can be used again, and must report for a retest. This is the kind of control which could (and should) be introduced. Generally it is essential to use the law-making process to achieve control, for until a thing is unlawful some people will persist in doing it. We therefore find that in most areas of business activity there are laws that have to be obeyed and penalties can be imposed for breach of them. Some of the areas where controls have been imposed are as follows:

1   Controls over the form of business – with particular reference to a limited liability company.

2   Controls over health and safety at work.
3   Controls over food and the methods of production and processing of foods.
4   Measures to protect consumers.
5   Measures to control the use of vehicles.
6   Measures to protect the environment.

22.3   Environmental controls and planning

Generally speaking, the influences of business on the environment are protected by the 'planning authorities which have a general responsibility for ensuring that businesses which may have undesirable environmental effects, are not allowed to set up without adequate measures to protect the environment. This is partly secured by zoning regulations, and the system of County Plans. These are long-term forecasts of the likely future needs of the population and the economy and include the designation of certain areas as business areas, residential areas and green-belt areas (areas of countryside around towns which are not to be built on, but are to be kept as agricultural areas). Any request for development is looked at in the terms of the County Plan, and whether it is a desirable development or not.

The proposal then has to be notified to the public by a series of notices in prominent places which give people a chance to object to the proposed development, while those most likely to have an objection are circularized personally to ensure that they are aware of the proposals. The plans may be seen at the local council offices, and objections may be lodged for consideration at the next planning meeting. All objections are carefully considered and if necessary a public enquiry may be held. Ultimate power lies with the Minister, who will often accept the advice of the Chairman of the public enquiry, but not always.

The whole procedure takes time, and causes delays to the development, but this is inevitable, and probably desirable. Bear in mind though that you cannot always change the location. If coal is discovered at a particular site we cannot mine it anywhere else and if it is an area of natural beauty we must weigh the loss of that beauty against the loss of energy if we decide not to mine it. Perhaps we can landscape the mine to make it less obtrusive, or insist on restoring the area once the coal has been removed (which may take years). Similarly oil wells and natural gas deposits may – after an initial period of disruption while the drilling takes place – become relatively well-disguised industrial sites which are not offensive to the local people.

The work of 'pressure groups' can be very important in such

matters. The environmental lobby is well-organized and local support is easily aroused. (The term 'lobby' refers to the entrance hall in the House of Commons where members of the public and other interested parties are able to meet Ministers and Members to express their points of view.)

Once the planning stages are over many enterprises need continuous monitoring to ensure that the promises made at the planning stage are actually carried out in the construction period, and in the operational period once the plant has been commissioned. Not only are inspections carried out by building inspectors during the construction stage but these checks are continued by the quality control procedures as soon as the plant comes on stream, and long-term operational activities are subject to scrutiny. In the construction stage, for example, the public must be excluded from building sites while work is in progress and secure walls to keep them out are quickly knocked together from panels of chipboard and similar materials. Complaints from the public are promptly taken up and firms can be served with orders to close down processes which are being carried out improperly.

Appropriate authorities monitor environmental changes, in many cases on a continuous basis – as where rivers are monitored by telemetry to detect changes in water quality or where 'returns' are required by health authorities. Thus owners of public swimming pools must submit returns showing the taking of water samples on a daily basis for analysis, and detailed reports on the results.

22.4   Consumer protection

Consumer protection is a very important part of control, and the current piece of legislation is the Consumer Protection Act, 1987. The Act deals with three main subjects. They are:

1 *Liability for defective products*   This part states that the person who produces a product is the person liable for any harm that it does. If the product is not produced in the UK it is the importer of the product who is liable. This prevents importers blaming the defect on a foreign supplier whom the dissatisfied customer would find difficult to pursue for redress of his/her grievance.
2 *Consumer safety*   The Act makes it an offence to supply consumer goods which fail to comply with the **general safety requirement**. The requirement is that goods shall be reasonably safe, having regard to all the circumstances, and must not contain any defective substances or infringe regulations about that sort of product. The Secretary of State may issue **prohibition notices** and **notices to warn** manufacturers about the safety of their products.

3   *Misleading price indications*   This part of the Act makes it an offence to give misleading price indications of any sort – such as where the price is said to be less than it in fact is, or where a price is said to cover a package of items (for example the supply and service of an article) but in fact a separate charge will be made at a later date. The Office of Fair Trading has published a detailed 'Code of Practice' for Traders on Price Indications which lays down what may, and may not, be done about marking prices. The local Weights and Measures Office are empowered to enforce the Code of Conduct, and will always advise traders if they are in any doubt about the procedures they should follow in marking prices, special offers, etc.

The Minister of State for Consumer Protection may publish regulations from time to time, in consultation with all interested parties, to ensure the safety of products. Examples are The Electrical Appliances (Safety) Regulations 1978. There are many such sets of regulations, and about twenty sets are added each year.

22.5   Controls over the forms of business

This subject has been referred to earlier in Chapter 6, but is worth reiterating here. Because sole traders and partners are legally liable to the limit of their personal wealth for the debts and the wrongs that they do to others there is little need to control them. Where a company operates, however, the shareholders have limited liability and cannot lose more than the value of the shares they have purchased in the company, nor can the directors be sued personally for wrongs of the company which is an independent body in its own right – an incorporation. For this reason controls over companies are very extensive indeed. The current Act, the Companies Act, 1985 has 747 sections and 600 pages of text. Almost every section ends with the words:

If an officer of the company knowingly and wilfully authorizes or permits the omission of any requirement of this section he is liable to a fine, and for continued contravention, to a daily default fine.

Clearly it is impossible to go into such a large number of controls, but they are a very important matter for company directors who should buy a copy of the Act and study it carefully.

22.6   Controls over health and safety at work

There have been (since about 1890) controls of one sort or another over health and safety at work, but the Health and Safety at Work

Act, 1974 introduced a new approach. It laid down broad obligations on employers about their duties to provide a safe system of work. Some of the points laid down were:

1 The employer must provide and maintain plant and systems of work which are, so far as is practicable, safe and without risks to health.
2 This also applies to the use, handling, storage and transport of articles and substances.
3 Staff must be informed, trained and supervised in such a way as to ensure, so far as is practicable, health and safety of all employees.
4 Premises, access to premises and departure from premises must be made as safe as possible.

To ensure that these ideas are followed codes of practice and guidance notes are issued by the Health and Safety Executive.

No charge may be made to employees for any protective clothing or other equipment required by the Act.

Statements of policy

If an employer has five or more employees he/she must draw up a **Statement of Policy on Health and Safety at Work**. The policy must cover:

1 The general policy.
2 The organization provided to back up the general policy.
3 The arrangements for carrying out the policy.

Although guidance notes are issued the essential thing is for the statement to fit the needs of that particular workforce in that particular trade or industry.

How firms are controlled

Essentially controls must be the result of legislation, that is Parliament considers a 'bill', a proposal by the Government, or possibly by a private member, and after passing through all the stages in both the House of Commons and the House of Lords, it receives the Royal Assent and the 'bill' becomes an Act of Parliament.

The stages of passing a bill are as follows:

1 The First Reading – the name of the bill is read and copies are made available to members.
2 The Second Reading – this is a debate in front of the whole house, on the general principles of the bill.
3 The Committee Stage – where every line of the bill is considered point by point, and amendments are discussed and either

accepted or rejected. Very important bills may be discussed in a Committee of the Whole House.

4   Report stage – the final bill is accepted.

Some bills start in the Commons and after the Report Stage go on to the House of Lords. Other bills start in the Lords and finish up in the House of Commons.

After the Royal Assent the Act of Parliament comes into force on a designated day, though some parts of it may wait until a Commencement Order is issued by the appropriate Minister.

Subordinate legislation

Nearly all Acts empower Ministers and others to make 'orders' which have the force of law and must be obeyed. Such orders are often called **delegated legislation** because the power to make them is delegated by Parliament to the Minister of State concerned, and through him/her to lesser ranks. They may be emergency matters – such as a cattle restriction order in an outbreak of foot and mouth disease – or they may be routine matters, like a periodic review of a statistical nature. This kind of 'order' is where much of the control is exercised, because orders are very specific; they name the firm, and the matter that is giving cause for concern and require it to be put right. Failure to comply can mean a fine, or imprisonment, or both.

22.7   The influences of independent organizations and statutory bodies

There are so many influences at work on businesses that it is impossible to mention them all, and many of them have been referred to elsewhere in this book. A few words about some of the more important ones are given below.

The Office of Fair Trading

This is a very important body with a Director General which has done much to improve the climate of business activity, and make the relationship between suppliers and customers fairer. The most important aspects of this are the regulations made under the Consumer Credit Act, 1974. The requirement to give the Annual Percentage Rate (APR) on all credit documents, credit cards, etc. enables us all to know what the true rate of interest is and thus to be able to compare one type of borrowing with another type.

Other aspects concern the power of the Director General to ask the Minister to refer to the Monopolies and Mergers Commission any takeover bid which it is felt will significantly reduce competition in a particular industry.

The Advertising Standards Authority

This body, as its name implies, seeks to ensure that advertising reaches a good standard. Its catchphrase 'is it legal, decent, honest and truthful' embodies much of what the authority feels constitutes desirable behaviour by advertisers.

Chambers of Commerce

These bodies have important parts to play in ensuring that international agreements are observed in such matters as the origin of exports, and the value of exports. Many countries, for one reason or another, erect barriers to, or embargoes on, the goods of other nations. Thus European countries might exclude goods from some Third World countries and many countries exclude South African goods, because of the apartheid policy. If goods from South Africa were exported to the UK and then re-exported as British goods, it would be clearly against the wishes of many countries. Therefore a system of Certificates of Origin, which have to be approved by the local Chamber of Commerce, applies. Similarly many countries object to 'dumping' (the sale of goods to foreigners at a cheaper price than they are sold at home, just to earn foreign currency). Clearly such goods undercut the home products being manufactured in the importing country and this is unfair. Chambers of Commerce, as members of the ICC (The International Chamber of Commerce) are the recognized bodies to certify the true value of goods sold abroad.

The Confederation of British Industry

This has already been mentioned as the largest employer's organization in Britain, with 250,000 businesses represented either directly, or indirectly. Together these firms employ half the working population. The Confederation provides useful statistical evidence of how employers see the economy: are they taking on staff or turning them away; are they investing in more plant and machinery or divesting themselves of such assets as they can dispose of; are interest rates too high, etc? The Confederation is a powerful pressure group on behalf of industry; it represents the UK in the Union of Industries in the European Community, and it nominates the employer's representatives in ACAS, the Advisory, Conciliation and Arbitration Service.

The Consumers Association

The Consumers Association is a private body, financed by subscriptions from its members, which tests products and recommends 'Best Buys'. Its magazine, *Which?*, features not only products of various types but also such matters as the provision of credit, the quality of holiday packages, the problems of divorce, the making of wills and similar matters. It acts as a powerful pressure group on firms and on the government on consumer affairs.

The British Standards Institute

Based at Milton Keynes, the British Standards Institute lays down standards for a wide variety of products and certifies them as being safe by awarding the 'Kite Mark' to goods which meet its specifications as to quality, durability and safety.

The Citizen's Advice Bureau (CAB)

These independent bodies receive some funding from central and local government sources. They exist to give free advice on all matters worrying the ordinary citizen – consumer affairs, marital problems, financial problems, etc. They are run by volunteers who have undertaken a certain amount of voluntary training, but also bring to the bureau a great deal of professional experience from their own walks of life.

22.8   Conclusions about Business Studies

We are coming to the end of a long book about Business Studies, and the reader is no doubt coming to the end of a long course of study. The conclusion we must inevitably draw is that there is much that we have not covered, and that so far from reaching the end, we have only reached the end of the beginning of a full study of the subject.

The most important thing to say about business activity is that it is **an intricate pattern of activities**, and the more intricate the pattern the higher the quality of life that can be sustained if we make the right choices. Every new business moves into its particular niche in the whole display of enterprise, and starts to contribute to the total output of goods and services which alone justify business activity. The cycle of production rolls on – each business takes its share of land, labour and capital and creates goods or services which are needed to satisfy human wants. The consumption of these goods, and the use of these services, means that another cycle of production must begin again next day, and next week, and next month for ever.

That there are many things wrong with the world most people would agree, but in general business activity is not one of them. Some of the things done in the name of business are no doubt reprehensible; there are mistakes made in every field of human endeavour; but on the whole business is a beneficial activity. Business alone can provide goods and services in the right quantity, at the right time, in the right condition and at the right place at the right price for the citizens of the world.

The author wishes readers the very best in their future careers and hopes you will pursue your studies to full professional qualification in the discipline you eventually select. The important thing is to make as high a contribution to the creation of wealth as your talents permit, whatever the frustrations encountered. In that way you will earn reasonable rewards for yourself, while ensuring that there is plenty for everyone else, with as little damage to the biosphere, which is our mutual inheritance, as possible.

22.9 A project on the control of business activity

Business activity may be controlled by a wide variety of measures, but they arise from legal powers conferred by Acts of Parliament. One of the best ways of understanding these legal controls is to make a collection of actual cases. There are certain cases reported in the *Times* as they occur which digest the important facts of cases and make interesting (if rather difficult) reading. More lively perhaps are the full reports of cases in the local and national press of firms and companies which have been charged with offences. It is well worth while appointing one or two members of a class to collect a scrapbook of reports on a particular case, and report back to the class on the whole matter. Such a report should cover the following facts:

1 Who were the parties charged?
2 What were they charged with? In particular of what piece of legislation had they been in breach?
3 What were the actual facts of the case?
4 What defence did they offer?
5 What was the final result?

Remember, if the case is a local one in particular, that while what is said in Court is privileged, and no one can be sued for what they say in Court, the same is not true outside the Court. Everyone is innocent until proved guilty, and if you report back to the class you should report carefully, stating only what the Court case revealed, without embellishment or personal viewpoints.

22.10   Rapid revision

Answers	Questions
–	**1 Why are controls over business activity necessary?**
1 (a) Because any business based on profit-making will seek to avoid costs which can be passed on to the general public as social costs; (b) to prevent unsatisfactory methods of work and the marketing of dangerous products.	**2 What are 'social costs'?**
2 Costs borne by the general public to save the manufacturer expense, such as noise pollution, air pollution, water pollution, and other adverse environmental effects.	**3 How are environmental effects controlled?**
3 Partly through the planning procedures, to ensure that plants are set up in proper places according to any zoning arrangements. Actual construction and operations are subject to monitoring activities by inspectors.	**4 What Act protects the consumer?**
4 The Consumer Protection Act, 1987	**5 What are its chief points?**
5 (a) It makes the manufacturers liable for defective goods, but if it is an imported item it is the importer who is liable; (b) it introduces a general safety requirement with which all goods must comply; (c) it enforces a body of Practice on Price Indications to prevent the public being misled.	**6 Which form of trading organization is most closely controlled?**

Answers		Questions	
6	The limited company, because since the shareholders have limited liability they are more likely to abuse the privileges Parliament has accorded to them and must be restrained by a sound code of laws.	7	**What is that code of laws?**
7	At present it is the Companies Acts, 1985–89.	8	**What is the purpose of the Health and Safety at Work Act?**
8	To promote safety at work by imposing a sound body of laws upon employers to provide a safe system of work. This is embodied in a clear Statement of Policy drawn up by all employers of five or more people.	9	**How are firms controlled?**
9	By legislation. There is a wide variety of Acts of Parliament covering both general activities and specific activities of particular industries. Not only must firms comply with the legislation but also with a host of 'orders' and othe subordinate (sometimes called delegated) legislation.	10	**What is the chief feature of free enterprise business activity?**
10	Its intricate nature: an involved pattern of major and minor industries, with numerous smaller firms occupying a 'niche' somewhere in the system. A centrally-controlled economy (such as a communist economy) cannot develop this intricate pattern of enterprises, because of the huge bureaucracy that would be needed to plan everything.	11	**Go over the test again until you are sure of all the answers. Then try the questions in Section 22.11 below.**

22.11   Questions on Chapter 22

1   What are private costs? What are social costs? Give examples of each, referring to a particular industry you are familiar with.

2   Organic Chemicals PLC proposes to establish a fertilizer plant at the mouth of an English river. What controls operate to ensure that this is an acceptable idea. What controls will operate once the plan is approved?

3   (a)   What are the rules about liability for defective products under the Consumer Protection Act, 1987.

   (b)   Parent, whose child has been made seriously ill by eating rubber imitation sweets sold to her by Trader, has sued Trader for damages, claiming the suffering of the child and her own distress. The sweets were actually made by Man Lee Products of Kysumu, and were imported by Funtoys of Camside Ltd. Advise Trader of the legal position.

4   What is an Act of Parliament? How does a piece of legislation finally reach the statute book?

5   A new set of regulations called 'The Employment of Disabled Persons Regulations' is about to be published. What steps should the Managing Director of a company take when he/she hears of the imminent appearance of the regulations.

6   'It is no good throwing up your hands in horror as if it is all too much for you. Parliament has imposed certain duties upon you and you must find out what they are, and carry them out.' – speaker at a meeting of people interested in setting up in business, referring to the VAT regulations. How would one set about finding out all about VAT. (*Note:* Teachers who would like to show classes one simple method of keeping VAT records may send for a free copy of their VAT book to George Vyner Ltd, Mytholmbridge Mills, Holmfirth, Huddersfield HD7 2TA.)

Appendix: Professional organizations

The following bodies either set examinations in subjects which include Business Studies of various sorts or are professional bodies prepared to accept students for student membership with a view to their passing the professional examinations and achieving full membership. Such full membership cannot usually be secured without practical experience in the industry concerned, but students intending to enter the field concerned are of course welcomed, and guidance will be given about options on degree courses etc. most likely to be helpful to students in the future.

Your aim should be to obtain full qualifications in the professional body of your choice, after concluding any academic course you are presently embarked on. For those in employment already, not possessing the necessary qualifications for entry to a professional body guidance will usually be given about subjects to study. The Made Simple series contains most of the books you will need, and 6–12 months study is usually enough to qualify for student entry. Write well in advance to educational bodies whose examinations you wish to sit, so that you do not miss vital deadlines for entry.

A businesslike approach to such studies is essential – buy the books; enrol on courses in your own locality if you can; if not study hard on your own and work systematically.

Professional bodies whose names and addresses are not included in this list are invited to submit details for inclusion in the next edition. The author apologizes in advance for any such omission. Mention of this textbook as a set book for students, or as a 'recommended-reading' book would be appreciated.

Acronym	Name of institution	Address and telephone number
AAT	Association of Accounting Technicians	154 Clerkenwell Road, London EC1 5AD Tel: (071) 837 8600

Acronym	Name of institution	Address and telephone number
ABE	Association of Business Executives	William House, Worple Road, London SW19 4DD Tel: (081) 879 1973
ACCA	Chartered Association of Certified Accountants	29 Lincoln's Inn Fields, London WC2 Tel: (071) 242 6855
BTEC	Business and Technician Education Council	Central House, Upper Woburn Place, London WC1H 0HH Tel: (071) 388 3288
CA	Institute of Chartered Accountants in England and Wales	Moorgate Place, London EC2P 2BJ Tel: (071) 628 7060
CAM	Communications, Advertising and Marketing Educational Foundation	Abford House, 15 Wilton Road, London SW1 1NJ Tel: (071) 828 7506
CBSI	Chartered Building Society Institute	See address for Chartered Institute of Bankers
CIB	Chartered Institute of Bankers	Emmanuel House, Burgate Lane, Canterbury, Kent CT1 2XJ Tel: (0227) 762600
CII	Chartered Insurance Institute	20 Aldermanbury, London EC2V 7HY and 31 Hillcrest Road, London E18 2JP Tel: (081) 989 8464
CIM	Chartered Institute of Marketing	Moor Hall, Cookham, Maidenhead, Berkshire SL6 9QH Tel: (062) 85 24922
CIMA	Chartered Institute of Management Accountants	63 Portland Place, London W1N 4AB Tel: (071) 637 2311
CIPFA	Chartered Institute of Public Finance and Accountancy	3 Robert Street, London WC2N 6BH Tel: (071) 895 8823

Acronym	Name of institution	Address and telephone number
CIPS	Chartered Institute of Purchasing & Supply	Easton House, Easton on the Hill, Stamford, Lincs P69 3NZ Tel: (0780) 56777
CIT	Chartered Institute of Transport	80 Portland Place, London WC1 Tel: (071) 636 9952
CLE	Council of Legal Education	Inns of Court School of Law, 4 Gray's Inn Road, London WC1R 4AJ Tel: (071) 404 5787
FOA	Faculty of Actuaries	23 St Andrews Square, Edinburgh EH2 1AQ Tel: (031) 557 1575
GCSE	1 Southern: Associated Examining Board	Stag Hill House, Guildford GU2 5XJ Tel: (0483) 506506
	2 Midland: Cambridge University Examining Board	Syndicate Buildings, 1 Hills Road, Cambridge CB1 2EU Tel: (0223) 61111
	3 Welsh: Welsh Joint Education Committee	245 Western Avenue, Cardiff CF5 2YX Tel: (0222) 561231
	4 London: East Anglian Examining Board	The Lindens, Lexden Road, Colchester, Essex CO3 3LR Tel: (0206) 549595
	5 Northern: Joint Matriculation Board	Manchester, M15 6EU Tel: (061) 273 2565
A Level exam boards	Associated Examining Board	Stag Hill House, Guildford GU2 5XJ Tel: (0483) 506506
HCIMA	Hotel, Catering and Institutional Management Association	191 Trinity Road, London SW17 7HN Tel: (071) 627 4251
IAM	Institute of Administrative Management	40 Chatsworth Parade, Petts Wood, Orpington, Kent Tel: (0689) 875555
IAS	Institute of Agricultural Secretaries	NAC Stoneleigh, Kenilworth, Warwickshire CV8 2LZ Tel: (0203) 696592

Acronym	Name of institution	Address and telephone number
ICM	Institute of Commercial Management	PO Box 125, Bournemouth, Dorset BH2 6JH Tel: (0202) 290999
ICOMA	Institute of Company Accountants	40 Tyndalls Park Road, Bristol BS8 1PL Tel: (0272) 738 261
ICS	Institute of Chartered Shipbrokers	3 Gracechurch Street, London EC3V OAT Tel: (071) 283 1361
ICSA	Institute of Chartered Secretaries and Administrators	16 Park Crescent, London W1N 4AH Tel: (071) 580 4741
IDPM	Institute of Data Processing Management	21 Russell Street, London WC2B 5UB Tel: (071) 240 8891
IHSM	Institute of Health Service Management	75 Portland Place, London W1N 4AN Tel: (071) 580 5041
IFF	Institute of Freight Forwarders	Redfern House, Browells Lane, Feltham, Middlesex TW13 7EP Tel: (081) 844 2266
IMS	Institute of Management Services	1 Cecil Court, London Road, Enfield, Middlesex EN2 6DD Tel: (081) 363 7452
IOA	Institute of Actuaries	Staple Inn Hall, High Holborn, London WC1V 7QJ Tel: (071) 242 0106
IOS	Institute of Statisticians	43 St Peter's Square, Preston PR1 7BX Tel: (0772) 204237
IOTA	Institute of Transport Administration	32 Palmerston Road, Southampton SO1 1LL Tel: (0703) 31380

Acronym	Name of institution	Address and telephone number
IOX	Institute of Export	Export House, 64 Clifton Street, London EC2A 4HB Tel: (071) 247 9812
IPM	Institute of Personnel Management	IPM House, Camp Road, Wimbledon, London SW19 4UX Tel: (081) 946 9100
IQPS	Institute of Qualified Private Secretaries	126 Farnham Road, Slough, Berks SL1 4XA Tel: (0753) 522395
IRTE	Institute of Road Transport Engineers	1 Cromwell Place, Kensington, London SW7 2JF Tel: (071) 589 3744
LCCI	London Chamber of Commerce and Industry	69 Cannon Street, London EC4 Tel: (071) 248 4444
MRS	Market Research Society	15 Northburgh Street, London EC1V OAH Tel: (071) 490 4911
NEBSM	National Examinations Board in Supervisory Management	76 Portland Place, London W1N 4AA Tel: (071) 278 2468
OPR	Operational Research Society	Neville House, Waterloo Street, Birmingham B2 5TX Tel: (021) 643 0236
PITMAN	Pitman Tutorial College	29 Waterloo Place, Royal Leamington Spa, Warwickshire Tel: (0926) 332 071
RSA	Royal Society of Arts	Progress House, Westwood Way, Coventry CV4 8HS Tel: (0203) 470033

Index